# British World Policy and the Projection of Global Power, c.1830–1960

A fundamental truth about British power in the nineteenth century and beyond was that Britain was a global power. Her international position rested on her global economic, naval and political presence, and her foreign policy operated on a global scale. This volume throws into sharp relief the material elements of British power, but also its less tangible components, from Britain's global network of naval bases to the vast range of intersecting commercial, financial and intelligence relationships, which reinforced the country's political power. Leading historians reshape the scholarly debate surrounding the nature of British global power at a crucial period of transformation in international politics, and in so doing they deepen our understanding of the global nature of British power, the shifts in the international landscape from the high Victorian period to the 1960s, and the changing nature of the British state in this period.

T. G. Otte is Professor of Diplomatic History at the University of East Anglia. Among his latest books are *July Crisis: The World's Descent into War, Summer 1914* (2014), *The Age of Anniversaries: The Cult of Commemoration, 1895–1925* (ed., 2018) and *Statesman of Europe: A Life of Sir Edward Grey* (2020).

# British World Policy and the Projection of Global Power, c.1830–1960

*Edited by*

T. G. Otte

*University of East Anglia*

CAMBRIDGE
UNIVERSITY PRESS

# CAMBRIDGE
## UNIVERSITY PRESS

University Printing House, Cambridge CB2 8BS, United Kingdom

One Liberty Plaza, 20th Floor, New York, NY 10006, USA

477 Williamstown Road, Port Melbourne, VIC 3207, Australia

314-321, 3rd Floor, Plot 3, Splendor Forum, Jasola District Centre, New Delhi - 110025, India

103 Penang Road, #05-06/07, Visioncrest Commercial, Singapore 238467

Cambridge University Press is part of the University of Cambridge.

It furthers the University's mission by disseminating knowledge in the pursuit of education, learning and research at the highest international levels of excellence.

www.cambridge.org
Information on this title: www.cambridge.org/9781316648322
DOI: 10.1017/9781108182775

First published 2019
First paperback edition 2022

*A catalogue record for this publication is available from the British Library*

*Library of Congress Cataloging in Publication data*
Names: Otte, Thomas G., 1967– author.
Title: British world policy and the projection of global power, c.1830–1960 / T.G. Otte.
Description: Cambridge, United Kingdom ; New York, NY, USA : Cambridge University Press, 2019. | Includes bibliographical references and index.
Identifiers: LCCN 2019008742 | ISBN 9781107198852 (alk. paper)
Subjects: LCSH: Great Britain – Foreign relations – 19th century. | Great Britain – Foreign relations – 20th century. | Great Britain – Politics and government – 19th century. | Great Britain – Politics and government – 20th century.
Classification: LCC DA530 .O88 2019 | DDC 327.41009/034–dc23
LC record available at https://lccn.loc.gov/2019008742

ISBN 978-1-107-19885-2 Hardback
ISBN 978-1-316-64832-2 Paperback

*In memoriam* Keith Neilson

# Contents

*Notes on the Contributors*                                    *page* ix
*Preface and Acknowledgements*                                         xiii

Introduction: British World Policy and the White Queen's
Memory                                                                   1
T. G. OTTE

1   The War Trade Intelligence Department and British
    Economic Warfare during the First World War                        24
    JOHN ROBERT FERRIS

2   The British Empire and the Meaning of 'Minimum Force
    Necessary' in Colonial Counter-Insurgencies Operations,
    c.1857–1967                                                        46
    DAVID FRENCH

3   Yokohama for the British in the Late Nineteenth Century:
    A Hub for Imperial Defence and a Node of Influence for
    Change                                                             67
    HAMISH ION

4   'The Diplomatic Digestive Organ': The Foreign Office As
    the Nerve Centre of Foreign Policy, c.1800–1940                    90
    T. G. OTTE

5   Financial and Commercial Networks between Great
    Britain and South America during the Long Nineteenth
    Century                                                           111
    KATHLEEN BURK

6   Britain through Russian Eyes: 1900–1914                           129
    DOMINIC LIEVEN

7   Imperial Germany's Naval Challenge and the Renewal of
    British Power                                                    147
    JOHN H. MAURER

8   Views of War, 1914 and 1939: Second Thoughts                     174
    ZARA STEINER

9   The Ambassadors, 1919–1939                                       201
    ERIK GOLDSTEIN

10  The Tattered Ties that Bind: The Imperial General Staff
    and the Dominions, 1919–1939                                     226
    DOUGLAS E. DELANEY

11  Seeking a Family Consensus? Anglo-Dominion Relations
    and the Failed Imperial Conference of 1941                       245
    KENT FEDOROWICH

12  Imperial Hubs and their Limitations: British Assessments
    of Imposing Sanctions on Japan, 1937                             276
    G. BRUCE STRANG

    *Index*                                                          305

# Notes on the Contributors

KATHLEEN BURK is Professor Emerita of Modern and Contemporary History at University College London. Her general field is international history, concentrating on politics, diplomacy and finance. Among her publications are *Troublemaker: The Life and History of A. J. P. Taylor* (2002), *Old World, New World: Great Britain and America from the Beginning* (2009), and *The Lion and the Eagle: The Interaction of the British and American Empires 1783–1972* (2018).

DOUGLAS E. DELANEY holds the Canada Research Chair in War Studies at the Royal Military College of Canada, where he lectures in the military history of Canada and the British Commonwealth, strategic studies and the two World Wars. His books include *The Soldiers' General: Bert Hoffmeister at War* (2005), *Corps Commanders: Five British and Canadian Generals at War, 1939–1945* (2011), *Turning Point 1917: The British Empire at War* (2017) and *The Imperial Army Project: Britain and the Land Forces of the Dominions and India, 1902–1945* (2017).

KENT FEDOROWICH is Reader in British Imperial History at the University of the West of England. His research covers the fields of Empire Migration, prisoners of war, civilian internment, Anglo-Dominion relations and the British World. He has published widely on these subjects in learned journals and scholarly collections of essays. Among his publications are (with Bob Moore) *The British Empire and Its Italian Prisoners of War, 1940–1947* (2002) and (ed. with Andrew S. Thompson) *Empire, Migration and Identity in the British World* (2013).

JOHN ROBERT FERRIS is Professor of History at the University of Calgary, where he is also a Fellow at the Centre for Military and Strategic Studies, and where he teaches nineteenth- and twentieth-century imperial, international and intelligence history. He has published numerous articles and essays in scholarly journals and edited collections. His books include *The Evolution of British Strategic Policy, 1919–*

*1926* (1989), (ed.) *The British Army and Signals Intelligence During the First World War* (1992) and *Intelligence and Strategy, Selected Essays* (2005).

DAVID FRENCH is Professor Emeritus of History at University College London. His interests centre on British military history, especially since the late nineteenth century. Among his publications are *British Strategy and War Aims* (1986), *Raising Churchill's Army: The British Army and the War against Germany, 1919–1945* (2000), *Military Identities: The Regimental System, the British Army and the British People, c.1870–2000* (2005) and *The British Way in Counter-Insurgency* (2011).

ERIK GOLDSTEIN is Professor of International Relations and History at Boston University. He is the founder-editor of the journal *Diplomacy & Statecraft*. His publications include *Winning the Peace: British Diplomatic Strategy, Peace Planning, and the Paris Peace Conference, 1916–1920* (1991), *Wars and Peace Treaties* (1992) and *The First World War's Peace Settlements: International Relations, 1919–1925* (2002, Italian translation, 2004). He has co-edited *The End of the Cold War* (1990), *The Washington Conference, 1921–1922: Naval Rivalry, East Asian Stability, and the Road to Pearl Harbor* (1994), *The Munich Crisis: New Interpretations and the Road to World War II* (1999), *Power and Stability: British Foreign Policy, 1865–1965* (2003) and *Guide to International Relations and Diplomacy* (2002).

HAMISH ION is Professor Emeritus of History at the Royal Military College of Canada. His publications concentrate on modern Japanese and Chinese history, Middle Eastern history, imperial and post-colonial history, Canadian and European history and the politics of the Third World. Among them are *The Cross and the Rising Sun* (2 vols., 1990–1993), *The Cross in the Dark Valley: The Canadian Protestant Missionary Movement in the Japanese Empire, 1931–1945* (1999), *American Missionaries, Christian Oyatoi, and Japan, 1859–73* (2010) and (ed. with Keith Neilson) *Elite Military Formations in War and Peace* (1996).

DOMINIC LIEVEN is Professor of Russian History at the London School of Economics and Senior Research Fellow at Trinity College, Cambridge. His numerous works include *Russia and the Origins of the First World War* (1983), *Russia's Rulers under the Old Regime* (1988), *Aristocracy in Europe* (1992), *Nicholas II: Emperor of All the Russias* (1993), *Empire: The Russian Empire and Its Rivals* (2001), (ed.) *The Cambridge History of Russia*, volume 2 (2006), *Russia against Napoleon: The Struggle for Europe, 1807–1814* (2009), *Towards the Flame. Empire,*

*War and the End of Tsarist Russia* (2015) and (ed. with Janet M. Hartley and Paul Keenan) *Russia and the Napoleonic Wars: War, Culture and Society, 1750–1850* (2015).

JOHN H. MAURER is Alfred Thayer Mahan Professor of Sea Power and Grand Strategy at the United States Naval War College, Newport, Rhode Island, and a Senior Fellow of the Foreign Policy Research Institute's Program on National Security. In recognition for his service and contribution to professional military education, he has received both the US Navy's Meritorious Civilian Service Award and Superior Civilian Service Award. His research covers the causes of war, arms control and Winston Churchill as statesman and war leader. Among his innumerable publications are (ed. with Erik Goldstein) *The Washington Conference, 1921–1922: Naval Rivalry, East Asian Stability, and the Road to Pearl Harbor* (1994) and *The Outbreak of the First World War: Strategic Planning, Crisis Decision Making, and Deterrence Failure* (1995).

T. G. OTTE is Professor of Diplomatic History at the University of East Anglia. He is the author or editor of seventeen books. Among the more recent ones are *The China Question: Great Power Rivalry and British Isolation, 1894–1905* (2007; Chinese translation, 2018), (with Keith Neilson) *The Office of the Permanent Under-Secretary for Foreign Affairs, 1854–1946* (2009), *The 'Foreign Office Mind': The Making of British Foreign Policy, 1865–1914* (2011), (ed.) *An Historian in Peace and War: The Diaries of Harold Temperley, 1900–1939* (2014), *July Crisis: The World's Descent into War, Summer 1914* (2014) and (ed.) *The Age of Anniversaries: The Cult of Commemoration 1895–1925* (2018).

ZARA STEINER is an Emeritus Fellow of Murray Edwards College, Cambridge. Among her books are *The Foreign Office and British Foreign Policy, 1898–1914* (1969), *Britain and the Origins of the First World War* (1977, second ed. with Keith Neilson, 2003), *The Lights That Failed: European International History, 1919–1933* (2005) and *The Triumph of the Dark: European International History, 1933–1939* (2011).

G. BRUCE STRANG is Professor of History at Brandon University. His research specialism lies in the fields of international history c.1870–1990, fascist ideology and twentieth-century British history. He has contributed numerous articles and chapters to learned journals and collections of essays. Among his publications are *On the Fiery March: Mussolini Prepares for War* (2003) and (ed.) *Collision of Empires: Italy's Invasion of Ethiopia and Its International Impact* (2013).

# Preface and Acknowledgements

At the end of the First World War, in the famous quip by Sellar and Yeatman, America had 'clearly [become] top nation, and History came to a .' Or so it seemed at the time. History, of course, did not come to an end then or later. What the war of 1914–18 did, however, was, in the words of Keith Neilson, to 'cast a retroactive shadow over historical studies'.[1] It skewed scholarly assessments of pre-war British foreign policy by privileging an Anglo-German perspective that was quite alien to the thinking of Britain's foreign policy elite in the long nineteenth century. And it helped to entrench a 'declinist' cast of mind that has tended to see Britain after 1919 as slowly and steadily retreating from global power.

The waxing and waning of British influence in the world, and the nature of the elements of power that underpinned the nation's international position and the nature of their interaction, has been the subject of enduring fascination for historians, academic and lay alike. It is also at the core of Keith Neilson's scholarly *œuvre*. A native of Alberta in western Canada, from his vantage point at the Royal Military College of Canada in Kingston, Ontario, he brought an 'imperial' perspective to studies of Britain's external relations. His work did not neglect the fundamentally European setting of British policy, however. On the contrary, it is remarkable for its finely balanced appreciation of the global nature of British policy. While appreciating the more extraneous, ephemeral even, cultural or ideological aspects of the subject – entirely befitting for someone of his fine literary sensibilities – Keith Neilson nevertheless placed political and material power at the heart of his studies.

These elements lie also at the heart of the essays brought together in this volume. Keith Neilson spent his life, which was tragically cut short within a year of his retirement from RMC, in learning and teaching, in thinking and writing about history and in sustaining his family and friends. Several of his friends and former colleagues have joined in producing this

---

[1] K. Neilson, *Britain and the Last Tsar: British Policy towards Russia, 1894–1917* (Oxford, 1995), xi.

collection of studies which they offer to Joan, Anne, David and Susan as a token – a slight and, I fear, wholly inadequate one – of their deep and continued respect and affection. These essays serve to underline both the varieties and the essential unity of history; and they justify the vocation of the man in whose memory his friends have written them.

I am grateful to all my fellow contributors for their dedication and efforts. All but two of them stayed the course, and their absence is noted with regret. I am most grateful to Michael Watson at Cambridge University Press for his steady support and sagacious advice during this volume's elephantine gestation period.

# Introduction: British World Policy and the White Queen's Memory

## T. G. Otte

This tendency to read history backwards – in effect, to have the White Queen's memory – has led to a misunderstanding of events.

Keith Neilson[1]

Writing at the end of 1901, Sir Francis Bertie, a senior Foreign Office official, advised against abandoning Britain's established policy of limiting liabilities abroad, because it would entail 'the sacrifice of our liberty to pursue a *British world policy*'.[2] In its specific contemporary context, it was a thinly veiled comment, dripping with heavy irony, on Wilhelmine Germany's pretensions at *Weltpolitik* and their potentially disruptive effect on British interests. Yet it also touched on a fundamental truth about British power in the long nineteenth century and beyond, well into the first half of the twentieth. Alone amongst the powers of the day, Britain was a global power. Her national interest was defined with reference to a wider global setting; her international position rested on her global economic, naval and political presence; and her foreign policy operated on a global scale. However, if Bertie reasserted the global range of British interests and policy, his comments were also suggestive of the constraints placed on the country's ability to pursue such a world policy.

Scholars of Britain's external relations in the nineteenth and twentieth centuries readily acknowledge the global nature of their subject. Yet in practice, they tend to dissect it along bilateral lines or with an exclusive focus on the imperial periphery. The tension between Britain's global strategic interests and its ability to safeguard them has likewise long been

---

[1] K. Neilson, *Britain and the Last Tsar: British Policy towards Russia, 1894–1917* (Oxford, 1995), 367.

[2] Memo. Bertie, 9 November 1901, G. P. Gooch and H. W. V. Temperley (eds.), *British Documents on the Origins of the War, 1898–1914* (11 vols., London, 1928–38) ii, no. 91; see also the draft version, n.d. [27 Oct. 1901?], The National Archives (Public Record Office), Kew, FO 64/1539, which is pithier than the printed version.

the subject of scholarly debates, invariably accompanied by more or less explicit assumptions about the nation's decline in the twentieth century. Already Arnold J. Toynbee, in reflecting on the origins of the Second World War, contrasted Britain's assumed position as 'the arbiter of Europe' from around the time of the War of the Spanish Succession at the beginning of the eighteenth century until the final years of peace before 1914 with the country's reduced circumstances in the interwar period.[3] In a similar manner, more recent works, such as Corelli Barnett's declinist trilogy or Paul Kennedy's account of the rise and fall of Great Powers, take as their starting point the British empire as the greatest power in the world.[4] And yet, such assessments exaggerate both the extent to which Britain reigned supreme and the degree and speed with which the country's power and influence seeped away. As Keith Neilson argued in a seminal article in 1991, notions of Britain's decline as a Great Power at the beginning of the twentieth century are 'greatly exaggerated'.[5] Assumptions of British dominance, however, are no less overstretched.

This volume takes its inspiration from Neilson's insight, and seeks to throw into sharper relief the material elements of British power but also its less tangible components. Historically, the most obvious, the most prominent, though not consistently the most effective, element of British power was the projection, and indeed the use, of military force. Until the period between the two world wars, naval power was the main instrument of safeguarding the country's strategic interests and protecting its global possessions. Naval dominance was also used to contain, through the threat or the actual deployment of force, any power with ambitions for continental hegemony.[6] In the decades after the Second World War successive British governments considered the nation's now more

---

[3] A. J. Toynbee, *The Eve of War, 1939* (Oxford, 1958), 47.

[4] C. Barnett, *The Collapse of British Power* (London, 1972), *The Audit of War: The Illusion and Reality of Britain as a Great Nation* (London, 1986) and *The Lost Victory: British Dreams and British Realities, 1945–50* (London, 1995); P. M. Kennedy, *The Rise and Fall of the Great Powers: Economic Change and Military Conflict from 1500 to 2000* (London, 1988); for a broader discussion of 'declinism' see R. English and M. Kenny, 'Public Intellectuals and the Question of British Decline', *British Journal of Politics and International Relations* 3(3) (2001), 259–83; for a recent revisionist take on the subject see D. Edgerton, *The Rise and Fall of the British Nation: A Twentieth-Century History* (London, 2018).

[5] K. Neilson, '"Greatly Exaggerated": The Myth of British Decline before 1914', *International History Review* 13(4) (1991), 695–725.

[6] See *inter alios* P. M. Kennedy. 'The Influence and Limitations of Sea Power', *International History Review* 10(1) (1988), 2–17; K. Neilson, '"The British Empire Floats on the British Navy": British Naval Policy, Belligerent Rights, and Disarmament, 1902-09', in B. J. C. McKercher (ed.), *Arms Limitation and Disarmament: Restraints on War, 1899–1939* (New York, 1992), 21–42; N. A. M. Rodger, *The Command of the Ocean: A Naval History of Britain, 1649–1815* (London, 2004).

precarious influence to rest on its nuclear capability.[7] However much the global reach of Britain's armed forces continued to diminish, the ambition of most cabinets remained – in the memorable phrase of the then foreign secretary Douglas Hurd (1990–95) – to 'punch above our weight'. It articulated a sentiment that continued to shape British policy until the beginning of the twenty-first century.[8]

Force projection as an enabling instrument of foreign policy required material foundations of its own. It is generally held as axiomatic that 'wealth is ... needed to underpin military power'.[9] The two are mutually reinforcing. It is no crude materialism to conclude that wealth was needed to maintain armed forces, and that armed forces were used to protect and, oftentimes, to acquire yet more wealth. From the seventeenth century onwards, Britain's trading prowess and her financial capacity, the facility it gave – through paper instruments, credit devices and bills of exchange – to transfer large funds over distances and between countries or continents, reinforced her naval power.[10] The growing commercial empire and the country's early industrialization placed it in an advantageous position. Above all, they were convertible into political coinage. British guineas not only kept the Royal Navy in gunpowder, they also helped to equip the country's continental allies and to lubricate the alliances with them.[11]

---

[7] For some of the complex discussions see M. S. Navias, '"Vested Interests and Vanished Dreams": Duncan Sandys, the Chief of Staffs, and the 1957 White Paper', and P. Nailor, 'The Ministry of Defence, 1959-1970', in P. Smith (ed.), *Government and the Armed Forces, 1856–1990* (London, 1996), 217–34 and 235–48; L. Freedman, *The Politics of British Defence Policy, 1979–1998* (London, 1999); R. Self, *British Defence and Foreign Policy since 1945: Challenges and Dilemmas in a Changing World* (Basingstoke and New York, 2010).

[8] D. Hurd, 'Making the World a Safer Place: Our Five Priorities', *Daily Telegraph*, 1 January 1992. The sentiment continued to influence British policy until the early years of the twenty-first century, see C. Hill, 'Putting the World to Rights: Tony Blair's Foreign Policy Mission', in A. Seldon and D. Kavanagh (eds.), *The Blair Effect, 2001–2005* (Cambridge, 2005), 384–409. Since 2016, there has been some uncertainty on this point, see 'PM Declines to Pledge UK Will Remain "Tier One" Power', *Financial Times*, 22 June 2018.

[9] Kennedy, Rise and Fall, xvi; W. H. McNeill, *The Pursuit of Power: Technology, Armed Force and Society since AD 1000* (Chicago, 1984 (pb)).

[10] J. Clapham, *The Bank of England: A History* (2 vols., Cambridge, 1944) remains the *locus classicus* for some of this; see also R. Davis, *The Rise of the Atlantic Economies* (London, repr. 1988), 231–49; and J. Brewer, *The Sinews of Power: War, Money and the English State, 1688–1783* (London, 1989).

[11] For some discussion of this see J. M. Sherwig, *Guineas and Gunpowder: British Foreign Aid in the Wars with France, 1793–1815* (Cambridge, MA, 1974); see also R. Lodge, 'The Continental Policy of Great Britain, 1740-1760', *History* xvi, 64 (1931), 298–304, and C. S. B. Buckland, *Metternich and the British Government, from 1809 to 1813* (London, 1932).

Conversely, financial muscle, later referred to as the 'fourth arm of defence', enabled Britain to meet the challenges of other powers in peacetime, such as the Anglo-Russian antagonism in Central Asia, the most persistent and significant long-term threat to British interests. Here nineteenth-century governments were imbued with a sense of British strength. Lord Salisbury was even prepared to embark on what amounted to a revolutionary policy, using Britain's financial leverage to force Russia to curb her expansionism in the region: 'We must lead her into all the expense that we can in the conviction that with her the limit of taxation has almost been reached, & that only a few steps further must push her into revolution over which she seems to be constantly hanging.'[12] Similarly, it was more than a characteristic flourish of hyperbole when, as Chancellor of the Exchequer, David Lloyd George assured the German ambassador in 1908 that he was ready to expend the gigantic sum of £100 million to maintain Britain's relative naval superiority.[13]

In the course of the long nineteenth century Britain's economic dominance was slowly eroded as other nations caught up with her industrial development.[14] The demands of international competition meant that the sinews of power were more important than ever before, but also that military power now began to consume a larger share of the country's wealth; and this at a time when Britain's political class was reluctant to tap into the existing financial wealth, for instance, by means of progressive taxation. Britain's defensive strength, noted the Chancellor of the Exchequer in 1903, rested 'upon our financial not less than upon our military and naval resources, and I am bound to say that in the present condition of finance it would ... be impossible to finance a great war, except at an absolutely ruinous cost'.[15] Shortly afterwards, he became more alarmed still: 'however reluctant we may be to face the fact, the

[12] Salisbury to Morier (private), 16 September 1885, Morier MSS, Balliol College, Oxford, box 21/1; for reflections on the persistence of the Russian threat see Neilson, *Britain and the Last Tsar*, 368–69 *et passim*.

[13] See M. G. Fry, *Lloyd George and Foreign Policy: The Education of a Statesman, 1890–1916* (Montreal and London, 1977), 94–95.

[14] D. H. Aldcroft, 'British Industry and Foreign Competition, 1875-1914', in D. H. Aldcroft (ed.), *The Development of British Industry and Foreign Competition, 1875–1914* (London, 1968), 11–36, and other essays in this volume.

[15] Memo. Chamberlain, 'The Financial Situation', 7 December 1903, Chamberlain MSS, Cadbury Research Library, University of Birmingham, AC 17/2/17; for some of the context see A. L. Friedberg, *The Weary Titan: Britain and the Experience of Relative Decline, 1895–1905* (Princeton, NJ, 1988). For the underlying 'objective' financial strength of the British economy see the arguments developed by P. J. Cain and A. G. Hopkins, *British Imperialism: Innovation and Expansion 1688–1914* (London, 1994), who do not, however, contemplate the reluctance of government to mobilize that wealth.

time has come when we must frankly admit that the financial resources of the United Kingdom are inadequate to do all that we should desire in the matter of Imperial defence'.[16] Technological advances and more sophisticated industrial production methods as well as growing manpower demands ate into Britain's maritime predominance. The greater financial outlay now entailed in naval construction programmes no longer guaranteed quantitative advantage of the kind enjoyed by the Royal Navy at the beginning of the century.[17]

Global conflict exacerbated the situation, so much so that, by the middle of the First World War, Britain's financial dominance had evaporated.[18] Fighting the war and preserving the alliance with France and Russia entailed exporting significant amounts of gold reserves to America to secure loans 'for the joint purposes of the Allies'.[19] It meant maintaining what was in effect 'an inverted pyramid standing on the Dollar exchange'.[20] Not to keep that pyramid upright was no option either. Cutting down on military supplies, the Minister of Munitions argued, 'because these three great rich countries cannot afford to incur another hundred million debtedness [sic] to America is the height of stupidity'.[21] The shift in financial power also had political consequences: 'We cannot get on without America either during or after the war. For the moment let us keep very quiet ... '[22]

The exigencies of war left Britain in a more precarious financial position. If she was not yet altogether financially hamstrung, she had nevertheless ceded her position in global finance to the rising power of America. Threadneedle Street receded into the deepening shadow cast by Wall Street. Ensuring international financial and thus political stability was now a matter for America to ponder. It lay beyond Britain's capacity, as Lloyd George impressed on President Woodrow Wilson in 1919: 'If Great Britain could shoulder any considerable share of the responsibility

---

[16] Memo. Chamberlain (confidential), 30 April 1904, Chamberlain MSS, AC 17/2/24.

[17] See J. T. Sumida, *In Defence of Naval Supremacy: Finance, Technology and British Naval Policy* (London, 1989), 1–17; G. C. Peden, *Arms, Economics and British Strategy: From Dreadnought to Hydrogen Bombs* (Cambridge, 2007), 17–48.

[18] D. C. M. Platt, *Finance, Trade, and Politics in British Foreign Policy, 1815–1914* (Oxford, 1968), xvii; K. Burk, *Britain, America and the Sinews of War, 1914–1918* (London, 1985), 77–96; A. Tooze, *The Deluge: The Great War and the Remaking of Global Order* (London, 2014), 46–49.

[19] Preamble of Anglo-French Boulogne Agreement, 22 August 1915, The National Archives (Public Record Office), T 172/256.

[20] M. Farr, '"A Compelling Case for Britain": Alternative Strategy, 1915-1916', *War-in-History* 9(3) (2002), 302–03; also P. Miquel, *La Grande Guerre* (Paris, 1983), 447–49.

[21] Memo. Lloyd George, 29 June 1916, Asquith MSS, Bodleian Library, Oxford, MS Asquith 30.

[22] Min. Hardinge, n.d., on report of the Committee on 'Dependence of British Empire on United States', 13 October 1916, FO 371/2496/63430/205593.

she would do so. As she cannot, the responsibility must rest principally on the shoulders of the United States.'[23] There, of course, it rested on uneasy sufferance. Even so, in 1939, Neville Chamberlain still thought it possible to use finance to deter Hitler and to use the prospect of credit and strengthened commercial ties as an inducement for the German leader to moderate his policy: 'We have at last got on top of the dictators.'[24] The relative recovery in the 1930s notwithstanding, the war had transformed finance from a facilitating element of international power into a constraining one.[25] The Second World War worsened matters further. Almost from the outset of the war it was recognized that it would be necessary 'to bring in the USA' for financial reasons and with a view to America's superior industrial capacity.[26] Matters were not helped by post-war piecemeal fiscal tinkering. In consequence, financial constraints shaped British policy in the short twentieth century.[27]

The third material factor underpinning Britain's ability to pursue her own world policy lay in London's ability to mobilize imperial resources, raw materials and manpower reserves, more especially so in times of war. They supported British war efforts in limited colonial campaigns and, more especially, during the two world wars in the twentieth century. The Empire's contribution in both these conflicts was a significant force multiplier. It amplified Britain's war-making prowess, and it her gave greater political influence in the wartime alliance.[28]

---

[23] Lloyd George to Wilson, 26 June 1919, Lloyd George MSS, Political Archive, House of Lords, F/60/1/16.

[24] Chamberlain to Hilda Chamberlain, 19 February 1939, Chamberlain MSS, NC 18/1/1086. For the context see R. A. C. Parker, *Chamberlain and Appeasement: British Policy and the Coming of the Second World War* (New York, 1993), 193–97; D. E. Kaiser, *Economic Diplomacy and the Origins of the Second World War: Germany, Britain, France, and Eastern Europe, 1930–1939* (Princeton, NJ, 1980), 284–315.

[25] K. Neilson, 'The Defence Requiremenets Sub-Committee: British Strategic Foreign Policy, Neville Chamberlain and the Path of Appeasement', *English Historical Review* 118(447) (2003), 651–84; G. C. Peden, *The Treasury and British Public Policy, 1906–1959* (Oxford, 2000), 247–302.

[26] Memo. Dalton, 'Note on the Present Position and Probable Future of Economic Warfare', 27 June 1940, Dalton MSS, LSE Library Archives and Special Collections, ser. II, 7/2.

[27] M. Daunton, *Just Taxes: The Politics of Taxation in Britain, 1914–1979* (Cambridge, 2002), 176–93 *et seq.*; also P. M. Kennedy, 'Strategy *versus* Finance in Twentieth Century Britain', *International History Review* 3(1) (1981), 45–61, though the focus here is on the early part of the century.

[28] For some of this see e.g. A. Offer, 'The British Empire, 1870–1914: A Waste of Money?', *Economic History Review* 46(2) (1993), 215–38; J. Winter, 'Migration, War and Empire: The British Case', *Annales de Demographie Historique* 1(1) (2002), 143–60. The Empire's contribution could be a mixed blessing, as the Canadian contribution to the First World War demonstrates, see R. G. Haycock, *Sam Hughes: The Public Career of a Controversial Canadian, 1885–1916* (Ottawa, 1986), 177–312.

The fourth element of British power bore no material aspect – diplomacy. Yet despite its elusive nature, it was scarcely less significant than the material elements. To no small degree, its reach and effectiveness were determined by them. Britain's naval power or financial prowess leant greater weight to the words of the government in London and its representatives abroad. If British guineas kept wartime allies furnished with gunpowder, it was diplomatic nous that helped to facilitate the peaceful adjustment or settlement of disputes. Frequently, it forged peacetime combinations with other powers, or groups of powers, to preserve peace wherever possible and to defend British interests abroad whenever necessary. Usually, its 'essential business', as the diplomat Sir Rennell Rodd commented in the 1920s, was 'vigilance to maintain the balance of power'.[29]

The different strands of Britain's global power can easily be dissected and separated under the historian's powerful magnifying lens. But that would be to miss their most important aspect. Each of the strands on its own was important, but their practical effectiveness and overall historical significance rested on their being interwoven through a myriad of hubs and nodes. In this they resembled the curious and amorphous nature of the British empire itself. Whether, as Sir John Robert Seeley famously quipped in the 1880s, Britain had 'conquered and peopled half the world in a fit of absence of mind', remains debatable.[30] That there was something haphazard and elusive about Britain's imperial possessions and her wider, global presence will hardly be contested.[31] Both were characterized by a blend of the formal and the informal. From the late Victorian period onwards, the empire took on a more formal aspect, with direct rule over imperial subjects, often conquered peoples, at its core. But it also had a significant accretion of 'white' Anglo-European settlements, in effect a form of 'reproduction of British society overseas through long-range migration', predominantly but not exclusively from the British Isles.[32] Alongside these formal elements were looser networks and informal

---

[29] Sir R. Rodd, *Diplomacy* (London, 1929), 47. Rodd had been Britain's long-serving ambassador to Italy.

[30] J. R. Seeley, *The Expansion of England: Two Courses of Lectures* (London, 2nd edn. 1897 [1st 1883]), 10.

[31] See e.g. W. J. Mommsen's valiant attempt at a structural analysis of the Empire, W. J. Mommsen, 'Das Britische Empire: Strukturanalyse eines imperialistischen Herrschaftsverbandes', *Historische Zeitschrift* 233(2) (1981), 319; for a recent synoptic reinterpretation see J. Darwin, *The Empire Project: The Rise and Fall of the British World-System, 1830–1970* (Oxford, 2009).

[32] J. Belich, *Replenishing the Earth: The Settler Revolution and the Rise of the Anglo-World, 1783–1939* (Oxford, 2009), 21 *et passim*; see also H. I. Cowan, *British Emigration to North America: The First Hundred Years* (Toronto, rev. ed. 1961).

systems of long-range interaction in the shape of commercial and financial ties as well as information and knowledge transfer.

The mixture of formal and informal, material and intangible, solid and more volatile elements lies also at the heart of this volume of essays. Its contributors cast their nets widely and let them drag at deeper levels to haul up some of the elusive aspects of British power. Maritime dominance and the industrial and technological head start enjoyed by Britain in the nineteenth century underpinned also some of the cultural aspects of the British world system. Ideas and information were disseminated by books, magazines and newspapers and, later on, by news communications technology, such as submarine telegraph cables and then wireless.[33] London, as the imperial metropolis, was the political and commercial centre of the Empire, and it enjoyed a form of information hegemony which gave greater cohesion to the British-controlled world. Conversely, it derived a significant portion of political and other intelligence from outlying parts overseas. Intelligence gathering and processing capabilities were one element of British power in the period examined in the essays in this volume.

The theme of Britain's physical location at an information crossroads is taken up by John Robert Ferris in his examination of war trade intelligence efforts during the First World War. Processing and applying relevant, trade-related information supplied by signals intelligence shaped British intelligence for economic warfare. Here, as in so much else, the 1914–1918 war acted as a powerful stimulant. Before August 1914, the British authorities misunderstood the nature and the value of modern economic warfare. Indeed, beyond broad but vague assumptions about the necessity of blockade measures, they scarcely recognized the imperative need for systematic intelligence gathering for them. It was almost the flipside of the Nelsonian myth that so dominated naval thinking of the period. There was a profound irony in all of this. Immediately following the outbreak of war, official policy collapsed.[34] Yet Whitehall swiftly responded to the challenge, not so much because officials recognized the full extent of the problems involved in economic warfare, but because of Britain's position in global communications and information processing. They did not know it, but the British authorities had at their disposal intelligence fit for economic warfare. Between 1914 and 1919 no fewer

---

[33] For an in-depth study of the impact of such technology see D. R. Headrick, *The Invisible Weapon: Telecommunications and International Politics, 1851–1945* (New York, 1991); also D. R. Headrick and P. Griset, 'Submarine Telegraph Cables: Business and Politics, 1838-1939', *Business History* 75(3) (2001), 543–78.

[34] On this point see K. Neilson, *Strategy and Supply: The Anglo-Russian Alliance, 1914–17* (London, 1984), 43–48; and K. Neilson and B. J. C. McKercher, '"The Triumph of Unarmed Forces": Sweden and the Allied Blockade of Germany, 1914-1917', *Journal of Strategic Studies* 7(2) (1984), 178–99.

than 80 million telegraphic messages were intercepted by war trade intelligence. If the authorities had not expected to have to wage an intelligence-led campaign of economic warfare before 1914, they were none the less in a position to fight it. They were able to draw on a loose network of non-governmental experts, mobilizing their commercial and technical expertise for the economic war effort.[35] The Trade Clearing House was a case in point. Its offices were populated by academics and barristers, commercial lawyers and commodity traders, literary types and city gents who coordinated and disseminated commercial intelligence from all sources. The intelligence digests produced by this motley crew of secret economic warriors helped to inform senior officials and ministers about the war effort of the Central Powers; and they shaped Whitehall preparations for post-war commercial competition in the event of a stalemate peace. In this manner, war trade intelligence amplified Britain's war-making capabilities. It also facilitated – yet another unanticipated consequence of the war – gender equality. Some 15 per cent of war trade intelligence officers were female, and – more remarkably still – they were given equal pay.

Secret information of a different type was the main staple of foreign policy. The gathering and utilizing of information was a vital function of Britain's foreign policy apparatus, as T. G. Otte shows in his chapter on the Foreign Office as a 'knowledge-based' organization. The growth of modern diplomacy brought with it the need for an institutionalized, central administrative machinery to conduct and control foreign policy. Progress in that direction was haphazard and slow, and it was not until 1782 that the Foreign Office was established as the organizational hub of British foreign policy. Throughout its history the department showed great flexibility in its internal arrangements. In many ways, indeed, its nature and development reflected the growth of the modern British state. Its principal concern, however, was with the effective gathering, processing, storing and retrieving of information relevant to foreign policy. In that sense the Foreign Office was a 'knowledge-based' organization.

Knowledge, as such, is an amorphous concept, influenced by all manner of assumptions about what is worth knowing and how and why it should be known. While the canon of subject-specific knowledge was liable to evolve in relation to changing external requirements, the Foreign Office remained the central repository of arcane knowledge and controlled access to it. This also explains why the registry was central to

---

[35] See also the general reflections on the use of expert knowledge – here with reference to the Second World War – offered by P. M. Kennedy, *The Engineers of Victory: The Problem Solvers Who Turned the Tide in the Second World War* (London, 2013), 353–74.

the efficient functioning of the department. It was vital to the storing and distribution of knowledge. As with other parts of the Whitehall machinery, wars or the prospect of conflict acted as an important spur in the growth of the Foreign Office as a knowledge organization. The Napoleonic wars drove home the need for systematic and standardized internal procedures. Throughout the nineteenth and twentieth centuries, however, there was a mismatch between the necessities of international diplomacy and what the Foreign Office was equipped to achieve; and in this respect, too, it reflected the general nature of the British state. Its staffing levels remained static from 1848 until the outbreak of the First World War. In the face of repeated demands for additional personnel the Treasury proved habitually deaf. Registering despatches and other policy papers thus fell into arrears, and this hampered the Foreign Office's ability to function as the nerve centre of British diplomacy. It was not until the great internal reform of 1905 that the department's machinery was overhauled. The 1905 arrangements were chiefly about enhancing the Foreign Office's functionality as a knowledge organization that could swiftly receive, classify, analyze, archive and distribute information for practical policy purposes. Even so, Treasury stinginess saw to it that the department's staffing requirements were cut down. In consequence, the finely adjusted machinery designed in 1905 broke down during the First World War, and the Foreign Office become something of a '"pass-on" Department'.[36] The emergence of prime ministerial diplomacy and of other, competing bodies further diminished the Foreign Office's role in foreign policy analysis and decision making. Peace in 1919 brought reforms, but the department never regained its influence. The Second World War further reduced its role. It was now just one of the Whitehall departments involved in policymaking.

Secret information was – and still is – in the possession of a professional or political elite. Yet information and perceptions of the outside world also influenced the wider public, as the two chapters by Zara Steiner and Dominic Lieven show. The nexus of public sensitivities and political decision making is crucial to any understanding of British foreign policy, more especially so in the period of the two world wars.[37] Before 1914, Zara Steiner reminds us, the newly emerging tabloids, catering for the

[36] Bertie to Hardinge (private), 25 June 1916, Hardinge MSS, Cambridge University Library, vol. 22.

[37] For some reflections on this see Neilson, *Britain and the Last Tsar*, 84–109; and Neilson, 'Tsars and Commissars: W. Somerset Maugham, Ashenden and Images of Russia in British Adventure Fiction, 1890-1928', *Canadian Journal of History* 27(3) (1992), 475–500; also P. M. H. Bell, *John Bull and the Russian Bear: British Public Opinion, Foreign Policy and the Soviet Union*, 1941–5 (London, 1990), 17–24.

semi-literate classes, produced a steady drumbeat of imperial patriotism.[38] 'Penny-dreadfuls' and 'shilling-shockers' of the William Le Queux variety chimed in with the obsession with national efficiency that dominated the contemporary public discourse.[39] Even so, the clamour for military preparedness, proliferated by a host of patriotic and army leagues – themselves a reflection of the vibrant strength of extra-parliamentary lobby groups in Edwardian Britain – did not indicate national bellicosity. Indeed, in the end, their activities were marked by failure. Popular suspicions of military Praetorianism and the military states on the continent were deeply rooted. In the end, there was no conscript army and the Royal Navy remained the backbone of imperial defence. In British political culture Wellington and Nelson might have been national heroes, but they had lived in exceptional times, and the Edwardians, for all the crises that afflicted them, did not consider their times to be that extraordinary.[40] Even in the summer of 1914, notions of war enthusiasm were greatly exaggerated.

The experience of the carnage on the western front and an enlarged post-war electorate ensured that the pendulum swung in the other direction after 1919. This helps to explain, at least in part, the slow and often hesitant response to the provocations by the revisionist powers in the 1930s. In the 1920s there was still a consensus that 'the League must be part of the general foreign policy of the country'.[41] In the face of the many challenges posed by the dictators in the following decade, the dream of a new world order based on collective security gradually revealed itself as a utopian illusion.

There was also the fear that – in Stanley Baldwin's striking phrase – 'the bomber will always get through'.[42] That dread reverberated through contemporary literature, too. Some prescient writers, like George Orwell, wove popular fears of the aerial threat into their fiction: 'There

[38] Z. S. Steiner and K. Neilson, *Britain and the Origins of the First World War* (Basingstoke and New York, 2nd ed. 2003), 33–34.

[39] Most famously in Le Queux's two starkly different and yet remarkably similar invasion fantasies, *The Great War in England in 1897* (London, 1897) and *The Invasion of 1910* (London, 1906). The former fictionalized a Franco-Russian onslaught, the latter a German 'bolt from the blue'.

[40] I. Pears, 'The Gentleman and the Hero: Wellington and Napoleon in the Nineteenth Century', in R. Porter (ed.), *Myths of the English* (Cambridge, 1992), 216–36; and A. Lambert, *Nelson: Britannia's God of War* (London, 2004), 339–62.

[41] Cecil to Curzon, 24 May 1923, Curzon Papers, British Library Oriental and India Office Collection, London, MSS. Eur. F.112/229.

[42] Stanley Baldwin, House of Commons speech, 10 November 1932, *Hansard Parliamentary Debates (House of Commons)*, 5th ser., vol. cclxx (10 November 1932), col. 632. Baldwin sought to shock domestic and international opinion into addressing the problem of aerial disarmament, see also P. Williamson and E. Baldwin (eds.), *Baldwin Papers: A Conservative Statesman, 1908–1947* (Cambridge, 2004), 303.

was a bombing plane flying low overhead ... In two years' time, one year's time, what shall we be doing when we see one of those things? Making a dive for the cellar, wetting our bags with fright?'[43] The steady build-up of international tensions made the late 1930s quite unlike the years before 1914. Revulsion at the *Kristallnacht* excesses and outrage at the German annexation of rump Czechoslovakia hardened public opinion, but there was no decisive shift from pacifism to jingoism. It even hardened Neville Chamberlain's line to a degree, though he continued to cling to the idea – a desperate hope – that the dictators could still be deterred.[44] In September 1939, there were few signs of war enthusiasm. There was, instead, rather a weary, yet determined, acceptance of the inevitable struggle that lay ahead and that would be long and arduous.

A sport, in the horticultural sense, is offered by Domenic Lieven's examination of Russian elite perceptions of Britain before the First World War. Views of foreign countries, frequently filtered through the policymaking elite's own preoccupations and prejudices, have always played a significant part in foreign policymaking. They were not static but dynamic, liable to be changed by the wider policy context and, in turn, to reflect it.[45] Thus, Russian elite perceptions of Britain throughout the second half of the long nineteenth century tended to be the reverse of views of Imperial Germany. For the eighteenth-century Russian aristocracy, Britain's perceived stability and the organic development of society and politics there were an inspiring role model. In Russia, as elsewhere amongst the continental nobility, Anglomania produced many exotic blooms.[46] After the Napoleonic wars, however, Anglo-Russian relations were dominated by rivalry, especially so in the so-called Eastern Question and further afield in Central and Eastern Asia. An altogether different picture now emerged of Britain. Her policies were seen to be greedy, selfish and egotistical, and her elites as unreliable. Although the rise of Germany after 1870 brought about some revision

---

[43] G. Orwell, *Coming up for Air* (Harmondsworth, Mdx., repr. 1986 (1st 1939)), 19–20.

[44] Z. S. Steiner, *The Triumph of the Dark: European International History, 1933–1939* (Oxford, 2011), 776–77 and 819–23.

[45] Fundamental on this Neilson, Britain and the Last Tsar, 51–83; Neilson, '"That Elusive Entity British Policy in Russia": The Impact of Russia on British Policy at the Paris Peace Conference', M. Dockrill and J. Fisher (eds.), *The Paris Peace Conference 1919: A Peace without Victory?* (London, 2001), 67–103; and Neilson, *Britain, Soviet Russia and the Collapse of the Versailles Order, 1919–1939* (Cambridge, 2006), 13–23.

[46] See A. Cross, 'Russian Perceptions of England, and Russian National Awareness at the End of the Eighteenth and the Beginning of the Twentieth Centuries', in A. Cross (ed.), *Anglo-Russica: Aspects of Cultural Relations between Great Britain and Russia in the Eighteenth and Early Nineteenth Centuries* (Oxford and Providence, RI, 1993), 93–112. The phenomenon is captured brilliantly in I. Buruma, *Voltaire's Coconuts, or Anglomania in Europe* (London, 1999).

of that view, suspicions of British perfidy were deep-seated. A shift towards friendlier sentiments came in the wake of Russia's humiliating defeat at the hands of Japan in 1904–05. The growing hostility towards Germany and political cooperation with liberal Britain and republican France were now seen as 'constitutional Russia' at last coming of age. This view was the reverse of British perceptions of Russian foreign policy. There was a general consensus at the Foreign Office and amongst senior embassy staff in St. Petersburg that its course was determined by an ongoing struggle for the levers of power between 'reactionaries' and 'reformers'.[47] Conversely, Russian views of Britain were often refracted through competing visions of Russia's place in the world, her projected future geopolitical development and anticipated broader changes in international politics. Friendly sentiments were not easily translatable into political action, however. While Count Alexander von Benckendorff, the ambassador in London, and his political master at the Choristers' Bridge, Sergei D. Sazonov, might have been complete Anglophiles, mistrust of 'perfidious Albion' was instinctive and deeply rooted in Anglo-Russian history. A preference for English habits, West End clubs and Savile Row suits did not prevent Russian expansionism or interference in Persian affairs in the years immediately preceding the outbreak of the First World War. In an intriguing mirror image of British perceptions of Russian policy being determined by domestic developments, the Russians were convinced that Britain's unreliability rested on a popular 'spirit of insularity', geopolitical naivety and a general ignorance of international affairs.

Informal influence and the material underpinnings of Britain's world policy are examined in Hamish Ion's study of Yokohama as an imperial defence and trade hub and a node of influence for change in Japan. It is a story of dynamic change. Yokohama began as an outpost of British naval power following the partial opening of that country to British trade and influence in 1858. There was, however, also a strong strand of continuity in British attitudes towards Japan and the Yokohama base. The strategic position of the Japanese archipelago in relation to both the Asian mainland and the trans-Pacific shipping lines made Japan an object of British policy. This was no less true during this early, 'quasi-colonial period' than during the interwar years. Japan, in fact, was a significant factor in the development of Britain's strategic foreign policy from the late nineteenth century to the 1930s. Naval capabilities determined policy in the region

---

[47] Instructive K. Neilson, '"My Beloved Russians": Sir Arthur Nicolson and Russia, 1906-1916', *International History Review* ix, 4 (1987), 521–54; for the context, D. C. B. Lieven, 'Pro-Germans and Russian Foreign Policy, 1890-1914', *International History Review*, 2(1) (1980), 34–54.

and underlined the centrality of the imperial-maritime nexus in the history of Britain in East Asia.[48] Yokohama was an important part of a chain of ports on which British naval and commercial power in the region rested.

Yokohama, however, was also a node of internal influence for change. Britain's presence in the port and its environs transmitted British cultural, social and, indeed, sporting ideas into Japanese society as well as industrial concepts. Yokohama offered the Japanese Anglo-Saxon society in microcosm. Trade held the various elements of British influence together. Yokohama was the key entrepôt for British import and export trade in Japan. It was an integral part of a network of ports, naval stations and logistical facilities, including Singapore, Hong Kong and Shanghai, which connected East Asia to other British interests in the Indian Ocean, Australasia and beyond.

Britain's interest in Yokohama was not static. It changed in accordance with the strategic balance in East Asian waters. However close or remote British foreign secretaries wished Anglo-Japanese relations to be, the emerging Japanese sea power helped to assuage concerns about Russian ambitions in Asia and so brought the two countries together. The Royal Navy remained the armed wing of British diplomacy in the region. Its function was to ensure that a global financial and commercial empire was able to use the maritime highways. The rise of Japan as a regional power thus took place in the context of a changing British and Western imperial presence in the Far East. It emphasizes further, as Ion demonstrates, the place of Japan within the overarching British interests in continental East Asia and the China trade. Yokohama, then, was part of the dynamics of that informal imperialism which shaped the trans-maritime geopolitics of the Asia-Pacific region, and it also acted as a stimulant in Japan's modernization of its transport infrastructure and commercial and financial practices. The Royal Navy's presence in Japanese waters and the British garrison at Yokohama allowed Britain to project an image of strength, not least also through the deployment of the pomp and circumstance of military parades and marching bands. In all these respects Britain's physical presence in the port, as well as its manifold commercial interests centred on it, backed the country's strategic foreign policy at the local level.

Britain's naval presence in the waters of East Asia helped to project her global influence and to protect her regional commercial and strategic

---

[48] See *inter alia* K. Neilson, 'The Anglo-Japanese Alliance and British Strategic Foreign Policy 1902-1914', in P. P. O'Brien (ed.), *The Anglo-Japanese Alliance* (London and New York, 2004), 48–63; K. Neilson, 'Defence and Diplomacy: The British Foreign Office and Singapore, 1939–40', *Twentieth Century British History* 14(2) (2003), 138–64.

interests. Neither there nor in home waters did her maritime predominance remain unchallenged. In the years after 1900, and even more so after 1905, Germany emerged as a serious competitor at sea. Intriguingly, her challenge, as John Maurer shows, led to the renewal of British sea power. Maritime dominance enabled Britain to maintain an empire that was stretched around the globe and linked together by a vast network of finance and trade, communications and naval power. By staying ahead of naval rivals, Britain secured command of the sea and its position as a world power.[49]

The Anglo-German naval race also suggests that there were limits to British naval power. Periodic bouts of the 'Copenhagen syndrome' notwithstanding, Britain's naval prowess was not sufficient to deter Imperial Germany's leadership from pressing ahead with their own naval programme. This opened tensions within the British cabinet. 'Economists' frequently now clashed with 'navalists'. Lloyd George might have railed against the vociferous demands for 'building gigantic flotillas against mythical Armadas', yet he provided the money needed.[50] In this way, Britain kept ahead of her rival. Indeed, if anything, the 'Dreadnought gap' was in her favour. By overreacting to uncertainty about German intentions, the British government gave a clear demonstration of Britain's material strength and political resolve to see off all comers. She had the financial reserves, industrial capacity and access to cutting-edge technology to build as strong a navy as any in the world. Britain in the years before 1914 was no 'weary titan'. She was a formidable Great Power, fully capable of beating back peacetime challengers.[51]

Historians have given particular attention to Britain's naval power, befitting the Royal Navy's position as the 'senior service'. Military force projection, however, was also a key factor, as David French explains in his contribution to this collection. In the twentieth century Britain's global position was challenged from two different directions. Other powers threatened Britain from the outside, while disparate nationalist movements sought to subvert British rule from within the Empire.[52] By the middle of the century, both had undermined the material strength and economic prosperity that buttressed the Empire. The notion that, until then, Britain had maintained its overseas possessions through a maximum of political

---

[49] See Neilson, 'The British Empire floats on the British Navy', 21–42; K. Neilson, '1914: The German War?', *European History Quarterly* 44(3) (2014), 395–418.
[50] Lloyd George budget speech, *Hansard Parliamentary Debates*, 5th ser. vol. iv (29 April 1909), col. 480.
[51] See Neilson, 'Greatly Exaggerated', 705 *et passim*; Steiner and Neilson, *Britain*, 51–63.
[52] For pertinent reflections on the external dimension of this, see Neilson, *Collapse of the Versailles Order*, 9–13.

cajolery and with the minimum of physical force has the patina of a posthumous myth. It was not entirely untrue, however; and this for no other reason than that the high costs of employing European officers to administer the Empire made it desirable to co-opt indigenous political and other elites in the imperial enterprise. But when faced with violent challenges to their authority, British officials, both metropolitan and in the locale, were ready to meet violence with violence. Britain, at any rate, had never relied on what became known in the later twentieth century as a 'hearts and minds' strategy to win over local populations. The various and repeated punitive expeditions against recalcitrant tribes on India's Northwestern frontier or the Ashanti kingdom in West Africa serve as reminders of this fact, if it requires reminding.

It was only in the aftermath of the 1914–1918 war that public concerns grew about the perceived excessiveness of the use of force by British troops in the Empire. Already before then, public opinion had recoiled at Kitchener's 'methods of barbarism' in the struggle against the Boers. Now, German reprisals against Belgian civilians had sensitized the public further to the complexities of using military force to maintain public order in conflict zones. Here, too, public opinion played a significant role. In practice, in colonial campaigns, British commanders in the field tended to act with some degree of restraint. This was not so much out of deference to legal niceties – local legal frameworks, indeed, made provisions for emergency legislation – but more with a view to pragmatic calculations. They did not shy away from using exemplary violence to impress on insurgents, and those suspected of harbouring insurrectionary ambitions, Britain's ruthless determination to uphold her position. Once that impression had been made, however, they sought to initiate a process of conciliation. Force, after all, was an expensive way of running the Empire, and usually effective only in the short term. The British had understood well enough that, over time, bayonets made for uncomfortable sitting.

Excesses were not entirely a thing of the past, as the occurrences at Amritsar or Croke Park demonstrated. After 1945, the application of the principle of minimum force was not the army's default position. If anything, it had to be forced upon it by its political masters in Whitehall and by public opinion. In effect, the notion of minimum force as a concept of military doctrine was so ill defined as to constitute no effective guidance for action. The same pragmatic considerations that applied before 1914 were also in operation after 1945. Some degree of physical violence was considered to be necessary to degrade and disrupt the insurgents' organization and to sap their morale. Too much violence, by contrast, was likely to stiffen resistance and make a negotiated settlement more difficult, if not impossible, to achieve. Minimum force was thus a supple linguistic construct that cloaked the complex realities of imperial policing. It had to be elastic because, ultimately, the British authorities did not wish to define it precisely – and in that respect it was rather like the Empire as a whole.

Kathleen Burk turns her attention to wealth as a factor underpinning British power, more especially here the commercial and financial networks in South America in the nineteenth century. As one middle-ranking diplomat, on declining the offer of a posting to Central America, noted a little indelicately, 'screwing money out of shady Dagoes' was 'the main preoccupation' of British diplomacy in that region.[53] There was, in fact, a kernel of truth in this blunt statement. British interests in South America were overwhelmingly commercial and financial. Indeed, Britain enjoyed a degree of economic dominance in several countries of the region. Even so, the authorities in London preferred to hold aloof from any active interference in the affairs of a region that, its economic potential aside, was even richer in internal and external squabbles. For much of the long nineteenth century, British governments refrained from any kind of intervention even to secure contracts and concessions for British banks and merchants. In contrast, for instance, to Persia there was no external pressure to force British diplomacy to adopt a more forthright attitude. The Royal Navy had the command of the sea in the Atlantic and kept other European nations out of South America, and the United States were as yet of little consequence there.[54] The extent of corrupt practices amongst the local political and commercial elites, moreover, suggested that it was better for British diplomats to remain above the fray of commercial competition.

Silver mines and agriculture as well as engineering were the mainstays of Britain's economic presence in the region. Banks, especially Barings Brothers and N.M. Rothschild, had the most extensive and effective networks of contact there, often using family ties. There were great profits to be made in Latin America. Equally, losses on a gigantic scale were no rarity, as readers of Trollope novels knew only too well, and as the near folding of Barings in 1890 might have reminded them.[55] British business kept a tight grip on the Argentine economy throughout the period. It and the southern half of the western hemisphere remained a lucrative market for British companies. Indeed, on the eve of the First World War

---

[53] Rumbold to Rumbold sr., 14 August 1913, Rumbold MSS, Bodleian Library, Oxford, Ms. Rumbold dep. 16.

[54] D. C. M. Platt, *Latin America and British Trade, 1806–1914* (London, 1972), 3–23; J. Smith, *Illusions of Conflict: Anglo-American Diplomacy toward Latin America* (Pittsburgh, PA, 1979).

[55] In *The Way We Live Now* (London, 1875), Augustus Melmotte, Trollope's main character, a financier with a suitably mysterious past, is ruined by his speculative South Central Pacific and Mexican Railway scheme.

somewhere between a fifth and a quarter of all British overseas investments were made in Latin America. The war ended Britain's commercial and financial hegemony over South America. Investments there were offered as collateral to secure wartime loans on the New York money markets or sold there to raise funds for the allied war effort.[56] In the process, Britain lost some 15 per cent of her national wealth. No matter how extensive and effective the various British financial and commercial networks in Latin America had been, they all fell victim to the profound shift in material power towards the United States brought about by the war.

Material and economic power not only facilitated and amplified British policy; economic assessments of other powers also shaped policy towards them, as Bruce Strang's examination of British views of Japan in the later 1930s shows.[57] Since the nineteenth century, long-established networks of business groups and other interested parties had lobbied Whitehall on China and East Asian matters. Following the escalation of Sino-Japanese fighting in 1937 and the acceleration of Japanese aggression on the Asian mainland, policy discussion in London revolved around the question of whether or not to impose economic sanctions to force Japan to moderate its behaviour.[58] Various Whitehall departments contributed assessments of their own. Japan, it was generally acknowledged, was dependent on Britain and America for various kind of iron and non-ferrous metals as well as oil, but had begun to stockpile vital commodities. A further consideration, which weighed against the sanctions weapon, was the appreciable effect of the loss of any export markets. The conclusion, pressed more especially by the Treasury, was that the more effective the sanctions were, the more of an incentive Japan had to go to war.

The problem of containing Japanese expansion in East Asia was exacerbated by the need of having to deal simultaneously with the difficulties posed by other revisionist powers in Europe. In Asia, Britain's interests were more closely aligned with those of the United States. Both countries were broadly in favour of preserving the regional status quo. There were significant differences, however. Washington was reluctant to assume a more active role in either Europe or Asia. Its contribution to a status quo policy was stronger on rhetoric than on practical assistance. Anthony Eden's conclusion at the time that 'we must lose no opportunity of

---

[56] See also Neilson, *Strategy and Supply*, 191–94, for some of the manoeuvring to secure such loans.

[57] For a complementary study see K. Neilson, '"Pursued by a Bear": British Estimates of Soviet Military Strength and Anglo-Soviet Relations', *Canadian Journal of History* 28(2) (1993), 189–221.

[58] Neilson, *Collapse of the Versailles Order*, 188–90.

cooperating with [the] US gov[ernmen]t' reflected the basic assumptions about British policy in the Asia-Pacific region since well before 1914.[59] In the circumstances of 1937, however, it was a further reason to move with circumspection. Sanctions were likely to prove ineffective, especially if America did not adopt a similar regime, and would thus only antagonize Japan.

There was, as Strang notes, considerable cognitive dissonance amongst the British foreign policy elite in the matter of Japan. Britain's relative decline and imperial overstretch were readily recognized; and so was the fact that, faced with difficulties in Europe, 'if they can only cause us some embarrassment . . . the Japanese will seize the opportunity to attack us in the Far East, Treaty or no Treaty'.[60] That investments in China could not be defended was not a matter of dispute.[61] At the same time, senior officials did not consider it necessary for the country to cut its East Asian cloth in accordance with its more reduced circumstances. Indeed, they indulged in wishful thinking in their attempts to secure that rarest of political commodities – time. Chinese resistance to Japanese aggression was bound to grow, it was hoped, and the fighting on the Asian mainland would ultimately exhaust Japan's resources.[62] This was not an altogether unreasonable assumption. Even so, declining powers, it seems, cannot simply scuttle. Britain could not retreat into isolation. There was a range of choices before it, but the country no longer had the power sufficient to secure its aims. There was no appeasement of Japan. British policy did not make any substantive concessions to the Japanese, but nor did it mount an effective defence of British interests in East Asia.

If Britain was hamstrung in Asia, elsewhere the Empire, more especially in the shape of the so-called white settler Dominions, acted as a multiplier of British global power. Mobilizing raw materials and manpower reserves was vital to the war effort in the two global conflicts in the twentieth century as well as in countless colonial campaigns. The Empire's support for Britain's global defence policy was less urgent and so less visible in peacetime, but it was no less significant, as Douglas E. Delaney shows in his account of the interwar Imperial General Staff.

[59] Min. Eden, 30 July 1937, TNA (PRO), FO 371/20952/F4890/9/10.
[60] Min. Cadogan, 21 November, on memo. Sargent, 19 November 1938, FO 371/21639/C14523/14209/62.
[61] See also the reflections offered by Neilson, *Collapse of the Versailles Order*, 219–20; also K. Neilson, 'Orme Sargent, Appeasement and British Policy in Europe, 1933 to 1939', *Twentieth Century British History* 21(1) (2010), 1–28; and 'The Royal Navy, Japan and British Strategic Foreign Policy, 1932-1934', *Journal of Military History* 75(2) (2011), 505–32.
[62] Tels. Clark Kerr to Halifax (nos. 569–570 immediate), 19 June 1939, FO 371/23400/F6017/1/10.

In 1919, Britain found herself encumbered with more liabilities and commitments than had been the case before the war; and this meant that the Dominions' contribution would remain important. Demands by the military authorities to maintain at least the semblance of some sort of war readiness swiftly ran into the brickwall of post-war political reality. Neither in Britain nor in the Dominions was there much appetite for anything that smacked of military adventurism. There were practical achievements, however. Above all, interoperability between the different Empire armies was maintained. In financial and political terms this was cheap – an important consideration given that the 'Geddes axe' hovered ominously over the armed forces. Close cooperation between staffs, facilitated by the continued existence of the Imperial General Staff, a commitment to standardized equipment and coordination of military education made no significant demands on the Exchequer. In practical terms, however, they laid the foundations for the later expansion of Commonwealth armies in the Second World War.

Given the desiccated condition of the military establishments across the Empire, retaining and refining the machinery for raising and expand-ing armies in the eventuality of war was all that could be achieved. Here, too, there were continuities over a longer period of time. The Imperial General Staff was a loose coordinating mechanism based on consensus rather than on a metropolitan hierarchy. It reflected the peculiar nature of the evolving Empire, but also that of the pre-war metropolitan Committee of Imperial Defence. Significantly, consensus facilitated by common education and training produced a similar, if not uniform, military outlook. In this respect, the Imperial Defence College was estab-lished in 1927 specifically to foster compatibility and familiarity. But already prior to its creation, the dissemination of ideas and habits of mind amongst Dominion forces was aided by instructors, the majority of whom had graduated from the Staff College at Camberley.[63] Officer exchanges were another inexpensive means of solidifying and deepening military compatibility. Fostering it furnished the slimmest of foundations of joint endeavour. Yet these were strong enough and durable enough to turn the idea of a Commonwealth war effort into reality in 1939.

Interoperability at the political level in wartime, by contrast, was noticeable largely by its absence, as Kent Federowich shows in his account of the plans for an imperial conference in 1941. The complex interplay of intra-Empire politics and calculations of a global war-fighting

---

[63] See also A. Godefroy, 'Professional Training Put to the Test: The Royal Military College of Canada and Army Leadership in the South African War, 1899-1902', *The Army Doctrine and Training Bulletin* 6(2) (2002), 5–13.

strategy conspired against such plans. It reflected the Empire's somewhat amorphous nature. Demands for greater consultation underscored the growing consciousness on the part of the Dominions of their own worth and importance. For now, the exigencies of war kept them together, but the clashes with London foreshadowed the centrifugal forces after 1945. Conversely, the Dominions' position was complicated by the piecemeal constitutional development in the years since the end of the First World War. Suggestions of a reconstituted imperial war cabinet, thus, sat awkwardly with earlier demands for greater autonomy.

The fissiparous internal politics of, for instance, Canada complicated matters further. Conscription had deeply divided the country in 1917 along ethno-linguistic lines, and it was widely expected to do so again in the event of another war. In Australia, a general election was looming on the horizon. Even so, Dominion leaders understood the need for an effective voice in London to have any kind of influence on the broad questions of strategy. For Britain's wartime prime minister, especially during the difficult months of 1941, the mooted imperial conference was a means of demonstrating resolve and strength, not least with a view to the still neutral United States, when the course of the war seemed to suggest nothing but weakness. Ironically, indeed, American lend-lease was soon to be overshadowed by the Dominions' contribution to the war effort.

Discussions about an imperial conference consumed much time, but ultimately proved fruitless. It was not until 1944 that the Dominion leaders collectively met with Churchill. Superficially, the meeting validated claims of Dominion equality in the imperial war effort. In the cold light of day, matters looked rather different, for Churchill brooked no interference in matters of strategy, not then and not later. The abortive gathering of Empire leaders leaves the student of British world policy with a paradox. Underneath the carapace of imperial unity, the conference 'that never was' underlined that each of the Dominions conducted its own foreign policy within the context of an evolving, fluid and now multi-centred Commonwealth alliance.

That Britain and her Empire were undergoing significant change in the first half of the short twentieth century is underscored also by Erik Goldstein's study of the fifty-one paladins, the diplomatic representatives who attained the position of ambassador between the two world wars. As in the nineteenth century, senior diplomats had a strong sense of being the representatives abroad of Britain and its values.[64] In the period after the

---

[64] Crucial for this aspect K. Neilson, '"Only a D ... d Marionette"?: The Influence of Ambassadors on British Foreign Policy', M. Dockrill and B. J. C. McKercher (eds.), *Diplomacy and World Power: Studies in British Foreign Policy, 1890–1951* (Cambridge, 1996), 56–78.

First World War the service faced a growing threat of politicization and diminution of its influence on policy. Even the survival of a professional service was in doubt, especially when Lloyd George, always disdainful of professional advice, sought to fill senior posts with his cronies. Maintaining service morale was an ongoing struggle. The First World War had been a watershed moment for the Foreign Office and the diplomatic service. The influence of professional diplomats reached a low ebb after 1916. There was a degree of recovery in the mid-1920s under the foreign secretaryship of Sir Austen Chamberlain, ably assisted by his Permanent Undersecretary, Sir Eyre Crowe.[65] A succession of weak and often neophyte foreign secretaries and then the advent of Neville Chamberlain, a Prime Minister bent on pursuing his own foreign policy objectives, reduced the department's role once again. The fate of Sir Robert Vansittart was exemplary in this respect. He was moved in a sideways arabesque from being Permanent Undersecretary to the newly created post of Chief Diplomatic Adviser, only for his advice to be carefully and deliberately ignored.

The First World War had disrupted the ordinary career progression of many diplomats, a significant number of missions abroad being out of circulation for the duration of the conflict. After 1919, as new states proliferated, so the number of missions increased. There were also more embassies than before 1914, though for status and financial reasons London was anxious not to increase their number by too much.[66] In 1938, Chamberlain, a former Chancellor of the Exchequer who knew the price but not the value of diplomacy, halted the creation of new embassies. In practice, of course, certain embassies were more important than others. For reasons of *realpolitik* and in terms of individual careers Latin America remained the graveyard of professional diplomats. Brussels and Lisbon were clearly less significant than Paris, Rome and Berlin. Washington and Moscow were problematic for different reasons throughout the interwar years. Successive British governments responded to the rise of the United States during the First World War with a series of not always successful non-professional appointments. As for the Soviet capital, none of the three ambassadors there before 1939 was 'among the most prominent in the diplomatic service'.[67] There was only a small pool of Russian linguists, and fewer diplomats still were ready to endure the austere life in the citadel of Bolshevism. Whatever their shortcomings and

---

[65] K. Neilson and T. G. Otte, *The Permanent Under-Secretary for Foreign Affairs, 1854–1946* (London and New York, 2009), 205.

[66] Balfour to Curzon (private), 22 January 1919, Curzon Papers, MSS.Eur. F.112/208A.

[67] Neilson, *Collapse of the Versailles Order*, 25.

whatever the challenges to the diplomatic service as a whole, the ambassadors were part of the machinery that assisted Britain in maintaining her position in world politics; and they were also part of an empire in transition.

The chapters in this volume shed new light on the full panoply of British power in its global setting in the nineteenth and twentieth centuries. They examine the different instruments at the disposal of British governments and the range of choices that confronted them. Appreciating the instruments and their varied suitability for their tasks furnishes a powerful antidote to the White Queen's memory syndrome that can so easily afflict historians.

# 1 The War Trade Intelligence Department and British Economic Warfare during the First World War

*John Robert Ferris*

The best-known element of signals intelligence during the First World War is work against the operational traffic of armies and navies, centring on cryptanalysis and traffic analysis. However, overwhelmingly its largest element during that conflict, and the area where signals intelligence was most frequently used, lay in economic warfare. This instance was perhaps the case in history where communications intelligence worked best without the aid of cryptanalysis. It was the first case where both communications intelligence and powerful and sophisticated modes of analysis were applied to strategy and economic warfare. These issues were fundamental to a central part of the Great War: the blockade.[1] Studies of the blockade routinely mention communications intelligence, but rarely treat it systematically. Thus, a key dimension in the history of the blockade, and signals intelligence, is overlooked. Between 1914 and 1918, British intelligence intercepted and read 80,000,000 telegrams, 25,000,000 radio messages and 630,000,000 postal packets, possibly involving over 1,000,000,000 letters, since business packages routinely carried many messages. These are big numbers. They dwarf any collection of communications, or intelligence, ever known before 1914. These messages were processed in real time and applied effectively to economic warfare. Without this power in collection and assessment, the blockade would have taken a different form. It might have failed. This chapter illuminates

---

[1] Useful accounts of the blockade include Archibald C. Bell, *A History of the Blockade of Germany and of the Countries Associated with Her in the Great War, Austria, Bulgaria and Turkey, 1914–1918* (London, 1937); Marion Siney, *The Allied Blockade of Germany, 1914–1916* (Ann Arbor, 1957); Nicholas A. Lambert, *Planning Armageddon, British Economic Warfare and the First World War* (Cambridge, MA, 2012), 60–100; Avner Offer, *The First World War: An Agrarian Interpretation* (Oxford, 1989); Eric W. Osborne, *Britain's Economic Blockade of Germany, 1914–1919* (London, 2004), 34–41. For my interpretation, see J. R. Ferris, 'The Origins of the Hunger Blockade: Irony, Intelligence and International Law, 1914-15', in Michael Epkenhans and Stephen Huck (eds.), *Der Erste Weltkrieg zur See* (Berlin and Boston, 2017), 83–98; for parallel views, Matthew S. Seligman, 'Failing to Prepare for the Great War?: The Absence of Grand Strategy in British War Planning before 1914', *War in History* 24(2) (2017).

that matter by examining the greatest instance of information processing in history before 1939: the work of the War Trade Intelligence Department (WTID) between 1915 and 1918.

\* \* \*

Between 1898 and 1914, despite many problems, Britain outstripped every other power in preparations to process and apply information for operational and strategic decision making. These systems shaped British intelligence for economic warfare during the First World War, though they were not intended to aid that effort, and developed apart from each other before 1914. So to enable informed action, the army and the Royal Navy (RN) adopted the General Staff model and reconfigured their C3I systems for operations, while the Foreign Office developed a new approach toward information processing.[2] These models, well suited to handling massive amounts of reports and data, helped Britain address economic warfare quickly and well during the Great War. So did the creation of means to collect intelligence from international communications. The Boer War illustrated the power of cable censorship in times of war and illuminated its requirements. Britain generalized these experiences into a policy and a structure. It aimed to prevent any enemy from communicating in war, and to control and exploit messages sent on British cables. Several interdepartmental committees formulated policy on censoring cable, wireless and mail. Thinking globally and acting locally, they integrated complex technical issues into every decision. These committees defined protocols, applied them across the empire, and established a structure to embody these ideas. Its skeleton was strong, but this structure needed much more muscle than Whitehall realized.[3] Decision makers over-generalized experiences from the Boer War, when traffic was easily controlled and targets identified, into preparations for a world war, when every message must matter, but be processed in the context of them all. Planners could not conceptualize the sort of struggle they would confront, an existential war involving every nation on earth,

---

[2] Nicholas Black, *The British Naval Staff in the First World War* (Woodbridge, 2009); Z. S. Steiner, *The Foreign Office and Foreign Policy, 1898–1914* (Cambridge, 1969), 80–82; T. G. Otte, 'Old Diplomacy: Reflections on the Foreign Office Before 1914', *Contemporary British History* 18(3) (2004), 31–52; John Gooch, *The Plans of War: The General Staff and British Military Strategy, c. 1906–1916* (London, 1974). Martin Daunton (ed.), *The Organisation of Knowledge in Victorian Britain* (Oxford, 2005), provides useful context.

[3] Report of Censorship of Cable and Wireless Committee, 7 July 1908, CAB 17/92; Admiralty Intelligence Division, August 1911, 'Regulations for the Censorship of Radio-Telegraphy in Time of War', FO 371/1283/38965; GS 1906, A 1039, 'Censorship of Submarine Cables in Times of War', and 1907 version, and 'Second Meeting, Censorship of Submarine Cables', 26 October 1910, L/MIL 7/13581.

and all of their communications. Not until overwhelmed by data could planners understand the problems of bulk processing, and their solutions. They mistook the amount of traffic they must handle, and the numbers of people, and the range of skills, required to do so. They overlooked the need for analysis, assuming that messages should be understood easily.

Planning for censorship emphasized military security and intelligence. Planners barely considered what became intelligence's greatest role, that of economic warfare, although they knew they would handle commercial traffic. This indifference probably reflected the view that control of contraband would be tertiary in economic warfare. Before 1914, British authorities misunderstood the nature and value of economic warfare, and scarcely recognized the idea of intelligence for it. Yet Britain possessed powerful means to achieve these ends. Intelligence was preadapted to the problem of contraband, not because a problem was recognized and solutions were followed, but through Britain's position in world communications and information processing. British authorities had intelligence fit for economic warfare without realizing it – for a campaign they did not expect to fight.

## The Birth of Economic Warfare, 1914–1915

In 1912, leading members of the Liberal government defined a policy for economic warfare based around the recommendations of the Desart committee. That policy broke almost as soon as it was adopted, without anyone knowing the fact. It assumed that the Declaration of London (DOL), which aimed to rewrite maritime law, and close blockade would govern economic war with Germany. The RN would effectively close German ports in the North Sea, preventing imports or exports of any items through them. Few items would be termed contraband, so minimizing the need to seize neutral goods, especially those of American firms, thus angering the neutral governments. Britain would regulate its exports to neutrals. Between 1912 and 1914, however, the DOL became stalemated, and lacked legal standing. Sailors abandoned close blockade, without informing landsmen, and adopted distant blockade. The latter could prevent any trade by German ships and reduce neutral exports to Germany, but was not legally effective. In war, no German ports would be blockaded effectively, leaving neutrals free to trade with them. Contraband, conversely, was not legally redefined. It could cover any item which any belligerent cared to name. In August 1914, no British decision makers knew what contraband would be, nor how to control it. The idea of regulating British trade during war remained controversial – civil departments wanted little control, and the Admiralty much.

Many ministers and the public were ignorant of the idea. Means to exercise these regulations remained undefined.[4]

When war began, British policy for economic warfare collapsed. Britain needed a new one. That endeavour involved Britain's relations with every neutral state, national firms and its own. These issues caused controversy among decision makers. Initially, they wished to respect international law and neutral rights, and to minimize restrictions on British exports and control over contraband. This approach would ease Germany's ability to import and export goods through neutrals, and blunt a blade against it. The diplomats, intelligence officials and naval officers who managed economic warfare soon developed a different view. Britain must prevent Germany from importing any item useful to its war economy, including any raw material used by industries, and also food. Britain must control the export to neutrals alongside Germany of any goods produced within the empire. British policy slowly drifted in this direction, against much resistance. It was far from those ends until Germany declared unrestricted submarine warfare in February 1915. After this declaration, Britain sought to prevent Germany from importing or exporting anything at all. It treated as contraband all items which neutrals imported or exported to the Central Powers.

This aim was easier to announce than to achieve. Between August 1914 and February 1915, Britain developed powerful means to wage economic warfare, but the authorities did not understand how easily or suddenly they could be combined.[5] Several departments created units to handle economic warfare, like the Contraband Department of the Foreign Office, under Sir Eyre Crowe, and the Naval Trade Division (NTD) of the Admiralty. The RN controlled trade across the Atlantic Ocean. Britain coerced neutral firms into accepting its regulation of their activities. It developed intelligence services able to detect contraband: diplomats in neutral countries, and the censorship of cables, wireless and post. They provided masses of information, much worthless, all requiring analysis, which initially no one could do. Confusion emerged as these services and units learned how to work and to cooperate. Several departments created Black Lists, delineating foreign businesses with which Britons could not work, on varying principles, naming different people. The wireless censors gave the Naval Staff some messages about contraband, which the cable censorship did massively and rapidly through a 'trade section' under Major Phillips. Intelligence directed some seizures of cargoes. Communications intelligence provoked a key event in Britain's campaign of economic warfare: to block shipments of copper

---

[4] Ferris, 'Hunger Blockade', for details.    [5] Ibid.

to Germany, guided by one of the first analysts of economic and communications intelligence in history, Frederick Leverton Harris, of the NTD.[6] Generally, however, suspicion produced seizures that could not be justified. Too many innocents were delayed, too much contraband passed. This situation rapidly improved as regards sources, assessments and process, as the regulatory system simplified contraband control. By February 1915, intelligence was strong enough to reduce the political difficulty of stopping too many neutral ships, but not to solve the central matter in law and practice, of seizing specific cargoes, and providing evidence to condemn them before the Prize Court. Compared to the intelligence system at its maturity, the postal censorship was weak, sources were uncoordinated, layers of analysts and data retrievers were lacking. Neutral governments resisted British expansion of its claims to control contraband, though the greatest of them, the United States, was willing to accept its practices, so long as they did not prevent Americans from doing well out of the war.

Unrestricted submarine warfare created a crisis in sea power. So did British retaliation, in a form combining diplomacy, intelligence and law. Supporters of hard practices feared these might not be feasible. During March 1915, reflecting its respect for the power of law and the United States in economic warfare, the Admiralty believed that inadequate intelligence would cripple control of contraband. The solution was more and better spies. No-one mentioned communications intelligence, not even those who had used it for economic warfare. The First Lord of the Admiralty, Winston Churchill, did not refer to it, because he did not know about that use, and thought the limits to intelligence forced a cautious start to blockade. 'Prima facie, I do not favour the wholesale arrest of ships. We should proceed selectively where we have clear cases, and operate by a deterrent effect on others who may think they come near the line.' The RN should seize 'at least a dozen ships sailing within the next week, for arrest on grounds outside the penalties of international law', while rapidly developing spy networks 'so that we get really good information of cargoes which are German tainted, and do not have to rummage ships unnecessarily'. The Admiralty's experts on economic warfare shared these views. Commander Longdon, the NTD's head on contraband, held that before the Prize Court proof of contraband status, such as proving '*probable enemy destination*', was essential. 'These cases should for the present be comparatively few in number, and vessels

---

[6] J. R. Ferris, 'Reading the World's Mail: British Censorship, Communications Intelligence and Economic Warfare, 1914–1919', in J. R. Ferris, *Issues in British and American Signals Intelligence, 1919–1932* (Fort George G. Meade, MD, 2015), 1–21.

should not be sent to discharge cargo unless the information is considered sufficiently definite to ensure condemnation in the Prize Court.'[7]

Sailors saw law and intelligence as a problem matching submarines in economic warfare, which would grow the more contraband was seized. Hence, retaliation must be restrained. These views were widespread, but misconstrued the power of intelligence in economic warfare. Three great sources were effective – cable and wireless censorship, and official reports; while another was starting, postal censorship; and a minor source, espionage. Good intelligence and means to crosscheck it were increasingly available. Modes of data processing were about to improve. The combination of communications intelligence and the WTID solved the problem of blockade intelligence with astonishing speed, and unanticipated effect. It provided strong bases of intelligence and evidence, as Britain intensified its control of contraband throughout 1915–16.

### Toward the War Trade Intelligence Department, 1914–1915

These solutions emerged through an episode, often seen as a curiosity, which was central to British intelligence during the Great War. In November 1914, the Director of Naval Intelligence (DNI), Admiral Reginald Hall, heard inaccurate stories that espionage messages were passing the postal censorship, and accurate ones that only 5 per cent of mail bags were examined. He met General George Cockerill, who had just become the Director of Special Intelligence, in charge of censoring the press, mail and cables. Cockerill noted that his men were overwhelmed.

It was necessary to create something out of nothing and at the very beginning opposition from more than one quarter had to be faced. The available staff remained lamentably small. On a recent visit to Mount Pleasant Col: Cockerill admitted that he had found something like chaos: piles of letters awaiting special attention, cheques strewn about the floor, dozens of bags which had not yet been examined at all.

Hall offered Cockerill a small staff for free to examine '*all* the foreign mails' (in fact, this involved just letters sent directly between Britain and European neutrals, not transit mails between two neutrals passing through Britain). Cockerill, replying 'In other words a little private censorship of your own!', accepted the offer for a two-month trial. Hall organized a staff through a friend, Colonel Frederick Browning, later

---

[7] Minute by Churchill 3 March 1915, memoranda by DTD, 4 March 1915, and Longdon, 6 March 1915, FO 800/909.

deputy commander of the Secret Intelligence Service (SIS). Browning delegated the task to friends at the National Service League (NSL), a pressure group which favoured conscription and had, as Stephen McKenna, later associated with these efforts, stated, 'premises, furniture, a staff' and no functions. 'A press gang of two, working the clubs of London and the colleges of Oxford, established the nucleus of a staff; and the first recruits were given, as their earliest duty, the task of bringing in more recruits', McKenna reported, the men paid 'stealthily each week, like a member of some criminal association, with a furtive bundle of notes'. This 'press gang' was Browning and probably Henry Penson, a well-known economist and statistician, or else H. W. Carless Davis, medieval historian and later Regius Professor of Modern History, from Worcester and Balliol Colleges. This inspection found no signs of espionage. It did find masses of information about how German and neutral businesses handled contraband. Penson and Davis reported to Cockerill and Hall on the topic. Then, Reginald McKenna, the Home Secretary, discovering this activity, called Cockerill and Hall onto the carpet. McKenna told Hall that his actions were illegal, which the Admiral and his subordinates thought was true. Cockerill, however, rightly defended Hall as operating under his own authority. They persuaded McKenna that the work on commercial letters should be continued officially, under Cockerill.[8]

For the first time, senior intelligence officers appreciated the significance of communications intelligence to economic warfare. Cockerill and Hall advocated aggressive postal censorship, against great resistance throughout 1915, and the coordination of intelligence on economic warfare. Histories of the WTID emphasize that they insisted on establishing 'a central bureau of war trade and economic information which would receive intelligence from all available sources; would examine, collate, and re-issue it in a convenient form to all the departments interested'.[9] They furthered their ambitions by exploiting circumstance. In January 1915, war trade was in chaos. Applications to export items overwhelmed the system to manage them, which damaged the economy and angered firms. So significant was the problem of maximising safe exports that the Prime Minister, Herbert Henry Asquith, chaired a meeting to

[8] Chapter on 1914–15, draft memoirs of Admiral Hall, Reginald Hall Papers, Churchill College, Cambridge Hall 3/2. For other references to this episode, cf. H. W. Carless Davis, 'History of the Blockade: Emergency Departments', n.d. (1920), MUN 5/113/600/25, 58–59; Stephen McKenna, *While I Remember* (London, 1921), 165; Stephen McKenna, *Tex: A Chapter in the Life of Alexander Teixiera de Mattos* (New York, 1922), 7 and 10.

[9] Carless Davis, 'History of the Blockade', MUN 5/113/600/25, 144; Unsigned, n.d., 'Origin and History of the War Trade Intelligence Department', 'A' [Penson], n.d. [c. November 1917], BT 61/12/7.

solve it. Adopting ideas from the secretary of the Committee for Imperial Defence, Maurice Hankey, who was guided by Cockerill and Hall, a War Trade Department (WTD), chaired by a minister, Lord Emmott, was created. This department, inaugurated on 1 February 1915, received a specialist staff, including a Trade Clearing House (TCH) to coordinate and disseminate commercial intelligence to all comers from all sources.

## The Trade Clearing House, 1915

Carless Davis and Penson later suggested that all worked smoothly from the start. The 'superior staff was carefully selected on the principle that the first essential was a mind trained to deal critically with evidence and to draw conclusions' from it. The TCH

benefitted by nothing so much as by the practical independence of its position. For a considerable period it stood outside the ordinary and inevitable rivalries and contentions of the older departments. It was considered to be a central clearing house for information, and was treated by all the departments which possessed such information with the greatest frankness and generosity.[10]

In fact, initial expectations about the TCH were divided. Emmott thought it would help maximize exports to neutrals, by delineating safe from suspect importers. Hall and Cockerill thought it would help stop any shipment of contraband, which they defined harshly. They understood that masses of material on commercial matters were involved, while communications intelligence must be coordinated and exploited with all sources. These officers were 'unfeignedly relieved' to hand the task of analyzing this material to the TCH, Davis wrote, perhaps because they found it daunting, and beyond their expertise.[11] Their backing was the trump card for the TCH in its early days, until it proved itself, though a weaker player, Emmott, supported them equally. Officials from other departments did not understand the situation, in part because they were not formally told of the TCH's role until March. On 21 February, Crowe did not know what the TCH was. Irritated by its informal modes of requesting that his department have consuls acquire information on specific firms, through letters headed 'For the Foreign Office (Trade Section)', he opposed cooperation with it until procedures were placed on a 'proper footing'. One of his subordinates, Robert Vansittart, persuaded him otherwise. The TCH was an official body tackling an

[10] Memorandum by Carless Davis, 'The Need for a Permanent Trade Intelligence Bureau' (Strictly Confidential), 21 November 1916, Emmott Papers, Nuffield College, Oxford, Box 6.
[11] Carless Davis, 'History of the Blockade', MUN 5/113/600/25, 144.

important task. 'I really think we shd. make enquiries of this nature when they ask it. We cannot boycott them.'[12] Soon the TCH adopted more conventional modes of correspondence, while Vansittart became its liaison with the Foreign Office, so beginning an education in intelligence, which marked British policy during the 1930s.[13]

The TCH's title suggests that many thought it would focus on creating a Black List, so easing decisions on exports to neutrals. However, it worked mostly for the units controlling contraband, as Cockerill and Hall intended. The TCH's procedures were left to the people who ran it, Penson and Davis, its chairman and deputy chairman, titles unusual for Whitehall, but not for the unofficial committees to which they were accustomed. Davis and Penson were selected because of their work with Hall's censorship. Emmott, a fellow statistician, appointed Penson, who selected the first members of his staff. Probably Penson started with veterans of Hall's censorship, who later recruited among their contacts. They created the most academic of British intelligence agencies during the Great War, or ever before, and matched only by Hut Three at Bletchley Park since. They became the largest group of communications intelligence analysts the world had ever known, and among the best on record.

Whereas Cambridge and the City dominated personnel for Room 40, the RN's communications intelligence bureau, Oxford and the Temple were the pillars of the TCH. In Britain between 1914 and 1918, economic warfare was the only area where civilian analysts dominated intelligence, and the one most involving women. One member of the TCH, Stephen McKenna, a novelist, nephew of Reginald McKenna and deputy head to the Intelligence Section, described its staff as being the successor to the NSL. A 'small and amazingly harmonious body, contributing diverse experience and callings from many countries, established a freemasonry with hard-driven men in other departments'. Recruits were almost entirely 'overage or unfit', excluding anyone 'who could turn to private account any knowledge that could come to him in his official capacity'. The TCH included 'dons and barristers, men of letters and stockbrokers, solicitors and merchants', some disabled officers, but no civil servants. In a few days they were 'acclimatized to the universal office-equipment of trestle-tables and desk-telephones, of card indices and steel filing-cabinets, of "in" and "out" trays, of rubber stamps and "urgent"

---

[12] Minute by Crowe, 21.2.15, FO 382/304/19085; cf. ibid., 19082.
[13] J. R. Ferris, '"Indulged in all too little?": Vansittart, Intelligence and Appeasement', in J. R. Ferris, *Intelligence and Strategy: Selected Essays* (London, 2005), 45–98.

labels'.[14] Emmott, describing the personnel in similar words, emphasized
that

The work demands qualities of an exceptional kind and experience of a varied
nature ... The peculiarly confidential nature of the material dealt with has made it
desirable that nobody should be engaged who could directly or indirectly benefit
by the knowledge gained in connection with the work. This has made it impossible
to accept offers of assistance from men actually engaged in banking or other forms
of business, however valuable their assistance would have been. Such men have
been consulted as experts but they have no access to the information collected in
the Departments.[15]

In 1917, about thirty, or 7 per cent of the WTID's members worked
for free, while others accepted only expenses.[16] Among them were
dons from many – probably all – British universities, but especially
Oxford, a striking proportion being historians, such as Robert
Sangster Rait, then the Professor of Scottish History and Literature
at the University of Glasgow. Alexander Teixeira de Mattos, a Dutch
national of Portuguese-Jewish descent and convert to Catholicism,
famous as translator into English of works by Danish, Flemish,
Dutch, French, German and Norwegian authors, including Emile
Zola and Maurice Maeterlinck, headed the 'Intelligence Section' –
even before he became a British subject. Relations between officers
followed academic models of collegiality. They, like civil servants and
military officers, shared a schoolboys' love for nicknames, practical
jokes and mediocre verse.

Though Penson said that 'what was needed were copyists, filers, and
really intelligent men of capacity', his organisation included many
women of that description. Two areas where women made particular
inroads among the executive branches of Whitehall were in departments associated with the blockade, and agencies based in London,
especially those involving data processing and communications intelligence. These departments had no established staff, men were required
to fight, women recognizably had the skills needed to work, and legally
were paid less than men. The Treasury pressed intelligence to hire
women. Women came close to numerical parity with men in the civilian
agencies responsible for blockade, and made up perhaps 33 per cent of
those in communications intelligence worldwide. 'Girls' matched men
in the strength of the Postal Censorship. Several hundred women

---

[14] McKenna, *While I Remember*, 163–65.
[15] Emmott, 'Memorandum to Lord Curzon', 9 August 1915, Emmott Papers, box 5.
[16] 'A' [Penson], 'Origin and Development of the War Trade Intelligence Department', n.d.
   [c. November 1917], BT 61/12/7.

worked in the War Trade Department, though, as Emmott noted, their presence was hampered by 'unfair rates of pay'. The Treasury rules prevented a woman being paid above the bottom rung of the starting salary of a man in the First Division, even though she 'may have higher academic honours, greater ability and sounder judgment'.[17] Women, with undergraduate or graduate degrees, served as translators or analysts, like one Australian, Trixie Geraldine Whitehead, previously Secretary for the National Union of Women's Suffrage Societies.[18] In its quest for the finest data processors in Britain, the TCH hired the indexing staff of *Encyclopaedia Britannica*, predominantly female, and paid at the same rates as men. By 1918, eight (or 15 per cent) of the WTID's intelligence officers were women.[19] Signals intelligence agencies enabled women to use their brains for their country, more than any other branch of the British state.

### The Trade Clearing House and the Evolution of Economic Intelligence, 1915

Models existed for their work, in the Commercial Intelligence Branch (CIB) of the Board of Trade, the Black Lists and the indices created for economic warfare by the NTD, the Contraband Department and Phillip's trade section, but why Penson, Davis and their staff choose to collect, index, disseminate and retrieve data as they did, is unclear. From their backgrounds, Penson understood information processing and commerce, as Davis did preparing studies from primary evidence. Their staff had similar skills and more. Davis and Penson had experience in collecting and analyzing this material; given the greater yield of letters than cables, they had already become Britain's leading analysts of communications intelligence on commercial matters, matched only by Leverton Harris. In its first months, the TCH created indices, an archive and analysts of commercial intelligence. As an internal account noted later, it 'always' aimed 'to centralise, record, and re-distribute to the proper quarters, all "war trade" information. With this object various indexes and files were instituted at the very beginning, e.g. a complete card index of the status and reputation of neutral traders; files of documents bearing on this question; files of commodities; etc. etc.' The TCH began with thirty members, divided into an 'Intelligence Section', extracting material from information received, and a Report Section,

---

[17] Memorandum by Emmott, 27 March 1919, CAB 15/6/4.
[18] Gabrielle Kemmis, 'Trixie Geraldine Whitehead and the First World War', http://expert nation.org/2017/01/24/trixie-whitehead-intelligence-and-the-first-world-war.
[19] Memorandum by Emmott, 27 March 1919, CAB 15/6/4.

for 'editing the information and distributing it where it would be most useful'.[20] Initially, it focused on publishing a 'General Black List' (GBL) including everything on the various departmental lists, and more, which took its first form as *Who's Who in War Trade*, first issued in June 1915. That handbook collated brief précis of all reports on every person and firm in war trade, enemy, friendly or neutral, based on proper names in alphabetical order. Each entry gave a broad sense of the information available. Any reader who wished to pursue a matter further could examine the still more detailed précis on the 'Traders' Index', the central instrument of the TCH, intended for every analyst in economic warfare, managed by a 'barrister of long experience', or the dossiers which contained the original reports on suspects. To confuse matters, the Contraband Department also maintained a separate 'Traders' Index'.

The compilation of these reports required much time, especially the first ones. Penson emphasized that 'the amount of verification of the information that comes in is very heavy; every name and address has to be verified; in addition to which the printers make such extraordinary mistakes in these foreign names, and the work of examining the proofs is in consequence very heavy'.[21] The TCH gathered information from millions of records, giving communications intelligence pride of place, and published material in forms convenient for distinct audiences. Whenever it scented new suspects, it had consuls find information on them. The TCH acted immediately, informally and precisely, asking authorities to acquire information, making itself the centre of a data collection, processing, analysis and distribution system. Its members directly contacted the analysts on economic warfare in every department, collating and disseminating their opinions. The NID and the Directorate of Special Intelligence (DSI) made the TCH their analytical organisation for commercial intelligence, and dissemination service for communications intelligence on economic matters. The TCH received communications intelligence from all sources and collated and disseminated it to all consumers.

The TCH, later renamed the WTID, became Britain's finest intelligence assessment body of the war, and perhaps of the century. The Minister of Blockade, Lord Robert Cecil, described its work as 'admirable', no mean compliment in an age of understatement.[22] After the war, other consumers had similar views. The WTID's internal histories

[20] Anon., 'Origin and History of the War Trade Intelligence Department', n.d., BT 61/ 12/7.
[21] War Lists of Traders, 12 September 1915, FO 382/366/173491.
[22] Minute by Cecil, 20 October 1916, FO 382/945/208145.

suggest this success was continual. In fact, months passed before the TCH became effective. Completing a GBL proved particularly difficult. Every neutral firm on earth was involved, the departmental Black Lists used different 'tests of undesirability' while the TCH, convinced that the Prize Court or foreign states might challenge its judgments, wanted its version to rest on 'scientific principles' and 'on evidence which amounted to legal proof'. This standard, reflecting the influence of lawyers and academics, created a characteristic problem for intelligence, where the search for perfect knowledge damages the use of the good. The inability to be certain about most suspects proved an enduring condition for Black Lists. The TCH used the Customs' Black List as an interim guide for a GBL, updated through its Traders' Index, which collected and analyzed masses of data on firms. Though at any time the TCH had a good idea of the blackness of firms, consumers could gain from it only by asking, which they often did not do, or by making their own judgments from the complicated evidence in *Who's Who*. The TCH also insisted on being the final judge about all decisions on blacklisting firms, around which confusion became common and publicly embarrassing.

In August 1915, Crowe claimed to have 'never discovered anything useful' the TCH did. One of his subordinates damned the TCH for having yet failed to produce a GBL, of which 'much was expected' and promised, 'under headings indicative of total blackness, moderate blackness, and potential blackness'. Instead, 'after months of momentous labour (the TCH) has produced a ridiculous compilation called Who's Who, filled with names with cryptic indications attached to them which is avowedly not a "Black List". It is of some use as an Index, or Directory, but that is all'. Phillips also found *Who's Who* 'not very useful' for his censors, 'who have to work at very high pressure', and needed clarity about suspects.[23] These comments from major consumers are telling. Yet they do not reflect the evidence showing how the Contraband Department, the Contraband Committee and the Procurator General's Department (PGD), which prosecuted cases in the Prize Court, already used material from the TCH, or an understanding of the value of an index which directed readers through a million reports. In 1916, the PGD held that because of the Cable Censors Handbook of Phillip's organisation and *Who's Who*, 'laboriously compiled', the censors missed just 'a small proportion of important' messages. The Cable Censors Handbook essentially became a simplified version of *Who's Who*. By 1918, the Military Intelligence Department regarded *Who's Who* as 'indispensable' for economic warfare, through its 'logical and intelligible' organisation of masses

---

[23] War Lists of Traders, 12 September 1915, FO 382/366/173491.

of complex information.[24] In any case, during 1915, more sensibly than some of his colleagues, Cecil Hurst, the Assistant Legal Advisor at the Foreign Office and a central figure in economic warfare, doubted that 'this abuse is justified'. The TCH had done tolerably well at a difficult task, assigned to it by the 'Intelligence Divisions'. No one was likely 'to have made a much better job of the black list'. No one could restart its work. If it was not doing its job, the TCH must be made to do so. Notably, the Foreign Office followed his line, not that of Crowe, and did not officially criticize the TCH.[25] Instead, the departments finally cooperated to produce a GBL, based on communications intelligence and TCH analyses, which blacklisted firms in two categories, which were those really best suited to the issue: (A) businesses against which stood conclusive evidence of serious behaviour and (B) those under suspicion.[26]

### The WTID at Work, 1915–1917

Meanwhile, the TCH guided economic warfare. By March 1915, it occasionally provided reports from several sources on suspects. By April, that practice was routine. Its intelligence helped to destroy major contraband organisations, especially those run by the German embassy in the United States. By May, the TCH's familiarity with firms, their communications and trade, and the increasing power of data retrieval through the Traders' Index, enabled it to offer powerful analyses regularly. By June, the TCH settled into a pattern which continued through the war. Its basic sources were official reports, newspapers and intercepted cables, with some wireless messages between neutral and German firms which, 'edited and studied by a special staff, proved to be specially constructive'. Agents' reports were small in number, and used only with care, after their accuracy was crosschecked with other sources.[27] Intercepted transit letters were the prize source, regularly receiving detailed analyses and widely circulated. The head of the Report Section wrote in early 1916:

The Transit Letters are the most valuable evidence that the Censors bring to light. Cables are usually ambiguous; letters to and from this country are written in the

---

[24] Memorandum by C. D. Webb, 'The Censorship with Particular Reference to the Work of the Procurator General's Department', 19 June 1916, TS 13/138 A; anon. memorandum for DMI, n.d. [c. December 1918], BT 61/12/7.

[25] Minutes by Hurst, 27 July 1915, and 2 August 1915, FO 382/349/100372.

[26] Carless Davis, 'History of the Blockade', 146; War Lists of Traders, 12 September 1915, FO 382/366/173491.

[27] Carless Davis, 'History of the Blockade', 143–48; for the Scandinavian background see Keith Neilson and B. J. C. McKercher, '"The Triumph of Unarmed Forces": Sweden and the Allied Blockade of Germany, 1914-1917', *Journal of Strategic Studies* 7(2) (1984), 178–99.

expectation that they will be censored. It is only in the Transit Letter, which he thinks may not be opened, that the enemy frankly and fully reveals the details of his business. The evidence derived from Transit Letters is invaluable to the Contraband Committee, and the Procurator General. The Transit Letters are also of good value to the War Trade Department, both in dealing with licences and in answering the inquiries of British firms about their neutral customers.[28]

Though the NTD and Phillips also worked in this area, the WTID became the core of information processing for economic warfare. It developed a threshing wheel to separate wheat from chaff – to find intelligence and to avoid information overload. Power and precision in collection aided that for analysis, and vice versa. The WTID gave the censors names to monitor, so making collection more effective and less annoying to the innocent. Between 1914 and 1919, the censors read 80,000,000 cables, of which 11,000,000 (often 40,000 per day) were temporarily or permanently stopped after being sent to government departments for action.[29] From about 450,000,000 envelopes touched between June 1915 and September 1917, the postal censors detained just 1,300,000 for examination, while the TCH generated only 15,516 Transit Letters.[30] By August 1918, another series of letter intercepts, probably for the WTD, reached the number WTD 81,431.[31] This winnowing enabled effective information management and intelligence analysis. At its peak, in the winter of 1916–17, the WTID received roughly 1,000 cables and 23 letters per day. Material on firms was constantly updated in the Traders' Index, which had 250,000 cards by the end of 1915. It grew by 4,000 to 5,000 cards each week, probably reaching 1,000,000 by the end of the war. Every month the TCH published updated and expanded versions of *Who's Who* and, from October, of the GBL. Every day, it (and the NTD) provided long compilations of cables relating to the names on cargo manifests, and crew and passenger lists, of all ships brought in for inspection, to aid the Contraband Committee, which decided which cargoes on ships should be detained or let pass. Every day, the TCH offered detailed analyses of transit letters

[28] Memorandum by Trade Clearing House and Trade Branch, Postal Censorship 'Memorandum on the Censoring of Transit Mails', n.d. [c. 1 January 1916], David Stevenson (ed.), *British Documents on Foreign Affairs*, Part II, Series H, *World War I, 1914–1918*, Volume VI, *Blockade and Economic Warfare*, Part II, *July 1915–Jan. 1916* (Frederick, MD, 1989), 385–94.
[29] 'The History of Cable Censorship, 1914–1919' (1919), 106–17 *et passim*, DEFE 1/130; 'The History of Postal Censorship, 1914–1919' (1919), DEFE 1/131.
[30] TL 15516, German Post Office Shanghai to Denmark, 6 August 1917, FO 382/1770; 'The History of Postal Censorship', 71, 328, 331, DEFE 1/131.
[31] Minutes of meeting on Swedish Black List Cases, 16 August 1918, TS 13/689.

on specific cases of contraband, and *ad hoc* memoranda, including copies of intercepted messages, with and without analysis attached.

O. R. A. Simpkin, a Chancery barrister and leader in blockade intelligence, later wrote, 'the ultimate sanction of the Blockade is the Prize Court', a national court which enforced international law. Seizure of goods required 'evidence, or at least a strong presumption, of intended enemy destination or origin such as would satisfy a Court of Law'. Intelligence confronted 'a two-fold problem: namely (a) the collection of facts constituting evidence or creating a presumption, of enemy destination or origin; and (b) the application of these facts accurately and rapidly' to ships and cargoes.[32] Analysts did so through what contemporaries called an 'evidentiary' system, using all the information at hand. The standard of proof varied between intelligence and evidence. The Contraband Committee looked for suspicion enough to justify seizure. Mere hints sufficed – for example, that a cargo negotiated through Rotterdam was sent via Copenhagen, or a Swedish firm advertised in German newspapers its ability to provide items which might not even be contraband in origin. The PGD needed to make a legal case before the Prize Court, though it had time to do so, and the opportunity to direct intelligence against its target. The PGD's briefs to the Prize Court rested on WTID analyses and communications intelligence.

The WTID was essential to this collection and collation of intelligence and evidence. For the Contraband Committee and the PGD, the TCH established 'a special section ... to investigate the true destination' of cargoes across the Atlantic Ocean to Scandinavia, based on analysis of communication intelligence. The TCH analyzed the import of all commodities to border neutrals, as background to contraband and the enemy's war economy, issues which particularly concerned the NID. The TCH reported to the WTD on every neutral firm mentioned in any export license, often reaching 15,000 names per week. Through the Board of Trade it advised British firms concerned about the blackness of any neutral business with which they might wish to deal. The TCH sent immediate reports on new suspects to the Contraband Department and the Contraband Committee, and analyses of transit letters to the PGD and the postal censors. It replied to all simple queries, and for information on manifests, in only a few hours. The TCH became experts in the jargon of all seaborne trades and about the firms which conducted them. It collated all current information, gave reasoned daily statements to the Contraband Committee and retrieved and assessed data about specific questions with remarkable speed and thoroughness. The TCH aimed to

---

[32] Carless Davis, 'History of the Blockade', 23–32.

be objective, and declare a firm or transaction innocent, as well as guilty.[33] Its analyses were nuanced, sophisticated and trusted by its consumers. More than any other source or agency, communications intelligence and the TCH underpinned the regulatory system, by showing whether neutral firms were honouring promises or cheating on them, and reminding key collaborators that their actions were observed. In particular, the TCH and Phillips constantly crosschecked the reports of the British minister in Copenhagen, Sir Gerard Lowther, on whether individual Danes were trustworthy, providing information to query his judgment on matters central to blockade and ask that he justify his views. Thus, they showed that four of the five Danish firms Lowther cleared as safe recipients of lard in early 1915, actually were trading with Germany.[34] The Contraband Department took these reports seriously, which damaged Lowther's reputation, and perhaps shaped his replacement in 1916, by a minister ordered to take a harsher line on contraband and Copenhagen.

During late 1915, the TCH increased its power. In September, its members copied by hand the cards from the Contraband Department's index.[35] Then, through titanic labour, they indexed the millions of unindexed cables from the start of the war, and re-indexed the older data on blockade intelligence, as well as all incoming material. The TCH organized all cables on one numerical system, and based its index around the names of individuals, senders and receivers, firms and ships, in alphabetical order. Ultimately, the indices contained hundreds of thousands of names, cross referenced to highlight their connections. Every reference to any name from millions of intercepts automatically appeared on the index, which was updated constantly, and widely circulated. The relevant records could be retrieved immediately when in dossiers, in their tens of thousands, and within hours for a new topic.[36] Cards represented data in many ways. By late 1917, for example, the WTID created a special index on 'the preparations of the Central Powers for trade after the war' Brief reports were pasted on cards: long ones were represented by a précis. Cards addressing general topics were white, those on German imports red, and exports yellow. Cards represented the title of a report, the subject heading and country: for example, 'Reported Sale of German Ships, Shipping, Switzerland' and 'Proposed German Industrial Bank in China, Financial, China'.[37]

[33] Ibid.    [34] Arnold Forster, 54–55, ADM 186/603.
[35] War Lists of Traders, 12 September 1915, FO 382/366/173491.
[36] 'History of Cable Censorship', DEFE 1/131.
[37] Memorandum by Penson, 28 November 1917, BT 61/12/7.

In 1916, when the Contraband Department became the Ministry of Blockade, Cecil brought the WTID under his control and drove it to attack. Carless Davis and Penson appreciated their 'most cordial' relations with Cecil and his ministry, which were 'of greatest assistance' to their work, but noted that 'certain channels of information which were formerly open to us are now closed or not so constantly open as they were before, because we are said to be "practically a branch of the Foreign Office"'.[38] Undoubtedly, they were referring to the Admiralty, which battled the Ministry of Blockade throughout 1916 over assessments of how much contraband was reaching Germany, from the Naval Attaché in Scandinavia, Captain Consett, and the RN's human sources there. Perhaps this closure of information involved these sources. If so, the loss to the WTID was minor. More significantly, after the Ministry of Blockade was formed, the Admiralty placed its blockade intelligence department and its Cable Index within the TCH, which prized it as a 'very considerable source of intelligence'. When the NID expressed fear that this arrangement might weaken its ability to acquire or guide intelligence, Penson replied, 'the only object of a Department of this kind was to be useful and therefore any way in which it can be made more useful was always welcome. It was for them to do what they were asked to do.' The TCH could replicate the 'way in which Trade information is worked up by the Admiralty', and meet other needs of government. All agreed that the NID should liaise closely with the TCH.[39]

Penson met his promise. This meeting disclosed the difficulty which the NID faced in aiding the Contraband Committee about ships' manifests, because of the limited time to retrieve and analyze data on reports cabled to and from ports of control. Simpkin, then head of the NTD's Cable Index and later of the Blockade Department of the WTID, 'stated such information as he had, he could not get through to the Contraband Committee in time ... With regard to the dossiers of the ships it was merely a question of time and typists. To get the telegraphed manifest from the Customs dissected and worked up in time, was very difficult.' Longdon hinted at information overload: 'the Contraband Committee was obliged to look at an average of 100 cards a day'. Significantly, however, after the war Simpkin noted that 'the index never became too cumbersome for easy reference'.[40] The TCH sidestepped information

---

[38] Memorandum by Carless Davis, 'The Need for a Permanent Trade Intelligence Bureau' ('Strictly Confidential'), 21 November 1916, and Penson to Emmott, 22 November 1916, Emmott Papers, Box 6.

[39] 'Conference held at the Trade Clearing House on Monday March 13th, 1916, at 11 a.m.', ADM 137/2735.

[40] Carless Davis, 'History of the Blockade', p. 26.

overload by improving the speed and thoroughness of reports, and by collating evidence given to the Contraband Committee, though the adoption of the NAVICERT system provided the real solution. Ships with manifests pre-cleared in the United States and telegraphed to Britain passed rapidly through ports of control like Ramsgate, Falmouth and Kirkwall, because intelligence already had been applied to their cargoes, crew lists and the individuals and firms related to them. Communications intelligence was applied to every ship Britain inspected. Cargo, crew and passengers were scrutinized both through physical means by Customs and intelligence, via what one old hand, William Arnold-Forster, called 'a vast hinterland of organization engaged in the critical evaluation of manifests and cargoes'.[41]

### The WTID and Economic Warfare, 1915–1918

Between 1915 and 1918, the WTID became the central element in blockade intelligence, and in assessing the enemies' economies.[42] The WTID was Britain's sole interdepartmental body for intelligence analysis and the only one addressing strategic issues – perhaps the only one fulfilling these functions on Earth. Other communications intelligence agencies were sources, which simply provided intelligence. The WTID, and two bodies placed within it, the Admiralty's blockade intelligence unit and the intelligence section of the PGD under Clive Lawrence, were analytical agencies, especially focused on communications intelligence. Leverton Harris, Simpkin, Lawrence and Carless Davis, financer, barristers and don, were the world's most experienced and able analysts of communications and economic intelligence. The WTID processed and analyzed vast quantities of communications intelligence effectively in real time and enabled an elaborate machine to operate with remarkable efficiency. This was the triumph of data processing for intelligence in the age of the card index.

The WTID's personnel rose in size, to 67 Higher Grade and 73 clerks and typists in September 1915, to 376 members by April 1918, housed in temporary buildings erected in St. James Park, its lake drained for the duration.[43] As a sign of its importance, the WTID always had enough of scarce resources – typewriters and typists – to disseminate its material, whereas members of the Contraband Department routinely transcribed

---

[41] W. E. Arnold-Forster, 'The Economic Blockade, 1914–1919', n.d., 108, ADM 186/603.
[42] 'Meeting at Trade Clearing House', 11 March 1916, ADM 137/2735; 3rd Ministry of Blockade Committee meeting, 1 February 1917, FO 902/36.
[43] Anon., 'Origin and History of the War Trade Intelligence Department', n.d., BT 61/12/7; Carless David, 'History of the Blockade', 142–55.

reports by hand. The WTID's structure changed to meet its tasks. By late 1917, the Intelligence Section 'was divided into small groups dealing with particular commodities' and a 'special sub-section' for wireless intercepts. The Report Section created sub-sections for serving the Admiralty and War Office. Special reports were written for many authorities, but all went through the editorial hands of Carless Davis, 'who is thus able to exercise control over their matter and form'.[44] By late 1918, when it switched attention to postwar conditions, the WTID had 333 members, including 40 to 50 seconded from the Admiralty and the PGD, to handle work related to their departments and the Admiralty's Cable Index. The two largest sections – 'Carding', which entered data on cards and maintained the index, and 'Editorial', which disseminated material through regular reports – had 46 and 79 personnel, respectively. The personnel of smaller sections included: History (16); War Office (including guidance for SIS and liaison with French offices, 9); Commodities (9); Contraband (30); Export Licences (49); Commercial Enquiries (20); Censorship (20); Black List (20); Italy (15); and Africa (9).[45]

***

The WTID helped decision makers to understand the effect of economic warfare. Analysts and translators of newspapers provided material for several newssheets which the WTID issued throughout Whitehall, like 'Daily Notes of Economic Information' and 'Secret Weekly Bulletin'. The WTID also provided the material used in the widely circulated and influential reports about the socio-economic impact of the blockade on the Central Powers, written by a former consul general in Budapest, William Grenfell Max-Müller.[46] The WTID and communications intelligence served other reports which guided economic warfare. The Admiralty's 'Jottings from Intercepted Cables' or the 'Daily Summary of Intelligence' by MI6b, the military agency for economic warfare, consisted primarily of excerpts from letter, wireless and cable intercepts, to illustrate how firms were coping with or evading the blockade, and German efforts to escape it.[47] The WTID produced shrewd and well-received reports on the economic condition of the Central Powers, for example, on how little the collapse of Rumania would improve calories for Germans. In 1917–18 it assessed the economic condition of the Central Powers weekly for the War Cabinet. The WTID helped decision makers understand the real economic position of Germany. Blockade had

---

[44] 'A' [Penson], 'Origin and Development of the War Trade Intelligence Department', n.d. [c. November 1917], BT 61/12/7.
[45] Ibid.    [46] His sources are well illustrated by FO 382/1311.
[47] For examples see WO 208/3568.

damaged the German economy, and pressed its people to malnutrition, which would multiply the effect of any defeats suffered by the German army, but not on its own start a deluge.[48] The WTID shaped Britain's decision to take blockade measures which would drive the border neutrals to slaughter their livestock in 1917, so increasing the calories available to Germany in that year, but denying them that prospect for 1918. The WTID also backed a policy which never had to be executed, but decision makers took seriously: how to prepare Britain and its firms for competition with Germany and its businesses, in case of a stalemate peace. Its final work was to write the monographs on the economics of Europe prepared for the British delegation at the Paris Peace Conference.

When the war ended, so did the WTID. Most of its files were destroyed, save those the PGD needed for prize cases, but key reports were preserved. Commissioned by Cecil, Carless Davis wrote a good history of the WTID and the blockade departments but, unfortunately, not his proposed study of diplomacy and blockade. Histories of all aspects of the blockade and blockade intelligence guided the basis for the Ministry of Economic Warfare (MEW) in 1939. During 1916, Carless Davis and Penson advocated that a permanent body based on the WTID become 'an economic General Staff working in close touch with military and naval experts and concerning itself with problems prescribed by the varying contingencies of the political situation' or to aid the 'basis of Foreign Economic Policy and lend precision to all schemes of an economic nature that may be prepared in view of the possibility of future wars'.[49] These far-seeing proposals were not followed, but the work of the WTID influenced two later creations. The intelligence work of the Department of Overseas Trade, Britain's effort to integrate economic issues into diplomacy, was based primarily on the CIB, but created by people familiar with the WTID. The Industrial Intelligence Centre (IIC) of the SIS followed many of the proposals which Carless Davis and Penson advocated. Though their ideas had no influence on that decision, probably memories of the WTID did. When the MEW was founded, the IIC immediately was placed within it, to serve the same function as the WTID had done. Britain passed on lessons from one Great War to another in economic warfare, and intelligence for it. Moreover, the WTID's techniques were applied to one of the key Anglo-American

---

[48] Memorandum by WTID, 'Summary of Blockade Information, June 22–28 1917', GT 1225, 29 June 1917, CAB 24/18.

[49] Penson, 'Memorandum for Lord Emmott', 23 November 1916; memorandum by Carless Davis, 'The Need for a Permanent Trade Intelligence Bureau' ('Strictly Confidential'), 21 November 1916, and Penson to Emmott, 22 November 1916, Emmott Papers, Box 6.

intelligence successes of the Cold War. Between 1946 and 1956, British and American signals intelligence acquired 70,000,000 plain text messages from Soviet radio networks, which illuminated all aspects of the Soviet Union's economy, including its nuclear programme. When American signals intelligence personnel encountered WTID techniques for the first time, in 1946–47, they were staggered by the power, and adopted them.[50]

The WTID illuminates the history of intelligence, information, economic warfare and the First World War. From 1914, the moment signals intelligence started, it involved mass data and bulk collection, which intelligence services forged into tools of state through advanced means of information processing. The communications intelligence collected and assessed for economic warfare between 1915 and 1918 resembles contemporary practices, more than does that produced by Room 40. Students of the history of information and intelligence tend to ignore each other, but the WTID illustrates how far these topics overlap, and mattered. Between 1914 and 1918, economic warfare was not merely a matter of navies, but of the interaction between sea power, intelligence and international law. Blockade was a battleaxe rather than a scalpel. It could wreck relations with states and firms in a counterproductive fashion. Intelligence guided this battleaxe so as to minimize the damage to Britain while maximising that on the enemy. That outcome might have been different without the WTID.

---

[50] Carol P. Davis, *Candle in the Dark, COMINT and Soviet Industrial Secrets, 1946–1956* (Fort Meade, 2018) (United States Cryptologic History, ser. VI, vol. 12).

# 2 The British Empire and the Meaning of 'Minimum Force Necessary' in Colonial Counter-Insurgencies Operations, c.1857–1967

*David French*

Britain's position as a global power from the middle of the nineteenth century onwards was challenged from two directions. External enemies, principally Russia, France and Germany, emerged as increasingly powerful rivals. Internally disparate groups of nationalists coalesced at different times and in different places to try to subvert British rule. By the middle of the twentieth century these two forces united to help undercut the props that had sustained the empire, with the result that between 1945 and 1970 the British shed most of their remaining colonial responsibilities. But in doing so they also developed a narrative of colonialism that explained both how they had governed their empire, and why they were willing to surrender it. Britain's imperial mission was to bring the rule of law and good governance to peoples who would not otherwise have enjoyed such benefits. To accomplish that mission they had ruled their empire with the maximum of political cajolery and the minimum of physical force. This story was not entirely a myth. The high cost of employing large numbers of European civil servants, not to mention soldiers or policemen, had indeed placed a premium on the need to incorporate local indigenous elites into the governance of the empire. However, recognition of that should not be allowed to hide the fact that when the British were faced by violent challenges to their rule from within their empire, they were more than capable of meeting violence with violence.

The British armed forces did not exist just to fight the empire's external enemies. They also had a role in helping to maintain order within the empire. How they went about doing this has in recent years generated some controversy. In 1966, Sir Robert Thompson, a former senior civil servant in Malaya, published his classic study of British counter-insurgency operations in that country, *Defeating Communist Insurgency: The Lessons of Malaya and Vietnam*. Thompson claimed that the British had discovered a way of employing a combination of political persuasion –

winning 'hearts and minds' – combined with the carefully targeted and calibrated use of physical force, to defeat armed insurgencies. Starting with the notion that an insurgency was a struggle waged between the colonial authorities and the insurgents to establish which side should enjoy political legitimacy in the eyes of the civil population, he argued that the government could only win if it employed the minimum necessary physical force, avoided harming innocent bystanders, and ensured that its soldiers and policemen never strayed beyond the boundaries of the law.[1] This was a seductive analysis. Not only had the British remained in control of the process of decolonisation, but they had discovered how to make western liberal notions of what was right and wrong compatible with the demands of fighting a war amongst the people. Thus, force could be used effectively but with discrimination to avoid harming the innocent. These arguments have provided the intellectual framework for numerous studies of British counter-insurgency operations.[2] However, this interpretation has not gone unchallenged.[3] Some historians have argued that British counter-insurgency campaigns had a much grimmer hue. Rather than being intent on employing only the minimum necessary force, they readily committed all the force they could muster, and were often not overly careful against whom they applied it.[4]

This chapter will explore this debate by focusing on what has been claimed to be one of the central tenets of the army's counter-insurgency doctrine: it is that troops involved in operations in aid of the civil power were, like civilians, always subject to the common law injunction that they should never employ more than the minimum force necessary to achieve their immediate objective in suppressing riot or rebellion. It will develop

---

[1] Sir R. Thompson, *Defeating Communist Insurgency. The Lessons of Malaya and Vietnam* (St. Petersburg, FL, 2005 [originally published 1966]).

[2] See, for example, T. R. Mockaitis, *British Counterinsurgency, 1919–60* (London, 1990); J. A. Nagl, *Learning to Eat Soup with a Knife: Counterinsurgency Lessons from Malaya and Vietnam* (Chicago, 2002–2005); R. Thornton, 'The Role of Peace Support Operations Doctrine in the British Army', *International Peacekeeping* 7(1) (2000), 41–62; R. Thornton, 'The British Army and the Origins of Its Minimum Force Philosophy', *Small Wars and Insurgencies* 14(2) (2004), 83–106; R. Thornton, 'Minimum Force: A Reply to Huw Bennett', *Small Wars and Insurgencies* 20(4) (2009), 215–26.

[3] The first significant attempt to question it was J. Newsinger, Review of T.R. Mockaitis, 'British Counterinsurgency 1919–1960', *Race and Class* 34(1) (1992), 96–98; see also J. Newsinger, *British Counterinsurgency from Palestine to Northern Ireland* (London, 2002).

[4] D. Anderson, *Histories of the Hanged: Britain's Dirty War in Kenya and the End of Empire* (London, 2005); C. Elkins, *Britain's Gulag: The Brutal End of Empire in Kenya* (London, 2005); H. Bennett, *Fighting Mau: The British Army and Counter-Insurgency in the Kenya Emergency* (Cambridge, 2013); P. Dixon, '"Hearts and Minds"?: British Counter-Insurgency from Malaya to Iraq', *Journal of Strategic Studies* 32(4) (2009), 353–81; A. Marshall, 'Imperial Nostalgia, the Liberal Lie, and the Perils of Post-Modern Counterinsurgency', *Small Wars and Insurgencies* 21(3) (2010), 233–58.

two closely related arguments. The first is that troops called out in aid of the civil power operated under a variety of legal codes. It is a mistake to assume that the same common law legal regime which constrained their conduct when called upon to suppress a riot in the United Kingdom also constrained their actions when confronted by a full-blown armed insurgency in a colony. Both the law and the situations within which it was applied were significantly different. The second argument that this chapter will explore is that the period immediately following the First World War represented something of a tipping point in the ways in which the security forces acted when confronted by armed insurgents. There had been some public disquiet expressed in Britain about the use of apparently excessive force to suppress colonial insurgencies before 1914. But it was only after the First World War that they achieved a significant degree of political purchase. Even so, colonial authorities did not lose their ability to employ force to suppress their opponents. Instead they found new ways to disguise the sometimes brutal reality of counter-insurgency. The chapter will conclude by examining some of the ways in which they did so.

\*\*\*

Since the early 1870s senior officers had been lobbying for a statement from the government defining the purposes for which the British army existed. They finally got it in 1888. Lord Stanhope, the Secretary of State for War, told them that the army had to perform four functions. They were, in order of priority, 'the effective support of the civil power in all parts of the United Kingdom', to provide a garrison for India and Britain's fortresses and coaling stations abroad, to provide for the needs of home defence and to fulfil the remote possibility that Britain might have to send an expeditionary force to the continent of Europe.[5] Stanhope had good reason to place giving aid to the civil power at the top of his list of priorities. Between 1869 and 1908 the army was called out to support the police in England and Wales on no fewer than two dozen occasions.[6] It was usually the case that the mere presence of troops at the site of a riot was sufficient to quell disturbances. But on a handful of occasions mob violence was so serious that soldiers did open fire. As a result, by the end of the nineteenth century a body of case law had developed which was codified in successive volumes of the *Manual of Military Law* and *King's Regulations*. The 1899 edition of the *Manual* told the soldier that under the common law it was the duty

---

[5] See also I. F. W. Beckett, 'Edward Stanhope at the War Office, 1887-1892', *Journal of Strategic Studies* 5(2) (1982), 299.

[6] E. M. Spiers, *The Late Victorian Army 1868–1902* (Manchester, 1992), 209.

of every citizen, be he soldier or civilian, to come to the aid of the civil power in repressing riot or rebellion, that in doing so they must not use more than the minimum force necessary and that what constituted that level of force was something that could only be decided by the man on the spot. In 1908, Lord Haldane, a distinguished lawyer and Secretary of State for War, explained to a Parliamentary Select Committee examining the employment of the military in cases of disturbances that soldiers summoned to give aid to the civil power were 'not entitled to use more force than is necessary to assert the cause of law and order'.[7] This placed the soldier in a potentially difficult legal bind. If he was asked by a civil magistrate to open fire on a rioting mob and he refused to do so, he could be prosecuted in the civil court for failing in his duty as a citizen. But if he did fire, *King's Regulations* warned an officer in command of troops sent to quell a riot that he should, 'exercise a humane discretion in deciding both the number of rounds and the object to be aimed at'.[8] If, however, it was later held that he had used excessive force, he could be prosecuted for murder or manslaughter.[9]

In their discussion of what might or might not constitute the appropriate degree of force that soldiers could employ when summoned to give aid to the civil power, the legal authorities who composed the *Manual* and other relevant instructions entered two important caveats. The first was explicit. They made a sharp distinction between how soldiers should behave when faced by a violent riot, and how they should behave when confronted by a full-scale insurrection. In the case of a riot, 'a tumultuous disturbance of the peace by three or more persons assembling together', they insisted that 'deadly weapons ought not to be employed against the rioters, unless they are armed, or are in a position to inflict grievous injury on the persons endeavouring to disperse them'.[10] However, in the case of an insurrection, which was defined as an undertaking which involved 'an intention to levy war against the Queen', they asserted that 'an armed insurrection would justify the use of any degree of force necessary effectually to meet and cope with the insurrection'.[11]

The second caveat was that the rules contained in the *Manual* and *King's Regulations* only pertained to troops operating in the United Kingdom. This was implicit in the *Manual*, which nowhere made any mention of what soldiers should do if they were operating in India or any other colony. It was explicit in *King's Regulations*, which stated that 'when

---

[7] War Office, *MML 1914* (London, 1914), 226.
[8] War Office, *KR 1912* (London, 1912), 186.
[9] War Office, *MML 1899* (London, 1899), 270–84; War Office, *MML, 1907* (London, 1907), 211–21; War Office, *MML, 1914* (London, 1914), 216–22.
[10] MML 1899, 271 and 280.    [11] Ibid., 271–72 and 281.

troops are called out in aid of the civil power at home . . .'[12] But what were they to do when they were operating in the colonies? The British army was slow to develop an explicit doctrine for what today would be termed counter-insurgency operations. The closest it came before 1914 was Colonel C. E. Callwell's seminal study, *Small Wars: Their Principles and Practice*.[13] Callwell mentioned several political factors that might constrain the kind and the degree of violence a commander in the field might employ in suppressing an insurrection. But he made no mention of legal constraints.[14] It was only in the 1930s that the military authorities addressed this issue explicitly in two manuals, *Notes on Imperial Policing, 1934* and *Duties in Aid of the Civil Power, 1937*. Produced by the General Staff to guide officers in their duties, they repeated the strictures about the application of the common law to all operations in aid of the civil power in the United Kingdom, but then added that 'the law in relation to duties in aid of the civil power is not the same in India and the colonies as in the United Kingdom. Officers employed on these duties abroad should be guided by such instructions as are issued by the military authorities concerned.'[15] *Notes on Imperial Policing* told officers that if troops were summoned to give assistance to the civil power to suppress a riot, the civil power did not abdicate and hand control over to the army. Rather, the ordinary civil law remained in force, and officers should remember that 'the principle which has consistently governed the policy of His Majesty's Government in directing the methods to be employed when military action in support of civil authority is required may be broadly stated as the use of the minimum force necessary'.[16] But in the event of more serious disturbances amounting to an insurrection, it was assumed that a governor would declare martial law, which would entail 'the suspension of ordinary law and its supersession by military rule during war or rebellion, and amounts merely to the exercise of the will of the military commander upon whom has fallen the task of ensuring the safety of the State and the restoration of law and order'.[17] In such circumstances, 'the

[12] *KR, 1912; KR, 1926*, 353; *KR, 1940*, 448.

[13] C. E. Callwell, *Small Wars: Their Principles and Practice* (London, repr. 1914 [1st 1906]); see also D. Whittingham, '"Savage Warfare": C. E. Callwell, the Roots of Counter-Insurgency, and the Nineteenth Century Context', *Small Wars and Insurgencies* 23(4–5) (2012), 591–607.

[14] Callwell, *Small Wars*, 40–41.

[15] WO 279/470, General Staff, *Duties in Aid of the Civil Power, 1937: Reprint Incorporating Amendments (No. 1) 1945* (London, 1945).

[16] WO 279/796, *War Office: Notes on Imperial Policing 1934* (London, 1934), 41.

[17] Ibid., 29. For an excellent analysis of the issues involved in the administration of martial law see C. Townshend, 'Martial Law: Legal and Administrative Problems of Civil Emergency in Britain and the Empire, 1800-1940', *Historical Journal* 25(1) (1982), 167–95.

principles enunciated above will not, however, apply in time of guerrilla warfare or rebellion to bodies of the enemy or rebels engaged in hostilities'.[18]

Although before 1914 troops summoned to suppress a riot were expected to employ only the 'minimum force necessary', in India the degree of force they were permitted to employ actually increased around the turn of the century. Driven by fears that communal rioting was becoming interwoven with nationalist agitation against the Raj, the Indian authorities were frightened into adopting sterner measures than those employed hitherto. Rather than try to frighten mobs into dispersing by firing blank cartridges in the first instance, after 1894 soldiers were expected to fire live rounds. This, it was hoped, would be more humane because it would ensure that the rioters dispersed at once.[19] Furthermore, by the eve of the First World War, *King's Regulations* forbade the firing of warning shots over the heads of rioters because doing so 'has the effect of favouring the most daring and guilty, and of sacrificing the less daring, and even the innocent'. Officers in command of troops sent to suppress a riot were expected to do their utmost to inform the crowd 'that, in the event of the troops being ordered to fire, their fire will be effective'.[20]

Troops called on to suppress a full-scale insurrection operated under even fewer meaningful legal constraints. In operations against 'savage' enemies, the army was enjoined to act boldly, and to take the offensive in order to bring operations to a successful conclusion with the utmost rapidity. If the enemy had a capital, or some holy place that it held dear, troops should advance towards it. Their opponents were bound to defend it, and would thus open themselves to defeat. But, as the *Field Service Regulations, 1909* advised, 'should the enemy refuse to make any organized resistance, the occupation of his country, the seizure of his flocks and supplies, and the destruction of his villages and crops may be necessary to obtain his submission'.[21] What this meant in practice was demonstrated during the Indian Mutiny in 1857. In May and June 1857 the Governor General of India, Charles Canning, gave British officers and civil officials in disaffected areas of India the legal power to crush the insurgency. These included the right to declare martial law and to imprison or execute captured insurgents. The retribution that the British

---

[18] WO 279/796, *War Office, Notes on Imperial Policing 1934*, 41.

[19] M. Doyle, 'Massacre by the Book: Amritsar and the Rules of Public-Order Policing in Britain and India', *Britain and the World* 4(2) (2011), 256–58.

[20] *KR, 1912*, 186–87.

[21] War Office, *Field Service Regulations*, Part 1, Combined Training (London, 1905), 150; General Staff, *Field Service Regulations*, Part 1, Operations, 1909 (London, 1909), 191–92.

meted out to captured insurgents during the Indian Mutiny has recently been described by one historian as 'swift, public and fearsome'.[22] In September 1857, for example, *The Times* reported that:

At Mooltan, disaffection having shown itself in the disarmed 69th, the Subahdar-Major [the most senior Indian officer in the regiment] was tried by court-martial under the Presidency of the commanding officer of the Bombay Fusiliers, and, being convicted on the clearest evidence, was blown from a 9-pounder gun on 24 July in presence of the whole brigade.[23]

Such exemplary punishments, handed out after drumhead courts martial or summarily without any pretence of a trial, were deemed necessary by the authorities because they had few troops with whom to restore order. They believed that they had to make a deep and quick impression on one locality before moving on to repeat the process at the next one. 'A Drum Head Court Martial sat immediately on the 78 prisoners taken by Major Orr's people', one British officer wrote in his diary in November 1857:

They were sentenced to be shot. We paraded that evening at 5pm. 74 prisoners had their hands tied behind them, their eyes bandaged were shot by one detachment [of the] 86th. most fell dead instantly, some having their brains shot out, others shot through the heart, the blood came pumping out, and some shot in ye abdomen showed signs of agony afterwards & so received an extra bullet. I walked past them lying in a bloody line. We dined in the open air . . .[24]

The focus of their retribution varied. On some occasions whole villages were subject to indiscriminate destruction. Elsewhere retribution was focused on disloyal sepoys. The aim of the British was to punish those most obviously guilty of rebellion, not to propel those on the margins of it into outright resistance to British rule.[25]

In the second half of the nineteenth century on the North West Frontier of India, when other means of maintaining peaceful relations had been tried and failed, troops conducted numerous punitive expeditions against recalcitrant tribesmen inhabiting the political no-man's land that lay between India and Afghanistan.[26] Such operations typically involved

---

[22] B. Collins, 'Counter-Insurgency in the Bombay Presidency during the Mutiny-Rebellion, 1857', *British Journal of Military History* 1(2) (2015), 41; T. Downs, '"Putting the Saddle Back on the Right Horse": British Suppression of Rural Insurgency in the Benares Division during the Indian Revolt of 1857–58', *South Asia: Journal of South Asian Studies* 37(2) (2014), 308–09.

[23] *The Times*, 19 September 1857. This was not an isolated incidence, see, for example, ibid., 17 August 1857.

[24] J. H. Sylvester Diary, 17 November 1857, quoted in B. Robson (ed.), *Sir Hugh Rose and the Central India Campaign 1858* (Stroud, 2000), 9.

[25] Downs, 'Putting the Saddle Back on the Right Horse', 309–10.

[26] Anon., 'Punjab Frontier', *The Times*, 3 January 1878.

columns of troops burning the villages, although taking care to avoid destroying places of worship, and razing the crops and destroying the livestock of tribesmen believed to have attacked targets on the Indian side of the frontier.[27] The British occupation of Zululand in 1879 followed a similar pattern. Troops were ordered to burn the inhabitants' *kraals*, their cattle were killed and their wounded sometimes summarily despatched as part of a conscious policy of terrorising the population into submission.[28] After the occupation of Pretoria in June 1900 and the annexation of the Transvaal and the Orange Free State by the British in October, several thousand Boer Commandos refused to surrender, and mounted a guerrilla campaign against the occupying British forces. Legally, at least in the eyes of the British, these men were British subjects and could be treated as rebels. Lord Roberts, the commander-in-chief of the army in South Africa, declared in September 1900 that 'unless the people generally are made to suffer for misdeeds of those in arms against us the war will never end'.[29] He was echoing the same sentiments uttered by Lord Chelmsford, who had commanded the British army in Zululand twenty years earlier. 'I am satisfied', Chelmsford wrote to the Secretary of State for War, 'that the more the Zulu nation at large feels the strain brought upon them by the war, the more anxious will they be to see it brought to an end.'[30] Roberts' successor, Lord Kitchener, made sure that the Boers suffered.[31] The army destroyed as many as 30,000 farms, and then placed their inhabitants in a series of overcrowded and unsanitary concentration camps, where nearly 28,000 Boer women and children and perhaps 20,000 Africans died.[32] As the total white population of the two Boer republics only amounted to about 220,000, this represented a massive demographic loss.

---

[27] See, for example, the account of a punitive expedition sent into Waziristan in the winter of 1894–95 in *The Times*, 24 and 31 December 1894, and 10, 17 and 18 January 1895. More generally T. Moreman, *The Army in India and the Development of Frontier Warfare, 1849–1947* (London, 1998).

[28] M. Lieven, '"Butchering the Brutes All over the Place": Total War and Massacre in Zululand, 1879', *History* 84(276) (1999), 614–32; J. P. C. Laband (ed.), *Lord Chelmsford's Zululand Campaign, 1878–1879* (Stroud, 1994), 148, 201–02, 212.

[29] S. B. Spies, 'Women and the War', in P. Warwick and S. B. Spies (eds.), *The South African War* (London, 1980), 165.

[30] Lieven, 'Butchering the Brutes', 621.

[31] Circular memorandum No. 29, reproduced in A. Wessels (ed.), *Lord Kitchener and the War in South Africa, 1899–1902* (Stroud, 2006), 60–61.

[32] Spies, 'Women and the War', 169–70; D. Low-Beer, M. Smallman-Raynor and A. Cliff, 'Disease and Death in the South African War: Changing Disease Patterns from Soldiers to Refugees', *Social History of Medicine* 17(2) (2004), 223–45; F. Pretorius, 'The Experience of the Bitter-Ender Boer in the Guerrilla Phase of the South African War', in J. Gooch (ed.), *The Boer War: Direction, Experience and Image* (London, 2000), 167–86.

However, the willingness of the British authorities to employ force to secure their ends stopped short of genocide. This owed little to an acceptance of legal niceties, and a great deal to some pragmatic political calculations. Exemplary violence of the kind the British practised had a purpose: to spread an impression of ruthlessness allied to unbeatable power far beyond the epicentre of an insurgency. But once that impression had been established in the minds of the insurgents, and any would-be insurgents, the British went about the process of conciliation. Force was a way of ruling an empire, but it was expensive to employ, and it only worked in the short term. It was far more efficacious, and cheaper, to transform malcontents into contents through the practice of judicious negotiation. But doing so presupposed that force had been used with a certain care and discrimination in the first place. As Callwell explained, 'expeditions to put down revolt are not put in motion merely to bring about a temporary cessation of hostility. Their purpose is to ensure a lasting peace. Therefore, in choosing the objective, the overawing and not the exasperation of the enemy is the end to keep in view.'[33] Thus, at the end of July 1857, when he had become aware that some local commanders were misusing the powers granted to them under martial law with sometimes reckless brutality, Lord Canning issued instructions to rein them in. He thus eared for himself the derisory nickname 'Clemency Canning'.[34] After the Mutiny, troops called upon to assist the civil power in suppressing riots inside India were expected to employ 'as little force, and do as little injury, as may be consistent with dispersing the assembly'.[35] Punitive expeditions on the North West Frontier were invariably accompanied by British political officers. Their job was to negotiate with the tribesmen in order to bring each expedition to a satisfactory conclusion as soon as possible. Negotiations usually involved the surrender of weapons, and sometimes hostages, in exchange for the withdrawal of troops, and perhaps the granting of a financial allowance.[36] One reason why Kitchener created concentration camps in South Africa in 1900 was to provide shelter and security for Boer families

---

[33] Callwell, *Small Wars*, 41–42 and 147.

[34] T. R. Metcalf, 'Canning, Charles John, Earl Canning (1812–1862)', Oxford Dictionary of National Biography, online ed. www.oxforddnb.com/view/article/4554 (accessed 8 August 2016).

[35] *Army Regulations India, 1904*, vol. 2, 76, quoted in D. Omissi, *The Sepoy and the Raj. The Indian Army, 1860–1940* (London, 1994), 217.

[36] C. Tripodi, *Edge of Empire. The British Political Officer and Tribal Administration on the North-West Frontier 1877–1947* (Farnham and Burlington, VT, 2011), 49–108; H. Beattie, 'Negotiations with the Tribes of Waziristan 1849–1914 – The British Experience', *Journal of Imperial and Commonwealth History* 39(4) (2011), 571–87; idem, 'Hostages on the Indo-Afghan Border in the Later Nineteenth Century', *Journal of Imperial and Commonwealth History* 43(4) (2015), 557–69.

whose farms he had destroyed.[37] The fact that so many people died in them reflected the grossly negligent way in which they were administered, rather than any genocidal malice on the part of the British. The peace settlement negotiated at the end of the war offered the Boers not only a wide measure of political autonomy, albeit within the British empire, but also generous compensation for the physical damage they had suffered.[38]

Even before 1914 Callwell knew that burning villages and executing rebels found under arms was liable to outrage humanitarian sentiments.[39] A handful of radical British newspapers were critical of the atrocities that British troops inflicted on captured insurgents in India in 1857–58, but they were the exception, not the rule.[40] The imposition of martial law by Governor Eyre on Jamaica in 1865, which led to the execution of 439 people, occasioned a furious debate amongst prominent Victorian intellectuals and politicians about the political, legal and moral rights and wrongs of what he had done.[41] The Aborigine Protection Society complained at the widespread ill treatment of Zulu tribesmen in 1879, only to be fobbed off with the excuse that any ill treatment had been meted out by African auxiliaries, not British soldiers.[42] In 1885 the Liberal statesman, Lord Rosebery, damned British punitive expeditions on the North West Frontier of India as a policy of 'butcher and bolt' and 'meaningless massacre'.[43] There were also radical critics on the left of British politics who questioned both the reasons why the British were fighting in South Africa and the means they were employing. In 1901, the leader of the Liberal party, Sir Henry Campbell Bannerman, famously condemned the ways in which the army was herding Boer refugees into concentration camps as waging war using 'methods of barbarism'.[44]

But a more typical public response to news that British forces were taking stern measures to suppress rebellious subjects was afforded by a *Times* leading article, which told its readers in June 1857 that

Whatever be the moral causes of an insurrection, the only safe remedy lies in a ready appeal to arms. On this point we are happy to say that there are no grounds

---

[37] Circular memorandum No. 29, reproduced in Wessels (ed.), *Kitchener and the War in South Africa*, 52–53 and 60–61.
[38] D. Judd and K. Surridge, *The Boer War* (London, 2002), 298, 300; B. Nasson, *The South African War, 1899-1902* (London, 1999), 231–32.
[39] Callwell, *Small Wars*, 40.    [40] Spiers, *Army and Society*, 131.
[41] Townshend, 'Martial Law', 168–70; B. A. Knox, 'The British Government and the Governor Eyre Controversy, 1865–1875', *Historical Journal* 19(4) (1976), 877–900; C. Hall, 'The Economy of Intellectual Prestige: Thomas Carlyle, John Stuart Mill, and the Case of Governor Eyre', *Cultural Critique* (12) (Spring 1989), 167–96.
[42] Lieven, 'Butchering the Brutes', 626.    [43] *The Times*, 2 April 1885.
[44] Ibid., 15 June 1901.

for despondency. We can only hope that the suppression of the mutiny will be speedy and decisive. As for the expression of a wish that it may not be accompanied with bloodshed, we feel that it would be an unworthy affectation. Justice, humanity, the safety of our countrymen, and the honour of the country demand that the slaughter of Delhi shall be punished with unsparing severity. Asiatics are not the people to whom rules can safely grant immunity from crime.[45]

Forty years later, 'pro-Boer' critics of the war in South Africa were openly accused of giving aid and comfort to the enemy, of committing treason, and saw their meetings sometimes broken up by mob violence.[46]

\*\*\*

It took the experience of the First World War to begin to produce a significant change in public attitudes towards what was or was not acceptable behaviour for troops called upon to quell an insurgency. In 1914, Britain went to war against Germany as a more or less united nation not just because the German invasion of Belgium represented a direct threat to British security. It was also an affront to what the British regarded as the right way to conduct international affairs. Those British voices which had been raised to condemn the policy of burning villages on the North West Frontier and farms in South Africa were articulating the belief shared by many people that wars should be waged between soldiers, and that innocent civilians should, if possible, escape harm. Reports that German troops had committed a series of atrocities against civilians as they marched through Belgium and northern France, exaggerated only to some extent by the British press, were an affront to that belief.[47] That the British were fighting the war to rid the world of Prussian militarism quickly became a deeply rooted conviction.[48] Indeed, it was so deeply rooted that it coloured the ways in which the British public regarded the methods employed by their own armed forces to repress the series of insurgencies that confronted the British empire in the post-war era.

Between 1919 and 1921 there were several episodes when troops fired on rioters and were then held up to public condemnation for doing so. The most egregious occurred in India, Ireland and Egypt. In Egypt, on 30 March 1919, a platoon of British soldiers executed out of hand five

---

[45] Ibid., 29 June 1857.

[46] S. C. Cull, 'Protesting against Modern War: A Comparison of Issues Raised by Anti-Imperialists and Pro-Boers', *War in History* 3(1) (1996), 66–76.

[47] On the behaviour of the German army in 1914 see J. Horne and A. Kramer, *German Atrocities 1914: A History of Denial* (New Haven, CT, and London, 2001). For British reactions to these and other German attacks on civilians see A. Gregory, *The Last Great War: British Society and the First World War* (Cambridge, 2008), 40–69.

[48] M. Sanders and P. M. Taylor, *British Propaganda During the First World War, 1914–1918* (London, 1982), 137–66.

village notables suspected of leading an attack on a group of their com-
rades. On 13 April 1919, Brigadier General Reginald Dyer ordered troops
to fire on a peaceful demonstration in the Punjabi city of Amritsar. Ten
minutes later, 379 Indians were dead and about 1,200 wounded. And in
November 1920, troops opened fire indiscriminately at a Gaellic football
match in Croke Park, Dublin, killing twelve people, while on the night of
11–12 December 1920 British paramilitary 'Black and Tans' and
Auxiliaries sacked the centre of Cork.[49] Such behaviour might have
been acceptable in 1857. But it seemed ill-suited to the new era that the
British empire had supposedly entered after 1918. The term
'Commonwealth' was increasingly used to describe the self-governing
white Dominions, which were seen as bastions of liberal, democratic
values in a world where such values seemed to be under threat. No longer
were the dependent colonies retained by right of conquest. Rather, they
were held in trusteeship for the benefit of their peoples.[50] But to the
government's critics these changes were cosmetic. The ways in which
the British acted to suppress nationalist movements in Ireland, India and
Egypt between 1919 and 1922 smacked all too much of those which the
British themselves had denounced when they had been employed by the
Germans in Belgium and France. They were the very negation of what the
British had been fighting against. They had not endured the horrors of
a world war merely to see some of those same horrors replicated within
their own empire.[51] As one MP told the House of Commons in
April 1920:

You cannot preach to the people of the rest of the world that you are in favour of
the greatest possible franchise and the right of small nationalities to decide their
own destiny, and at the same time say to four and a quarter million people in

---

[49] J. E. Kitchen, 'Violence in Defence of Empire: The British Army and the 1919 Egyptian
Revolution', *Journal of Modern European History* 13(2) (2015), 249–67; N. Lloyd, 'The
Amritsar Massacre and the Minimum Force Debate', *Small Wars & Insurgencies* 21(2)
(2010), 382–403; CAB 23/23, memo. Churchill, 'The Irish situation', 3 November 1920;
D. Leeson, 'Death in the Afternoon: The Croke Park Massacre, 21 November 1920',
*Canadian Journal of History* 38(1) (2003), 43–67; D. Leeson, *The Black and Tans. British
Police and Auxiliaries in the Irish War of Independence 1920–21* (Oxford, 2011), 157–222.

[50] A. Thompson and M. Kowalsky, 'Social Life and Cultural Representation: Empire in the
Public Imagination', in A. Thompson (ed.), *Britain's Experience of Empire in the Twentieth
Century* (Oxford, 2012), 256; T. R. Mockaitis, *British Counterinsurgency, 1919–60*
(London, 1990), 18.

[51] J. Lawrence, 'Forging a Peaceable Kingdom: War, Violence, and Fear of Brutalisation in
post-First World War Britain', *Journal of Modern History* 75(3) (2003), 557–89;
A. Gregory, '"Peculiarities of the English"?: War, Violence and Politics: 1900–39',
*Journal of Modern European History* 1(1) (2003), 44–59; S. R. Grayzel, *At Home Under
Fire: Air Raids and Culture in Britain from the Great War to the Blitz* (Cambridge, 2012),
20–63.

Ireland under your very noses that you are going to use the same Prussian methods you have been fighting for five years to destroy.[52]

In India, Egypt and Ireland the British followed their customary practice of combining the use of exemplary force with negotiations and political concessions. But they also realized that they needed new ways of responding to colonial insurgencies if they were not to incur the financial costs and political opprobrium they had faced between 1919 and 1921. New technologies offered only half an answer. On the margins of the empire, in parts of the Middle East, in the more remote regions of Africa and on the North West Frontier of India, air power offered a swift and cheap way of meting out retribution to unruly imperial subjects.[53] The problem was how to respond to critics who insisted that bombing and machine-gunning people from the air was an indiscriminate and inhuman application of violence that would hurt the innocent as well as the guilty.[54] The RAF's solution was to claim blandly that their critics were wrong, that they took all possible precautions to avoid innocent casualties and that air power achieved its effect not by inflicting physical damage but by the moral effect it had on those under attack.[55] The reality was different. The 1922 edition of the RAF's *Operations Manual* did insist that 'endeavour should be made to spare the women and children as far as possible, and for this purpose a warning should be given, whenever practicable'. But it also recommended that delayed action bombs should be used, 'so that the enemy people will not feel safe in returning to their villages even after the departure of aircraft; livestock should be attacked with machine gun fire and crops burnt by means of incendiary bombs'.[56] On the ground, tear gas might offer a more humane solution compared to rifle fire in controlling a rioting mob. But until the middle of the 1930s British governments were reluctant to adopt it for fear of a public relations backlash growing out of the widespread public abhorrence of the use of lethal gas during the First World War.[57] It was only after much hesitation

---

[52] Hansard, HC vol. 12, col. 981 (26 April 1920).

[53] D. Killingray, '"A Swift Agent of Government": Air Power in British Colonial Africa 1916–39', *Journal of African History* 25(4) (1984), 430–35.

[54] J. L. Cox, 'A Splendid Training Ground: The Importance to the Royal Air Force of Its Role in Iraq, 1919–32', *Journal of Imperial and Commonwealth History* 13(2) (1985), 171–73; CAB 63/27, Hankey to Lloyd George, The garrison of Mesopotamia, 28 May 1920.

[55] D. E. Omissi, *Air Power and Colonial Control: The Royal Air Force 1919–1939* (Manchester, 1990), 150–77.

[56] CD22. Air Ministry, *Operations Manual, Royal Air Force (Provisional)* (London, 1922), 128.

[57] S. Shoul, 'British Tear Gas Doctrine between the Two World Wars', *War in History* 15(2) (2008), 168–90.

that the Labour government permitted its use to disperse rioters in Malaya and Java in 1945. Their sensitivity that they might be accused of using weapons banned by the Geneva Convention was illustrated by the fact that commanders in the field were ordered to refer to it as 'tear smoke'.[58]

But new technology did not mean that governments could avoid the need sometimes to make a frank admission that they had so badly mismanaged matters that they had no option but to declare martial law. The last occasion when they did so was in 1947, when they briefly imposed it on Jerusalem and Tel Aviv. But they quickly discovered that it was both a propaganda gift to their opponents and that it imposed a heavier burden on the army than it could carry.[59] However, a solution was already at hand. In 1934, *Notes on Imperial Policing* had asserted that 'the British Empire has nothing equivalent to what is called in France the "declaration of a state of siege"'.[60] That was wrong, and indeed the manual hinted as much by explaining that colonial legislatures could enact emergency legislation to 'delegate extraordinary powers of a special character to the chief military commander'.[61] As long ago as October 1896 the government in London had used its prerogative powers to promulgate an Order in Council that permitted the governors of the fortress colonies of Gibraltar, Malta, Hong Kong and Ceylon to issue proclamations giving them control of all property and persons in their colony, and making the latter liable to trial by a court martial.[62] In 1916 the scope of the Order was extended to other colonies and protectorates, and in 1928 the legislation was consolidated and remained on the statute book until 1939. It was then replaced by the Emergency Powers (Colonial Defence) Order in Council, 1939.[63] This enabled colonial governments to solve the problem of how to crush an insurgency without bringing down on their own heads the political odium of declaring martial law and remain within the orbit of the law. The legitimacy of an Order in Council did not rest on parliamentary

---

[58] WO 106/5176, Wilson, AFHQ Mediterranean to War Office, 4 December 1944; WO 106/5176, ALFSEA to Cabinet Office, 7 November 1945; WO 106/5176, COS to ALFSEA, 9 November 1945.
[59] CAB 129/18/CP(47)107, Chiefs of Staff, Palestine, Imposition of Martial Law, 26 March 1947.
[60] WO 279/796, *War Office, Notes on Imperial Policing*, 30.
[61] WO 279/796, *War Office, Notes on Imperial Policing 1934*, 31.
[62] CO 323/1594/3, Order in Council, 21 October 1896.
[63] CO 323/1594/3, The British Protectorates (Defence) Order in Council, 1916; CO 323/1594/3, The Defence (Certain British possessions) Order in Council, 1928; CO 323/1594/3, W. L. Dale to Sir G. Bushe, 13 January 1938.

legislation but on the exercise by the government of the Crown's prerogative powers. The 1939 Order in Council gave a colonial governor the power to declare a state of emergency and then make such regulations as he thought 'necessary or expedient for securing the public safety, the defence of the territory, the maintenance of public order and the suppression of mutiny, rebellion and riot'. With the permission of the Colonial Office in London, a governor could then suspend or amend any law that he chose. The one thing that he was specifically forbidden from doing was to establish military courts to try civilians. But given the wide-ranging powers he now enjoyed, he had little need to do so.[64] The declaration of a state of emergency was usually followed by the publication of a battery of regulations giving the security forces wide-ranging powers. Control regulations gave them the right to use exemplary force to intimidate the civilian population and disrupt the insurgents' organisation by limiting the movements of people and goods, imposing curfews and compulsory identity checks, restricting the possession of foodstuffs and censoring the media. They also gave them the right to search premises and arrest suspects without a warrant, to mount cordon and search operations and to impose collective punishments. Counterterrorist regulations gave security forces the power to hold suspects in detention without trial, and in some colonies to enforce wholesale population resettlement and create free-fire zones where the security forces could shoot suspects on sight.[65] As one Colonial Office official admitted in 1948, such regulations amounted to 'police state controls'.[66]

\*\*\*

After 1945, the application of the principle of minimum necessary force was not the army's default setting. It had to be imposed on them by their political masters. Soldiers who had fought in the Second World War had learnt that massive firepower won battles, and their initial instinct was to follow the same practice when they confronted insurgents. In 1944–45, in the face of insurgencies in Athens and Surabaya in the Netherlands East Indies, they had no hesitation in employing artillery, naval gunfire support and ground attack aircraft, and they took little care to discriminate

---

[64] CO 822/729, Emergency Powers (Colonial Defence) Order in Council, 9 March 1939; A. W. B. Simpson, 'Round up the Usual Suspects: The Legacy of British Colonialism and the European Convention on Human Rights', *Loyola Law Review* 41(4) (1995–96), 629–711.

[65] D. French, *The British Way in Counter-Insurgency, 1945–1967* (Oxford, 2011), 76–81.

[66] CO 111/736/4, Note of a meeting held on security matters in British Guiana in Mr Seel's room, Church House, on 28 October 1948.

between armed insurgents and civilians.[67] In Athens troops were told that they 'must NOT be squeamish about killing anyone carrying a weapon – civilian, woman or child. All occupants of a house from which fire has been coming must be arrested or killed.'[68] They wanted to continue such practices thereafter. In August 1945 the Commander-in-Chief's committee in the Middle East asked the Cabinet for permission to be allowed to use aerial bombs, naval gunfire, mortars and artillery to quell serious disturbances in Britain's Middle Eastern empire.[69] A horrified Cabinet refused.[70]

The concept of minimum force, as it was set forth in successive editions of *King's* and *Queen's Regulations*, the *Manual* and the army's doctrinal manuals was so ill-defined that it could not constitute an effective guide for actions by troops on the ground. There could be no better illustration of that than the fact that when in 1919 Brigadier General Dyer was called upon to defend his actions at Amritsar before a public inquiry, he insisted that he believed that he had obeyed both the letter and the spirit of the doctrine.[71] Plenty of British officials and private individuals, both in India and at home, shared Dyer's conviction that by his timely action he had saved India from a second Mutiny, although that was by no means a universal interpretation. What is certain is that his actions did lead to an important amendment to the army's formal doctrine. Dyer was held by his critics to have acted vindictively and to have continued firing on an unarmed crowd because he wanted to send a message throughout the disaffected areas of India that the Raj was not to be toyed with.[72] Henceforth, soldiers were warned that 'he must on no account use force with a view to its deterrent effect elsewhere or in the future'.[73] After 1945, troops were usually issued with a short statement spelling out the circumstances in which they could or could not open fire. But even this did not always provide clear rules. This was illustrated by a covering note issued by a brigade commander in Kenya during the Mau Mau insurgency in 1953: 'The

---

[67] WO 204/1909. Operations in Greece, 15 October 1944 to 7 January 1945, 23 Armoured Brigade. On the fighting in Indonesia see R. McMillan, *The British Occupation of Indonesia, 1945–1946* (London, 2005); CAB 69/7/DO(45)42, Note by the Secretary, Situation in Java, 1 December 1945 and enc. report by Lieutenant Colonel G. S. Nangle.

[68] WO 204/1909. *Lessons from fighting in Greece*, n.d. (c. 15 January 1945).

[69] CAB 69/7/DO(45)40, Note by the Secretary, Use of appropriate weapons in the Middle East, 30 November 1945.

[70] CAB 69/7/DO(45)17, Meeting, Cabinet Defence Committee, 12 December 1945.

[71] Doyle, 'Massacre by the Book', 249–50.

[72] R. Johnson, 'Command of the Army, Charles Gwynn and Imperial Policing: The British Doctrinal Approach to Internal Security in Palestine 1919–29', *Journal of Imperial and Commonwealth History* 43(4) (2015), 571–72.

[73] *MML, 1940*, 256.

principle of the "minimum force necessary" must apply in all circumstances and each of the cases described below. This principle is not really restrictive; in fact the minimum force necessary might be the maximum force a soldier or party of soldiers could muster.'[74] In 1958, the Secretary of State for War, Christopher Soames, added to the confusion when, in a reference to operations on Cyprus against EOKA, he told MPs that 'it is known by every soldier in Cyprus that, whatever action he is called upon to take, he has to do it with the minimum of force'. But he added, 'we must never forget that the role of the security forces is to conquer terrorism, and there will be many incidents when the minimum force necessary will be quite a lot of force'.[75]

It was understandable that members of the security forces on the ground were resentful at a law that was so ill-defined and which placed them in jeopardy of being punished for obeying their orders. One junior officer thought that putting the onus in this way on the soldier or policeman on the spot was just 'a most convenient umbrella for the politician and for the civil power, leaving the military holding the baby. If anything went wrong the military could be held to blame, for using either too much or too little force, or for not taking action or, alternatively, using no force when it should have done so.'[76] The authorities issued plenty of declarations that members of the security forces had to maintain strict discipline and avoid the use of excessive force, no matter what provocation they encountered.[77] Some members of the security forces were punished for using excessive force.[78] But many others got off scot-free, because there were limits beyond which the authorities understood they must not go for fear of undermining the morale of their men on the ground.[79] The law was a tool which could be used not just to protect innocent civilians from excessive military force. It could also be used to protect soldiers from the civil justice system. Thus, in 1949 the Malayan government rewrote one of its own emergency regulations to give retrospective legal cover to troops who were alleged to have massacred two dozen Chinese rubber

[74] WO 32/21721, OC, 39 Infantry Brigade to CO's 1/Buffs, 1/Devons, 1/Lancashire Fusiliers, 20 April 1953.

[75] *The Times*, 7 July 1958.

[76] Major V. Dover, *The Silken Canopy* (London, 1979), 128.

[77] See, for example, WO 169/19521, *Middle East Training Pamphlet No. 9*, Part XIII, *Notes for Officers on Internal Security Duties* (May 1945); WO 169/19745. HQ British Troops Palestine and Transjordan, Operational Instruction No. 21, 23 October 1945; CO 1015/1523, Nyasaland Government, *Instructions to Civil Officers, Military Officers, and Police Officers on the use of Armed Force in Case of Civil Disturbances, 1958* (1958).

[78] French, *British Way in Counter-Insurgency*, 140–41.

[79] An outstanding example of this was the case of Major Roy Farren, who was tried and found innocent by a court martial in Palestine of the murder of a Jewish insurgent, see D. Cesarani, *Major Farran's Hat* (London, 2009).

tappers at the village of Batang Kali.[80] Governors were also usually careful to place the troops under their command in a state of active service under the Army Act, because once they had done so they were immune from prosecution in the civil courts.[81] They could only be tried by courts martial for their misdemeanours, and military officers sitting on a court martial were more likely than civil judges or a civilian jury to show leniency to a soldier who had transgressed. As a senior officer wrote in 1957, when troops were facing rioters or insurgents,

the possibility that fire is mistakenly opened without complete legal justification cannot be excluded particularly as junior ranks frequently have to assess the situation and make a decision in this connection for themselves. I am sure you will agree that it is therefore essential that all ranks should feel that if their actions in this respect are thought to contravene the established legal principles involved in the use of force, they should be held accountable to a court technically equipped to adjudicate not only on the legal principles but on the military considerations also involved. Whilst this is not in any way intended as a reflection on the civil courts it is clear that the possibility of trial before a civil court can induce hesitancy when decisiveness is essential.[82]

Military considerations, meaning the overriding need to ensure that soldiers obeyed their military superiors, had to trump legal considerations. Perhaps the most egregious instance of this occurred in Kenya in 1955, when the authorities amnestied members of the loyalist home guard for a series of crimes they had committed lest they go over to the insurgents themselves.[83] Nor were responsible politicians above bending or ignoring the law if it suited their wider purposes. In September 1957, Cabinet ministers put pressure on a senior judge on Cyprus to tone down criticism he had made in an official report on army misdeeds.[84] Three months later the Prime Minister, Harold Macmillan, deliberately hid the truth from the House of Commons about a recent breakdown in discipline amongst troops in Famagusta that had left three civilians dead and more than two hundred injured. He feared that if he yielded to demands for an independent inquiry, 'we shall break the spirit of the security forces'.[85]

---

[80] French, *British Way in Counter-Insurgency*, 166–68.
[81] WO 169/19745, HQ British Troops Palestine and Transjordan, Operational Instruction No. 21, 23 October 1945.
[82] FCO 141/4578, Campbell to Henry, 15 October 1957.
[83] H. Bennett and D. French (eds.), *The Kenya Papers of General Sir George Erskine, 1953–1955* (Stroud, 2013), 251–312.
[84] FCO 141/4487, Record of a meeting held in the Colonial Office at 11 a.m. on Friday, 5 September 1958; FCO 141/4487, Bower to Foot, 21 October 1958; FCO 141/4487, Foot to Lennox-Boyd, 4 November 1958.
[85] P. Catterall (ed.), *The Macmillan Diaries*, Vol. 2, *Prime Minister and After, 1957–60* (London, 2011), 173.

The ways in which the British conducted counter-insurgency operations in the two decades after 1945 showed what Soames' definition of 'the minimum force necessary' meant in practice. In the Suez Canal Zone and, albeit to a lesser extent, in Aden, casualties between the insurgents and the security forces were roughly equal. In Palestine and Cyprus, security forces suffered significantly heavier losses than did the insurgents. But in Malaya, Kenya, Nyasaland and the Brunei-Indonesian Confrontation the reverse was the case, and the security forces inflicted far more casualties on the insurgents than they suffered themselves. This suggests that there were two kinds of counter-insurgency campaigns. In Palestine, the Canal Zone, Cyprus and British Guiana, the security forces did operate under constraints that limited the amount of lethal force they employed. But in Malaya, Kenya, Oman, Nyasaland and Eastern Malaysia, those constraints were much weaker. (Aden was situated somewhere between these two categories.) The differences were partly a product of the way in which the security forces understood the tactics that their opponents were employing. They showed a greater degree of restraint if their opponents confined themselves to terrorism, sabotage and individual assassinations than if they combined these tactics with guerrilla operations. Thus the degree of violence that the security forces employed was, in a rough and ready way, proportionate to the violence that was being applied against them. However, in Kenya and Nyasaland another factor was at work, which ratcheted up the readiness of the security forces to use force. That was the determination of European settler-dominated regimes to stamp their authority unmistakably on insurgents they regarded as posing a mortal threat to their privileged position.[86] Finally, the same pragmatic political imperatives that had operated before 1914 continued to operate after 1945. Some degree of violence was essential to disrupt the insurgents' organization and degrade their morale. But too much violence would drive them to desperation and stand in the way of what was usually the government's goal: the best possible negotiated settlement.[87]

*** 

The rhetoric of the 'minimum force necessary' thus concealed a complex reality. It was an elastic concept that defied precise definition because the authorities themselves did not want to define it precisely. It provided

---

[86] These findings have been explored at much greater length in French, *British Way in Counter-Insurgency*, 105–16.

[87] K. Hack, 'Negotiating with the Malayan Communist Party, 1948–89', *Journal of Imperial and Commonwealth History* 39(4) (2011), 607–32; H. Bennett, *Fighting the Mau: The British Army and Counter-Insurgency in the Kenya Emergency* (Cambridge, 2013), 135–46.

a convenient shield that could hide the sometimes nasty reality of counter-insurgency operations. The reality was that whatever legal regime was in operation, be it martial law or regulations promulgated under the 1939 Order in Council, the security forces were able to employ as much or as little coercion as the authorities on the spot believed to be necessary, and their political masters in London thought would be acceptable to British political and public opinion. That freedom really only began to be constrained in the second half of the 1950s when, for the first time, British colonial authorities found themselves answerable not only to British public and political opinion, but also to the court of international public opinion.[88] In 1953, as part of their Cold War campaign to demonstrate their championship of human rights, the British government had extended the scope of the European Convention on Human Rights to cover most of their colonies. They hoped this would be little more than a propaganda gesture, for they had negotiated two safeguards. They could opt out of its provisions should they wish to do so, and they denied their colonial citizens the right of individual appeal under the Convention.[89] But foreign governments could launch appeals under the Convention, and once the EOKA insurgency erupted on Cyprus the British government could do nothing to prevent the Greek government from bringing down upon them the maximum possible political embarrassment by raising the Cyprus crisis at the United Nations, and lodging complaints on behalf of the Greek Cypriot population with the European Court at Strasbourg.[90] At a time when they were waging a vigorous campaign to

---

[88] This is not to say that the British had not been subject to international criticism for their conduct in earlier years, or that it had been without effect. In Palestine, Zionist propagandists were highly effective in publicizing misdeeds by the security forces, see G. Goodman, '"Troops Were then Forced to Fire": British Army Crowd Control in Palestine, November 1945', *Small Wars & Insurgencies* 26(2) (2015), 271–91.

[89] K. Sellars, 'Human Rights and the Colonies: Deceit, Deception and Discovery', *The Round Table* 93 (2004), 709–10; Convention for the Protection of Human Rights and Fundamental Freedoms as amended by Protocol No. 11. Rome, 4 November 1950. Article 63, www.conventions.coe.int/Treaty/en/Treaties/Html/005.htm (accessed 4 November 2007); K. Vask, 'The European Convention of Human Rights beyond the Frontiers of Europe', *The International and Comparative Law Quarterly* 12(4) (1963), 1210; Universal Declaration of Human Rights, www.un.org/en/documents/udhr/ (accessed 7 February 2010); *The Times*, 27 October 1953.

[90] CO 936/294, Permanent Representative of Greece to the Council of Europe, Petition from the Greek government concerning the violation of human rights and fundamental freedoms in Cyprus, 7 May 1956; A. W. B. Simpson, *Human Rights and the End of Empire. Britain and the Genesis of the European Convention* (Oxford, 2004), 929–32 and 1022–30; *The Times*, 20 February 1957; *Manchester Guardian*, 22 February 1957; CO 936/495, Vallat to Roberts-Wray, 31 July 1957; E. Johnson, 'Keeping Cyprus off the Agenda: British and American Relations at the United Nations, 1954–58', *Diplomacy & Statecraft* 11(3) (2000), 227–55; E. Johnson, 'Britain and the Cyprus Problem at the United Nations, 1954–58', *Journal of Imperial and Commonwealth History* 28(3) (2000) 113–30.

win the hearts and minds of the growing number of former colonies which had joined the international community on independence, the British could ill afford to ignore the charge that they were acting inhumanely in one of their remaining colonies. They were able to contain the Greek 'lawfare' campaign by some deft legal manoeuvres of their own. But doing so came at a cost. In 1957, they had to dispense with several of the more objectionable practices they had regularly employed during emergencies, including the imposition of collective punishments and the birching of juveniles.[91] The ways in which the British could conduct counter-insurgency had now entered a new era. In the past they had been judge and jury in their own court. Henceforth that was no longer the case.

## Abbreviations used in the text and notes:

* All Cabinet, Colonial Office, Foreign Office and War Office documents were drawn from materials in the collections of The National Archives (TNA), Kew.

| | |
|---|---|
| CAB | Cabinet |
| CO | Colonial Office |
| FCO | Foreign and Commonwealth Office |
| KR | King's Regulations and Orders for the Army |
| MML | Manual of Military Law |
| WO | War Office |

---

[91] D. French, *Fighting EOKA. The British Counter-Insurgency Campaign on Cyprus, 1955–59* (Oxford, 2015), 200–02, 216; FCO 141/4324, Martin to Macpherson, 6 December 1956; FCO 141/4324, Sinclair to Harding, 6 December 1956; FCO 141/4324, Harding to Colonial Office, 16 December 1956; FCO 141/4324, Lennox-Boyd to Harding, 18 December 1956.

# 3    Yokohama for the British in the Late Nineteenth Century: A Hub for Imperial Defence and a Node of Influence for Change

*Hamish Ion*

Japan may be called the 'Gem of the Sea' from her geographical position, her magnificent harbours and inland sea, the approaches to which might be rendered impregnable. It is a rich country, with mines of coal and iron, fisheries, and a vast maritime population. Japan is coveted alike by Russia, America and France; and its possession would enable the power holding to monopolise the whole trade in China.

Sir Henry Keppel (1868)[1]

Much of the attraction of Japan[2] to Keppel and to the long succession of other naval officers who left memoirs was its striking natural beauty and generally temperate climate, especially in comparison with that of coastal China, as well as the probability of a good run ashore. Yet, Keppel also understood that the strategic position of the Japanese archipelago in relation to both continental East Asia and to the trans-Pacific shipping lanes meant Japan was the object of international Great Power rivalry. British policy toward Japan was limited, merely directed to maintaining the territorial integrity of Japan, and utilizing her dominant trading

---

[1] Admiral of the Fleet the Hon. Sir Henry Keppel, *A Sailor's Life under Four Sovereigns* (London, 1899), 3 vols., vol. 3, 191. Keppel was Vice Admiral in command of China Squadron between 1867 and 1869. For a brief biographical sketch of Keppel and Japan, see Robert T. Morton, 'Sir Henry Keppel (1809–1904): "Probably the Most Universally Popular Naval Commander Ever Sent by England to the East"', in Hugh Cortazzi (ed.), *Britain & Japan: Biographical Portraits*, vol. IX (Folkestone, 2015), 513–23.

[2] For an excellent short survey of early Anglo-Japanese relations, see Derek Massarella, 'Anglo-Japanese Relations, 1600–1858', in Ian Nish and Yoichi Kibata (eds.), *The History of Anglo-Japanese Relations*, vol. 1, The Political-Diplomatic Dimensions, 1600–1930 (Basingstoke and New York, 2000), 1–30. See also W. G. Beasley, *Great Britain and the Opening of Japan 1834–1858* (London, 1951); Gerald S. Graham, *The China Station: War and Diplomacy 1830–1860* (Oxford, 1978). For Anglo-Japanese relations in the late nineteenth century, see Grace Fox, *Britain and Japan 1858–1883* (Oxford, 1969). For details concerning Royal Navy operations in Japanese waters, see William Laird Clowes, *The Royal Navy: A History from the Earliest Times to 1900* (7 vols., London, 1997 [1897–1903]), especially volumes 5, 6 and 7.

position in East Asia to ensure that she would benefit most from any treaty that she or other Great Powers signed with Japan.

The impact of Japan on the development of British strategic foreign policy in East Asia from the late nineteenth century to the 1930s was a consistent but subordinate theme in Keith Neilson's writings. Neilson stressed that naval capacities helped to determine British Far Eastern policy, and underlined the centrality of imperial maritime history in the history of British–East Asian relations. This case study of the British and Yokohama[3] in the late nineteenth century will show that the high policies of Admiralty, Treasury and Foreign Office that Neilson so astutely illuminated also had at the local level an impact and often a lasting influence that went beyond military, economic and diplomatic affairs into the social and cultural realms. It stresses the importance of international relations at the local level and the role of the individual and individual organizations of which the Royal Navy's China squadron was one in Anglo-Japanese relations.

At the treaty port Yokohama level, various different factors were at work. Yokohama came to serve not only as an informal hub in the external network of British imperial defence and trade throughout the Asia-Pacific region, but also as a node of internal influence for change through which British cultural, social, sporting and industrial ideas were transmitted into the surrounding broader Japanese society. Trade was the glue that held together the various elements that made up British interests in Yokohama. This paper concentrates on the relationship between the Royal Navy's China squadron and Yokohama during the nineteenth century, with special emphasis on the quasi-colonial period between 1864 and 1875 when a British military garrison was stationed there to protect the British Legation and British community and to ensure the provisions of the Anglo-Japanese treaty of 1858 were upheld.

Even though it was not a colony, Yokohama quickly became an integral part of the network of ports and logistical facilities that included Singapore, Hong Kong and Shanghai, which connected East Asia to the other British interests in the Indian Ocean region,

---

[3] For the purpose of this paper, treaty port Yokohama is seen to include Yokosuka, the site of the French-built naval dockyard and arsenal as well as the much smaller foreign settlement at Tsukiji where the naval training establishment, Kaigun Heigakkô (海軍兵学校, Naval Academy) was opened by the Meiji government in 1870. Although permission from the Japanese authorities was usually needed to travel to Kamakura, Hakone and Miyanoshita Hot Springs and Enoshima, those places where many Britons from Yokohama holidayed should also be included.

Australasia and beyond.[4] Yokohama was a hub for imperial defence and trade. Yokohama as the major Japanese port for international trade was still important for the British, and it was in their interest to avoid any damage to British trade or to the business interests of British merchants. While there were other treaty ports in the Japanese archipelago, among which Nagasaki was traditionally the most important, and Osaka and Kobe in the Kansai were commercially valuable, Yokohama, both in terms of trade and geographically as it was close to the seat of the Japanese government, remained the most useful for the maintenance of the British naval presence.[5] In trade terms, the total value of trade through Yokohama exceeded that of Nagasaki from 1860. In that year, the value of Yokohama trade was almost four times that of Nagasaki, some 76.89 per cent to 20.4 per cent of the total value of the Japanese national trade. The gap in trade between Yokohama and Nagasaki had widened to thirteen times in Yokohama's favour by 1865. In 1860, British commerce in Yokohama comprised 55 per cent of the total trade there; by 1865, the British share of Yokohama's imports and exports had increased to 85 per cent.[6] Yokohama was the western terminus for the P&O Lines and its regular service to Shanghai and beyond, and after 1891 the first trans-Pacific port of call for the Canadian Pacific Steamship Lines.[7] After the First World War, trade was bolstered by Japan's appetite for Canadian grain and lumber as well as goods and services from Britain, India and other parts of the British Empire.[8] Tôyama Shigeki has argued that Britain regarded the prospects of trade with Japan as less important than either China or India, in part

[4] Robert Bickers, in studying Hugh Hamilton Lindsay (1802–81), the China trade merchant and lobbyist, points out that by 1855 Lindsay had a vision of a British Asia that joined up Labuan, Singapore, Hong Kong and Shanghai as hubs and out-stations of an integrated system. See Robert Bickers, 'The Challenger: Hugh Hamilton Lindsay and the Rise of British Asia, 1832–1865', in *Transactions of the Royal Historical Society*, Sixth Series, XXII (2012), 141–69, 164. With the signing of the commercial treaty with Japan in 1858 and the beginning of the treaty port system there, Yokohama can be added.

[5] For the British in Nagasaki, see Brian Burke-Gaffney, *Nagasaki: The British Experience, 1854–1945* (Folkestone, 2009). For Kobe, see Peter Ennals, *Opening a Window to the West: The Foreign Concession at Kôbe, Japan, 1868–1899* (Toronto, 2014).

[6] Noell Wilson, *Defensive Positions: The Politics of Maritime Security in Tokugawa Japan* (Cambridge, MA, 2015), 201–02. The value of French trade was second to Britain at 8 per cent, the Dutch trade at 4 per cent and American trade at 1.5 per cent.

[7] In 1891, the Canadian Pacific advertised the passage from Yokohama to London would take twenty-one days. See Yokohama Kaikô Shiryôkan hen, *Yokohama & Bankuba: Taiheyô o koete* (Yokohama, 2005), 8.

[8] For British Commonwealth trade with Japan from the mid-1920s to the mid-1930s, see Michiko Ikeda, *Japan in Trade Isolation 1926–37 and 1948–85* (Tokyo, 2008), chapter 4, 118–76. In the wake of the 1923 earthquake, which devastated Yokohama and Tokyo, Japan bought a billion board feet of lumber from Canada between 1924 and 1926. See Anne Shannon, *Finding Japan: Early Canadian Encounters with Asia* (Vancouver, 2012),

because the sale of opium was prohibited by treaty.[9] Although Japan could offer both tea and silk, these commodities could also be found, possibly cheaper and in greater quantity, in China. This has led Gordon Daniels to argue that 'successive British governments always viewed Japan as an area of far less commercial potential than China and consequently were unwilling to commit armed forces to action there in anything but the most extreme circumstances'.[10] However, the enormous growth of British trade at Yokohama meant that some attempt to placate the anxieties of the British community there about their exposure to attack from the dreaded Japanese swordsmen should be made.

British interest in Yokohama was not static, however, and understandably changed in accordance with the strategic balance in East Asian waters, the proclivities of Anglo-Japanese relations and the overriding concerns of different Foreign Secretaries, First Lords of the Admiralty, Chancellors of the Exchequer and governments in Westminster. The English-language newspapers in Yokohama were alive to the ramifications of British naval and government policies for their expatriate community and not adverse to expressing their opinions. As Marvin Swartz has pointed out about British foreign policy in the era of Disraeli and Gladstone, finance and trade reinforced the strategic considerations of the Foreign Office as the expansionism of the other Great Powers challenged the British Empire.[11] The concern over Russian ambitions in Korea and in Manchuria, for instance, led to the search in the 1880s and 1890s for bases under British control, first at Port Hamilton and eventually at Weihaiwei, from which a closer watch could be maintained on Russian activities.[12] T. G. Otte, in his study of the China Question during the decade after 1894, stressed that a guiding principle of the Far Eastern diplomacy of the Liberal Party under Lord Rosebery (Archibald Philip Primrose, 1847–1929) had been 'to have

---

148. Britain, its colonial and Dominion partners would continue to dominate Yokohama's trade and foreign life, at least until the end of the 1920s.

[9] Tôyama Shigeki, 'Independence and Modernization in the Nineteenth Century', in Nagai Michio and Miguel Urrutia (eds.), *Meiji Ishin: Restoration and Revolution* (Tokyo, 1985), 29–42, 31.

[10] Gordon Daniels, 'The British Role in the Meiji Restoration: A Re-Interpretive Note', *Modern Asian Studies* 2(4) (1968), 292.

[11] Marvin Swartz, *The Politics of British Foreign Policy in the Era of Disraeli and Gladstone* (Houndmills, 1985), 145.

[12] See T. G. Otte, '"Wee-Ah-Wee"?: Britain at Weihaiwei, 1898–1930', in Greg Kennedy (ed.), *British Naval Strategy East of Suez 1900–2000: Influences and Actions* (London, 2005), 4–34.

Japan on our side'.[13] Japan, however, only played a secondary role in the foreign policy calculations of Lord Salisbury (Robert Arthur Talbot Gascoyne-Cecil, 1830–1903), Rosebery's Conservative successor as British Prime Minister.[14] Yet, as the eventual signing of the Anglo-Japanese Alliance in 1902 illustrated, the added reassurance given by emerging Japanese sea power was seen to help assuage British concerns about Russian ambitions in the central Asian hinterland.

The usefulness of Yokohama as an informal imperial outpost, which supported the British command of the Eastern Seas, did not depend solely on the comings and goings of the ships of the China squadron in those waters. This was clearly the case at a later date, during the First World War, when Yokohama still acted as a British imperial hub, but it was the Imperial Japanese Navy (IJN) that was projecting its power from there, rather than the Royal Navy, to protect British maritime interests in the Pacific, to guard the convoy lines from Australia through the Indian Ocean and Red Sea to Suez and even beyond into the Mediterranean to Valetta.[15] David Steeds has pointed out that the Anglo-Japanese Alliance (1902–23) at the very least worked in keeping Germany out of East Asia during the First World War.[16] The Great War also underlined the fact that the British community in Yokohama was part of an amorphous British world system and a resource not only to facilitate British trade, investment and influence in Japan, but also a reservoir of manpower in wartime, as the many names listed on the First World War Memorial unveiled by Edward, Prince of Wales in 1922 at the front gates of the Yokohama Foreign General Cemetery attests.

The late nineteenth century was for Yokohama a period of frenetic activity in the transmission of foreign ideas into Japan outside the gates of the treaty port, and perhaps at its zenith as a node of influence for change. Yokohama itself also provided the Japanese with a view of western society in microcosm (albeit, in its earliest days of rather a Wild West version) with all the paraphernalia of Victorian living, from the making of soap and

---

[13] T. G. Otte, *The China Question: Great Power Rivalry and British Isolation, 1894–1905* (Oxford, 2007), 14.

[14] Ibid., 19.

[15] See Hirama Yôichi, *Dai Ichi Ji Sekai Daisen to Nihon Kaigun: Gaikô to Gunji no rensetsu* (Tokyo, 1998); see also Ian T. M. Gow, 'The Royal Navy and Japan, 1900–1920: Strategic Re-Evaluation of the IJN' along with Yoichi Hirama, 'The Anglo-Japanese Alliance and the First World War', both in Ian Gow and Yoichi Hirama with John Chapman (eds.), *The History of Anglo-Japanese Relations, 1600–2000*, vol. III: *The Military Dimension* (Basingstoke and New York, 2003), 35–50, 51–70.

[16] Author's notes on paper by David Steeds, 'Formation of American Hegemony and the Anglo-Japanese Alliance' given in Session 1: Anglo-Japanese Alliance in World History at The Centenary of the Anglo-Japanese Alliance: Its Historical Impacts, Tokyo Conference held at International House of Japan, Toriizaka, Tokyo, 25 May 2002.

safety matches to the building of lighthouses and railways. Sixty years on, by the interwar years the British and foreign community in Yokohama serve as a reminder for the Japanese of the continued existence of British Great Power status even though its naval power was less often seen in Yokohama and Japanese waters. But it also, more negatively, suggested a colonial sense of entitlement and privilege among foreigners living in their midst who were no longer the purveyors of positive change. Similarly, any ability that British residents might have had to influence British public opinion about Japan at home had also disappeared with the rising tide of anti-Japanese feeling after 1937.

Yet such later issues are beyond the scope of this paper centred on the late nineteenth century. Andrew Lambert has pointed out that 'trade and market access were the critical imperial concerns, not land or people'.[17] The treaty ports, of which Yokohama was one,[18] were, Adarth Burks has stressed, 'in no sense a joint development. Rather they were imposed on the Japanese.'[19] As James Hoare has argued, 'the main purpose of the British establishment of links with Japan was trade. The treaty ports were nothing if not trading posts, and the British diplomats' function was to encourage and facilitate trade.'[20] Again, Lambert has stressed that the defence of empire 'was about using the sea for trade and communications, deterrence and war-fighting. The RN ensured that a global empire of trade and capital could use the sea.'[21] Commerce and force went hand in hand, and the Royal Navy showed in the two Anglo-Chinese Wars that it was prepared to use its power to open China to trade, also more reluctantly at Kagoshima in 1863 and the Shimonoseki Straits in 1864 to protect British interests. The British enjoyed in Yokohama all the benefits of an imperial outpost without the expense of colonial administration. In the early Meiji period, the British garrison and naval presence in Yokohama had an important impact on the transformation of Japan, the social and economic development of Yokohama as a treaty port, the transfer of military technology to the Japanese as well as its role in the maintenance of Britain's paramount position in East Asia.

---

[17] Andrew Lambert, 'The Royal Navy and the Defence of Empire, 1856–1918', in Greg Kennedy (ed.), *Imperial Defence: The Old World Order 1856–1956* (Abingdon, 2008), 112.

[18] The other Japanese treaty ports were Hakodate, Nagasaki, Kanagawa (Yokohama), Tsukiji (Tokyo waterfront), Osaka, Kobe and Niigata.

[19] Ardath W. Burks, review of J. E. Hoare, *Japanese Treaty Ports and Foreign Settlements: The Uninvited Guests 1858–1899* in *Journal of Japanese Studies* 22(2) (Summer, 1996), 446.

[20] James Hoare, 'The Era of the Unequal Treaties, 1858–99', in Nish and Kibata (eds.), *History of Anglo-Japanese Relations*, vol. 1, 115.

[21] Ibid., 129.

Much recent academic writings have been directed toward military service, maritime security and engagement with foreigners by Tokugawa Japan,[22] which would suggest that Japan was much more prepared for the onslaught of western powers after 1853 than perhaps previously thought. However, this study points to the need for continued attention to be paid to the rise of Japan as a regional power in the context of changing British and western imperial history in East Asia. It also emphasizes the place of Japan within Britain's overarching concerns in continental East Asia and the protection of its China trade. It was very much in the interest of Japan that the Royal Navy kept the sea open for trade. Catherine L. Phipps has argued in her study of Japan's ports and power in the late nineteenth century that Japan made effective use of the British and other empires in East Asia, including the precedents, infrastructure and markets that they provided, and 'the dynamics of informal imperialism helped shape trans-marine East Asia's geography of trade as Japan struggled to modernize its transportation infrastructure and stabilize finances through its unplanned and tumultuous, but ultimately successful, integration into the world economy'.[23] The success of the new Meiji government in its negotiations with Britain and the other Great Powers after the Restoration was completed, which has normally been seen as a result of Japanese diplomatic skill,[24] owes actually much less to that skill and much more to the fact that Britain had already achieved its limited foreign policy and military goals and aims in Japanese waters.

Yet all this was in the future when Yokohama first began to be an outpost for the British in the wake of the 1858 treaty between Britain and Japan.

### The China Squadron and Yokohama

The 1858 treaty protected the position of Britons and other foreigners within treaty port Yokohama. Extraterritoriality protected their legal rights both personally and commercially, and they also possessed freedom of worship. The British came to dominate the foreign settlements in Japan.[25] The British consul and the British merchant-controlled

---

[22] See, for instance, Constantine Nomikos Vaporis, *Tour of Duty: Samurai, Military Service in Edo, and the Culture of Early Modern Japan* (Honolulu, 2008); Wilson, Defensive Positions; and Robert I. Hellyer, *Defining Engagement: Japan and Global Contexts, 1640–1868* (Cambridge, MA, 2009).

[23] Catherine L. Phipps, *Empires on the Waterfront: Japan's Ports and Power, 1858–1899* (Cambridge, MA, 2015), 59.

[24] See for instance Michael R. Auslin, *Negotiating with Imperialism: The Unequal Treaties and the Culture of Japanese Diplomacy* (Cambridge, MA, 2004).

[25] Hoare, 'The Era of Unequal Treaties', 113.

Chambers of Commerce loomed large in Yokohama and treaty port life in Japan. Although attempts were made to move to Tokyo in the early 1860s, it was only in 1875 that the British Legation moved permanently from Yokohama. The British were unapologetic in maintaining a western type of lifestyle in Yokohama similar to that of Shanghai or Hong Kong, or even Masijid i-Sulaiman, that was essentially British colonial regardless of the claims of the local authorities and central government to control. The western community in Yokohama had briefly established a system of self-government like that of the International Concession in Shanghai, but rejected it as unnecessary in the circumstances of Japan. The race meetings, the clubs, the theatre, the athletics, the hotels and taverns, the churches, the foreign cemetery, parks, street lighting and housing show that treaty port Yokohama had a great many features in terms of its foreign way of life with the other great treaty or colonial ports that made up the network of British imperial outposts in East Asia.[26] Eventually outnumbered only by the Chinese,[27] British residents totalled 1,200 out of 2,500 of foreign residents in the Japanese treaty ports in 1885, and 1,750 out of 4,700 in 1895. James Hoare points out that it was not until the 1920s that Americans began to outnumber Britons.[28]

The China Station after its reorganization in 1863 stretched from Singapore and the straits of Malacca to the Bering Sea, and was divided into four divisions: the strait of Malacca, based at Singapore; south China, based at Hong Kong; north China, based at Shanghai; and Japan under the senior officer posted at Yokohama.[29] The real strength of the China squadron in comparison to the East Asian squadrons of the other Great Powers was not its numerical strength, which was always limited, but its logistical sinews provided by its imperial defence network, that allowed the British to move their naval and military assets with greater ease than their rivals. In 1863, the China squadron consisted of forty-seven ships, the majority of which were lightly armed wooden screw gun vessels built at the time of the Crimean War and carrying between one and four guns. At the bombardment of Kagoshima in August 1863,

---

[26] This can certainly be seen in the photographs, historical surveys, biographical sketches of leading members of the western community, businesses and institutions found in Yokohama Kaikô Shiryôkan hen, *Yokohama gaikokujin kyoryûchi* (Yokohama, 1998).

[27] Yokohama boasted a Chinese population of over 6,000 in 1910. By the 1880s, although it numbered still under a thousand, Yokohama's Chinese population had become self-sustaining and a distinct Chinatown within the treaty port boundaries had begun to form, see Eric C. Han, *The Rise of a Japanese Chinatown: Yokohama, 1894–1972* (Cambridge, MA, 2014), 11, 30.

[28] Hoare, 'The Era of the Unequal Treaties', 114.

[29] For its early history, see C. Northcote Parkinson, *War in the Eastern Seas 1793–1815* (London, 1954), and Graham, China Station.

the seven ships of the China squadron that were deployed included the three largest of its warships, a wooden screw frigate HMS *Euraylus* (thirty-five guns); the flagship, HMS *Pearl* (twenty-one guns), a wooden screw corvette; and HMS *Perseus* (seventeen guns), a wooden screw sloop.[30] In 1875 there were twenty-one Royal Naval ships in China waters with HMS *Iron Duke*, a double-screw armour plated iron ship with fourteen guns as the flagship. Beyond the flagship the only other significant warships on station were two steam corvettes, *Charybdis* and *Modeste*.[31] The simple fact was that the China squadron was not a powerful naval force. The same balance of one first-class cruiser as flagship backed up with two second-class cruisers and a flock of lesser warships and gunboats persisted throughout the period, as seen in 1894 when HMS *Imperieuse*, a twin-screw first-class armoured cruiser of 8,400 tonnes and fourteen guns flew the flag of Vice Admiral Sir E. R. Fremantle (1836–1929), and was supported by three second-class screw cruisers, *Leander*, *Mercury* and *Severn*, of approximately 4,000 tonnes and ten guns.[32] The Imperial Japanese Navy had no ships to rival the *Imperieuse*, but in the *Naniwa* and *Takachiho* had ships of similar strength to *Leander*, *Mercury* and *Severn*.[33] On the eve of the Sino-Japanese War, the IJN was ahead of the China squadron in numbers of ships (thirty-seven, excluding wooden ships, torpedo boats, transports and small steamers to twenty-two), and close to it in terms of naval strength.

In 1902, the Royal Navy had five battleships, two armoured cruisers, thirteen protected cruisers, six destroyers and sixteen gunboats in Asia; the Russians had five battleships, six armoured cruisers, two protected cruisers and two gunboats. The French, in contrast, had only one battle-ship, five protected cruisers and six gunboats.[34] In 1904, on the eve of the Russo-Japanese War, the IJN had six battleships (less than ten years old), seven armoured cruisers, thirteen protected cruisers, twenty destroyers and six gunboats.[35] From these figures, it would appear that the China squadron at the turn of the century was capable of meeting any naval challenge from the Russians or French, and strong enough to counter the Japanese long enough for British reinforcements to arrive from elsewhere.

---

[30] See Clowes, *Royal Navy*, vol. 7, 196–97; and A. Preston and J. Major, *Send A Gunboat! A Study of the Gunboat and Its Role in British Policy, 1854–1904* (London, 1967).
[31] See *China Directory 1863*, 22–23; *China Directory 1875*, 222–27.
[32] See *China Directory 1894*, 447–50.    [33] Ibid.
[34] See Kwong Chi Man and Tsoi Yiu Lun, *Eastern Fortress: A Military History of Hong Kong, 1840–1970* (Hong Kong, 2014), 36.
[35] See David C. Evans, Mark R. Peattie, *Kaigun: Strategy, Tactics, and Technology in the Imperial Japanese Navy 1887–1941* (Annapolis, MD, 1997), 90.

The eventual signing of the Anglo-Japanese Alliance in 1902 was not driven by the naval situation in East Asian waters.

During the late nineteenth century, under normal circumstances there was a seasonal progression made by the flagship of the China squadron from Singapore in winter, Hong Kong and the China coast in spring and early summer to Japan in the high summer with fleet manoeuvres off Hokkaidô. Likewise, ships and crews were rotated to allow them to spend time in Japanese waters where the climate was more temperate than the China coast. Hospital facilities available at Yokohama were important for ship crews escaping to healthy temperate Japan from the summer heat and fevers of the China coast. In April 1872, Vice Admiral Charles Frederick Alexander Shadwell (1814–88), who succeeded Vice Admiral Henry Kellett (1806–75) in the summer of 1871, wrote that he needed more ships, for other than his own flagship and a despatch ship, he claimed that he had only thirteen ships for the whole of the China station. Shadwell argued that both Singapore and Yokohama had gained in importance, the former because of the traffic coming through the Suez Canal and the latter because it had become the terminus of the American Mail Route. He wanted senior officers in both those places to be of post-rank and to have under their command corvettes of similar power to those that the Americans and Russians possessed.[36] For the Japan division, Shadwell had only two ships available to cover the ports of Yokohama, Nagasaki, Hiogo (Kobe) and Hakodate. Moreover, it was from Japan that ships were sent to check on the state of Russian settlements in the Gulf of Tartary. Indeed, Shadwell felt that the development of Vladivostok should be monitored from year to year as that port grew in importance.[37] This would mean that there would be greater demand for naval supplies from Yokohama.

A logistical constant was always evident in the requirement for coal and other naval supplies, which could be stored at Yokohama.[38] Considerable effort was made to find an adequate Japanese supply of coal for the Royal Navy, and there was much interest in the Takashima coalmine near Nagasaki.[39] Welsh coal, however, which was brought out as ballast to Japan, was considered the best but expensive. As well as coal storage, hospital facilities at Yokohama were also important to the China

---

[36] Shadwell to Admiralty, 16 April 1872, Admiralty (hereafter ADM) 125/21.     [37] Ibid.
[38] The British naval depot was on the waterfront at Yokohama Bluff lot 117 next to the P&O Coal Depot at Yokohama Bluff lot 183 on the one side, and Royal Navy Hospital at Yokohama Bluff lot 115 on the other. See *Yokohama gaikokujin kyoryûchi*, 4, 114, 115.
[39] A considerable amount of correspondence dealing with the question of Japanese coal between January 1872 and August 1873 can be found in ADM 125/19.

squadron. In January 1867, when discussing a proposal for a new civil hospital for Yokohama, *The Japan Times' Overland Mail* noted that Yokohama had 'now assumed the position of a *sanatorium* for India and China'.[40] In 1868, Keppel began a successful campaign to see the extension of the Contagious Disease Act to Yokohama, which called for the compulsory examination of Japanese prostitutes and the creation of a lock hospital supervised by a Royal Navy surgeon. By 1871 the Japanese government had acquiesced to this demand. It was followed in 1871 by a further demand from the China squadron for the mass vaccination of Japanese in Yokohama against smallpox. Both these demands were made in order to protect the health of British sailors and soldiers and the foreign community in Yokohama. The effort to control syphilis and smallpox, a feature of the outreach of western medicine to the east and to Japan, is a case of medical as well as sexual imperialism.[41] It also revealed how deeply embedded Yokohama had become into the network of ports used by the China squadron when controlling sea lanes and commercial routes throughout East Asia that it must abide by the medical rules that the Royal Navy was applying to all other parts of the network. In October 1868, Keppel hoped that on the completion of a permanent hospital the naval depot in Shanghai could be transferred to Yokohama.[42] In 1875, the Royal Navy was maintaining at Yokohama a victualling depot and a naval sick quarters as well as stationing naval accountants there. By 1883 there seemed to have been a reduction in the size of the Royal Navy victualling depot. However, the Royal Navy retained hospital facilities in Yokohama into the 1920s. There was also a Japanese government rifle range which could be used.[43] The Royal Navy used the dockyard at Yokosuka to repair its heavier ships. Shadwell's flagship, the *Iron Duke*, had been docked at Yokosuka in 1873 and 1874 and the Vice Admiral recommended the use of this facility for the repair of large ships with deep draughts over the dockyard at Hong Kong.[44]

The development of Hong Kong as a major fortified naval base with a dry dock capable of repairing large warships was achieved by the mid-1880s, by which time it was also becoming one of the major shipping and

[40] *The Japan Times' Overland Mail*, 18 January 1867.
[41] See A. Hamish Ion, 'Sexual Imperialism on the China Station during the Meiji Restoration: The Control of Smallpox and Syphilis at Yokohama, 1868–1871', *The International History Review* 31(4) (2009), 709–44.
[42] Keppel to Admiralty, 11 October 1868, ADM 125/78.
[43] This was also used by various rifle clubs including by Brennwald and the Swiss Rifle Club, see *Yokohama mono no hajime ko*, 134.
[44] Memorandum relating to China Station transferred by Vice Admiral Sir C. F. A. Shadwell to Vice Admiral A. P. Ryder, 1 February 1875, ADM 1/6342.

financial centres of Asia.[45] Sir John Colomb (1838–1909) noted in the late 1870s that the troops garrisoned in Hong Kong were there to defend the British communities in China and Japan as well as Hong Kong, but the residents of the treaty ports did not bear any of its costs while Hong Kong made a very considerable contribution to its defence.[46] Here it is important to remember, as Andrew Lambert has argued, that by the 1870s 'only Malta, Gibraltar and Bermuda were Imperial bases, naval fortresses entirely funded by the Imperial Government. Other bases were partnerships, like Sydney, Auckland, Halifax, Esquimalt, Hong Kong, Cape Town and Bombay. These partnerships were clearly and consistently established.'[47] While the Japanese did subsidize the British and French garrisons in Yokohama in terms of barracks, there was no financial or political partnership between the British and Japanese to offset costs such as occurred in the British colony of Hong Kong or at the Cape of Good Hope. Further, of course, the Meiji government was eager by the early 1870s for the British to withdraw all their troops from Yokohama.

### Protecting Yokohama

It was held important that the British in Japan did not yield in the face of violence or threat. In 1861, Sir Rutherford Alcock (1809–97), the British minister to Japan, had stressed that by

giving signs of weakness or by timidly recoiling before danger and menaces of violence. These people [the Japanese] are Asiatic in type … To yield a right, or retreat before violence, either the one or the other, bears but one construction, and they who give way are driven to the wall and trampled under foot without pity or hesitation, as objects of contempt. Every day supplies illustrations of this in Japan.[48]

Despite repeated pleas for greater protection for the British Legation and foreign community in Yokohama, the China squadron had been reluctant to supply a permanent guard for the minister until after the attack on the Legation (the Tôzenji Incident) in July 1861.[49] A pusillanimous

---

[45] See Man and Lun, *Eastern Fortress*, 21–35. The Cosmopolitan dockyard was completed in 1880. See Table 10 on 34 for a list of British dry docks east of Suez in 1914 and their dimensions.

[46] Captain J. C. R. Colomb, *The Defence of Great and Greater Britain: Sketches of Its Naval, Military and Political Aspects* (London, 1880), 150.

[47] Lambert, 'The Royal Navy and the Defence of Empire', 127.

[48] Alcock to Hope, 8 July 1861, ADM 125/116.

[49] See Ion 'Namamugi Incident', 4–5. See also J. E. Hoare, *The Tokyo Embassy: A Short History of the British Embassy in Japan 1859–1996* (London, 1995–1996), 7–10.

approach, however, still continued, for in February 1863 Nicholas Kingdon (1829–1903), an Englishman working for Dent Company in Yokohama,[50] wrote from Shanghai that 'Our Consul there [Yokohama, Neale] appears to be a veritable old woman and has made the Japanese have a small idea of British powers, by yielding every point in dispute.'[51] In May 1863, Kingdon, writing from Yokohama about the alarms that gripped the British community about potential night attacks or even their wholesale massacre in the aftermath of murder of Lennox Richardson on the Tôkaidô by retainers of the former daimyo of Satsuma (Namamugi Incident, 生麦事件, 14 September 1862), reported that Vice-Admiral Sir Augustus Leopold Kuper (1809–85) had only been prepared to land 20 men from a force of 1,500 afloat to protect the British merchants in the treaty port.[52] The British community in Yokohama had a mind of its own which was sometimes highly critical of the actions of their consuls and government policies as well as the inaction of the China squadron and its leadership, and perhaps in the case of the Namagumi Incident justifiably so. Happily, for Kingdon and those Britons in Yokohama, first some 250 French troops arrived in 1863. It was only in January 1864 that two companies of the 20th (Lancashire) Regiment arrived there and were reinforced in June 1864 by a Royal Marine battalion sent out directly from England.[53] The management of the crisis in Japan was very much conditioned by the ability of the Royal Navy to transfer ships and men from the China coast. In 1864, the British and French garrisons in Yokohama, which combined totaled 3,200 troops, guarded a foreign community of some 400. Ten years later there were only 400 troops guarding over 2,200 in the Yokohama foreign community.[54]

Prior to 1864, the army in China had been opposed to sending ground troops to protect the treaty ports in Japan because it was felt that it would be unable to reinforce the troops should they come under attack.[55] For its part, the Royal Navy itself, until Kagoshima in 1863, was also loath to

---

[50] Kingdon became a leading figure in the business community in Yokohama and was the founder of Kingdon, Schwabe and Company, and the President of the Yokohama United Club. He is buried with his wife in plot 18 in the Yokohama Foreigners Cemetery. In 1875, he was living at lot 16 on the Yokohama Bluff. See *Yokohama gaikokujin kyoryûchi*, 72.

[51] Quoted in Yokohama Kaikô Shiryôkan hen, *Shiryô de tadoru: Meiji Ishin shoki no Yokohama Eifutsu chûton gun* (Yokohama, 1993), 123.

[52] Ibid., 127.

[53] Of great use concerning the history of the British and French garrisons in Yokohama are the various articles in Yokohama taigaikeishi kenkyûkai hen, *Yokohama Eifutsu chûton gun to gaikokujin kyoryûchi* (Tokyo, 1999) and the research guide and materials in *Meiji Ishin shoki no Yokohama Eifutsu chûton gun*.

[54] Ibid., 272; *Yokohama Eifutsu chûton gun to gaikokujin kyoryûchi*, 17.

[55] See Brown to Neale, 19 May 1863, ADM 125/117.

become involved in full-scale hostilities against the Japanese not because of military difficulties of campaigning in Japan, substantial though they were deemed to be, but rather the deterrent for the British was the perceived belief that the Tokugawa government would be unable to raise and pay an indemnity to cover the British financial costs of making war on the Japanese.[56] Indeed, as Daniels has pointed out there were self-imposed constraints to the British use of force after 1864 because the Foreign Office insisted that force could only be used in response to a clear threat to British lives and property, and 'this tight restriction on the local use of force always limited the actions of British Ministers in Japan and, although the Royal Navy played an important role as a means of transport for diplomats, a source of intelligence, and a means of adding emphasis to British requests, it could never be freely used by British Ministers to intervene actively in Japanese internal events'.[57] In the light of the lacklustre performance of the French and Americans in their punitive expeditions against Korea in 1869 and 1871, respectively, and that of the Japanese against Taiwan in 1874, it was fortunate for the reputation of the China squadron that it had begun to stand aloof of reckless gunboat diplomacy following the successful but unauthorized actions of HMS *Algerine* in Taiwan in 1868.[58]

It was, however, not instantly clear after Shimonoseki that there would be no more major Japanese actions against the treaty ports in Japan or terrorist attacks on individuals. On 21 November 1864, Major Baldwin and Lieutenant Bird of 2nd battalion, 20th Regiment, were murdered near Kamakura. The difference between the many prior individual assassinations of soldiers and sailors and this attack was that the Tokugawa authorities quickly apprehended the perpetrator and executed him in front of the officers of the battalion, the first time a Japanese had suffered capital punishment for the murder of a foreigner.[59] A precedent had been set, and the number of attacks on foreigners began to decline. Constant calls were still made, however, on the China squadron to assist the minister in Japan in a variety of ways including helping to suppress the

---

[56] See Ion, 'The Namagumi Incident', 12–13. See Paget to Kuper, 3 February 1864, enclosure Memoranda of Michel and Hope, ADM 125/18.

[57] Daniels, 'The British Role in the Meiji Restoration', 292.

[58] See Gurdon to Jones, 2 December 1868, and Jones to Admiralty, 28 December 1868, ADM 1/6094. See also Hamish Ion, 'Gunboats, Independence Movements and War: Three Incidents Involving Missionaries on the Fringes of Diplomacy in the Late Nineteenth and Early Twentieth Centuries', in John Fisher and Antony Best (eds.), *On the Fringes of Diplomacy: Influences on British Foreign Policy, 1800–1945* (Farnham and Burlington, VT, 2011), 179–208, 183–90.

[59] Quoted in *Meiji Ishin ki no Yokohama Eibu chûton gun*, 76.

contraband trade in summer 1865,[60] and impressing upon the anti-foreign element in the Imperial Court the strength of western powers by assembling a large naval force in Osaka Bay in October of that year.[61] In July 1866, Sir Harry Parkes, the British minister, held that the free navigation of the Shimonoseki Straits should not be given up under any circumstances, and rejected a Tokugawa government request that all western ships should keep clear of the Straits during the hostilities between the Tokugawa government and Chôshû.[62] The presence of the garrison was useful. Above all, as Parkes stressed to Keppel, in late 1867 it was 'desirable that all classes in Japan should be satisfied of the ability of Her Majesty's Government to ensure respect for the engagements of the Treaties to which this country is pledged'.[63]

British neutrality during the Boshin War (戊辰戦争, 1868–69) served British interests well for it allowed for the triumph of the imperialist forces without the interference of the Great Powers. The change of central government in 1868, the subsequent defeat of Aizu (会津) and the Northern Alliance (北部同盟) and the successful siege of Hakodate led to a decline of French influence in Japan (because of the close identification of France with the losing Tokugawa side) to the benefit of Britain.

The biggest change that was taking place in the British military position in Japan was the question of the withdrawal of the British garrison from Yokohama. In December 1873, Parkes was in favour of the withdrawal of the Royal Marine battalion.[64] For its part, the Admiralty was prepared to replace the battalion with a new one sent out from England,[65] and the initiative to withdraw the Royal Marine presence was coming from Parkes and the Foreign Office. Parkes, as Hoare has pointed out, was previously opposed to the withdrawal of troops.[66] However, by June 1874 Parkes was suggesting that the marines not be withdrawn until the early months of 1875 because of the uncertainty of the political situation.[67] In July the Foreign Office decided that even though the Saga Rebellion in Kyûshû had been crushed, the Taiwan Expedition had followed it; and the time was not right for the marines to be sent home even though no decision had

[60] Fox, *Britain and Japan, 1858–1883*, 163.
[61] Parkes to King, 26 October 1865, ADM 1/5923; see also Parkes to King, 30 October 1865, ADM 125/119.
[62] Daniels, 'The British role in the Meiji Restoration', 301.
[63] Keppel to Admiralty, 4 December 1867, enclosure: Parkes to Keppel, 22 November 1867, ADM 1/6006.
[64] Parkes to Shadwell, 15 December 1873, ADM 125/21.
[65] Lushington to Shadwell, 20 January 1874, ibid.
[66] Hoare, 'The Era of Unequal Treaties', 112.
[67] Parkes to Derby, 16 June 1874, ADM 205/45.

been made as to when this might take place.[68] Shadwell himself thought that the presence of the marines at Yokohama 'gives great moral support to British Interests in Japan',[69] and thought their withdrawal in 1875 premature given that even though Japan was quiet at that time, 'elements of trouble freely exist in the discontent of the Samourai class, that is the disarmed retainers of the ancient Daimios, who are much dissatisfied with the recent political changes in Japan, and are generally of a turbulent disposition'.[70] Yet the Royal Marines had received their orders to leave.[71] In expressing his high regard for the contribution of the troops to peace in Japan, Parkes told Lieutenant Colonel Fleetwood Richards, 'the departure of your Corps terminates an occupation which, it is gratifying to all parties to believe, is no longer necessary'.[72] At the beginning of March 1875, HMS *Adventure* took them away.[73] Their departure meant that a very visible British presence in Japan had disappeared.

### Soldiers and Sailors As Teachers and Salesmen

The Royal Navy's relations with Japan were not simply those of a force that could descend on the Japanese coast at will and intervene with military force in Japanese affairs.

Indeed, within three years of the shelling of the Chôshû batteries on the Shimonoseki Straits in 1864 the first group of Royal Navy advisors to the embryonic Japanese naval forces, the Tracey Mission,[74] had appeared to be followed after the Meiji Restoration by the Douglas Mission[75] and a gaggle of naval helpers and advisors. A relatively large number of British instructors were employed with the Japanese navy in the 1870s and 1880s, as seen in the lists of names in the relevant years of the *Chronicle and Directory for China, Japan and the Philipines*. Lieutenant Albert

---

[68] Wolley to Shadwell, 14 July 1874, ADM 125/21.

[69] Shadwell to Admiralty, 22 June 1874, ibid.

[70] Memorandum relating to China Station transferred by Vice Admiral Sir C. F. A. Shadwell to Vice Admiral A. P. Ryder, 1 February 1875, ADM 1/6342.

[71] Richards to D. A. General, 22 February 1875, ADM 201/45.

[72] Parkes to Richards, 27 February 1875, ibid.

[73] See *The Japan Weekly Mail*, 6 March 1875.

[74] For a description of the Tracey Mission (1867–68) and its activities in Japan, see Admiral Sir Edward E. Bradford, *Life of Admiral of the Fleet Sir Arthur Knyvet Wilson Bart., V.C. G. C.B., O.M., G.C.V.O* (London, 1923), 22–27; see also Fox, *Britain and Japan 1858–1883*, 254–57.

[75] For the Douglas Mission (1873–79), see Fox, *Britain and Japan 1858–1883*, 265–67. See also Archibald C. Douglas, 'The Genesis of Japan's Navy', *Transactions and Proceedings of The Japan Society* 36 (1938–39), 19–28; Kaigun Rekishi Hozon Kai, *Nihon Kaigun Shi*, 123–28; Ikeda Kiyoshi, *Nihon to Kaigun*, 148–50, Ian Gow, 'The Douglas Mission (1873–79) and Meiji Naval Education', in J. E. Hoare (ed.), *Britain & Japan: Biographical Portraits*, vol. 3 (Richmond, Surrey, 1999), 144–57.

G. S. Hawes (1842–97) of the Royal Marine Light Infantry, who was a close friend of Sir Ernest Satow (1843–1929), was employed on the naval training ship *Ryujo* off Yokohama. Lieutenant John M. James RN, together with Lieutenant Francis Brinkley (1841–1912) of the British Army (Royal Engineers), were employed at the Kaigun Heigakkô from January 1870.[76] In 1886, Captain John Ingles was selected to help develop higher and technical naval education,[77] and he stands out for playing a significant role in the development of the naval doctrine of the late nineteenth-century Imperial Japanese Navy. Japan, of course, was not the only country which looked to the Royal Navy for naval advisors, as China and Korea did the same during this period.[78] It stands to reason that such a transfer of ideas and technology would not have been allowed if it was thought that the development of Japanese sea power would threaten British interests and lines of communication in the Pacific, something that was inconceivable before a solution had been found to the problem of *beri-beri* in the early 1880s.[79]

Beginning in 1884, when the Japanese government placed orders for the protected cruisers *Naniwa-kan* and *Takachiko-kan* with Armstrong-Mitchell, British shipyards garnered lucrative contracts to build large warships for the IJN as seen in the fact that the six principal battleships of the Japanese fleet at the onset of the Russo-Japanese War, *Fuji*, *Yashima*, *Hatsuse*, *Shikishima*, *Asahi* and *Mikasa*, were all built in British shipyards.[80] In 1912, a battlecruiser *Kongo* built by Vickers at Barrow-in-Furness was the last major warship built for the IJN, and would eventually see action against the Royal Navy in 1942. However, following the *Kongo* other heavy warships were built in Japanese yards

[76] For Hawes, see Kaigun Rekishi Hozon Kai, *Nihon Kaigun Shi*, 64–67. For other names of Royal Navy officers and men involved in the training of the Imperial Japanese Navy, see Fox, *Britain and Japan 1858–1883*, 263–68; see also Clowes, *The Royal Navy*, vol. 7, 77. Among those who taught English to Japanese officer cadets during the 1880s were Arthur Lloyd (Shukei Gakkô, Paymaster's School) and Basil Hall Chamberlain (Kaigunshô, Naval Department).

[77] The Ingles mission lasted from 1887 to 1893. For a brief account of Ingles influence on the Imperial Japanese Navy see Evans and Peattie, *Kaigun*, 12–13, 36, 48–49. See also Ian Gow, *Military Intervention in Pre-War Japanese Politics: Admiral Katô Kanji and the 'Washington System'* (London, 2004), 36.

[78] See for instance John L. Rawlinson, *China's Struggle for Naval Development 1839–1895* (Cambridge, MA, 1967).

[79] For the problem of *beri-beri* among crews in the Imperial Japanese Navy and the effective solution to this problem through the introduction of a new shipboard diet by 1883, see Sachiko Noguchi and Alan I. Davidson, 'The Mikado's Navy and Australia: Visits of His Imperial Japanese Majesty's Training Ships, 1878–1912', *Monash University Working Papers on Japanese Studies* 3 (1993), 19–20. In the early 1930s, the RN itself looked to the IJN to help find solutions to cases of scurvy in British ships.

[80] Marie Conte-Helm, 'Armstrong's, Vickers and Japan', in Ian Nish (ed.), *Britain & Japan: Biographical Portraits*, vol. 1 (Folkestone, 1994), 96 and 98.

based on British designs. One of the roles of the British naval attachés at the embassy in Tokyo prior to the First World War was to facilitate the sale of British-built warships to the IJN, which accounts for the design blueprints of the famous *HMS Warspite* and other new British warships being in the Japanese military archives.[81] By the end of the nineteenth century, Japan's example was contributing to the intellectual discussion within the Royal Navy concerning the changing nature of naval warfare, as was shown by the interest that Philip Howard Colomb (1831–99) took in the naval aspects of the Sino-Japanese War.[82]

### The Military Garrison and Life in Treaty Port Yokohama

David French has argued that 'the main role of the army in the colonies was to "project an image of strength" through parades and other imperial ceremonies, such as the arrival and departure of governors'.[83] This was also very true of the British troops garrisoned in Yokohama; instead of governors it was the visits of admirals, birthdays of European monarchs and celebrations of national days of the Great Powers that led to considerable expenditure of ceremonial gunpowder in salutes. Indeed, British military bands served to introduce military music into Japan with Bandmaster John William Fenton of 1st battalion, 10th (North Lincoln) Regiment in September 1870 training the Satsuma Military Band (薩摩藩軍楽隊), the forerunner of the IJN's Military Band.[84]

As an old resident of Yokohama recalled in 1902, 'the presence of the officers helped greatly the social part of the Community, as having plenty of spare time on their hands, they were available for rides, picnics, &c., whilst the civilians were all in their offices'.[85] *The Japan Times* complimented the 2nd battalion, 20th Regiment for its amateur theatricals, for

---

[81] Bôechô Kenkyûjo, Kaigun M30-38-38 Meiji 44. As well as the *Warspite*, there was a detailed description of the *Marlborough* including design drawings showing details of heel and armour plating, and description of the ventilation system on the *Centurion*. There was little that escaped the interest of the Japanese. The naval attaché files show that a most cordial and friendly relationship existed between British naval attachés and their Japanese counterparts in the Japanese Navy Ministry in the decade before 1914; this stood in very marked contrast to relations between British naval attachés and the Navy Ministry in the mid-1930s.

[82] See Colomb, *Naval Warfare*, especially 435–52. For a study of Colomb's intellectual ideas and their impact on the Royal Navy see the relevant chapter in D. M. Schurman, *The Education of a Navy: The Development of British Naval Strategic Thought 1867–1914* (London, 1965).

[83] French quoted in Man and Lun, *Eastern Fortress*, 35.

[84] Yokohama Kaikô Shiryôkan hen, *Yokohama mono no hajime ko* (Yokohama, 3rd ed. 2003), 23, 150.

[85] 'Yokohama in the Sixties by an Old Resident', 4 January 1902, *The Japan Weekly Mail*.

giving concerts and the Garrison Races,[86] which proved that many of the regiment's officers were hearty sportsmen.

If the officers spent their time socializing, the soldiers and their dependents could suffer. In late September 1865, the troopship HMS *Adventure* arrived in Yokohama from Hong Kong with an officer and 22 rank and file, 55 women and 78 children, dependents of members of the 2nd battalion, 20th Regiment, which had been part of the British garrison in Yokohama since January 1864, as well as 4 officers and 150 rank and file, 5 women and 8 children belonging to the 2nd battalion, 11th (Devonshire) Regiment.[87] A considerable number of the new arrivals were sick because of the unhealthy conditions in Hong Kong. Apparently, little effort was made by the British military authorities in Yokohama to take care of the sick or even to see that transportation, comforts and rations were available for the newcomers when they landed. For some three months during the summer, sickness and mortality had been very high among the Hong Kong garrison and its military hospitals and medical staff were overstretched. While health conditions in Hong Kong were going from bad to worse, *The Japan Herald* was 'astounded to find on enquiry, that during this state of things in Hongkong, nearly all the heads of departments are absent, and in Yokohama, grumbling at its dullness and enjoying the itziboo exchange'.[88] The newspaper was suggesting that the senior figures in the British Army in China were in Japan because they could make a profit out of the exchange rate and were neglecting their professional responsibilities to the troops they commanded in Hong Kong.[89] At the time the 2nd battalion, 20th Regiment left Japan in May 1866, it was in good health.[90] Its departure was especially regretted by *The Japan Times*, which admitted 'the staff of which is almost entirely drawn from the ranks of the corps'.[91] Francis Brinkley, who became the editor of *The Japan Mail* in 1881 and later a *Times* correspondent in Japan, was one of the journalists who came from an army background.[92]

Soldiers could also be plunderers and murders. In late November 1866, Casper Brennwald, the Swiss consul, wrote in his diary about the great fire that destroyed much of Yokohama that 'the behavior of the English soldiers

---

[86] See advertisements for 2/20th Regiment amateur theatricals on 13 November 1865 and the Yokohama Garrison Races of 2 December 1865 in *Meiji Ishin ki no Yokohama Eibu chûton gun*, 62–67.

[87] *The Japan Herald*, 23 September 1865.

[88] Ibid. See also *The Japan Times*, 22 September 1865; and also *Meiji Ishin ki no Yokohama Eibu chûton gun*, 61.

[89] *The Japan Herald*, 14 October 1865.    [90] *The Japan Times*, 19 May 1866.

[91] Quoted in *Meiji Ishin ki no Yokohama Eibu chûton gun*, 79.

[92] *Yokohama gaikokujin kyoryûchi*, 89.

of the garrison, the 9th [Norfolk] Regiment, was appalling, the city was actually in a state of pillage by the soldiers. They forced their way into houses everywhere, drank like pigs and plundered whatever they could lay their hands on.'[93] Such behaviour on the part of the garrison was, happily, not always the case for *The Japan Times* had earlier commended the 2nd battalion, 20th Regiment for its help in fighting fires and saving buildings during its tour of duty in Yokohama.[94] In early May 1874, the foreign community in Yokohama was shocked to learn a Royal Marine private had attempted to murder a European woman with whom he had been having a relationship and then committed suicide.[95] Such a tragedy could only help to diminish the reputation of the garrison. In the main, however, soldiers and ex-servicemen were law-abiding and useful members of the British community.

Space allows only the mention of three different figures who made significant contributions to welfare of the British community and the creation of a modern treaty port. One of the seemingly outlandish characters in Yokohama in the 1860s was William H. Smith, nicknamed 'Public-Spirited Smith', who had been a Royal Marine lieutenant and worked as manager of the well-subscribed Yokohama United (Services) Club. Smith was known for his antics, which gave Charles Wirgman (1832–1891) plenty of copy for *Japan Punch*,[96] such as riding a tricycle, being a member of the Yokohama Skating Club and being the founder of the Yokohama Washing Establishment which featured two European ladies doing the washing and mangling, owning a piggery and growing western vegetables in the Bluff Gardens. More seriously, he was also in 1870 on the committee to establish street lighting in the treaty port.[97] John Diack (1828–1900), who had served with the Royal Engineers in Hong Kong, arrived in Japan in 1870 to work on the railway being built from Yokohama to Shinagawa, and went on to design in the 1880s many western-style commercial and public buildings such as the Hong Kong Shanghai Bank branch, the Japan Post Office building, the Masonic Hall and the Japan Brewery building.[98] Major General Henry Spencer Palmer (1838–93) of the Royal Engineers was responsible for the construction of the waterworks that supplied Yokohama with water from the Sagami River, which was completed in October 1887 just after his retirement

[93] Ibid., 131.    [94] *The Japan Times*, 6 April 1866.
[95] *The Japan Daily Herald*, 11 May 1874.
[96] Wirgman had served in the army prior to coming to Japan in 1861, and founded the *Japan Punch* in 1862. See Haga Tooru et al. (eds.), *Wiguman sobyô korekushyun* (2 vols., Tokyo, 2002), and for Smith see, for instance, vol. 1, 107–08.
[97] *Yokohama mono no hajime ko*, 20, 22, 41, 43, 52–53, 91–92, 113, 135, 146.
[98] *Yokohama gaikokujin kyoryûchi*, 80.

from the army. Palmer went on to design waterworks for Osaka, Hakodate, Tokyo and Kobe, and was involved in constructing new harbour works in Yokohama when he died.[99] What Smith, Diack and Palmer were building in Yokohama was a little piece of Victorian Britain set on the flatland and Bluff at Yokohama which offered the Japanese a glimpse into its buildings, its street lights, waterworks, food and drink, and clubs of a possible future. It was commerce and trade, import and export through the port of Yokohama with its connections to Britain and the network of ports in the Asia-Pacific guarded by the Royal Navy that made such a transformation a possibility.

### Into the Future

Treaty port Yokohama came to an end in July 1899, and with it extra-territoriality. The British and foreign community in Yokohama still continued to exist and to prosper. A new relationship with Japan came with the promulgation of the Anglo-Japanese Alliance in 1902. Neilson held that the Alliance caused a systemic problem to the balance of power in Europe, which had natural balances that were upset when an East Asian power was introduced to deal with a European power in Russia. He held the view that the Alliance in reality weakened Britain's position in East Asia and unleashed a monster that resulted in the 1911 treaty being more to keep Japan in check than to benefit British interests.[100] However, there were naval benefits to the British war effort against Germany accruing from the Alliance despite the rise of anti-British feeling in the Japanese army and the actions of the Japanese government in China as seen in the Twenty-One Demands. Similarly, British naval influence on the development of the IJN, Japanese maritime heavy industry and naval aeronautical training would extend beyond the end of the Anglo-Japanese Alliance in 1923.

In the interwar years, a third different role was played by British Yokohama. This does not so much relate to British strategic foreign policy as to the social and cultural aspects of the British community in Yokohama. After the end of the First World War, Neilson pointed out the changed international system during the interwar period meant that 'Japan posed an insoluble problem for imperial defence.'[101] Ian Nish has emphasized that 1919 brought change in the conduct of international

[99] Jiro Higuchi, 'Henry Spencer Palmer 1838–1893', in Hugh Cortazzi (ed.), *Britain & Japan: BiographicalPortraits*, vol. 4 (London, 2002), 203–05.

[100] Author's notes on conversation with Keith Neilson on 3 September 2002.

[101] Keith Neilson, '"Unbroken Thread": Japan, Maritime Power and British Imperial Defence, 1920–32', in Kennedy (ed.), *Naval Strategy East of Suez*, 83.

relations particularly in regards to openness, questions in parliament, the role of the press in public relations and national propaganda, which was not to the liking of veteran Japanese diplomats who preferred the 'old diplomacy'.[102]

Neilson postulated that Britain's decline as a Great Power at the beginning of the twentieth century was greatly exaggerated. This study of Yokohama upholds this view. Yet what is also clear is that the strategic foreign policy, which according to Neilson framed British policies toward Japan and East Asia, was backed at the local level by a British physical presence in the network of ports and logistical support centres of which Yokohama was one. As well as a hub for imperial defence and trade, Yokohama proved itself to be a British resource for manpower and also served as a node of influence from which British ideas, some as seemingly picayune as driving on the left side of the road or a fondness for the English Garden Suburb as a model for city living – of which Denonchôfu (田園調布) in Ota Ward in southern Tokyo, close to Yokohama is an example – could be transmitted into the surrounding broader Japanese society.

Yet, the interwar British community in Yokohama was also a continuing reminder – more negative than positive perhaps for the Japanese – of continued British presence in Japan, and the physical existence of impressive British consular buildings a reminder of British Great Power status. This was reinforced by the social paraphernalia of an exclusive and wealthy western enclave in Yokohama (multinational in composition, but still predominantly British in its colonial inclinations) seen in its large western-style houses on the Bluff, its race course, the Yokohama Country and Athletics Club where cricket and rugby were played, the Yokohama Yacht Club, its English-language schools, Christian Churches, Foreign Cemetery and newspapers that fed a colonial sense of entitlement and privilege among its British and western residents.[103] The perception of British power in East Asia continued to persist in Japanese eyes until 1941, at least, in terms of anti-British propaganda. Ikeda Kiyoshi, a leading authority on the IJN, noted that when he was a middle schoolboy in Kagoshima (鹿児島) in the late 1930s, he heard and saw 'nothing but a tremendous outburst of anti-British fever' which he went on to say 'was in sharp contrast to my experience at sea during the latter half of the war when I saw only U.S. navy

---

[102] See Ian Nish, *The Uncertainties of Isolation: Japan Between the Wars: The Creighton Lecture 1992* (London, 1993), 9–10.

[103] The way of life of the Yokohama foreign community in the interwar period has recently been described by W. Puck Brecher, *Honored and Dishonored Guests: Westerners in Wartime Japan* (Cambridge, MA, 2017), 51–59.

sailors'.[104] As anti-British feeling in Japan mounted, the informal influence of the British community in Yokohama continued to inform Japanese perceptions of Britain and British perceptions of Japan until 1941. This was perhaps more negative than positive, for the British community was living in a time warp, and they missed the opportunity to counter the ethnocentricity in the views of military and naval attachés in regards to the Japanese army which was continuously downgraded from the First World War onwards, as was the Royal Navy's view of the talent of the IJN revised down as its threat to the British position in East Asia was revised up. After all, the British had to contemplate a Japanese navy that the Royal Navy could defeat. As their defeat in 1945 revealed, the Japanese, in precipitating war, made a cataclysmic miscalculation about their ability to defeat the global resources of the British Empire, but the peace brought the foreigners to Yokohama. It is the American Seventh Fleet that uses Yokosuka now, and Togo Heihachirô's flagship, *Mikasa* (三笠), encased in concrete the only reminder of those days when the workers at Vickers at Barrow-in-Furness built the best of battleships and the China squadron commanded the Eastern Seas.

[104] Kiyoshi Ikeda, 'Japanese View of the Royal Navy', in Ian Nish (ed.), *Anglo-Japanese Naval Relations*, International Studies 3 (London, 1985), 1.

# 4 'The Diplomatic Digestive Organ': The Foreign Office As the Nerve Centre of Foreign Policy, c.1800–1940

## T. G. Otte

*Scientia potentia est; sed parva; quia scientia egregaria rara est, nec proinde apparens nisi paucissimis, et in paucis rebus.*

Thomas Hobbes (1669)[1]

Foreign ministries form a central part of modern diplomatic practice. They emerged slowly and haphazardly from the late fifteenth century onwards. With the growth in scope – both geographical and temporal – and intensity of diplomacy came the need for a central organization that could control and coordinate policy at the seat of government.

In Tudor and Elizabethan England, too, the steady growth of diplomatic activity spurred on institutional change in the shape of the Principal Secretary of State. Initially, an officer of the royal household, executing the decisions of the monarch and the Privy Council, over time much of his business came to be focused on foreign affairs.[2] Indeed, towards the end of Henry VIII's reign there were now two such secretaries, a practice continued by Elizabeth I and later formalized with the establishment of the Northern and Southern Departments. This geographical division reflected practical needs, mostly geopolitical factors but also Europe's religious divide, the Northern Department dealing with primarily the Protestant powers. The many ambiguities and peculiarities of the *ancien régime* in general were thus reflected in it.[3] If it was premodern, it was nevertheless

---

[1] *Thomae Hobbes Malmesburiensis Opera Philosophica quae latine scripsit omnia*, ed. Sir W. Molesworth (4 vols., London, 1839–41) iii, 69.

[2] F. M. G. Evans, *The Principal Secretary of State* (Manchester, 1923) remains the standard account.

[3] Britain was not unusual in this, but lagged well behind France and Prussia; see the first volume of Jean Baillou's magisterial *Les Affaires Étrangères et le corps diplomatique français* (2 vols., 1984), which examines in detail the pre-1789 arrangements; for Prussia see R. Koser, 'Die Gründung des Auswärtigen Amtes durch König Friedrich Wilhelm I. im Jahre 1728', in R. Koser, *Zur preussischen und deutschen Geschichte: Aufsätze und Vorträge* (Stuttgart and Berlin, 1921), 64–109.

flexible. Both offices and the diplomats abroad communicated and coordinated policy across the established administrative-geographical boundaries. In practice, some secretaries easily eclipsed others and were foreign ministers in all but name. Bolingbroke, who in fact held both posts in conjunction at one point, Townshend, Stanhope or the elder Pitt spring to mind. George III, perhaps the most reform-minded British monarch, pushed hard for a sole secretary of state to conduct foreign affairs, but it was not until 1782 that a single department of state, the Foreign Office, was established.[4] It was a small outfit, no more than a dozen clerks supporting the Secretary of State and an undersecretary. But its creation meant that Britain had 'joined the other major states in providing herself with a single minister and administrative machinery designed to conduct and control foreign policy'.[5]

Although small in size, there was considerable flexibility in its internal arrangements. The number and remit of departments were frequently expanded or contracted, reshaped and remodelled as external and internal demands necessitated. George Canning's recognition of the Latin American republics, for instance, increased the volume of Foreign Office business by half, and so led to the establishment of a department dedicated to the affairs of the western hemisphere.[6] Whatever changes were made over time, the principal concern lay with the effective gathering and processing of policy-relevant knowledge. From its inception, the Foreign Office was a 'knowledge-based' organization.[7] It was the 'digestive organ' connected to the agents abroad as 'the diplomatic feeding organs', as Sir Robert Morier, one of the most prominent ambassadors of the high Victorian period, noted in typically colourful, if not entirely appealing, language.[8] The chief function of this *monstro simile* organism was the gathering, storing, retrieving and analyzing of policy-relevant information, geared towards practical ends to ensure informed, strategic decision making. What follows here is not an attempt at a survey of an administrative history of the Foreign Office or of policy views developed

---

[4] D. B. Horn, *The British Diplomatic Service, 1689–1789* (Oxford, 1961), 2.
[5] M. S. Anderson's apt comment, *The Rise of Modern Diplomacy, 1450–1919* (London, 1993), 76; for the Foreign Office at its inception see C. R. Middleton, *The Administration of British Foreign Policy, 1782–1846* (Durham, NC, 1977), 151–76.
[6] Middleton, *Administration*, 186–87. Canning instituted a series of reforms of Britain's diplomatic machinery, see H. W. V. Temperley, *The Foreign Policy of Canning, 1822–1827: England, the Neo-Holy Alliance, and the New World* (London, 1925), 258–96.
[7] For the concept of 'knowledge-based organizations' see N. Stehrs, *Knowledge Societies* (London and Thousand Oaks, CA, 1994), 109–14 and 172–74 *et passim*.
[8] Morier to father, as quoted in Rosslyn Wemyss, *Memoirs and Letters of the Right Hon. Sir Robert Morier, GCB, from 1826 to 1876* (2 vols., London, 1911) ii, 131.

by it. Rather, it seeks to establish how and why the department executed its principal function, and how and why it often failed to do so.

\*\*\*

Collecting and ordering data in a canon of knowledge was a particular concern of the nineteenth century. The taxonomy of the known world, thus established, was a means of imposing an intelligible order on it, and so controlling it. Rooted in enlightenment ideas, such thinking reflected the early Victorian scientific endeavours, stimulated by Newtonian physics and Darwinism, to identify laws of human behaviour and even to unlock the secrets of universal history.[9]

Knowledge is an amorphous and complex concept. It will not be necessary here to descend into Plato's cave or to head for the upper reaches of the philosopher's realm. Suffice it to note that, although connected to it, knowledge transcends information; that it has multiple meanings and often perplexing ramifications; and that it involves complex processes of perception, reasoning and communicating. It is a systematic set of statements of fact or of ideas, based on reasoned judgment and communicated in some systematic form. It has its own implicit limitations, unspoken assumptions that define what is worth knowing and what is not. Knowledge as a paradigm is a temporal construct and a contested one, reflecting the prevailing preoccupations of the time and so liable to change with time. What was considered worth knowing amongst early Victorians was not necessarily regarded in the same light in, say, the 1930s, and vice versa.[10]

Change is thus inherent in the concept of knowledge, and it underscores its instrumental character. Knowledge constitutes 'a faculty or capacity for action'. It enables an actor to employ it, in conjunction with control over the contingent circumstances of action, 'as a means of power, as a justification for a decision, as a means of orientation, or as

---

[9] See H. T. Buckle's *History of Civilization in England* (3 vols., London, repr. s.a. (1857)) as an extreme form of 'scientific' history.

[10] For some philosophical ideas see Richard Rorty's controversial *Philosophy and the Mirror of Nature* (Princeton, NJ, 1979); D. Bell, 'The Social Framework of the Information Society', in M. L. Dertouzos and J. Moses (eds.), *The Computer Age: Twenty-Year View* (Cambridge, MA, 1979), 162–211; for the social sciences and historical scholarship see M. Poovey, *A History of Modern Fact: Problems of Knowledge in the Sciences of Wealth and Society* (Chicago, 1998); B. Barry, 'A Hundred Years of Studying Politics: What Have We Got to Show for It?' and D. Cannadine, 'What Is History Now?', in J. Morrill (ed.), *The Promotion of Knowledge: Lectures to Mark the Centenary of the British Academy, 1902–2002* (Oxford, 2004), 9–28 and 29–52; and M. Bentley, 'The Evolution and Dissemination of Historical Knowledge', in M. Daunton (ed.), *The Organisation of Knowledge in Victorian Britain* (Oxford, 2005), 173–97.

a means or rationalization'.[11] In the context of this chapter, knowledge is also arcane, in the original sense of the word. What was worth knowing for the Foreign Office was closed to outsiders. That in itself was a function of the nature of international politics and of the modern state as such.[12] The question of who generated, possessed and disseminated knowledge, and how this was done, is vital also to understanding the growth of the British state in general.[13] Similarly, in the context of the empire, knowledge derived from indigenous sources helped to underpin the cultural authority and influence of British colonial officials in the *locale*.[14]

The Foreign Office may be seen, then, as an epistemological site of arcane knowledge. It was – and still is – a 'knowledge-based organization', with its own hierarchies of power and authority. It also acted as a 'gatekeeper', controlling access to special knowledge and disseminating insights derived from it. In its internal organization the Library and the Registry occupied a central position. As an investigation of the Office's business noted in 1918, a 'Registry is not an end in itself. It is a necessary . . . means of facilitating the rapid and smooth working of a large administrative machine. The efficiency or otherwise of the Registry is reflected in all the work of a department.'[15] Its organizational structures were designed to enhance the gathering, storing and utilizing of practical knowledge, geared towards foreign policy action. It meant collecting, organizing, sifting and interpreting data thus gathered in a constant effort to extract further meaning from them. The understanding of politics that underpinned the apparatus was essentially pragmatic, rooted

[11] N. Stehr, *Practical Knowledge: Applying the Social Sciences* (London and Newbury Park, CA, 1992), 2–3; N. Stehr and R. Grundmann, 'How Does Knowledge Relate to Political Action?', *Innovation – European Journal of Social Science Research* 25(1) (2012), 29–44; the *locus classicus* is K. Mannheim, 'Das Problem einer Soziologie des Wissens', *Archiv für Sozialwissenschaft und Sozialpolitik* 57(3) (1925), 577–652.

[12] The etymological root of the word is the Latin verb *arcanere*, 'to shut up', but also 'to keep at a distance'; also *arca*, 'chest or box', so that the *arcana imperii*, the secrets of power, really are locked up. Intriguingly, the Greek αρκεω has a similar meaning, but may also mean 'to be of use'.

[13] See the essays in G. Sutherland (ed.), *Studies in the Growth of Nineteenth-Century Government* (London, 1972); see also M. Wright, *Treasury Control of the Civil Service, 1854–1874* (Oxford, 1969), 329–51. Instructive also R. Davidson and R. Lowe, 'Bureaucracy and Innovation in British Welfare Policy, 1870–1945', in W. J. Mommsen and W. Mock (eds.), *The Emergence of the Welfare State in Britain and Germany* (London, 1981), 263–95, and G. C. Peden, 'Economic Knowledge and the State in Modern Britain', in S. J. D. Green and R. C. Whiting (eds.), *The Boundaries of the State in Modern Britain* (Cambridge, 1996), 170–90.

[14] See the important work by C. A. Bayly, *Empire and Information: Intelligence Gathering and Social Communications in India, 1780–1830* (Cambridge, 1996).

[15] Report of Inter-Departmental Committee, 'Reorganisation of Foreign Office Register' (confidential), 14 November 1918, app., Foreign Office, Librarian's Department, Correspondence and Memoranda, vol. 6, 1919–1930. I am grateful to the departmental records officer at the Foreign and Commonwealth Office for permission to quote from material held there.

in assumptions about Britain's national interest. Its principal concern was with making the outside world intelligible and its workings calculable to a degree. Capturing the full complexities of Great Power politics in a manageable manner would remain a constant challenge for the Foreign Office.

\*\*\*

As a repository of arcane knowledge, the Foreign Office structured that knowledge in a certain manner and distributed it in relation to external requirements. Its administrative structure reflected this. The political departments formed the Office's organizational spine, around which were grouped various non-political departments, mostly, though not exclusively, concerned with consular and commercial matters. Without the effective organization and internal transfer of knowledge, none of the departments could function; and this made some central knowledge repository necessary. The need for informed policymaking became more pressing during the wars against Napoleonic France. This led to the appointment, in January 1801, of the first Foreign Office Librarian, Richard Ancell, an illegitimate royal offspring, married to one of George IV's cast-off mistresses and in receipt of a pension for life. Under his guidance the entire diplomatic correspondence from 1780 onwards was transferred from the State Paper Office, where it had been left to moulder, to be reassembled and housed in a separate building in St. James's Park under Foreign Office control and available for reference in the conduct of the Office's daily business. By the time Ancell retired in 1810, the Library had organized a mass of papers into a systematic, searchable and thus useable collection.[16] The Library itself, with its expanding collection of reference and other works, remained a less effective resource. Until it found a new home in George Gilbert Scott's florid cinquecento Foreign Office palazzo in 1868, it was dispersed all over the department's old buildings in the warren of smaller streets abutting the Downing Street cul-de-sac and made up of small, dark offices and labyrinthine passages. 'In fact, the whole arrangement was so inconvenient and unsatisfactory' that a parliamentary committee was established to examine it. Books were kept wherever space could be found in niches and passages between offices, usually several rows deep. This proved unexpectedly beneficial

---

[16] Memo. Hertslet, 'Access of historians and others to the F.O. archives', n.d. (c. December 1878), Foreign Office, Librarian's Department, Memoranda, vol. 3; memo. Sherwood, 'Supplementary Departments of the Foreign Office', 28 July 1914, ibid., vol. 34; see also *First report of the Royal Commission on Public Records appointed to inquire into and report on the state of the public records and local records of a public nature of England and Wales: minutes of evidence* i, pt. III (1912) (C. 6396), qq. 1565–67.

in 1848, when it was feared that the great Chartist demonstration might turn violent: the windows facing Downing Street were filled with books, loopholes being left to pass rifles through.[17]

Such serendipitous uses of disorder aside, the Library's collection of books and pamphlets was not a useful resource; there was not even a catalogue. The careful archiving of official papers, however, meant that the Office had the means of producing serious foreign policy analyses. It also had its domestic uses. When, for instance, a vote of censure was moved against Palmerston over the 'Don Pacifico Affair', officials trawled through some 3,000 volumes of departmental papers spanning some twenty years to compile a comprehensive rebuttal.[18] It was 'by no means unusual', noted an internal minute three decades later, 'for other Departments of the Gov[ernmen]t to apply to this Dep[artmen]t for information on a variety of subjects'.[19]

Retrieving policy-relevant information was a question of effective archiving, but also of rigorous, systematic internal processes and discipline. Considerable effort was devoted to inculcating the habit of standardized procedures into clerks. This was a particular concern to Edmund 'Dictator' Hammond, the Office's first proper permanent undersecretary. On assuming the post in 1854, he drafted a memorandum on the system of conducting official business, later known as 'The Adventures of a Paper in the Foreign Office'. It described a hierarchical organization, and gave a detailed account of the internal paper trail, how despatches and telegrams were received, registered and then, if sufficiently important, passed up to the Foreign Secretary; how a policy decision was then framed and a draft reply prepared; and how, finally, the draft replies were communicated internally before being sent to the relevant mission(s) abroad.[20] The departmental 'Order Book' gave further detailed procedural guidance to senior clerks to place the transaction of business on a regular footing.[21] All

---

[17] Sir E. Hertslet, *Recollections of the Old Foreign Office* (London, 1901), 20–21 and 67–69.

[18] Ibid., 72–73; see Parl. Debs. (series 3) vol. 112, col. 444. (25 June 1850).

[19] Min. anon., January 1884, Foreign Office, Librarian's Department, Correspondence and Memoranda: General, vol. 4, 1879–1889.

[20] 'Memorandum respecting the System under which the Business of the Foreign Office is conducted', 31 March 1886, FO 366/724. This is a marginally altered version of Hammond's original memorandum of 1854. For the 'Adventure' title see M. A. Anderson, 'Edmund Hammond: Permanent Under-Secretary of State for Foreign Affairs, 1854-1873' (PhD thesis, London University, 1955), 65; for Hammond's PUS-ship see also K. Neilson and T. G. Otte, *The Permanent Under-Secretary for Foreign Affairs, 1854–1946* (London and New York, 2009), 5–31.

[21] Min. Hammond, 22 February 1859, 'Order Book', Foreign Office, Librarian's Department, Correspondence and Memoranda, vol. 7. Only a handful of pages of the original were preserved by the then FO Librarian Stephen Gaselee, see min. Gaselee, 7 March 1939, ibid.

these guidelines aimed at ensuring that internal procedures were well-designed and smoothly operating so that there was a constant flow of information from the agents abroad to the nerve centre in London and within it, and the Library was crucial to its functioning. It was 'scarcely possible to over-estimate the important nature of ... [the Library], which [is] ... second to none appertaining to the Political Departments of the Office'.[22] Nowhere else had 'the Librarian's Department ... to report on such questions as the right of the British Crown to Islands or Possessions abroad, or transactions connected with European Conferences, or the interpretation of Treaties, or such like questions of vital importance'.[23] Indeed, without the Library's register, 'it would be impossible to carry on the work of the Foreign Office in a satisfactory manner'.[24]

Hammond's 'Adventures of a Paper' remained the blueprint for the intradepartmental information flow. The methods of business remained substantially the same, though smaller labour-saving devices were added over time.[25] As a knowledge-producing and consuming machinery the Foreign Office coped well enough in ordinary times. At moments of crisis, the increased volume and speed of business overstretched its capacity. In 1874, for instance, it received a total of 57,316 despatches and telegrams. The number peaked at 71,493 papers in 1878 at the height of the Great Eastern Crisis. It rose even further in the following year to 78,307 as a result of the problems left unresolved by the Berlin Congress and the wars in South Africa and Afghanistan. By 1882, business had subsided somewhat, but the department still had to process some 67,620 papers.[26]

---

[22] Wylde to Hammond, 27 January 1871, ibid., vol. 3, 1868–1878; also evidence Otway, *Report from the Select Committee on Diplomatic and Consular Services with Minutes of Evidence, 1870* (Cd. 382) VII (1870), qq. 1118–19.

[23] Hammond to Granville, 9 March 1872, Foreign Office, Librarian's Department, Correspondence and Memoranda: General, vol. 3, 1868–1878. He later noted that the Library's 'most important and responsible duty ... is that of preparing *Reports* and *Memoranda*', memo. Hertslet, January 1884, ibid., vol. 4, 1879–1889.

[24] Memo. Hertslet, 'Further Memorandum respecting the Librarian's Department of the Foreign Office', 24 June 1874, ibid.

[25] A scheme for colour-coding correspondence according to urgency or importance, min. Lister, 18 April 1878, FO 366/678. For the business of the Office see Currie's evidence (12 November 1889), *Fourth Report of the Royal Commission Appointed to Inquire into the Civil Establishments of the Different Offices of State at Home and Abroad: Minutes of Evidence* (C. 6172) (1890), q. 26062.

[26] Figures from memo. Hertslet, 'Memorandum respecting the present Condition of the Librarian's Department of the Foreign Office', January 1884, FO 881/4905; memo. Villiers, 'Memorandum respecting Arrears in the Registration and Indexing of MS. in the Librarian's Department', 10 November 1883, FO 881/5452. The volume grew steadily. In 1826, a mere 12,402 papers had been received or sent, 'Return of the Number of Despatches Received and Sent from the Foreign Office, in each year, from 1826 to 1872', encl. in Hammond to Granville, 9 March 1873, Foreign Office, Librarian's Department, Correspondence and Memoranda: General, vol. 3, 1868–1878.

While the Office's workload had thus grown by between 20 and nearly 40 per cent at its peak in 1879, there was no concomitant increase in personnel. In consequence, the registering of papers fell behind, so that an internal estimate suggested that the number of arrears was in the order of just under 564,000. The Foreign Office was no longer a fully functioning knowledge-based organization. Indeed, attempts to remedy the situation by appointing a technical expert as permanent registrar in the Commercial Department to deal with the backlog there ran into Treasury opposition; and with no additional funding available, the arrears remained.[27] The Treasury was perhaps less than helpful in suggesting 'that the larger proportion of ... [documents] might ... be usefully destroyed after a comparatively early date'. Such weeding brought with it the risk of losing departmental knowledge: 'The Registrar and Archivist are specially valuable members of each Department, as they necessarily acquire at least a general knowledge from the fact that all papers go through their hands.'[28]

The growing volume of business caused other problems. The mass of unprocessed papers impeded foreign policy analysis, and so weakened more especially the PUS's role as chief foreign policy adviser. Lord Tenterden found it 'a constant strain to keep clear'.[29] All of this mattered because the Office's permanent head was the channel of communication between London and the diplomats abroad. His semi-official letters, his 'Vade mecums', transmitted a combination of analyses and practical guidance.[30] His 'ideal' was that departmental heads *should* ... make themselves masters of the history of the Relations with the Countries under their several Dep[artmen]ts and of all subjects connected with it'. This could only be done if the relevant knowledge was ordered and retrievable: 'I do not see how this is to be arrived at if their official memories are to be clipped every first of January [by a suggested removal of correspondence].'[31]

Internal reforms, aimed at rationalizing procedures, were meant to ensure that the Office's machinery was better placed to cope with the

---

[27] Tenterden to Lingen, 17 March 1882, and min. Lingen, 22 May 1882, T 1/13229/5227; memo. Villiers, 'Registration and Indexing of MSS in the Foreign Office', 10 November 1883, Foreign Office Librarian's Department, Correspondence and Memoranda: General, vol. 4, 1879–1889.

[28] Lingen to Fitzmaurice, 22 December 1883, and memo. Villiers, 7 January 1884, ibid.

[29] Tenterden to Derby (private), 15 January 1875, Derby MSS, Liverpool Record Office, 920DER 16/2/10. Later in the year the PUS was given a private secretary to ease some of the burden on him.

[30] Dufferin to Tenterden (private), 5 May 1879, Tenterden MSS, FO 363/1/2; see also Z. S. Steiner, *The Foreign Office and Foreign Policy, 1898–1914* (Cambridge, 1969), 8.

[31] Tenterden to Green (private), 24 January 1871, Foreign Office, Librarian's Department, Correspondence and Memoranda, vol. 3, 1868–1878.

increased volume of business. But it was also a matter of ensuring that relevant information could be retrieved and used more expeditiously and effectively. This was the object of a major reorganization in 1882, which in essence remained in place until the First World War. Its centrepiece was the reduction of the political divisions to three, but with extended geographical remits. By far the largest of the new units was the Western Department, with altogether ten clerks, double the size of the two old departments that preceded it. The Turkish Department was renamed Eastern, but retained its focus on the Ottoman dominions, the Balkans and Russia. The third and smallest department was that dealing with the Americas and Asia. The non-political divisions were also reorganized, now consolidated in two larger departments, the Consular and African (East and West) Department and the Commercial and Sanitary Department.[32] Reducing the number of political divisions allowed for an increase in the actual working size of the new departments.[33] The reform aimed at enhancing the Office's ability to handle its constantly growing work load and to produce pertinent advice. Ambition and reality, however, were uneasily matched. The battle with the ever-increasing volume of business was unceasing. In the 1880s, the number of papers received or sent by the Office rose by 24 per cent. The Library had fallen in arrears with the registering, indexing and archiving of correspondence. This circumstance hampered the department's ability to function as the nerve centre of British foreign policy, and only the most pressing business was prioritized. Limited resources scarcely allowed for longer-term strategic planning.[34]

Efficiency and swiftness in processing information were the twin concerns here. The memorandum on the 'Use and Abuse of Red

[32] Min. Granville, 21 December 1882, FO 366/678. Subsequent changes were marginal, see Currie to Salisbury, 13 March 1889, Salisbury MSS, Hatfield House, 3M/E/Currie; memo. Currie, 'Office Arrangements', Apr. 1889, FO 366/724. A useful survey of the frequent changes in the functions of the administrative departments can be found in M. Roper, *The Records of the Foreign Office, 1782–1968* (London, 2nd ed. 2002), 82–117.

[33] The increased use of lower division clerks, known as second division clerks from 1890, in the non-political departments allowed mainstream officials to concentrate on political tasks, see memo. Pauncefote et al., 'Preliminary Report of the Committee appointed to enquire into the State of the legal and general business of the Foreign Office', 21 July 1886, FO 97/499; also memo., 'Return of the Number of Despatches, etc., from 1826 to 1886', 1 January 1887, FO 97/505. A useful picture of the humdrum routine work of the Office is given in R. B. Mowat, *The Life of Lord Pauncefote, First Ambassador to the United States* (London, 1929), 63–70.

[34] Memo. Villiers, 'Arrears in the Registration and Indexing of MS. In the Librarian's Department', 10 November 1883, FO 881/5452; memo. Hertslet, 'The Present Condition of the Librarian's Department', 12 January 1884, FO 366/392.

Tape' by Sir Thomas Sanderson, the last of the old-school permanent undersecretaries and 'a walking encyclopaedia of Foreign Office lore',[35] testified to this. 'Red Tape', he wrote, 'like drill in the army, is only the means to an end. It is the method by which a huge machine is made to move – rather ponderously – but steadily and without confusion.' It was imperative that officials understood and controlled this machine. But it was not 'so high and holy and beautiful a thing in itself that one cannot have too much of it. And it is certainly not intended either to deprive us of the power, or to relieve us of the duty, of using our intellects and improving our knowledge.' Individual thought and action were important: 'You cannot invent a machine into which documents can be put at one end and conclusions ground out at the other by turning a handle.' Initiative had to be tempered by 'industry and integrity, but also intelligence, sympathy, and good broad common sense'. Legible handwriting, careful docketing of incoming despatches, the systematic archiving of official papers and the careful drafting of documents were dull but necessary. Docketing was to enable busy superiors to identify relevant papers easily and speedily: 'A false docket is therefore a serious crime. And it is almost an equal offence to scribble down a series of hieroglyphic abbreviations.' Similarly, officials had to understand which papers were 'material to the point at issue'. Relevant documents had to be archived with 'regularity and method' and following a 'recognized system': 'The fundamental principle of a well-managed Department is that a certain amount of trouble should be systematically taken in order to avoid recourse to violent and ineffectual effort upon an emergency. To leave papers to accumulate till the mass becomes intolerable, and then to have a grand clearing up, is a direct contravention of this elementary rule.' None of this could substitute for individual initiative: '[E]ndeavour to think and to take an intelligent interest in the work.' Without it, 'it turns our daily bread into dry bones, and after a time the steel pen enters into the soul, and the individual becomes a mere official (who is a dismal creature), or loses vigour, and sinks into hopeless mediocrity'.[36]

Managing the growing flow of information and processing it remained a challenge, as the Ridley Commission noted in 1890. The

---

[35] Sanderson obituary, *The Times*, 22 March 1923.
[36] Memo. Sanderson, 'Observations on the Use and Abuse of Red Tape for the Juniors in the Eastern, Western, and American Departments' (private), October 1891, Foreign Office Library; see also memo., 'Departmental Instructions', 10 May 1898, FO 881/7034*. Excerpts from the 'Red Tape' memorandum were still circulated in the 1930s, see memo., 'Draft-Writing', n.d. (c.1931), Foreign Office, Librarian's Department, Correspondence and Memoranda: General, vol. 7, 1930–1940.

fact that clerks in the Librarian's Department were often employed on other tasks meant that the indexing and registering of correspondence were about ten years behind. Senior officials were opposed to a centralized registry as separate departmental registers allowed for the speedier retrieval of information in the departments.[37] Ultimately, a compromise was agreed. The compilation of daily registers of correspondence was handed to departmental clerks, leaving it to the Library to draw up more detailed indexes two years later, when current correspondence was transferred there.[38] It was little more than a sticking plaster solution. Pressure for reform was building up in the 1890s, feeding off the contemporaneous debate about 'National Efficiency' and eventually leading to the great reform of 1905. 'The existence of a central source of information, embracing every subject and covering every quarter of the globe cannot fail to be acknowledged', noted a clerk in the Librarian's Department in outlining a scheme for reforming what, tellingly, he envisaged to be the 'Library and Intelligence Department'.[39] The changes instituted in 1890 had condemned the old system of registering correspondence, 'perhaps, by theoretical principles rather than by knowledge of its working'. The multiplicity of systems and the want of uniformity in keeping registers made the retrieval of information almost impossible. Insufficient staffing meant that significant arrears in indexing had built up, and the Foreign Office Librarian warned of an imminent 'deadlock with which a continuance of the present system of indexing seems to threaten it [foreign policy]'.[40] An internal review established the full extent of current shortcomings. Different departments operated by different standards. The Western Department, for instance, did not index correspondence relating to countries outside its geographical remit, while the Eastern Department did not record later correspondence after the first entry, nor did it register any memoranda: 'Consequently it is to be feared that a good many important despatches are not entered ... at all, and a thorough overhauling of the Library will eventually be necessary.' Departmental indexes, moreover, were made 'with a view to current requirements' rather than to

[37] Evidence Currie and Hertslet (12 November and 12 December 1889), *Fourth Report: Minutes*, qq. 26054–55 and 27536–39; see also memo. 'Instructions to Index-Makers', Dec. 1890, FO 366/724.

[38] Min. Pauncefote, 20 December 1890, FO 366/724; Sanderson to Treasury, 11 August 1892, Foreign Office, Librarian's Department, Correspondence and Memoranda: General, vol. 5, 1890–1918; *Fourth Report*, 7.

[39] Memo. Oakes, 24 December 1894, ibid., vol. 3A. A.H. (later Sir Augustus) Oakes was the Office's Librarian, 1896–1904.

[40] Memo. Oakes, 22 November 1897, ibid., vol. 5, 1890–1918.

their longer-term uses.[41] Given the rapid increase in the volume of business, such failings were hardly surprising. The number of despatches rose by 40 per cent from 102,000 in 1898 to 143,208 in 1906, while the staffing had remained static since 1848.[42]

Pressure soon came to a head. Various reform schemes were floated.[43] They included plans for a significant 'devolution of work ... downward' from departmental heads to junior clerks, with non-political and mechanical work delegated to the administrative departments. Preserving and enhancing the Office's functionality as a knowledge-based organization was at the heart of the planned reforms.[44] Unsurprisingly, the committee established to oversee them made the establishment of a single General Registry, as opposed to the existing departmental registers, and a more systematized method of archiving and retrieving correspondence the core of its recommendations. Paper-keeping was thus moved away from the 'Executive Departments' to 'specially trained staff'. Amongst a range of other measures the committee also encouraged a regular system of producing memoranda, continually kept up to date, on current affairs.[45] The aim was to transfer most routine work to second-division clerks to ensure that junior officials received 'a better training for higher and more responsible duties later on'. Only by liberating them from the humdrum and stultifying chores of paper-keeping could the department's arcane knowledge be allowed practical application. Following suggestions by the indefatigable Eyre Crowe, it was decided to introduce separate minute sheets for every paper received, so that all information could be contextualized and analyzed with a view to its practical significance. Comprehensive annual reports on foreign countries supplemented the quest for more efficient knowledge management.[46]

As a result of the reorganization, which became effective from 1 January 1906, the Office acquired a Central and three Sub-Registries,

---

[41] Memo. Dallas and Oakes, 15 June 1898, ibid. No indexes were kept for the years 1891–1900, and those for 1900–1905 were 'not comparable with the more carefully compiled registers ... from 1810 to 1890', Report of Inter-Departmental Committee, 'Reorganisation of Foreign Office Register' (confidential), 14 November 1918, ibid., vol. 6, 1919–1930.

[42] Memo. Sanderson, 27 May 1903, ibid., vol. 3A.

[43] Min. Sanderson, 2 May 1903, ibid.

[44] Villiers to Sanderson, 27 April 1903, and min. Sanderson, 2 May 1903, ibid.; R. A. Jones, *The Nineteenth-Century Foreign Office: An Administrative History* (London, 1971), 114–17.

[45] Min. Sanderson, 17 June 1903, Foreign Office, Librarian's Department, Correspondence and Memoranda, General, vol. 3A; report by Cartwright, Oakes, Maxwell, and Langley, 18 May 1904, T 1/10369/4480.

[46] Memo. Crowe (confidential), 5 January 1905, T 1/10369/4480; for a discussion of these matters see Jones, *Foreign Office*, 111–34, and Steiner, *Foreign Office*, 78–82.

the latter attached to different political departments. The former was the 'distributing centre' where all incoming and outgoing correspondence was classified, numbered and 'recorded in the first register', before being passed on for docketing and re-entry in the subordinate registries.[47] The 1905 reform was more than a clerical revolution. It reinvigorated the Office as the knowledge-based nerve centre of foreign policy, and it revolutionized its place in the policymaking process. Officials were given a free rein to record their views and offer advice to ministers. The new minute sheets swiftly became playing fields for future policy advisers. Junior clerks were encouraged to acquire specialist knowledge in international affairs, while senior officials took a larger share in framing policy.

At least for a while, the advising function was concentrated in the hands of the PUS. 'Important questions have often trivial beginnings', decided Sanderson's successor, Sir Charles 'Capability' Hardinge, 'and the difficulty has been pointed out to me of deciding what is or may develop into a question of political importance. It seems to me therefore best that *all* work . . . should pass through me to the Secretary of State'.[48] 'The Grand Panjundrum'[49] sought to strengthen his own grip on the department, but he appreciated the need to improve the quality of analyses and to disseminate information across the service.[50] Both were needed to enhance the effectiveness of the Office as the hub of Britain's foreign policy. Yet the new machinery was no Rolls-Royce engine. The Library scarcely produced papers 'recording the events of recent or contemporary history' and offering 'reasoned summaries of past diplomatic negotiations and discussions'.[51] The staff requirements of 1905 were 'materially cut down' by the Treasury; and there was no additional physical space to house the

[47] Quotes from memo. Hiscock and Behrens, n.d. (c. 10 May 1911), T 1/11278/5434, and Report of Inter-Departmental Committee, 'Reorganisation of Foreign Office Register' (confidential), 14 November 1918, Foreign Office Librarian's Department, Correspondence and Memoranda: General, vol. 6, 1919–1929, both of which described the workings of the 1906 system in great detail; see also memo. Crowe, 'Provisional Instructions for the General Registry' (confidential), 1 January 1906, FO 881/8550.

[48] Min. Hardinge, 3 February 1906, FO 366/761.

[49] Rumbold to father, 15 February 1908, Rumbold MSS, Bodleian Library, Oxford, MS. dep. Rumbold 13; for Hardinge's career see also K. Neilson, *Britain and the Last Tsar: British Policy and Russia, 1894–1917* (Oxford, 1995), 23–26.

[50] Thus, for instance, the legation at Berne, usually a sleepy backwater, found itself the recipient of such information largesse, min. Hardinge, n.d. (14 May 1909), FO 371/799/18210; see also mins. Crowe and Nicolson, 15 March 1912, FO 371/1557/11104.

[51] Memo. Crowe, 'Memorandum respecting the future organization of the Treaty Department and Library', n.d. (1910), FO 366/782; see also min. Crowe, 28 April 1909, on memo. Brant, 'Suggestions for the Improvement of Indexing', 15 April 1909, FO 371/799/16051.

growing archives. Indeed, a 1918 investigation concluded that there had been a 'partial breakdown of the system' by 1913.[52]

\*\*\*

With the coming of war, the breakdown was complete. Hardinge's bureaucratic neo-absolutism proved 'an egregious failure. No one man can properly do the work which Hardinge's system entailed.'[53] The department's machinery was immediately recast. A new War Department subsumed the Eastern and Western Departments to deal with all the political aspects of the war, and the sub-registries were reallocated.[54] Given the nature of the conflict that now unfolded, the changes were necessary, but they were not sufficient to maintain the Office as the nerve centre of foreign policy. The volume of business and the pace of events were overwhelming. The war, moreover, introduced a number of matters that changed the focus of its work, many of them connected with the imposition of a naval blockade on the enemy coalition. A different kind of arcane knowledge pertained to them. To archive, process and apply it, all contraband work was hived off the War Department in September 1914. Crowe's Contraband Department brought order and purpose where there had been chaos and confusion.[55] It soon assumed also the war-related business of the Commercial and Treaty Departments, and grew rapidly, eventually to become the Ministry of Blockade in February 1916 with its own minister in the Cabinet.[56]

Separating such highly specialized work from its more general political work was one of the many changes that weakened the Foreign Office as the foreign policy nerve centre. It had become 'in great part a "pass

[52] Report of Inter-Departmental Committee, 'Reorganisation of Foreign Office Registry' (confidential), 14 November 1918, Foreign Office, Librarian's Department, Correspondence and Memoranda: General, vol. 6, 1919–1929. The Office found itself frequently in the position of supplicant, requesting further funding for the registries, see Nicolson (PUS) to Murray (Permanent Secretary, Treasury) (no. 3088/11), 17 March 1911, T 1/11278/5434. The Treasury declined the request, *vice versa*, 20 May 1911, ibid.

[53] Quote from memo. Bertie, 19 December 1914, Bertie MSS, TNA (PRO), FO 800/163; Steiner, *Foreign Office*, 164–71, and Z. S. Steiner, 'The Foreign Office and the War', in F. H. Hinsley (ed.), *British Foreign Policy under Sir Edward Grey* (Cambridge, 1977), 488–515 offer authoritative accounts of the changes.

[54] Min. Crowe, 7 August 1914, FO 366/786/40089.

[55] Memo. Crowe, 1 November 1914, FO 368/1192/66930; Sir J. Tilley and S. Gaselee, *The Foreign Office* (London, 1933), 178; see also B. J. C. McKercher and K. Neilson, '"The Triumph of Unarmed Forces": Sweden and the Allied Blockade of Germany, 1914-1917', *Journal of Strategic Studies* 7(2) (1984), 178–99.

[56] A. C. Bell, *The Blockade of the Central Empires* (London, 1961), 454–56; T. Kaarsted, *Storbritannien og Danmark, 1914–1918* (Odense, 1974), 93–97.

on" Department'. It had been 'ruined ... deprived ... of any initiative; made ... into a Correspondenz Bureau. How are we to train men & have them ready for the Peace negotiations when they come?'[57] Hardinge, reinstalled as PUS in mid-1916, soon found that the 'amount of work done is so stupendous' that the organization struggled with its policy-framing duties.[58] There were other changes that infringed upon its traditional territory. 'The secret service part has developed enormously', Hardinge noted, and the position of the blockade ministry, housed inside the Foreign Office but 'independent' of it, was 'curious'.[59]

The emergence of competing bodies during the war, not least Lloyd George's Downing Street 'kindergarten', undermined the Foreign Office as the principal provider of foreign policy analysis and advice. Indeed, as the war drew to a close, there was considerable competition between Downing Street and the Office to 'get the principal *locus standi* in regard to administrative matters during peace negotiations'.[60] To staunch the haemorrhaging of influence Hardinge poached the Department of Information's Intelligence Bureau, the Naval Intelligence's Historical Section and the War Trade Intelligence Department.[61] The aim of his 'piratical raid[s]' was to monopolize political advice to the Cabinet. It should come from a single source only, the Foreign Office.[62] The raids undoubtedly helped to slow the haemorrhaging of influence, but they were no lasting solution. Commercial matters remained a blind spot. Hardinge blocked the creation of a Foreign Trade Department, opting instead for a Department of Overseas Trade. It was a feeble entity from its inception and would hover uncertainly between the Foreign Office and

[57] Quotes from Bertie to Hardinge (private), 25 June 1916, Hardinge MSS, Cambridge University Library, vol. 22, and Oppenheimer diary (recording a conversation between Crowe and Lord Milner), 30 March 1918, Oppenheimer MSS, Bod., box 5; for an analysis of the Office's decline see R. M. Warman, 'The Erosion of Foreign Influence in the Making of Foreign Policy, 1916–1918', *Historical Journal* 15(1) (1972), 133–59.
[58] Hardinge to Bertie, private, 27 June 1916, Hardinge MSS, vol. 22.
[59] Hardinge to Errington, private, ibid.
[60] Parker to Hardinge (private), 9 October 1918, Foreign Office, Librarian's Department, Correspondence and Memoranda: General, vol. 5, 1890–1918; J. Turner, *Lloyd George's Secretariat* (Cambridge, 1980), 60–82.
[61] Mins. Drummond, Grey and Hardinge, 13, 14 and 18 July 1916, Foreign Office, Librarian's Department, Correspondence and Memoranda: General, vol. 5, 1890–1918; E. Goldstein, *Winning the Peace: British Diplomatic Strategy, Peace Planning, and the Paris Peace Conference 1916–1920* (Oxford, 1991), 23–24; E. Goldstein, 'Hertford House: The Naval Intelligence Geographical Section and Peace Conference Planning, 1917–1919', *Mariner's Mirror* 72(1) (1986), 85–88.
[62] See Erik Goldstein's pertinent comments, 'The Foreign Office and Political Intelligence 1918–1920', *Review of International Studies* 14(2) (1988), 276.

the Board of Trade, its two overseeing departments. Above all, it created a gap in the Foreign Office's own capabilities until the 1930s.[63]

After 1916 and in the aftermath of the war, there was greater outside interference with Foreign Office business. Lloyd George was wont to ignore its advice, and Lord Robert Cecil launched frequent forays onto its territory, so much so that Hardinge was advised to 'keep a good watch on the Downing Street door of the Foreign Office; and take care that it is not stormed by any Bolschevik [sic] politician with a bible in one hand a tomahawk in the other, to the cry of "Hatfield über Alles"!'[64] During the war the Office had 'suffered a good deal from divided authority', Lord Curzon complained: '[I]t has produced much confusion and overlapping from which I find the Office still suffering.'[65]

\* \* \*

The war had stretched the Office's capabilities: 'It has been like a somewhat antiquated & overweight motor car with several of its cylinders not working & its machinery out of place & the danger of pushing it too hard had been that it might stop dead!'[66] The flaws in its information-processing systems had become apparent, too. The five-fold increase in the volume of correspondence between 1913 and 1917 had pushed the system to the brink. '[T]he Foreign Office Registries will break down during the strain of peace negotiations unless the registry question is grappled with', warned Alwyn Parker, Librarian in 1918–19. The problem was 'an exceedingly complicated one on account of the vast multiplicity of subjects dealt with'. A system was required that combined 'uniting the greatest possible expedition in registration with accuracy, and ... securing that all competent authorities shall be apprised as soon as possible of the existence of papers'. Parker had examined registering systems in use in Whitehall and larger commercial enterprises, and devised a scheme, 'based on a combination of the existing Foreign Office system with the advantageous features of other systems'.[67]

---

[63] Victor Wellesley pressed for a commercial department at the Foreign Office, see memo. Wellesley, 'Memorandum on Commercial Policy', 28 June 1917, FO 371/5361/F2495/199/23; for a discussion of the lack of capacity in the 1930s see D. G. Boadle, 'The Formation of the Foreign Office Economic Relations Section, 1930–1937', *Historical Journal* 20(4) (1977), 919–36.

[64] Graham to Hardinge, private, 7 November 1919, Hardinge MSS, vol. 41.

[65] Curzon to Lloyd George (confidential), 18 January 1919, Curzon MSS, British Library Oriental and India Office Collection, MSS. Eur. F.112/211; G. H. Bennett, *British Foreign Policy during the Curzon Period, 1919–1925* (London, 1995), 9–10.

[66] Graham to Curzon (private), 5 September 1919, Curzon MSS, MSS. Eur. F.112/213. Sir Ronald Graham, the acting PUS, was a Hardinge protégé.

[67] Memo. Parker, 29 April 1918, Foreign Office, Librarian's Department, Memoranda, vol. 36.

An inter-departmental committee under Crowe finessed Parker's plans. The demands on information-processing were 'necessarily high. The Office is concerned with every country in the world, but the questions which it is called upon to handle are practically unending in their diversity, frequently complex and interrelated where this may at first sight be little expected, and of a nature to call for rapid decisions in a large number of cases.' The committee removed various existing processing bottlenecks and streamlined the registering by stripping out any duplication of effort. Archiving remained 'a most important operation and one of the main hinges in any registry'. A simple clerking error, such as the transposition of numbers, could lead to 'an error of sorting ... and for all practical purposes the document is lost'. To obviate the existing shortcomings, a new comprehensive Registry was introduced that consisted of three separate branches in charge of 'Classification', 'Archives' and 'Despatch' and used a new filing, docketing and précising system.[68]

Peace brought challenges of various kinds. Most of the war-time departments were disbanded, merged into new ones or subsumed in the political ones.[69] The gathering and application of knowledge was very much to the fore in the internal debates about the necessary peace-time adjustments. It lay at the heart of the decision to establish the new Central Department to deal with Germany, Italy and the newly independent states in Central Europe and the western Balkans.[70] The geographical configuration of the political departments was to undergo repeated changes over the years.[71] It proved difficult, however, to make up for ground lost during the war. Post-war financial constraints, for one, hampered the Office's ability to function properly even before the Geddes Axe descended upon Whitehall: 'Nothing can be done without more men, better pay, and doubled accommodation, and there will no doubt be the

---

[68] Report of Inter-Departmental Committee, 'Reorganisation of Foreign Office Registry' (confidential), 14 November 1918, ibid., Correspondence and Memoranda: General, vol. 6, 1919–1929. The appendix to this memorandum, seventeen densely printed pages, gives detailed instructions on the registering process, the Main Index, the card method of filing papers by subjects and the estimated staffing needs, ibid. A later memorandum refined procedures further, memo. 'Foreign Office Registry: General Procedure', July 1920, ibid.

[69] *Foreign Office List 1921* (London, 1921), 7; Z. S. Steiner and M. L. Dockrill, 'The Foreign Office Reforms, 1919–21', *Historical Journal* 17(1) (1974), 144–45; E. Maisel, *The Foreign and Foreign Policy, 1919–1926* (Brighton, 1994), 1–30.

[70] The exchanges between Hardinge and Crowe in October–November 1919 can be followed in FO 366/781.

[71] Mins. Vansittart, 13 June and 26 July 1933, and Norton, 22 December 1936, Foreign Office Librarian's Department, Correspondence and Memoranda: General, vol. 7, 1930–1940; V. Cromwell and Z. S. Steiner, 'Reform and Retrenchment: The Foreign Office between the Wars', R. Bullen (ed.), *The Foreign Office, 1782–1982* (Frederick, MD, 1984), 85–106.

usual Treasury obstruction.'[72] Hardinge's *ançien régime* was eventually dismantled by Crowe, who succeeded him in 1920. A 'radical change of the organization alone can enable me to carry on', he reasoned. The new arrangements, devolving responsibilities to the assistant undersecretaries, reduced the PUS's workload but facilitated the information flow within the Office. The observance of routine practices remained vital to it reestablishing itself as the foreign policy nerve centre. Slipshod filing, inaccurate references or imprecise drafting were cardinal sins that threatened to blunt the edges of foreign policy analyses.[73] Already soon after the Paris peace conference, clerks in the Eastern Department, weighed down by current work, were caught short-circuiting the registering system by colour-coding files 'green', strictly reserved for 'exceptional papers of supreme secrecy', and much time was wasted 'in vain searches'.[74] Pressure from within Whitehall complicated Foreign Office business further. Its activities remained focused on the production, analysis and application of knowledge relevant to the framing and execution of foreign policy. Its organizational structures reflected these concerns. All papers had to go through the Library, which was 'concerned with the collection of a great quantity of legal and historical data and precedents; and its utility to the Office at large depends on the completeness of its collections ... [made] accessible for present and future work'.[75]

Disseminating analyses and thus shaping decision making were hampered by interwar political realities. It would, reflected one former Foreign Office official, 'be to the eternal benefit of all if the FO people were brought more into contact with Political people, for the best FO people know a good deal and can form opinions on data which is not available to others'.[76] Too many of the politicians, however, preferred their own opinions. Lord Curzon, indeed, threatened to resign 'if any of my colleagues is at liberty to act in this way'.[77]

---

[72] Crowe to Clema, 6 April 1919, Crowe Mss, Bod., Mss.Eng.e.3024; The 1918 interdepartmental committee had estimated the registry staffing needs at around 184 clerks, *supra*. One of the victims of the Geddes Axe was the News Department at the Foreign Office, see Hardinge diary, 26 February 1922, Hardinge MSS, CUL, Add. I.28.

[73] Mins. Crowe, 16 September 1913 (recirculated September 1920), and 22 January 1924, Foreign Office, Librarian's Department, Correspondence and Memoranda: General, vol. 6, 1919–1929.

[74] Dunlop to Gaselee,16 March 1920, and mins. Gaselee and Tilley, 16 March 1920, ibid. Tilley was the culprit here.

[75] Min. Hardinge, 17 April 1920, ibid.

[76] Emrys-Evans to Crookshank, 11 February 1925, Emrys-Evans MSS, British Library, Add. MSS. 58238. Paul Emrys-Evans had served in the Foreign Office, 1916–22; MP (Cons.) South Derbyshire, 1931–45.

[77] Curzon to Baldwin (confidential), 8 August 1923, Curzon MSS, MSS.Eur. F.112/229. The object of his wrath was Robert Cecil.

Nothing highlighted the Office's declining influence as much as the divisions between the then PUS, Sir Robert Vansittart, and the new Prime Minister, Neville Chamberlain. The Office no longer occupied the position it had in the days before 1914, and 'Van' was destined to lose the struggle for influence with the Prime Minister. With his penchant for lengthy minutes and memoranda – likened by his eventual successor to 'dancing literary hornpipes' rather than straightforward expositions of policy – he had alienated more people than was prudent.[78] At the end of 1937 he bowed to the inevitable, agreeing to a sideways arabesque to become Chief Diplomatic Adviser.[79] Its grand title stood in inverse proportion to its occupant's influence. 'The new post ... will be very honourable & may be very useful', Chamberlain noted with satisfaction, 'but he will be removed from active direction of F.O. policies & I suspect that in Rome & Berlin the rejoicings will be loud & deep'.[80] Vansittart's new remit was extremely circumscribed. The notion that he still exercised any significant influence now was 'sheer moonshine'.[81] There was 'an ill-defined jumble of duties between Vansittart and Cadogan. Nobody ... knows where their respective duties lie.'[82] All papers were to be passed to his successor as PUS, and through him to the Secretary of State, Sir Anthony Eden, who would decide whether Vansittart's input was required. Nothing underlined his 'splendid isolation' more than Eden's stipulation that, in case of urgent action being necessary, the papers were to be sent to one of the AUSs concerned, 'with a slip

---

[78] Cadogan diary entry, 11 September 1936, Cadogan MSS, Churchill College Archive Centre, ACAD 1/5; D. Boadle, 'Vansittart's Administration of the Foreign Office in the 1930s', in R. T. B. Lanhorne (ed.), *Diplomacy and Intelligence during the Second World War: Essays in Honour of F.H. Hinsley* (Cambridge, 1985), 79–80.

[79] Eden to Chamberlain, 12 December 1937, Avon MSS, Cadbury Research Library, University of Birmingham, AP 20/5/14; for a discussion of Vansittart see also K. Neilson, *Britain, Soviet Russia and the Collapse of the Versailles Order, 1919–1939* (Cambridge, 2006), 29–31.

[80] Chamberlain to Ida (his sister), 12 December 1937, Chamberlain MSS, CRL, NC 18/1/1031. Chamberlain also thought that 'when Anthony [Eden] can work out his ideas with some slow man like Alick [sic] Cadogan he will be much steadier'. Vansittart had the effect 'of multiplying Anthony's natural vibrations'. Chamberlain and Vansittart had an early run-in in 1932 over trade with Soviet Russia, Vansittart to Chamberlain, 23 November 1932, and min. Chamberlain, 28 November 1932, T 172/1792.

[81] Hankey to Phipps (personal and confidential), 11 January 1938, Phipps MSS, CCAC, PHPP 3/3.

[82] Crawford to Wilson, 27 July 1938, Crawford MSS, National Archive of Scotland, Edinburgh, ACC 9769 97/9; see also the important article by K. Neilson, 'The Defence Requirements Sub-Committee, British Strategic Foreign Policy, Neville Chamberlain, and the Path to Appeasement', *English Historical Review* 118(477) (2003), 651–84.

bearing the words "Sir R. Vansittart after action"'.[83] The 'Grand Panjandrum' of yore had been emasculated. There was now no more internal obstacle in the way of Chamberlain's policy of seeking an accommodation with the dictators. In consequence, the Foreign Office voice was less authoritative and more muted in the foreign policy debates of the late 1930s. 'It is Hitler ... who does all the developing' now, noted one senior official.[84]

War once again forced changes upon the department. The most immediate effect of the war was the increase in cypher telegrams, which led to the enlargement of the existing Communications Department. It also forced Sir Alec Cadogan, the PUS, to issue an appeal for economy, 'both to avoid undue expense and to ensure speed in dispatch, receipt and distribution of telegrams'.[85] The Office took advantage of the corporate memory from the earlier conflict, and what had been planned in the inter-war period, to provide the skeleton staff for a separate Ministry of Economic Warfare. In addition, a number of new Departments were created: a General Department to deal with broader questions concerning the war; a Dominions Intelligence Department to deal with imperial matters; and a Political Intelligence Department.[86] Although frustrating for the PUS – 'I am suddenly told that a Department in the Ministry of Obfuscation has to be reorganized: it must come back "under control" of the Ministry of Circumlocution' – it was the inevitable result of wartime exigencies.[87] They also placed a premium on stricter adherence to agreed procedures. 'The contraction of [working] hours, due to the air raids', meant that all papers had to be dealt with on the day of their receipt.[88]

As already during the earlier conflict, the war weakened the Foreign Office as the organizational hub of foreign policymaking. Global war made foreign policy less of a departmental matter and more a matter of national survival. Senior military and naval officers occupied a more

---

[83] Memo. Eden, 'Status of Chief Diplomatic Adviser and Scope of His Activities' (confidential), 22 January 1938, Foreign Office, Librarian's Department, Correspondence and Memoranda, General, vol. 7, 1930–1940.

[84] Sargent to Emrys-Evans, 12 September 1938, Emrys-Evans MSS, Add. MSS. 58238; for Sargent's career K. Neilson, 'Orme Sargent, Appeasement and British Policy in Europe, 1933 to 1939', *Twentieth Century British History* 21(1) (2010), 1–28, is the authoritative account; see also C. Hill, *Cabinet Decisions on Foreign Policy: The British Experience, October 1938–June 1941* (Cambridge, 1991).

[85] Min. Cadogan, 11 September 1939, Foreign Office, Librarian's Department, Correspondence and Memoranda, General, vol. 7, 1930–1940.

[86] See e.g. mins. of Butler Committee (Ministry of Economic Warfare), 8 May 1940, FO 837/516; for staffing difficulties, Cadogan diary, 8 September 1939, D. Dilks (ed.), *The Diaries of Sir Alexander Cadogan, 1938–1945* (New York, 1971), 214–15.

[87] Cadogan diary, 6 October 1939, ibid., 221.

[88] Memo. Cadogan, 'Office Procedures' (confidential), 19 December 1940, Foreign Office, Librarian's Department, Correspondence and Memoranda, vol. 7, 1930–1940.

prominent role along with a wider range of political figures than had been the case in peacetime. As the war progressed, and more especially after Winston Churchill replaced Chamberlain, something akin to Lloyd George's Garden Suburb began to emerge, changing the Office's role and supplanting some of its functions.[89] From being the centre of foreign policymaking, it became just one of the departments involved in framing foreign policy.

\*\*\*

From its very beginnings the Foreign Office was an epistemological site of arcane knowledge. It was conceived as a 'knowledge-based organization'. Its internal structures and procedures were designed to ensure that policy-relevant information could be gathered, processed, archived, retrieved, and then applied to current problems. The Library and the registry were the hinges around which the rapid and smooth working of the Office revolved.

From the beginning also aspiration and reality were uneasily matched. At no stage did the Office offer a picture of Platonic perfection. Financial constraints and insufficient staffing levels meant that it never quite functioned as its senior officials intended it to do. Its organizational development thus reflected the nature of the state it served. Haphazard decision making forced it to make do with limited resources. This and sticking plaster solutions curtailed its capacity for strategic decision making: 'We never look more than 3 inches beyond our noses.'[90] That the Office nevertheless sought to frame policy with a view to long-term challenges is testimony to the intellectual calibre and fortitude of the people who staffed it.

The great 1905–06 reform revolutionized the Office's inner workings and its place in the policymaking process. Its Edwardian heyday could not, however, mask the partial breakdown of the system on the eve of the First World War. The vicissitudes of two global conflicts further diminished its role as 'gatekeeper'. Once the nerve centre of British foreign policy it had become one of a number of competing repositories of relevant knowledge, its position more peripheral and its influence no longer predominant. Its decline thus mirrored the decline of Britain.

---

[89] G. A. Craig, 'Wartime Diplomats and Diplomacy', G. A. Craig and F. L. Loewenheim (eds.), *The Diplomats, 1919–1939* (Princeton, NJ, 1994), 20–24; C. I. Hamilton, 'The Decline of Churchill's "Garden Suburb" and Rise of His Private Office: the Prime Minister's Department, 1940–1945', *Twentieth-Century British History* 12(2) (2001), 133–62.

[90] Sanderson to O'Conor (private), 15 April 1896, O'Conor MSS, CCAC, OCON 6/1/6.

# 5 Financial and Commercial Networks between Great Britain and South America during the Long Nineteenth Century

*Kathleen Burk*

During the century after independence, both governments and businesses in the countries of South America alternated between boom and bust. How was an investor back in Great Britain to know when to invest and in what? How was a merchant bank in the City of London to know to whom to lend money, whether it was a capital loan or the buying of an 'acceptance' from a merchant (by which the merchant received payment for his goods from the bank before the goods were paid for across the ocean)? And how was a new businessman in a South American country to know with whom he could safely deal? They all needed networks of information, contact with a firm or an individual whom they could trust to provide them with that information. This was particularly crucial in the decades before the laying of the transoceanic cable between Great Britain and South America, when months could elapse without contact. How were these networks of information established, and by whom? And were they always successful? The answer to the last question was, of course, no, but having them was better than not having them. What was also vital to the position of British business in South America was the strength provided by networks of interconnected services.

The relationships of Great Britain with South American countries in the nineteenth century were overwhelmingly financial and commercial. There was no particular government drive to conquer a physical empire, even though some colonies did result, but an economic or informal empire was another matter entirely. Even so, any expression of a desire for an 'empire' of any sort seldom crossed Foreign Office lips. What was desired was fair and equal treatment in trade, on the assumption, of course, that 'equality' would not preclude British commercial or financial dominance. They were not, however, prepared to take the defence of general British commercial interests as far as intervention in the internal affairs of South American countries. It is true that intervention in support of British commercial dominance was not wholly absent, but one episode in what was later Argentina so burnt the fingers of the Foreign Office that for the remainder of the century the government refused to accept this support as automatically one of their tasks.

This episode took place in the 1840s. It was not unusual to offer mediation in wars between Latin American states, but actual intervention was normally restricted to the protection of British lives and property. In this case, however, the British government slid into a mess. The dictator of Buenos Aires, General Juan Manuel Rosas, was fighting General Fructuoso Rivera of Uruguay, and the British commercial communities were very worried about the safety of their property and appealed to the British government for protection. It became very complicated. Lord Palmerston, then Foreign Secretary, offered mediation in July 1841, but both sides turned it down. In February 1842, the British invited the French to join them in another attempt at mediation, and this was offered the following month. It was also turned down. In June 1843, Sir Robert Peel assured the Commons that although the fighting could only retard the growing prosperity of those countries, and though Great Britain wanted to use all of the influence they had to put an end to them, and would use all their power to protect British subjects, Great Britain would not 'become a principal in the hostilities', nor would 'British forces . . . be brought to bear on the issue of the contest'.[1]

A year later the British were bombing Colonia on the River Plate, and Lord Aberdeen, the Foreign Secretary, 'whose ignorance of Latin American affairs was rivalled – among British Foreign Secretaries – only by [the Earl of] Malmesbury, had blundered into a costly and futile intervention'.[2] He was forced to defend himself in the House of Lords, directly after Lord Beaumont had stigmatized very strongly the intervention of France and England in the affairs of La Plate as unnecessary and unjust. Aberdeen responded that France and England had come together 'determined to offer mediation a third time, for the purpose of offering pacification in that part of the world; and, if that offer were refused, to attempt by coercive measures to attain that object'. He conceded that 'it was true that a blockade of Buenos Aires had been established, but that act, though approaching to a condition of hostilities, was not necessarily an act of war'.[3] Lord Palmerston, who later that year succeeded him as Foreign Secretary, changed the policy, telling the French Ambassador in

---

[1] Parl. Debs. (series 3) vol. 69 col. 1251 (2 June 1843); D. C. M. Platt, *Finance, Trade, and Politics in British Foreign Policy 1815–1914* (Oxford, rev. ed. 1971), 319–22; H. S. Ferns, *Britain and Argentina in the Nineteenth Century* (Oxford, 1960), 262–79.

[2] Platt, *Finance, Trade, and Politics*, 322.

[3] *Parl. Debs.* (series 3) vol. 83 cols 1158–59 and 1191 (19 February 1846).

London that 'the blockade is piracy ... I am very glad that we are out of such a system.'[4]

On the whole, during the nineteenth century, Great Britain maintained a policy of non-intervention in South America when it came to the gaining by British bankers and merchants of contracts and concessions. Indeed, there was relatively little pressure for intervention (although later in the century there was some grumbling that since Germany was helping their businessmen, it was a pity that the Foreign Office would not do more to help theirs). For one thing, there was no political rivalry with a major power (as in Persia), and no danger of physical partition and the closing of markets (as in China). Indeed, it could be positively dangerous for diplomats to become involved in financial promotions, as explained in 1886 by Sir Edmund Monson, a former Minister at Montevideo and Buenos Aires. His view was that the standard of commercial and political morality in South America was such that it was wholly undesirable for British diplomats 'to depart from their traditional policy of abstention in matters of business'. As he went on to explain,

in those countries every concession to foreign capitalists, foreign Companies, foreign syndicates, is made a matter of pecuniary bargaining. All speculations and enterprises ... taken in hand by foreigners, depend for their preliminary success upon the readiness of the promoters to bribe the wire-pullers of the Government. Commercial houses seeking contracts or simply desirous of increasing their ordinary operation, are driven to have recourse to the same measures. Individuals or associations who have wrongs to redress or claims to assert can only hope to succeed by paying blackmail to officials; and when such cases are taken up and carried to a successful issue by Diplomatic Agents, the latter can never escape suspicion of having received a share of the plunder.[5]

Over the remainder of the century, it was the case that occasional appeals were made to the government for aid. If a British subject was being treated in a manner that was illegal or unfair, an informal word to officials – 'good offices' – was sometimes used, with greater or lesser firmness. There was a good reason for going no further. Sir Edward Grey in July 1914 reiterated in the House of Commons the principle that had determined the approach of the British government to British business activities in South America: 'British financiers run their own businesses quite independent of politics, and, if we attempt to interfere, they naturally consider that we come under some obligation.' If they grant or withhold a loan at the request of the Foreign Office, then the Foreign Office comes under some obligation. 'But, generally speaking, and

[4] Ferns, *Britain and Argentina*, 279.
[5] Quoted in Platt, *Finance, Trade, and Politics*, 332–33.

especially in South America, these are things in which the Foreign Office do not interfere.'[6] If the government was not going to help, the businessman or financier was on his own, unless he had a little help from his friends.

For over 200 years, Europeans had seen Latin America as the home of almost unimaginable potential wealth, particularly of gold and silver.[7] British 'privateers, merchants and ministers' attempted to break into the Spanish and Portuguese monopoly while preventing the French, their commercial rivals, from doing the same. The British achieved their first success in 1810, when they negotiated preferential trading privileges in Brazil.[8] This was a *quid pro quo* for British support of the Portuguese royal family during the Napoleonic Wars; for example, when the Portuguese emperor and his family were fleeing Lisbon, a Royal Navy ship carried them safely to Brazil.

Between 1810 and 1825, the Spanish South American colonies struggled for independence, in which they were successful, and during which restrictions on trade with other countries than Spain gradually disappeared. The French were keen to take over the Spanish position there, inaugurating this with an invasion of Spain in 1823 to defeat the constitutional government and restore the Bourbon king Ferdinand VII to the throne (France itself again had a Bourbon monarch); this was to be followed, France hoped, by the placement of Bourbon princes on the thrones of former Spanish colonies such as Mexico, Gran Colombia, Peru and Chile. Britain, however, had not been idle. At the Battle of Trafalgar in 1805, the Royal Navy had pretty well destroyed the French and Spanish fleets, and the Navy's control of the ocean thereafter facilitated the safeguarding of British interests. After the end of the Napoleonic Wars, British commercial interests raced to take ship, while George Canning, the British Foreign Secretary from 1822 to 1827, supported them by sending out consular officials (as did the Americans).[9]

By 1823, according to a French official in Colombia, 'the power of England is without a rival in America; no fleets but hers to be seen; her merchandises are bought almost exclusively; her commercial agents, her clerks and brokers, are everywhere to be met with'.[10] 'The British mania for Latin America rose in a crescendo early in 1825, just after the

---

[6] *Hansard, HC* (series 5) vol. 64 cols 1448–49 (10 July 1914).

[7] During much of this period, Mexican silver dollars were the currency of European trade with China.

[8] Rory Miller, *Britain and Latin America in the Nineteenth and Twentieth Centuries* (London, 1993), 1–2.

[9] Kathleen Burk, *Old World, New World: The Story of Britain and America* (London, 2007), 249–50.

[10] Quoted in Wendy Hinde, *George Canning* (London, 1973), 345.

government's decision to grant formal recognition to some of the new nations. Merchants with cargoes of manufactured goods, particularly cotton textiles, established themselves in large numbers in ports along the Atlantic and Pacific coasts, while in London eager speculators invested their savings in loans to the young governments and in mining enterprises which promised a new El Dorado.'[11]

It is worth pointing out briefly the needs driving both the South Americans and the British, because these factors in one form or another would later reappear once memories had faded. Although the British had been dealing with the South Americans for some years, the crucial event which opened up the countries was the battle of Ayacucho on 9 December 1824, when the South American troops led by General Antonio Sucre decisively defeated the royalist army led by La Serna, the Spanish viceroy. In place of the empires of Spain and Portugal emerged two confederations, five republics, two federal republics, and one native empire (Brazil). But their victories were fragile: what if Spain gained the backing of France and the Holy Alliance to reconquer her colonies? Thus, the most immediate need was military supplies, including ships, for which war loans were required, but there was also the need to repair or build infrastructure, and to facilitate businesses and agriculture. Fortunately, it was thought, because they were now independent nations, they would be welcome in the London money market.[12]

Yet there were problems. For one thing, virtually all of the new nations adopted free trade policies because they believed that more trade would generate greater revenues; at the same time, they changed the colonial tax structures and eliminated a number of taxes. Greater revenues were indeed generated, but the elimination of the taxes also meant that there was an overwhelming dependence on import-export duties. This required a concomitant dependence on the honesty of those collecting them, a trust which was not always repaid. Furthermore, the need to pay for military goods meant that much of the money collected was not available for domestic investment, but was sent abroad. For example, between 1819 and 1825, Charles Ricketts, the British consul at Lima, reported that British men-of-war had carried off 27 million pesos of gold and silver from Peru.[13] It is also worth remembering that until mid-century, the

---

[11] Miller, *Britain and Latin America*, 2.

[12] Carlos Marichal, *A Century of Debt Crises in Latin America: From Independence to the Great Depression, 1820–1930* (Princeton, NJ, 1989), 12–22.

[13] During 1818–24, Birmingham became the major military supplier to Latin America, and 'had a field day disposing of surplus arms and uniforms from the Napoleonic Wars', Marichal, *Century of Debt Crises*, 17, n. 17, and 21 for gold and silver.

British Empire ran a colonial preference system, which could sometimes inhibit export-import possibilities.

On the other side, what drove the British? The answer to this is pretty straightforward: the desire to take advantage of the new opportunities to make lots of money. A real frenzy was stimulated in the early 1820s by the possibilities opening up for silver mining: as described by the *Annual Register* of 1824,

> all the gambling propensities of human nature were constantly solicited into action: and crowds of individuals of every description – the credulous and the suspicious – the crafty and the bold – the raw and the experienced – the intelligent and the ignorant – princes, nobles, placemen, patriots, lawyers, physicians, divines, philosophers, poets, intermingled with women of all ranks and degrees – spinsters, wives and widows – hastened to venture some portion of their property in schemes of which scarcely any thing was known except the name.[14]

By mid-1825, twenty-six different Latin American mining companies had been registered on the Royal Exchange, with their shares selling at awe-inspiring premia.

There was also a foreign loan boom. All of the imported goods had to be paid for, and investors were delighted to loan the money. There was also the chance to invest in infrastructure. Between 1823 and 1825, the total value of Latin American government bonds issued in London was more than £20 million.[15] In addition, there were the loans made to business start-ups as well as to established firms. This huge Royal Exchange boom coincided with a cyclical upswing in Great Britain, driven primarily by two factors. First of all, there was expansion of the cotton textile industry, encouraging hopes of growth; and secondly, the 1820s saw the widespread introduction of new technologies leading to the first-ever passenger railways, steam navigation companies and gas-lighting enterprises. Large and small investors from all over England invested madly, whether or not they truly understood the industries. The banker Alexander Baring was quoted as exclaiming that 'it seemed as if all Bedlam had broken loose on the Royal Exchange'.[16]

Given the frenzy, what might have been expected to happen happened. Admittedly, the goods sent to South America were cheap and of good quality. One reason that they were relatively inexpensive was that merchants had access to cheap loans, because the London money market was booming and they could extend cheap credit; furthermore, British shippers provided competitive shipping rates. Even with all of these

---

[14] As quoted in ibid., p. 24.
[15] Ibid., 28, Table 1, 'Latin American Government Issues Floated in England, 1822–1825'.
[16] As quoted in ibid., 13.

advantages, there were obstacles to safety. Part of the problem which developed with Latin American loans was caused by stupidity. For one thing, the huge number of exporters hugging the coasts frequently gave little thought to what they were sending to tropical Brazil, for example: wool blankets and bed-warming pans![17] Even for realistic exports, the less well-developed markets were soon saturated. The mining companies largely failed as well. This meant huge numbers of bankruptcies. Further, almost all of the new governments, because they were unable to raise the revenue necessary to pay the interest on their loans, defaulted. But what truly condemned countries and businesses dependent on funding in and by London was the ferocious European financial crisis, characterized in Great Britain by a run on the banks, and in response the banks demanded the repayment on all outstanding debts and, as Baring observed, 'by screwing almost to destruction every farmer, manufacturer and other customer in the country from whom they could get their money'.[18] Hundreds of mercantile and industrial firms went bankrupt and tens of thousands of workers lost their jobs. The result was full-scale economic depression. In the circumstances, Latin America received relatively little attention. Indeed, general commercial interest in Latin America lagged until the 1840s.

Sadly, even those individuals and firms who had built up a broad network of commercial and political alliances, with offices in both Great Britain and Latin America, might not survive: sometimes financial crises, at a time when governments did not rescue businesses, were just too overwhelming. A number of these were already present in various countries, and maintained commercial and political ties there with the political élites. One of these was Parish Robertson Brothers, who sometimes worked with Baring Brothers. They began a wide-ranging trading career at Buenos Aires in 1807, when the British occupied the port, and enlarged their activities to encompass other ports in Argentina and Paraguay. In 1817, by which year they had amassed a considerable fortune, they established a commercial house in Buenos Aires and opened an agency in Liverpool. During the 1820s they combined trade with a wide range of financial and commercial activities, promoting mining companies, establishing ranching companies and participating in the issuing of foreign loans for the governments of Buenos Aires and Peru; in the former loan, they worked together with Barings. Yet, overextended by a mining

---

[17] The same thoughtless mistake happened in China, where merchants sent, for example, pianos and cutlery, and then wondered why they did not sell.

[18] As quoted in Marichal, *Century of Debt Crises*, 45.

venture and an expensive colonisation scheme, they failed in 1827, brought down by the financial crisis.[19]

Others were more fortunate: Antony Gibbs & Sons had long been established in the Anglo-Spanish trade. In the 1820s they extended into Chile and Peru, subsequently becoming one of the most prosperous firms in the Pacific trade with Latin America. They developed into a major London merchant bank. Two other merchant banks of enduring fame, Barings and Rothschilds, issued a loan to Buenos Aires in 1824 and to Brazil in 1825, respectively, but they were careful as to how much they lent, that is, for how much of it they took responsibility. Parish Robertson took a larger part and made much larger profits, but they also speculated more heavily. Barings and Rothschilds were more careful. Both also had long-standing networks of information.

How did these networks develop? Probably the most important element was the development of the cousinhood: 'the extended business family was the private bankers' chief source of talent'.[20] Note that it was Gibbs and Sons, Baring Brothers, N.M. Rothschild and Sons. Family members – brothers, sons, nephews, cousins, sons-in-law – joined the business: the Rothschilds were famous as beginning with five brothers from Frankfurt, four of whom fanned out to other European cities. The Barings, too, were eminently a family firm. The First Lord Ashburton, born Alexander Baring, co-negotiator of the Webster-Ashburton Treaty in 1842 with Daniel Webster, US Secretary of State, had resided for years in the United States, part of the family business. It was normal for firms to send out agents in whose judgement and probity they had confidence to reside in the countries with which they carried out business; family members, presumably, eminently fulfilled that role. Less qualified or dependable relatives tended to be kept in London, where their work could be closely scrutinized, or they might be farmed out to the army or politics.

Naturally, there were also fellow firms which fulfilled that role of representative or agent. In 1833, Barings' new representative in Buenos Aires was Zimmerman, Frazier and Co. Johann Zimmerman was born in Germany, emigrated at an early age to the United States, and came to Buenos Aires around 1817, where with his relative Nalbro Frazer he founded the eponymous firm; in mid-century, they were still connected to Barings. At least part of his attraction for Barings was probably the significant role he played in Argentine politics; in 1826, he became a member of the first board of the National Bank of the Argentine

---

[19] Ibid., 34–42 and 50.
[20] Vincent Carosso, *Investment Banking in America* (Cambridge, MA, 1970), 16.

Republic. Nevertheless, Barings continued to send out specific agents for specific tasks, such as negotiating the repayment of loans or to scout out a new industry.

If you were new in the merchant or banking business, a new investor, an unknown young man chancing his arm, an unscrupulous fraudster, you had absolutely no chance of being supported by, or even seen by, Barings or Rothschilds or others of that standing. What to do? You asked your friends, you listened to rumours, you called upon relatives or associates of relatives who might know a bit more, or you might just go out yourself to look around. If you were not a my-word-is-my-bond man, you wanted to get hold of enough, whether government or company bonds, or, especially in the 1820s, mining stocks of companies that had not actually failed, and sell them on, buy them back, and sell them on, speculating madly and, ideally, making money hand over fist. During boom years, this sometimes worked: there were a lot of people around Great Britain who took their money and invested. If not as bad as the famous Dutch tulip frenzy, or the South Sea Bubble episode, it was bad enough. A century later, J. P. Morgan, Jr, sold out of his stock market holdings before the 1929 crash, because, he said, once his cab driver began giving him stock tips, it was time to depart.

What honest people required to navigate these shoals and rapids was good information. It was certainly useful to be in the country itself. As a young man, you could probably get a position as a clerk in a British firm in Buenos Aires or Lima or Montevideo or other growing cities in developing countries, ideally one where wars were not raging. What you needed to gain was experience, and links in the country, both with other British merchants and investors and with Argentinians or Brazilians or Chileans. A very important breakthrough would be links with influential men in politics, the élites, the decision-makers, knowing them and their friends, dining with them, going to their parties, perhaps marrying one of their daughters or nieces. After you had lived there for a while, perhaps having advanced to a position of some responsibility in the firm with a concomitant advance in salary, you might begin to make careful investments yourself, using judgement, never taking too great a financial position, only investing what you could afford to lose. This way you would gain experience as well as a growing reputation as a man who knew what he was about.

Eventually you would have to decide whether to remain in South America or to return to Great Britain. What might be the considerations? First of all, you might have developed a satisfactory life. Perhaps you had a South American wife and children whose only experience was living in a warm, comfortable environment; do you want to subject them to cold and rainy Great Britain? Perhaps you have a very nice house and estate: if you moved back home, would you be able to enjoy an equally comfortable life? Perhaps you enjoy a significant position in society and politics, given your connection with a British firm of some status: could this be replicated in London? Alternatively, you may be a single, very ambitious, young man, who is convinced that his future lies in the financial centre of the world, or the shipping centre, or the commercial centre, and who has little to lose.

This, too, may drive the possibly older family man. Given that he will no longer be the representative or agent in, say, Argentina of a powerful merchant bank, he can nevertheless look forward to a career as the man in London to know about that particular country – the politics, the legal system, who can be trusted and who cannot and, perhaps, who might take his own place. A partnership might beckon, although this might well depend on one's pedigree. The younger man will also have the knowledge and perhaps can look forward to a higher position in London with a concomitant increase in salary. In short, it was not necessarily a given that either ought to return to the centre. Presumably you will have an increased position in this network: the decision would be, at which end?

The financial crisis of the late 1820s had on the whole put paid to the ideas of substantial British merchant or financial houses investing in most of South America, although Brazil never defaulted on is loans. An exception was Huth and Co. of London, a bank which was established in 1809, and was apparently the only London merchant bank who decided to 'go global' before 1850. Establishing branch houses in Chile and Peru in the 1820s, it had correspondence links around the world: between 1822 and 1850, it had 814 in the Americas, 1,313 in the United Kingdom, 3,778 in Europe, 125 in Asia, 18 in Africa, 24 in Australia and 202 others (knowledge about which is 'not available'), for a total of 6,274. This global information and trading network enabled a significant and successful trading capacity, based as it was on local knowledge, trust and an ability to judge risks. As a result, Huth & Co., later Frederick Huth & Co., a significant player in Chile and Peru in this context, was a wealthy and respected house.[21]

It was not until the 1850s that interest in South America surged again. One influence was the growth in joint-stock companies and banks, the

---

[21] Manuel Llorca-Jaña, 'The Economic Activities of a Global Merchant-Banker in Chile: Huth & Co. of London, 1820s-1850s', *Historia (Santiago)* 45(2) (2012), 2 for quote; see also ibid., Table 1: 'Location of Huth's Correspondents. A sample for 1812-1850', 3, and Table 2: 'Location of Huth's correspondents, 1822', which numbered 665, 5. Frederick Huth & Co. remained a successful and independent bank until 1936, when it became part of British Overseas Bank.

latter of which benefitted from the Companies Acts of 1858–62, which extended the privilege of incorporation with limited liability to banks.[22] A joint-stock company differed from a partnership in that it spread the risk from the partners themselves, whose personal assets were always in danger of being swept up in a bankruptcy (but who also shared out the profits, paying other members of the firm a salary and giving them no control). A joint-stock bank issued stock and required shareholders to be liable for the company's debts – so far, so similar – but, unlike in a partnership, these shares could be traded on exchange, theoretically allowing shareholders to sell their shares if they saw a crisis coming (and if they could find buyers) and thereby ending their liability for the debts.

The 1860s saw a raft of new institutions set up to take advantage of relative stability in South America, and particularly in Argentina. One important one was that established in Buenos Aires by the London and River Plate Bank, whose history illuminates some of the advantages and dangers affecting these investments. In the late summer of 1862, *Bankers' Magazine* published the following announcement: 'An enterprise, to be called the London, Buenos Ayres, and River Plate Bank (Limited), with a capital of £500,000, in 5,000 shares of £100 each, and a power to increase, has been announced ... the promoters say that "they have the assurance of the representatives of those states that their respective governments would regard with favour the establishment of such an institution, as a powerful means of contributing to the advancement of commercial relations with Great Britain".'[23] The head office was opened at 40 Moorgate Street in the City of London, and the first chairman was Henry Bruce, a director of the Colonial Bank.

Bruce's experience led him to establish clear lines of management and strict rules for the banking activities of their new representative firm in Argentina, which had finally emerged from years of war. The intention was to extend banking facilities through the use of British capital to the cities of Buenos Aires and Montevideo. Each of the eight first directors, four from banks in London and four from merchants in London, Liverpool and South America, invested a significant amount in the new venture, while the chairman had invested £37,000 by the end of the second year. The willingness of the founders, all successful and reputable men, to subscribe so much of their own capital would reassure

---

[22] Ignacio Briones and André Villela, 'European Bank Penetration During the First Wave of Globalisation: Lessons from Brazil and Chile, 1878–1913', *European Review of Economic History* (10)(3) (2006) 334.

[23] David Joslin, *A Century of Banking in Latin America to Commemorate the Centenary in 1962 of The Bank of London & South America Limited* (London, 1963), 28. The subsequent relevant paragraphs are based on this book, 28–39.

possible investors, and by 1867 the new bank had a paid-up capital of
£600,000. What, then, was their procedure?

First of all, they needed to begin to build their networks of correspondents, both to provide information and to carry out other tasks that the
successful running of a bank required, such as making payments to the
River Plate or sending funds back to Europe. In London, the City Bank
became its banker, and a discount and drawing account was opened at the
Bank of England. Once arrangements in London had been set up, agents
to act for them were appointed in Paris (Bischoffsheim and Goldschmidt,
connected to the Rothschilds and with an office in London as well as in
Paris)[24] and, soon, in Hamburg, Amsterdam, Berlin, Genoa and
New York. In the River Plate itself, a further network of correspondents
and agents was needed to enable the bank to collect bills and extend the
circulation of its notes, which the agents were required to honour.

They then appointed a manager for their Buenos Aires office,
J. H. Green, who set out for Argentina on 9 October 1862, carrying
with him a copy of the bank's statutes to submit to President Bartolomé
Mitre. He also carried with him two boxes of gold doubloons, some
account books and letters of credit to enable him to secure the funds
necessary for the most basic needs on arrival. The bank, the first joint-
stock bank to operate in South America, opened on 1 January 1863.

From the first, Henry Bruce, who had shared responsibility for twenty
years for an overseas bank with many branches, kept a close eye on the
activities of their Argentine bank. He wrote to Green every fortnight (the
schedule of the steam packet to Argentina). As noted above, it took two
months for a return of letters, and Green's following of Bruce's advice and
instructions was crucial to the viability of the bank. These reflect some of
the problems and pressures experienced by Green. He had to learn
quickly, for example, that risks that he might make with his own capital
were not acceptable for a banker when trading with the deposits of his
customers. If local customers were angry because Green had to refuse
transactions contrary to sound banking practice, he had to cope with the
resultant unpopularity.

---

[24] Stanley Chapman, *The Rise of Merchant Banking* (London, 1984), 45–6. Between 1866
and 1875 their London house placed a sequence of loans for South American states.
However, according to Leland Hamilton Jenks, the report of the Commons, *Report on
Loans to Foreign States*, 1875, xlvi, its revelations 'concerning market-rigging, concerning
loan-issues made solely for the purpose of earning fat commissions, concerning interest
kept up solely out of the interest on the loans threw serious distrust upon several firms of
cosmopolitan bankers. This was cast especially upon Bischoffsheim & Goldschmidt, for
whose proceedings the committee considered that "a remedy ... ought to be found in the
tribunals of the country."' L. H. Jenks, *The Migration of British Capital to 1875* (London,
1938), 292.

When Green was pressed to make long loans to landowners supported by mortgages, he had to decline, because Bruce insisted that doing so would be unwise: land values went up and down wildly in a developing country, and such loans were therefore unsuitable for a commercial bank; would-be borrowers should go to a mortgage bank. This was, in fact, a common rule of the foreign banks: they were 'explicitly committed to privilege short-term credit and avoid long-term (for example, land securitised) loans'.[25] Another reason for not lending on land was that a rule of the bank, as articulated by Bruce, was that Green should not borrow short and lend long. Even a great landowner such as the former President of the Confederation, General Justo José de Urquiza, was refused, and doubtless made Green somewhat uncomfortable as a result.

There were a number of other problems with which Green and Bruce had to deal, especially in relation to the money market, but one of the most ticklish was what attitude should the bank take to requests for accommodation from the national government or the provincial governments, such as that of Buenos Aires? Green was allowed to invest some funds in their bonds and to make temporary advances. 'But he [Bruce] was fond of reminding the manager of the dangers which a foreign banker ran by lending to a government within its own territory – where it was effectively a party "beyond the reach of the law".'[26] Large and permanent loans had to be floated in London through an issuing house, normally a merchant bank, which the London and River Plate Bank was not.

Green's early months were fraught, since within two months of opening, he was hit by a severe commercial crisis, culminating in a panic and run on the bank. He survived, but there had been a serious imbalance between money travelling to Argentina to provide funds for the bank to use to make loans, and remittances from Argentina to London to meet these loans. Indeed, the crisis as it spread to London put a great strain on the London head office, which had itself to borrow to meet these obligations, as remittances continually failed to arrive. Once the crisis was over, Bruce insisted to Green that an international bank liable to simultaneous pressure both in Buenos Aires and in London could not run great risks: bullion or sterling bills on the ocean several weeks from port would be no help in a crisis.

One of Green's main duties was to act as the London bank's eyes and ears. He sent back credit ratings and detailed reports of the characteristics of local individuals and firms, he had to recognize the danger signals of 'unhealthy speculation'[27] and he needed to know the seasonal

---

[25] Briones and Villela, 'European Bank Penetration 1878–1913', 341.
[26] Joslin, *A Century of Banking in Latin America*, 35.    [27] Ibid., 21 for quote.

movements in both agriculture and the different trades. He was to refuse to deal with those native banks with dubious reputations. Finally, under no circumstances was he to loan against stocks, which tended to be, if that were possible, even more volatile than land speculation.[28]

The combination of Bruce and Green was a good one. Bruce died before the crisis of 1866 (the failure of the large London house Overend Gurney, which threatened to pull a number of other houses down with it) struck, but thanks to his instructions and guidance, the Argentine house concentrated on legitimate, mercantile business, essentially conservative and, possibly for that reason, successful. Bruce was very pleased with Green's work, and with what he saw as the successful development of the branch. What Bruce had accomplished was what a great number of houses who wished to expand in South America had to do: facing a great shortage of experienced men, they had to train up their own. Many tried to send out those with commercial experience with the expectation that they would pick up the necessary banking experience more or less on the hoof. This seldom worked, as many discovered to their annoyance and chagrin. They tried to send out more experienced men – when they could find them – and to begin, in some haste, to train up native Argentinians, Brazilians, Chileans and Uruguayans.[29]

The London and River Plate concentrated on commercial business, but what was growing in South America was corporate finance, particularly with the huge growth in the construction of railways, and sovereign loans, i.e. those made to countries rather than to individuals and firms. The last of those was the most prestigious, but often not the most profitable. In spite of information or rumours, the gambling desire to make huge profits, which was eminently possible with a successful loan, too often led the unwary to plunge beyond what the common sense of others might prevent, and they – or the investors whom they had talked into handing over their funds – suffered more often than not during the nineteenth century.

One London bank which decided to move into Latin America without establishing a subsidiary bank in one or more of the countries was J.S. Morgan & Co., a merchant bank which rose into the top rank of London

[28] Briones and Villela, 'European Bank Penetration, 1878–1913', 341.

[29] According to G. Subercaseaux, *Monetary and Banking Policy of Chile* (Oxford, 1922), 131, 'foreign banks [had] placed at the head of their administration thoroughly very competent men, who have seen to it that their functions are well performed; and in this way they have not only given the country the benefit of a good banking service, but at the same time have set a good example for the national banks, the administration of which has not always been equally commendable', as quoted in Briones and Villela, 'European Bank Penetration, 1878–1913', 341, n. 24.

banks during the period 1870–1914. Their initial interest was indeed in corporate finance, which accorded with the decision they had made in December 1873 to move into international securities. It is also true to say that until about 1885, corporate finance was a more important area for them than sovereign (government) loans: a list of the loans managed or co-managed by Morgans contains over twice as many foreign corporate issues, in particular for railways, as those of foreign governments (including municipalities), although the total nominal value of the government issues was considerably higher.[30] Nevertheless, to be in the front rank of British merchant banks, it was necessary to co-lead or lead in issuing sovereign loans, especially of the more important countries. In South America, these were Argentina, Brazil and Chile. Morgans *in toto* had the benefit of close links with related firms in London, New York, Philadelphia and Paris, as well as with allies in London amongst the other banks. To a great extent, the Morgan firms shared with each other assessments, information, some decisions and business; the same to a greater or lesser extent took place between the Morgan firms and their banking allies in London and New York. With the laying of the cables in the 1870s, information could pass quickly back and forth, but knowledge and judgement remained vital. It would be the lack of judgement shown by Lord Revelstoke, the senior partner of Barings, that would trigger the worst, though relatively short-lived, financial crisis in London since that of Overend Gurney in 1866. The reason was the same: their failure would have brought down numerous other houses.

Argentina by the 1890s was the major South American investment area by far for British investors. It was the strongest trading and investment market, and the British led against other countries.[31] The attraction of Argentina for investment was not surprising: there were high rates of profit available on both private and public investments; it was a very good credit risk; and in the 1880s, the per capita income of the eastern provinces of Argentina ranked on a level with those of Canada, the United States and Australia.[32] Unfortunately, this economic boom had been accompanied by speculation, price inflation and corruption and, frankly, by a general lack of ability, or disinclination, to view expectations through the filter of common sense. As Sir John Clapham, a historian of the Bank of England, wrote, the story of Argentina and the crisis might also 'have to include extensive and not too kindly reference to the then standard of

[30] Typescript in 'Loans and Options', Morgan Grenfell Papers, Guildhall Library, London, MS 21,793, no. 1; see Kathleen Burk, *Morgan Grenfell 1838–1988: The Biography of a Merchant Bank* (Oxford, 1989), 48.
[31] The British also led in Chile, Brazil and Uruguay.
[32] Marichal, *Century of Debt Crises*, 145.

probity among businessmen and statesmen in the Argentine',[33] although the drive to improve conditions by Argentine leaders also played a role. The resignation of the Argentine Cabinet in April 1890, when joined with a deteriorating economy, undermined the confidence of overseas investors and brought substantial losses to many of the London banks which dealt in Argentinian issues.[34] Barings was the most active in this market, engaging in activities more vast and more diverse than any of its rivals and, indeed, had indulged in 'wild speculations'.[35] Why?

In general, of course, the bank had with other banks been part of the drive to make profits that seemed easy to realize. But more importantly in this case, Revelstoke must carry much of the blame. He appeared to have complete faith in a man called C. H. Sanford, contrary to the opinion of the other partners. As the historian of Barings comments, 'this man, who could not be induced to act honestly and in whom Barings had no confidence, was not merely received by Lord Revelstoke, but listened to with respect and treated as a sound authority on the Argentine economy. He seems, indeed, to have been an uncommonly plausible trickster; not, perhaps, consciously a rogue, but carried away by his enthusiasm and with an alarming capacity to carry others away as well.'[36] Revelstoke was inclined to follow Sanford's advice and made substantial investments in risky enterprises.

Throughout the second half of October 1890, there had been growing suspicions in the City of London that Barings was in difficulty – Argentina would be the trigger, but not the only cause[37] – but it was not until 8 November that Revelstoke was essentially summoned to a meeting with William Lidderdale, the Governor of the Bank of England, at which he warned the Governor that Barings was in grave danger of failing. This meeting must have been distinctly uncomfortable, even humiliating, for Revelstoke, since Lidderdale did not bother to hide his indignation at Barings' conduct of affairs.[38] Knowledge of this was kept from the public until 15 November, and meanwhile the Bank of England mounted a rescue operation, secretly purchasing £1.5 million in gold from Russia, borrowing £3 million from the Banque de France and extracting from the British government a promise to share whatever losses the Bank might sustain until a guarantee fund was set up. This fund was organized

[33] Sir John Clapham, *The Bank of England: A History 1694–1914* (2 vols. Cambridge, repr. 1970) vol. II, 326.

[34] Burk, *Morgan Grenfell*, 53.     [35] Marichal, *Century of Debt Crises*, 147.

[36] Philip Ziegler, *The Sixth Great Power: Barings 1762–1929* (London, 1988), 239.

[37] Stanley Chapman, *The Rise of Merchant Banking* (London: George Allen & Unwin, 1984), 77–80, argues that, even without Argentina, mismanagement would have caused the collapse of Barings. This certainly does not obviate Revelstoke's responsibility.

[38] Ziegler, *Barings*, 246.

from amongst the whole banking community, and its purpose was to guarantee any losses sustained by the Bank through providing Barings with a loan. Within less than two hours the guarantee from other merchant banks was in place, and they were joined by the five principal joint-stock banks. As Barings had proved to be solvent, if embarrassed, this fund ensured that the firm had time to realize its assets over the following several years in order to pay off its creditors.[39] There was a lesson to be learned, or re-learned, which was to be careful to whom you listen and trust, and consider carefully both the judgement of others and your own.

One consequence, and this was not a bad one, was a dramatic awareness of the risks inherent in the international loan business, and certainly it moved at a much more modest pace for over a decade, when activity increased. By 1900, Argentina's exports were growing and the country's finances were sound.[40] Argentina remained extremely important to British commercial and trading activities in South America as a whole. Great Britain began to lose market share in South America from 1870, primarily because of the rise in competition from France, Germany and the United States, but the decline would have been more serious had she not kept a tight grip on the Argentine market, which by the end of the century was by far the most important Latin American economy in terms of foreign trade. British pre-eminence in foreign investment in Latin America was not seriously challenged before the First World War. It has been estimated that in 1913, British investments were worth £999.2 million compared with £333.9 million for the United States, £329 million for France and £185 million for Germany. In fact, between a fifth and a quarter of all British foreign investments were to be found in Latin America.[41]

It was the First World War which ended the commercial and financial hegemony of Great Britain in South America. By 1916, Great Britain had taken on the financial responsibility for her wartime allies' purchases in the United States, as well as for her own military and civilian population, and this placed an overwhelming financial burden on her. When the United States entered the war in April 1917, Great Britain tried urgently to convince the US to take over the responsibility for the purchases of the European allies; the United States, however, not being terminally stupid,

---

[39] Clapham, *Bank of England*, II, 327–38; Burk, *Morgan Grenfell*, 53–54.
[40] Miller, *Britain and Latin America*, 155.
[41] According to Irving Stone in 'British Direct and Portfolio Investment in Latin America Before 1914', *Journal of Economic History* 37(3) (1977), 691, Britain's Latin American holdings in 1913 represented about one-fifth of its overseas capital; according to Victor Bulmer-Thomas, 'British Trade with Latin America in the Nineteenth and Twentieth Centuries', *Institute of Latin American Studies, University of London, Occasional Papers* No. 19 (1998), 9, they represented one-quarter.

preferred that the world's major financial power retain the responsibility for the guarantees of the pre-April 1917 purchases to taking it on herself. Few of these debts to Great Britain were repaid. Great Britain in 1917 and 1918 was forced by her financial desperation to borrow from the United States, and the total of the resultant war debts was nearly $5 billion. By 1928, 40 per cent of the British budget went towards the paying of war debts of one sort or another. In addition, during the war, Great Britain had, by the use of penal taxation, 'encouraged' the British investing public to turn over their securities, including those related to investments in South America, in order that the Treasury could either use them for collateral for loans in the New York money market or sell them to raise funds.[42] Altogether, Great Britain lost 15 per cent of her national wealth because of the war.

In these financial circumstances, it was to be impossible for Great Britain to retain, or to re-establish, her position of economic supremacy in South America. It was the case that even in 1920, American banks found it virtually impossible to establish themselves there against the position of the British banks. But as the 1920s wore on, and the financial strength of the City of London declined while that of Wall Street soared, when the economic position of Great Britain in general declined relative to that of the United States, whose economy by the end of the decade was practically in overdrive (if one ignores the farmers, who were suffering), it is not surprising that the United States supplanted the position of Great Britain in South America.

This, then, illustrates the final lesson. No matter how strong and wide-ranging are the financial and commercial networks of businesses and banks, no matter how considered and intelligent the judgements made, even no matter how virtually impregnable the position of a country seems, all can fall victim to one factor: power and the associated circumstances of its exercise. Against the power of the continent, the country was forced to retreat.

---

[42] Kathleen Burk, *Britain, America and the Sinews of War, 1914–1918* (London, 1985), 45–48, 208–14 and 223.

*Dominic Lieven*

The aim of this chapter is to study Russian perceptions of Britain in the years before the First World War. Its focus will be on Russian elites – meaning the press, the legislature and naval, diplomatic and political leaders within the government – and it will confine itself to politics rather than to questions of culture. Particularly where policymakers were concerned, it is mistaken to look at their perceptions of Britain as if they were static and independent. On the contrary, context was crucial. This context was sometimes created by Russia's own decisions, such as the shift in foreign policy focus back from East Asia to Europe in 1907. On other occasions it was decisions by other countries that mattered: the Anglo-French *entente cordiale* is an important example. In an international system widely perceived to be dominated by Britain and Germany, Russian perceptions of Britain were often above all else a reflection of Russian views of Germany. About the one point on which all Russian observers agreed in these years was that Britain was of vital importance.

In the long eighteenth century that ended with the overthrow of Napoleon in 1815, Russia usually sided with Britain against France. Britain was Russia's main trading partner. France's clients in eastern Europe – Sweden, Poland and the Ottoman Empire – were Russia's main enemies and the targets of Russian expansion. Many Russian statesmen admired Britain's 'mixed constitution' and its management of public finance and economic development. The first generation of gentry Slavophiles praised England's organic development and the harmonious relationship between state and society, whose leading representatives were the landowning elite. In the nineteenth century, the British peerage was the richest, most powerful, most privileged and most free of all the aristocracies of Europe. Not surprisingly, it was a model that many Russian (and European) aristocracies wished to copy. Sometimes emulation took a political form as Russian aristocrats pressed for civil rights and political representation. On other occasions it was more superficial and sought to emulate British aristocratic fashion. In the 1890s, for example, one of the most exclusive sets in Petersburg high society were the so-called Russian-bred lords whose members prided themselves on even speaking Russian with English accents.[1]

After 1815, however, Britain and Russia were more often rivals than allies. Their competition centred on Asia. Its focus was initially the Ottoman Empire and central Asia, but by the 1890s it had spread to East Asia too. Though the two countries only went to war with each other in 1854–56, they came close to conflict on a number of occasions, and their rivalry was the most constant element in Great Power relations from the 1830s down to the end of the century. In 1900, the Russian Foreign Minister submitted a memorandum to Nicholas II which stated that 'during the last fifty years England has angered almost all the states of continental Europe by its greedy, selfish and egoistical policies. Exploiting its unique position as an island and its pre-eminence as a naval and commercial power, the English have sewn discord and confusion among the peoples of Europe and Asia which they have then used to their own material advantage.' Further confirmation of British intrigue and the damage it caused to Russian interests came with the signing of the Anglo-Japanese alliance in 1902, which was designed to check Russian policy in East Asia. Even nine years later, when tempers had cooled and Anglo-Russian relations had become friendly, a moderate, liberal and relatively anglophile Russian diplomat, Prince Grigorii Trubetskoy, could still write that London had encouraged Japan to attack Russia and was therefore to some extent responsible for the war.[2]

Nevertheless, despite continuing Russian resentment of Britain, by 1900–05 influential voices within the Russian government were beginning to argue for the possibility of détente with London. The instructions issued in 1902 to the newly appointed ambassador in London, Count Alexander Benckendorff, stressed that partly because of the growing

---

[1] On Russian-British relations and Russian attitudes to Britain from 1763 to 1815 see Dominic Lieven, *Russia against Napoleon. The Battle for Europe, 1807 to 1814* (London, 2009), especially chs. 2 and 3. For perspectives on Russian, English and German aristocracy see Dominic Lieven, *The Aristocracy in Europe, 1815–1914* (London, 1992). Specifically on Russian aristocratic constitutionalism see I. A. Khristoforov, '*Aristokraticheskaia' oppozitsiia Velikim reformam* (Moscow, 2002).

[2] The quote is from a memorandum dated 25 January/6 February 1900, in I. S. Rybachenok (ed.), *Korennye interesy Rossii glazami ee gosudarstvennykh deiatelei, diplomatov, voennykh i publitsistov* (Moscow, 2002), no. 22, 251. For Trubetskoy's comment see V. P. Ryabushinsky (ed.), *Velikaia Rossiia* (Moscow, 1911), vol. 1, 67–69. On the Great Game the best work in English remains D. Gillard, *The Struggle for Asia 1828–1914* (London, 1977) but major new monographs by Alexander Morrison and David Schimmelpennig van der Oye should soon be published; in Russian see E. Yu. Sergeev, *Bol'shaia igra 1856–1907* (Moscow, 2012) (translated as *The Great Game, 1856–1907: Russo-British Relations in Central and East Asia* (Washington, DC, and Baltimore, MD, 2013)).

challenge to Britain's global supremacy from Germany and the United States, Russia and Britain shared some common interests and could agree on a number of key issues. One important element in European politics was, for example, that Germany was replacing Britain as the key ally of the Ottoman sultan, a shift that had serious implications for Russian security on the Black Sea and on the empire's Caucasian frontier. A number of diplomatic, military and civilian observers were now arguing that growing German power on land and sea was a more serious threat than Britain to Russian security and vital interests.[3]

The Russo-Japanese war transformed both Russian foreign policy and public opinion in ways very difficult to predict at the war's outset. As the British prime minister, Arthur Balfour, noted on the eve of the war, if, as most people predicted, the war ended in a draw or a limited Russian victory then the threat of Japan's inevitable desire for *revanche* would tie down Russian resources in the East Asian theatre for the foreseeable future, thereby greatly reducing its ability to pursue an active policy in Europe.[4] The British embassy in Saint Petersburg added in retrospect that victory in the war would also probably have legitimized Russian Far Eastern policy in the eyes of much of public opinion.[5] But in a different context, humiliating defeat by Japan might have inspired a Russian desire for revenge. Enmity towards Japan's ally, Britain, might also have increased since London was widely credited in Russia with inciting Japan to war and then acting in a thoroughly un-neutral way during the conflict. Having concluded an entente with Britain on the very eve of the war, France might also have alienated Russian opinion. William II tried hard to exploit these possibilities. He failed partly because Russian public opinion reacted to defeat by blaming the whole Far Eastern fiasco on the autocratic regime. The priority accorded to East Asia by Russian foreign policy in the 1890s had never enjoyed much public support. The abject mismanagement which had resulted first in Russia blundering into the conflict and then in losing the war encouraged public opinion to turn its back on East Asia. Russian nationalists as well as much of the military leadership stressed that the poor performance of Russian reservists during the war showed all the dangers of pursuing a foreign policy which did not enjoy popular support. Those elements in Russian society which had always believed in Russia's mission as the leader of the Slav and

---

[3] Rybachenok (ed.) *Korennye interesy*, 332–57, Instruktsiia MID A.K. Benkendorfu, and N. N. Peshkov, *Rossiia i Germaniia v Turtsii*, 219–49; see also Sergeev, *Bol'shaia igra*, 261 ff.

[4] K. Neilson, *Britain and the Last Tsar: British Policy and Russia, 1894–1917* (Oxford, 1996), 240–44.

[5] 'Annual Report for 1908', The National Archive (TNA), Kew, FO 371/6057.

Orthodox world argued that only a return to this priority would regain public support for Russian foreign policy.[6] Aleksandr Izvolsky, appointed Foreign Minister in April 1906, was personally no great enthusiast for the Slav cause. But he believed strongly that foreign policy needed the backing of public opinion.[7]

The radical shift of Russian public opinion towards Britain had both positive and negative causes. Since Russian public opinion perceived Britain to be the leader of the anti-German camp in European politics as well as the only country sufficiently powerful to counterbalance Germany, pro-British sentiment was to a great degree the result of an outburst of Russian hostility to Germany. But a pro-British foreign policy was also popular for internal political and ideological reasons.

Britain was seen as a strong bulwark of European liberalism and democracy. This perception was strengthened by the Liberal victory in the 1905 election and by Britain's entente with republican France. Alliance with the democratic powers of western Europe against the authoritarian regime in Berlin was seen as a mark of constitutional Russia's coming of age and a pledge that liberal democracy would prevail both in Russia and throughout Europe. The British Foreign Office itself believed that Russian foreign policy was significantly influenced by domestic Russian politics. The return to power of 'reactionaries' might well in London's opinion spell the end of the Anglo-Russian entente. On the other hand, the support for the entente of moderate conservative and liberal opinion was seen as a powerful weapon in Britain's hands. The embassy in Saint Petersburg therefore kept a very careful watch on the Russian press and the parliament. In its opinion, though Britain's popularity waxed and waned on occasion, during the whole period between the signing of the Anglo-Russian convention in 1907 and the outbreak of war in 1914 all the most influential newspapers and the great majority of parties in the Duma fully supported the entente. All historians who subsequently studied Russian public opinion and Duma politics in this era agreed with this conclusion. Less of a consensus exists as regards public opinion's impact on the making of foreign policy, though clearly it was of some significance. My own view is that it is a mistake to make too sharp a distinction between government and public as regards the making of foreign policy. The men who dominated the Foreign Ministry and the Duma shared similar values, assumptions and priorities as regards Russia's place in the world. Prince Grigorii Trubetskoy could act in

---

[6] For further discussion see Dominic Lieven, *Towards the Flame: Empire, War and the End of Tsarist Russia* (London, 2015), 83–90 and 163ff.

[7] Gosudarstvennyi Arkhiv Rossiiskoi Federatsii (GARF), Moscow, Fond 559, Opis 1, Delo 86, ll. 20i–27ii.

1906–12 as a journalist and a key shaper of public opinion, and subsequently take up the crucial position as head of the Near Eastern and Balkan department of the Foreign Ministry.[8]

The strength of Russian public opinion's turn against Germany from 1906 onwards surprised all observers, often embarrassed the Russian government and was carefully monitored by the British embassy. Bernard Pares, who wrote reports for the embassy on Russian public opinion, commented in September 1908 that 'the partial emancipation of the Russian people has been accompanied by a most pronounced and almost universal outburst of feeling against Germans and Germany ... For instance, the "Novoye Vremya", which is an excellent weather-cock, now inserts violent attacks on the Germans, and no paper on the popular side has a word to say for them.' The embassy's Councillor, Hugh O'Beirne, endorsed Pares's view and explained the growth of anti-German feeling as in part simply reflecting the press's greater freedom to express such sentiments long bottled up. But he added that specific recent events had enflamed this feeling: 'Liberal politicians dislike the Germans, because they attribute many of the illiberal acts of the Administration to German influence', and because many of the provincial governors and generals who had repressed the revolution of 1905 and subsequently constrained civil rights bore German names. In addition, 'patriotic Russians of the reactionary type, hold Germany indirectly responsible for Russia's unfortunate adventure in the Far East. They see Germany as thwarting Russian aims in the Balkans, Asia Minor and Persia, and their resentment is embittered by a sense of the military weakness of Russia as compared with her powerful neighbour.' In subsequent years, O'Beirne wrote that although anti-German feeling had subsided somewhat since its highpoints in 1907–08 and after the Bosnian Crisis of 1909:

There are certain abiding causes of ill-feeling in this country towards Germany. Among them are the racial struggle that is proceeding in south-eastern Europe between Slavdom and Germanism: jealousy of the German superiority in culture, energy, and the moral qualities; the industrial intrusion into Russia; the fact that

---

[8] It is impossible to cite all the many reports by the embassy on the pro-British attitude of the press and the Duma parties: every annual report between 1908 and 1914 stressed this point, for example. *Nota bene* the marginal comment by the Foreign Office on a report by Sir Arthur Nicolson in May 1909 that 'the advent of a Reactionary to power must be the end of the entente': Nicolson to Grey, 7 May 1909, TNA, FO 371/730/17375. A good recent work on public opinion and foreign policy is E. G. Kostrikova, *Rossiiskoe obshchestvo i vneshnaia politika nakanune pervoi mirovoi voiny 1908–1914* (Moscow, 2007). Her view on the great influence of public opinion on foreign policy is not shared by Ronald P. Bobroff, *Roads to Glory. Late Imperial Russia and the Turkish Straits* (London, 2006); for my own views on this issue see Lieven, *Towards the Flame*, 128–33 and 178–81.

Germany thwarts Russian policy at various points in the Near and Middle East; and the dominant fact that Germany is a too powerful neighbour who seems occasionally to abuse her strength.[9]

For all his liberal sympathies and his belief that foreign policy needed to enjoy public support, Aleksandr Izvolsky's determination to turn the focus of Russian policy away from East Asia and towards Europe and the Near East owed nothing to a desire to court public opinion, still less to any wish to align Russia in an alliance with Britain against Germany. By far the best evidence of his strategic thinking is a speech he made on 10 February 1907 (Old Style) to the State Defence Council, the body set up in 1905 to coordinate diplomatic, military and naval strategy. His main opponent in the Council was Admiral Fedor Dubasov, who reiterated the principles that had underlain Russia's prioritisation of the East Asian theatre in the decade before the war with Japan. Dubasov argued that Russia's future lay in Siberia and the Pacific region. Its rapidly growing population needed to colonize this huge area and by so doing would guarantee Russia's long-term position as the greatest power in Eurasia. He added that, 'without the Far East Russia cannot exist and develop'. To realize their full potential, however, the Russians needed to industrialize Siberia, open Asian markets for their produce and guarantee access to the Pacific Ocean by building up their naval power. In comparison to these grandiose possibilities, to focus on the Slav cause or the acquisition of the Straits was to lead Russia down a dangerous blind alley. The Germans were already so well entrenched at Constantinople that it would take a full-scale European war to remove them. Nor would access to the Mediterranean do Russia much good. In Dubasov's opinion, Russian leadership of the Slav cause was a chimera: the Slavs themselves would reject this leadership. By pursuing this dream, Russia would involve itself in Balkan and central European quarrels that were far removed from its essential interests.[10]

Izvolsky rejected Dubasov's argument. He stated that for Russia to be a true Pacific power it needed a formidable Pacific fleet, and this was inconceivable in anything but a distant future. The Foreign Minister also rejected the fears expressed not just by Dubasov but also by many of the Council's generals that Japan was preparing to attack Russia. On the contrary, he retorted, the Japanese government was open to a compromise with Russia that would fully guarantee Russia's essential

[9] Memorandum by Bernard Pares, 4 September 1908, TNA, FO 371/532/14254; O'Beirne to Grey, 2 June 1908, FO 371/517/19622; O'Beirne to Grey, 8 September 1910, FO 371/980/32998.

[10] Rossiiskii Gosudarstvennyi Voenno-istoricheskii Arkhiv (RGVIA), Fond 830, Opis 1, Delo 170, ll.7i–7ii.

interests as well as peace in the region for at least the next ten years, and probably for longer. Whereas in East Asia it was within Russia's power to control events if it entered into an agreement with Japan, Izvolsky argued that this was not true either in Europe or in the Near East. This was because of the growing crisis of the Ottoman and Austrian empires, which was the result above all of internal developments though also complicated by geopolitical factors. Russia could neither control events in these empires nor stand aside if the Habsburg and Ottoman empires began to implode, as was likely to happen in the next ten to fifteen years. To fail to participate in the issues which would emerge as these two empires disintegrated would be to reduce Russia to the status of a Persia. Not just were immense Russian interests at stake but so too was her identity as a European great power, with all that meant in terms of the Russian elites' pride in their country's status and its place in history. Izvolsky explicitly linked Russian foreign policy to deeper issues of Russian identity. The Russians were a European people, he said. If Russia wished to prioritize its position as a Pacific power, then it should start by moving its capital to Tomsk or Chelyabinsk.[11]

In his speech to the State Defence Council, Izvolsky noted that better relations with Britain were very useful as regards restraining Japan and achieving an acceptable compromise with Tokyo. But his policy rested on his belief that he could end Russia's traditional conflict with Britain in Asia without alienating the Germans. Given current Russian weakness, he fully understood that angering Berlin would be extremely dangerous. In 1906–08 he therefore invested great effort in trying to assure the Germans that the agreement with Britain would not in any way infringe German interests outside Europe, let alone mean that Russia was joining an anti-German alliance within the European continent. Even at the time many commentators doubted Izvolsky's chances of success, given the extreme rivalry of Britain and Germany in these years and given Berlin's acute fears of a British-led policy of encirclement. In any case, by shifting the focus of Russian foreign policy from Asia to Europe, the Foreign Minister was prioritising areas where Germany and Austria were Russia's main rivals. In retrospect, Izvolsky acknowledged implicitly that his critics had been correct. In August 1911 he wrote to the Premier, Petr Stolypin, that in 1906–08 Russia really only had two options given the international context at that time and the mood that prevailed in Berlin. Either Russia could accept William II's pressure to rejoin the old *Dreikaiserbund* (the German–Austrian–Russian 'Three Emperors' Alliance') or it could stick to its existing alliance with

---

[11] RGVIA, Fond 830, Opis 1, Delo 170, ll.2i–8ii.

France. But Russia, especially in its current weakened state, must inevitably be the junior partner in any alliance with the two Germanic empires and would thereby forfeit its position as a truly Great Power able to pursue its own independent goals. Once Russia chose the alternative option, however, and held to the French alliance there was little choice but to draw closer to France's ally, Britain, as well. While on the one hand this created an unavoidable danger of war, if Germany decided to pursue a policy of expansion, on the other hand the Franco–British–Russian entente did represent a formidable deterrent power which could only grow as Russia regained its strength.[12]

The fundamental shift in international alignments that Izvolsky's policy represented was reflected perfectly in the thinking of Russia's naval leadership in the years between 1900 and 1914. Ever since the 1830s the navy had been at the cutting edge of Russia's rivalry with Britain, with all this implied given the greatly superior power of the British fleet. In 1900 the Naval Minister, Vice Admiral Pavel Tyrtov, wrote that on any international issue 'we can always be confident of finding England among the ranks of our enemies' and 'therefore any measure that leads to England's weakening in any way is of direct benefit to Russia'. In October 1906 the chief of the Naval General Staff, Captain Brusilov, wrote that Germany, Britain and Britain's ally, Japan, were all dangerous potential enemies of Russia. On the rare occasions in the past when Russia had aligned itself with Britain the latter had been the main beneficiary. This had, for instance, been the case with the destruction of Napoleon, which had opened the way to British global supremacy. At the time, European politics was dominated by acute Anglo-German naval and commercial rivalry. 'England now seeks an agreement with us, and maybe even an alliance. Its goal is to worsen our relations with Germany and to drag us into a war that will at the same time finally destroy our power on land and will weaken its rival, Germany, at sea.' Russia must avoid British enticement and stay out of the struggle, while leaning in Germany's direction. Thankfully, so long as Russia behaved with caution, 'the time for the final settling of accounts of the Slav world with Germany is still far away'. Meanwhile, even Saint Petersburg, let alone the western Russian borderlands were acutely vulnerable. Therefore 'it is in our interest ... to direct all our efforts towards maintaining the best relations with Germany, to strengthening our western front, and to sharpening tensions between Germany and England. We are being offered a rare

---

[12] Alexandre Iswolsky, *Au Service de la Russie: Correspondence Diplomatique* (2 vols., Paris, 1937–39), vol. 2, Addenda, No. III, Izvolsky to Stolypin, 21 July/3 August 1911, 299–304.

occasion when a very powerful country is aiming and preparing for war with England and we must do everything to encourage this.'[13]

Even when Brusilov wrote these words there were influential voices in the navy arguing that Germany was now a more dangerous threat than Britain to Russia's vital interests. After 1909 this view dominated the navy. To some extent this merely reflected the fact that naval leaders were aligning themselves with the state's foreign policy and seeking to maximize the budgetary benefits that the navy could derive from so doing. But there is good reason to believe that the naval leadership was wholly sincere in the arguments it advanced for a pro-British orientation. Their most complete expression came in a memorandum written in January 1912 by the new chief of the Naval General Staff, Vice Admiral Prince Alexander Lieven. Like almost all naval officers and most Russian observers of international relations, he saw Anglo-German rivalry as the key to European politics. Drawing on history, and especially on Alfred Mahan, Lieven believed that he was witnessing a new phase in the long naval struggle to control Europe's Atlantic trade routes. An Anglo-German war would be the inevitable result since neither Britain nor Germany could allow its rival to control the vital arteries on which its economic survival depended.

Lieven argued that Russia must take Britain's side in this struggle. In tactical and operational terms this was essential to draw most of Germany's navy out of the Baltic, and thereby avoid the danger of amphibious assaults on Russia's coastline and, above all, on Saint Petersburg. Far more important was the strategic perspective. Historically, Britain had played the key role in stopping any European land power from controlling the Straits and the Sound, which were Russian trade's two openings to the oceans. British naval power had in general served British commercial interests rather than any geopolitical goal. But if Germany triumphed over Britain, 'a completely different picture will emerge'. Should Germany succeed in excluding English influence from the issue of Central Europe's communications with the oceans, then 'having freed itself from all constraints on its economic development, it will achieve political hegemony in Europe and will surround us by a united ring of its power from the North Cape to Asia Minor. Already today Sweden, Austria and in part Turkey are under German influence.' As a result, 'it would depend on the goodwill of the German

[13] Tyrtov's statement is in *Korennye interesy*, no. 22.2, P. P. Tyrtov to M. N. Muravev, 14/27 February 1900, 272–76. Brusilov's comments are from a long report to Nicholas II on the state of the navy, dated 2 October 1906 (OS): Rossiiskyi Gosudarstvennyi Arkhiv Voenno-Morskogo Flota (RGAVMF), Fond 418, Opis 1, Delo 238, ll.24–48: the quotations are from ll.31–35.

Emperor whether to let us exist in our present state or to push us back from the coasts of the Baltic and Black seas into the depths of our steppe, where for us would begin a new era of life in the wild apart from civilisation that could last for centuries'.[14]

As one would expect of an aristocratic naval officer, Lieven's arguments were rooted purely in geopolitics with no shade of the ideological commitment to the Anglo-French *entente* that animated much of Russian public opinion. Indeed, his memorandum made clear his view that Germany's political system was superior to that of France. There was of course some irony in the strong commitment to the entente of a representative of one of the leading Baltic German aristocratic families who had himself been educated at the Royal Cadet Corps in Berlin and who had served as a page of the Bedchamber to the Queen-Empress Augusta of Prussia-Germany, the wife of William I. But the fact that a man of Lieven's background and views should nevertheless be a powerful advocate of friendship with Britain shows just how broad was the consensus behind Russia's foreign policy by 1914.

Military and naval officers tended towards a Darwinian view of international relations without ever necessarily having read a word written by Darwin. They assumed war's inevitability and focused on how to achieve victory. Civilian ministers were much more pacific, and in general Russian Finance Ministers were the most pacific of all. This was certainly true of Vladimir Kokovtsov, who served as Finance Minister from 1906 to 1914, simultaneously holding the position of Chairman of the Council of Ministers after Petr Stolypin's assassination in 1911. Kokovtsov's aversion to war went beyond the normal Finance Minister's concern to contain expenditure and concentrate resources on economic development. On the one hand, he shared Petr Stolypin's fear that war in the next decade would lead to revolution: on the other, he believed that the future belonged to Russia if only peace was maintained and she was able to sustain the current very rapid growth of her economy.[15]

Sir Arthur Nicolson, the British ambassador, first recorded a confidential conversation with Kokovtsov in the aftermath of the Bosnian Crisis. While considering the public attacks on Izvolsky to be unjust, Kokovtsov did admit that the Foreign Minister had been incautious in committing himself to a secret deal with Aehrenthal. 'By placing Russia in the forefront, M. Isvolsky had almost inevitably exposed himself

[14] RGAVMF, Fond 418, Opis 1, Delo 1289, ll.338–54. There is a copy of this memo in Arkhiv Vneshnei Politiki Rossiiskoi Imperii (AVPRI), Fond 138, Opis 467, Ed. Khr. 303/306, ll.17ff. See also the memorandum of Rear Admiral Count Heiden, *Korennye interesy*, A. F. Heiden, *Kakoi flot nuzhen Rossii?*, 383–422.

[15] This summarizes my discussion of Kokovtsov's views in *Towards the Flame*, 112–15.

to a diplomatic check.' Having discovered Aehrenthal's intentions, in Kokovtsov's opinion Izvolsky should have informed Britain and France and allowed them to take the lead since they too were the 'guardians of international treaties'. Kokovtsov added that although the German intervention in March 1909 could not be called an ultimatum, it did warn in sharp terms that unless Russia accepted the annexation Austria would almost certainly invade Serbia. But Kokovtsov added that the press greatly exaggerated the seriousness of Russia's defeat since Austria had alienated public opinion in the Balkans and 'had paid very heavily for what she had gained'. In reality, said Kokovtsov, it was 'absurd' for public opinion to argue that Russia had lost her position in Balkan affairs. But William II's response to the Tsar's request to moderate Austrian behaviour had not been 'very friendly', and the result of the crisis 'has certainly not been to improve the relations of Russia with Austria-Hungary, or indeed with Germany'. Vladimir Kokovtsov commented to Nicolson that he personally was very pro-British and that 'it was very necessary to maintain the Triple Entente'.[16]

While speaking in these terms in private to the British ambassador, in public Kokovtsov played a leading role in the government's push to defuse tensions with Germany and thereby reduce the danger of war. In August 1909, two months after his conversation with Nicolson, Kokovtsov gave an interview to the press about Anglo-Russian relations. The Finance Minister warmly endorsed the Anglo-Russian convention and cited the Russo-Japanese war as an example of the dangers Russia faced when relations with Britain were bad. He stressed too how much British capital could serve both its and Russia's interests by investing in the development of Siberia, and specifically in Russian railways. The challenge of developing Russia's huge potential resources was immense but exciting, remarked Kokovtsov, adding that 'we are now to do in a brief period what others have done gradually in centuries'. But the Finance Minister went out of his way to stress that it would be 'a very serious and a very foolish mistake' to imagine that better relations with Britain meant worse relations with any other country:

England, of course, can never be to us what Germany is; a glance at the map will show you why. England is too far away, and our land-frontiers with Germany are extensive. We cannot forget either the centuries past of friendship with Germany, and that we, equally with that country, have the greatest interest in maintaining the best and most sincere relations with our nearest neighbour.

[16] Nicolson to Grey, 1 May 1909, TNA, FO 371/729/1751; for Nicolson's views of Russia see the important analysis by Keith Neilson, '"My Beloved Russians": Sir Arthur Nicolson and Russia, 1906-1916', *International History Review* 9(4) (1987), 521–54.

Kokovtsov concluded the interview by claiming that Russia's circumstances made it the most pacific of all the great powers:

We have in Russia territory enough still to explore, we have still more that is unexploited, and we have problems enough on our hands for the development of this country and the reorganisation of our social structure under the new conditions without seeking any kind of forward policy for a great many years to come, if ever. Consolidation and not expansion is the key to our historical problem.[17]

At the time when Kokovtsov succeeded Stolypin as Premier in September 1911 the Foreign Minister, Serge Sazonov, was seriously ill and foreign policy was being directed by the deputy minister, Anatolii Neratov. The British embassy commented that neither Kokovtsov nor Neratov seemed to have a clear grasp of foreign policy and tended to handle issues in isolation as they arose. In one crucial respect, however, Sazonov's return to the Foreign Ministry did not improve matters since it was under his watch that Russia helped to arrange the Serb-Bulgarian alliance, in the process making a fateful contribution to Europe's slide towards the disaster of 1914. It was perhaps understandable that Kokovtsov, lacking any experience of Balkan affairs, accepted Sazonov's assurances about the alliance and reassured foreign diplomats that 'Bulgaria would never move without Russia's permission and that the Emperor was far too prudent to allow her to embark on a policy of adventure'.[18]

The outbreak of the First Balkan War in September 1912 came as a rude shock, and for the next year Kokovtsov gave crucial support to Sazonov in restraining Nicholas II, the military leadership and even the other civilian ministers from taking any measures that might exacerbate tensions with Vienna and risk precipitating a war. Uncertainty about British and French support contributed to their caution but so too did military unpreparedness and fears of internal unrest.[19] When the Liman von Sanders crisis erupted in the winter of 1913–14, Kokovtsov and Sazonov's positions began to diverge, with the former showing more understanding for German policy and greater aversion to any risk of war. Kokovtsov's more cautious line was in fact closer to that both of the British and French governments, and of Alexander Benckendorff, Russia's ambassador in London. Throughout 1912 and 1913 the German and Austrian ambassadors in Petersburg found Kokovtsov

---

[17] O'Beirne to Grey, 12 August 1909, TNA, FO 371/726/30738.

[18] 'Annual Report for 1911', BNA, FO 371/1468; Buchanan to Grey, 18 July 1912, FO 371/1470/31867; 'Annual Report for 1912', FO 371/1743/10175.

[19] See in particular the record of crucial meetings of the Council of Ministers to discuss military measures in December 1912: AVPRI, Fond 133, Opis 470, Delo 218, ll.2ff.

a constant voice of moderation, compromise and calm, the latter a particularly useful attribute given Sazonov's tendency to excitement. But Kokovtsov's commitment to the Triple Entente never wavered even though he was often very frustrated by what he saw as Britain's unrealistic enthusiasm for the constitutionalist cause in Persia, which the Premier believed to be a source of anarchy and a threat both to Russian trade and to the security of Russia's own Transcaucasian region. Kokovtsov told the British ambassador in May 1913 that although increased German military expenditure was a worry, he could not believe that Berlin would run the risks that war would entail for her economy and finances. But, he added, 'the one consideration which must give her pause' would be 'the fear of what England would do, for if she knew that England would in such case make common cause with France and Russia, Germany would never go to war'. To this statement Sir George Buchanan could only make the usual unsatisfactory and indeed frightening reply that 'England's participation in such a war would depend entirely on the circumstances which had brought it about, and the view taken of it by British public opinion'.[20]

As regards Britain's decisive role as a deterrent to German adventurism, Kokovtsov and Sazonov were in complete agreement. Aleksandr Izvolsky had chosen and groomed Sazonov to be his successor precisely because he knew that Sazonov shared his views on Russian foreign policy. Among the Russian ambassadors, Izvolsky's closest confidant was Alexander Benckendorff, who once described himself to Izvolsky as 'one of your oldest colleagues and friends'. The two men discussed in strict confidence how to ensure that the pro-entente policy to which they were both committed could best be guaranteed after Izvolsky retired as Foreign Minister. Serge Sazonov emerged as the best solution to this dilemma. Sazonov had served under both Benckendorff and Izvolsky, who trusted him and knew well his views on policy. With Sazonov as minister both ambassadors could be sure that their former subordinate would continue their policy line and lend a respectful ear to their advice.[21]

Sazonov was as complete an anglophile as Benckendorff. In his memoirs he wrote that 'I always felt that if there were two countries in the world

---

[20] Buchanan to Grey, 15 May 1913, TNA, FO 371/1745/22759. In September 1913, for example, after relating a particularly striking example of Kokovtsov's friendly moderation, the Austrian charge in Petersburg noted that the Germans also saw Kokovtsov as a patient and cautious man of finance 'who has no time for chauvinist adventures', Czernin to Berchtold, 30 August/12 September 1913, L. Bittner and H. Uebersberger (eds.), *Österreich-Ungarns Aussenpolitik von der Bosnischen Krise 1908 bis zum Kriegsaufbruch 1914* (8 vols., Vienna, 1930), vol. VII, no. 8614.

[21] Benckendorff to Izvolsky, 9/22 January 1908, and 20 July/2 August 1910, in Iswolsky, Au Service, vol. 2, no. 1, 117–20, and no.11, 287–89.

which nature itself intended for peaceful coexistence and collaboration, it was Russia and England.' In February 1908, Benckendorff had written to Izvolsky that Germany did not fear either Russia or France, but she did fear Britain, above all because conflict with the United Kingdom would rob Germany of her trade and overseas assets. On this point too Sazonov was in full agreement. In the winter of 1913–14 he stated that whereas Germany could shrug off the Russo-French threat, 'a war in which Britain was involved could prove fatal for Germany, which clearly recognizes the danger in that event of being reduced to total internal social catastrophe within six weeks'. Sazonov's views in this matter were almost certainly drawn from Ivan Bloch's work on the consequences of a future European war and in retrospect seem fanciful. To do the Foreign Minister justice, the British government did in fact have well-laid plans for undermining the German economy in precisely this time span but abandoned them in August 1914 for fear of wrecking Britain's own economy and alienating the United States.[22]

Most Russian observers agreed that Anglo-German rivalry was the single most important element in current international relations and that Britain was a country of immense and potentially decisive power. When asked by Petersburg in October 1909 about Italian views on any future Russian acquisition of the Straits, the ambassador in Rome, Prince Nicholas Dolgoruky, replied that the first instinct of Italian policymakers on all such questions was to discover London's opinion: 'I often hear in the course of conversations that if England agrees then the success of a given matter can be regarded as guaranteed ... the key to the Straits lies ... in the hands of the cabinet of Saint James.' Equally, the Russian military attaché in Berlin, Colonel Aleksandr Mikhelson, concluded an exceptionally well-informed report on German preparedness for war during the Bosnian crisis by emphasising 'England's decisive position' in international politics: Germany in his opinion was fully prepared for war and good political reasons existed for seizing the present opportunity to crush Russia and France. But unless convinced of British neutrality, 'Germany will sit quietly and will not dare to attack anyone on the continent'. In November 1912, Mikhelson's successor, Colonel Pavel Bazarov, noted that 'if on the one side the Germans believe that they can count on victory for the Triple Alliance (with Romania) in a war against Russia and France, on the contrary the possibility of

[22] S. D. Sazonov, *Vospominaniia* (Moscow, 1991), 24; Benckendorff to Izvolsky, 23 January/5 February 1908, Iswolsky, *Au Service*, vol. 2, 120–24; 'Tri soveshchaniia', *Vestnik N.K.I.D.*, 1919, 30; N. A. Lambert, *Planning Armageddon: British Economic Warfare and the First World War* (Cambridge, MA, 2012).

a simultaneous war with England inspires great fear in Germany and at the present moment is the best guarantee of peace'.[23]

Even supporters of the pro-entente line sometimes feared that Britain's support could not be relied on if a crisis came. The lack of firm guarantees set out in a formal alliance played to such fears. But they were also rooted in instinctive and historically rooted suspicions of 'perfidious Albion'. Of course, these suspicions were even stronger among Russians whose attitude to Russia's entente with Britain was more cautious. The Russian ambassador in Berlin, Count Nicholas von der Osten-Sacken, was no apologist for Germany and provided balanced reports on the factors that inspired Berlin's irrational and sometimes even hysterical attitude to Britain's perceived policy of encirclement. But he noted that Britain's extremely Machiavellian history of using and then abandoning continental allies in order to undermine the United Kingdom's rivals did provide some justification for German fears.

Inevitably, outright enemies of the Triple Entente were even more inclined to stress this point. In his famous memorandum to Nicholas II, Petr Durnovo wrote in February 1914 that, given the opportunity, Britain would use Russia to destroy Germany, would do little of the fighting in any future European war and would turn against Russia once victory had been achieved and its German rival disposed of. As with most of the so-called pro-Germans, Durnovo's memorandum also reflected his conservatism: in his view, even victory over Germany in alliance with the Western democracies would be counterproductive since it would encourage liberal and democratic currents in Russia whose triumph must result in the disintegration of the multinational empire and the destruction of the property-owning classes. Opposition to the Triple Entente was not, however, confined to conservatives. Among Russian diplomats Baron Roman Rosen provided the most impressive critique of the policy pursued after 1906. But Rosen was a liberal-conservative and a supporter of the new constitutional order. Though he shared Durnovo's acute fear of social revolution in the event of a European war, the main thrust of his argument was that for Russia the Asia-Pacific region was far more important than the Balkans and the Straits. German hegemony in western and central Europe was no threat to Russia's essential interests, so long as the latter were understood in a rational, sober and minimalist fashion. Moreover, in Rosen's views, Russians had to raise their eyes from the European to the global level if they were to be a Great Power in the

---

[23] Dolgoruky to Izvolsky, 29 September/12 October 1909, AVPRI, Fond 138, Opis 467, Delo 287/289, l.41i–41ii; Report of Military Attaché to Count Osten-Sacken AVPRI, Fond 138, Opis 467, Delo 280/282, ll.4ff, quotes in conclusions ll.10i–13ii; Bazarov to General Staff, 21 November 1912, RGVIA, Fond 2000, Opis 1, Delo 7255, ll.136.

twentieth century. By so doing they could see that the Anglo-Saxons were the true global powers, and that Germany's challenge to their supremacy could suit Russian interests.[24]

By 1913–14, worry and frustration marked Russian policymakers' view of Britain. In part this reflected signs of Anglo-German rapprochement. By 1913, Britain had won the naval arms race even if domestic political considerations made it impossible for Berlin to accept this publicly. Already in April 1908 Benckendorff had warned that financial pressures might well make naval competition unsustainable for Germany.[25] In February 1912, the Russian naval attaché reported a remarkable discussion with his British equivalent, Captain Watson. The latter had said that by the end of 1913 so many new British warships would be in commission and German finances would be so overstretched that it would be obvious to all rational Germans that the naval competition with Britain was pointless. Typically, the Russian officer's reaction was to suspect British skulduggery in stirring up German fears of Russia and thereby diverting German expenditure towards the army.[26]

In 1913, the British and Germans had at last come to an agreement on the Baghdad railway and a de facto demarcation of respective spheres of interest in Asia Minor and the Gulf. In the wake of the Balkan wars, German officers were rebuilding the Turkish army while British ones were performing the same task for the Turkish navy. Britain and Germany agreed on the need to prolong the life of the Ottoman Empire. Serge Sverbeev, Osten-Sacken's replacement in Berlin, reported frequently in 1912–13 on German belief that their relations with Britain were greatly improved. He added that a future Anglo-German entente could not be ruled out and rejoiced in the fact that Nicholas II had agreed to attend the marriage of William II's daughter. Had George V alone attended, in Sverbeev's view it would have been dangerous both in symbolic terms and because of the private conversations he might have with German leaders.[27]

Sazonov shared Sverbeev's fears that improving relations between Britain and Germany might in time evolve into an entente. His worries

[24] On Osten-Sacken, Durnovo and Rosen see Lieven, *Towards the Flame*, 133–39, 227–29, and 303–07.

[25] Benckendorff to Izvolsky, 16/29 April 1908, Iswolsky, Au Service, vol. 2, no. 14, 155–58.

[26] Lieven to Zhilinsky, enclosing a report by naval attaché in Berlin: 31 January/13 February 1913, RGVIA, Fond 2000, Opis 1, Delo 7255, ll.74i–80ii.

[27] It is not possible to cite all of Sverbeev's despatches: see e.g. Sverbeev to Sazonov, 1/14 March 1913, AVPRI, Fond 133, Opis 470, delo 215, l.38; Sverbeev telegrams, 25/7 April 1913, ll. 52, 55; Sverbeev to Sazonov, 11/24 December 1913, Opis 470, delo 23, l.5. On Anglo-German cooperation in the Ottoman Empire see G. Schöllgen, *Imperialismus und Gleichgewicht: Deutschland, England, und die orientalische Frage* (Munich, 2000), 399–416.

were stoked by a renewal of Anglo-Russian conflict over Persia. Four days before the assassination of Archduke Franz Ferdinand, Sazonov wrote in exasperation to Benckendorff that good relations with Britain 'had always been his dominant political preoccupation'. For this overriding goal he had sacrificed some Russian smaller interests in Persia. But Sazonov viewed British complaints about Russian military intervention in northern Persia as both unrealistic and hypocritical. Faced by the anarchy that was wrecking Russian trade and endangering stability in neighbouring Russian Azerbaijan, how else was Russia to act? The Persian constitutionalists so beloved of British public opinion had shown themselves incapable of preserving even basic order, let alone governing effectively. Sazonov asked Benckendorff to remind the British at a suitable moment that they had de facto annexed a vast swathe of territory around the Indian Ocean and the Persian Gulf in order to protect the approaches to their Indian empire. The native peoples of these areas enjoyed neither autonomy nor representative institutions.[28]

The core of Sazonov's discontent with Britain concerned disagreement on how to deter Germany. In February 1914, he wrote to Benckendorff that 'the peace of the world will not be secure until the day when the Triple Entente – whose real existence is no more proven than that of the sea monster – is transformed into a defensive alliance without secret clauses and made public in all the newspapers of the world. On that day the danger of German hegemony will be removed definitively and each of us can get on with our business in peace and quiet', which in the Russian case meant to 'secure internal unity (*nous consolider*) and to work on our economic transformation'.

Sazonov's frustration with the English was not improved by his conviction that, should war come, England would be dragged into the conflict willy-nilly. But although Benckendorff shared Sazonov's commitment to a policy of deterring Germany as the likeliest way to avoid war, in other respects his replies gave little comfort to the Foreign Minister. As regards transforming the Triple Entente into an effective alliance, he reported, 'the difficulty is immense'. Some British diplomats, and in particular the three last ambassadors in Russia, Hardinge, Nicolson and Buchanan, supported this policy, as did many generals and admirals. But in political terms the problems stretched well beyond opposition to tsarism in the Liberal Party or the present obsession with the affairs of Ireland. Fundamental were the public's 'terrible spirit of insularity', its naivety about European geopolitics and its unwillingness to think deeply about international relations until

---

[28] Sazonov to Benckendorff, 24/11 June 1914, *Mezhdunarodnye otnosheniia v epokhu imperializma* (MOEI), Series III, vol. 3, no. 343, 394–96.

a crisis exploded under its nose. In a subsequent private letter Benckendorff told Sazonov that Sir Arthur Nicolson had recently spoken to Lord Curzon, the likeliest Foreign Minister in a future Conservative government, about the need to turn the Triple Entente into an open alliance: 'Lord Curzon is said to have replied that on this point too he shared his [Nicolson's] position. But he added that he could not see how a Minister of Foreign Affairs could approach parliament with a treaty of alliance with a continental power in his pocket'.[29]

Serge Sazonov's protestations about the completely pacific nature of Russian policy were true in the short run. But Russia's wooing of Serbia and Romania posed a serious longer-term threat to Austria's existence, though perhaps the same might be said of Vienna's use of the Ukrainian and Polish cards against Russia. For those who feared future Russian ambitions at Constantinople, the presence at Sazonov's side of Prince Grigorii Trubetskoy was not comforting. Nevertheless, with the advantage of hindsight Sazonov's frustration with Britain seems reasonable to me. The Russian belief that for the present Germany feared Britain far more than France or Russia is borne out by German sources. Sazonov's prediction that Britain would be pulled into a war willy-nilly also proved true. Sazonov himself wrote subsequently that if Sir Edward Grey had made an unequivocal declaration of support for France and Russia at the outset of the July Crisis, then war would have been avoided. Perhaps this is the case, but British political realities made such a statement in defence of tsarist Russia on an issue arising in eastern Europe very difficult. Certainly, if Britain had signed a defensive military alliance with France and Russia previously and had put teeth into its commitment to Franco-Belgian independence by creating an army large enough to make a decisive impact in a future conflict, then events would have taken a different course. But in terms of British political realities in the early twentieth century this was to ask for the moon. If Britain did share some responsibility for the coming of war in 1914, then the culprit was not Edward Grey but the British people and the history and geography that had shaped their understanding of international relations and European realities.[30]

---

[29] Sazonov to Benckendorff, 8/9 February 1914, AVPRI, Fond 138, Opis 467, delo 235/236, ll.7–8; Benckendorff to Sazonov, 12/25 February 1914, ibid., ll.9–14, is the ambassador's official response and ll.19ff a subsequent follow-up and private letter.

[30] Not, of course, a very politically correct conclusion, but see Lieven, *Towards the Flame*, 298–302, 317, 332 and 337–42 for a broader discussion. For an Austrian view on Trubetskoy see Thurn to Berchtold, 13/26 April 1913, ÖUA, vol. 6, no. 6782; Sazonov, *Vospominaniia*, 45–46.

# 7    Imperial Germany's Naval Challenge and the Renewal of British Power

*John H. Maurer*

## I

Great Britain stood as the world's leading sea power at the beginning of the twentieth century. The British Empire stretched around the globe, the homeland, dominions, and colonies linked together by a vast network of finance, trade, communications, and naval power. Britain's leading role on the world stage, however, was threatened by rival Great Powers growing in industrial and naval strength. Defending against these rivals confronted British leaders with a daunting strategic problem. The famed scholar, academic leader, and policy commentator Sir Halford Mackinder asserted: 'At this moment all the great Powers are building fleets.' He warned: 'Nature is ruthless, and we must build a Power able to contend on equal terms with other Powers, or step into the rank of the States which exist on sufferance.'[1] Gerard Fiennes, a well-informed journalist covering naval affairs, echoed Mackinder's warning: 'the task before the [British] Empire is colossal. We, with about fifty-seven millions of white men, have to impose our peace on sixty-three millions of Germans, forty-five millions of Japanese, and a hundred million Americans, not to mention other Powers.'[2] The 'rise of the rest' during the first half of the twentieth century entrapped Britain in an intense struggle for naval mastery.[3]

The tale of Britain's search for naval security during the first half of the twentieth century has long fascinated historians, political scientists, foreign policy analysts, and opinion writers.[4] Was Britain facing inevitable

---

[1] H. J. Mackinder, 'Man-Power as a Measure of National and Imperial Strength', *National Review* 45(265) (1905), 139 and 143.
[2] Gerard Fiennes, *The Ocean Empire: Its Dangers and Defence* (London, n.d. (1911)), 159.
[3] I draw upon the language used by Fareed Zakaria, *The Post-American World* (New York, 2008).
[4] Corelli Barnett, *The Collapse of British Power* (New York, 1972); Paul Kennedy, *The Rise and Fall of the Great Powers* (New York, 1987); Paul Kennedy, *The Rise and Fall of British*

decline because it could not keep pace with rising Great Power challengers? Did British leaders assess accurately the driving forces transforming the international security environment, which brought increased danger to their country? Could Britain's leaders have staved off the collapse of British power by pursuing alternative courses of action in their foreign, defence, and economic policies? These questions have shaped and spurred debate among scholars who examine the British Empire's strategic predicament during this hideous age of hegemonic wars, when Britain slipped from the first rank of the Great Powers.

Keith Neilson weighed into this debate with gusto, making a valuable contribution to the international history of this era, arguing against the view that Britain was an enfeebled 'weary titan', inevitably doomed to decline and fall. In a provocative article on the myth of the Decline of Great Britain before 1914, he argued that the British Empire more than held its own in the intense international competition among the Great Powers.[5] He highlighted the importance of naval strength as a leading indicator of Britain's standing within the international system. By staying ahead of naval rivals, Britain secured its command of the sea and position as a world power.

This chapter will elaborate on Neilson's argument by examining British decisions and efforts to meet the growing naval threat from Imperial Germany. In 1908–09, Britain's leaders and the public received a rude shock when intelligence revealed that Germany was ready and able to build the latest generation of naval weaponry, challenging British dominance of the maritime commons. Britons, accustomed to thinking that their country ruled the waves, grew alarmed that Germany stood poised to overturn their naval lead. A public outcry and shrill partisan political posturing drove a heated debate over national security. Popular passion combined with faulty intelligence about German warship construction pushed a reluctant Liberal government into undertaking an extraordinary shipbuilding effort to stay ahead of Germany. The Conservative opposition, in a noisy public campaign, demanded nothing less than the start of eight large capital ships – battleships and battle cruisers – in a single year, or twice the number considered necessary by prominent Liberal leaders and their party rank and file. The battle cry of the Conservatives became

*Naval Mastery* (New York, 1976); Aaron L. Friedberg, *The Weary Titan: Britain and the Experience of Relative Decline, 1895–1905* (Princeton, 1988).

[5] Keith Neilson, '"Greatly Exaggerated": The Myth of the Decline of Great Britain before 1914', *The International History Review* 13(4) (November 1991), 661–880; also Keith Neilson, '"The Empire Floats on the British Navy": British Naval Policy, Belligerent Rights, and Disarmament, 1902–1909', in B. J. C. McKercher (ed.), *Arms Limitation and Disarmament: Restraints on War, 1899–1939* (Westport, CT, 1992), 21–41.

famous: 'We want eight, and we won't wait!'[6] To allay public fears, to confound the Conservative opposition, and to meet Germany's naval challenge, the Liberal government caved and sanctioned the start of the eight capital ships.

The political uproar in Britain showed there could no longer be any disguising that Europe's two leading Great Powers were vying against each other in an intense head-to-head struggle for naval dominance and command of the seas. Britain's Foreign Secretary Sir Edward Grey told the German ambassador: 'the whole world was now watching the rivalry between German and English shipbuilding'.[7] Across the Atlantic, the famous naval historian, strategic analyst, and public commentator on international relations, Alfred Thayer Mahan drew attention to the significance of the competition between Britain and Germany. Mahan told his readers: 'The rivalry between Germany and Great Britain today is the danger point, not only of European politics, but of world politics as well ... No such emphasized industrial and maritime competition between two communities has arisen since the time of Cromwell and the later Stewart kings, when England wrested from Holland her long possessed commercial supremacy, supported by a navy until then unconquered.'[8] The naval race also provoked the policy activist Norman Angell to write 'at a time of panic' his famous tract *The Great Illusion*, which begins with the ominous sentence: 'It is pretty generally admitted that the present rivalry in armaments with Germany cannot go on in its present form indefinitely.'[9] Assessing Britain's response to Germany's naval buildup thus contributes to the ongoing debate among scholars, in which Keith Neilson took so vigorous a part, over whether this era witnessed a decline or renewal of British power.

## II

Of the Great Powers challenging Britain's leadership at sea after the turn of the twentieth century, Germany posed the most immediate and serious threat. A new generation of German leaders dreamed of their country taking a larger role in international affairs, becoming a world power. Kaiser Wilhelm II championed this effort to transform the German

---

[6] This slogan is attributed to the Conservative Member of Parliament George Wyndham, see Arthur J. Marder, *From the Dreadnought to Scapa Flow*, vol. 1: *The Road to War, 1904–1914* (London, 1961), 167.

[7] Grey to Count de Salis, 18 December 1908, CAB 37/98, The National Archives (TNA).

[8] A. T. Mahan, *The Interest of America in International Conditions* (Boston, repr. 1918), 163–64. This book first appeared in 1910.

[9] Norman Angell, *The Great Illusion: A Study of the Relation of Military Power in Nations to their Economic and Social Advantage* (London, 1910), 3.

Empire from a European continental state into a global sea power. While the barriers to entry in mounting a challenge to Britain at sea were high, Germany's growing industry and technological prowess provided the wherewithal to compete. Theobald von Bethmann Hollweg, Germany's chancellor at the war's outbreak, told a confidante: '[The Kaiser's] first and basic idea is to break Britain's world position in favor of Germany; for this, a fleet is required ... . [The Kaiser's grandfather] founded the German empire with the army, he will establish Germany as a commercial and colonial power with the fleet.'[10] Wilhelm enthusiastically led the charge in making public appeals for building a powerful German navy. The eminent historian Friedrich Meinecke paid tribute to Wilhelm as the *Flottenkaiser*. The Kaiser, Meinecke intoned, 'ceaselessly converted the nation and enticed it out onto the water ... [and] he has the satisfaction of knowing that his conviction has become the conviction of the nation'.[11] Where the Kaiser led, the German government and people followed.

To serve as architect of Germany's naval buildup, the Kaiser picked Admiral Alfred Tirpitz as his navy secretary in 1897. Tirpitz was an ambitious, forceful character, politically savvy in domestic, bureaucratic, and interagency politics. His views were those of a nationalist extremist, stridently anti-British in outlook, believing that Britain stood as the principal obstacle to the emergence of Germany as a world power. When Colonel Edward House, President Woodrow Wilson's political confidant, met Tirpitz in Berlin before the war, he recorded in his diary that the German Navy Secretary 'evidenced a decided dislike for the British, a dislike that almost amounted to hatred'.[12] Tirpitz maintained: 'There was no way to the position of world-power than by building a fleet.'[13] Christopher Clark nicely summarizes the strategic objective of the German naval buildup: 'Tirpitz's Imperial Naval Office installed a massive long-term construction programme that would dominate German defence expenditure until 1912. Its ultimate objective was to enable Germany to confront the British navy on equal terms.'[14] Two navy laws put forward by the Kaiser's government, subsequently adopted by the Reichstag in 1898 and 1900, provided the legal basis for Germany's

---

[10] Baroness Hildegard von Spitzemberg Diary, 14 March 1903, in Rudolf Vierhaus (ed.), *Das Tagebuch der Baronin Spitzemberg* (Göttingen, 1960), 428.

[11] Thomas A. Kohut, *Wilhelm II and the Germans: A Study in Leadership* (New York, 1991), 191.

[12] Diary Entry for 23 May 1914, Edward House Papers, Sterling Memorial Library, Yale University.

[13] Alfred von Tirpitz, *My Memoirs* (London, 1919), vol. 1, 230.

[14] Christopher Clark, *The Sleepwalkers: How Europe Went to War in 1914* (London, 2012), 148.

naval buildup.[15] In the minds of Germany's leaders, their country's growing naval strength would act as 'yesterday's deterrent' in any trial of strength Britain. The German navy would so intimidate British leaders that they would concede rather than contest Germany's foreign policy aims. The battle fleet would serve as an instrument of coercion to compel British appeasement of Germany in the international arena.

In taking on Britain's Royal Navy, Tirpitz was going up against a formidable foe. Britain's naval leaders were alert to changes taking place in the naval balance of power and determined to beat back any challenger. Under the dynamic leadership of the legendary Admiral Sir John ('Jackie') Fisher, the British navy built a new generation of capital ships designed to surpass in combat power all existing types of battleships and armoured cruisers afloat. The result was the battleship named *Dreadnought*, carrying ten heavy guns as its main armament and propelled by turbine engines, and the Invincible-class battle cruisers. Qualitatively superior in gun power and in speed to the battleships and large cruisers planned by foreign navies, these warships established a new standard of naval strength and disrupted the efforts of competitors.[16]

Britain's decision to build the *Dreadnought* and *Invincible* confronted Tirpitz with the dilemma of either seeking substantial increases in the navy's budget to construct German 'dreadnoughts' or give up the competition in the building of the latest generation of large surface ships.[17] But the launching of the *Dreadnought* also provided Tirpitz with an opportunity to close the gap between Britain and Germany in battle fleet strength. In 1906, when Britain launched the *Dreadnought*, Germany's force of large armoured ships amounted to only a quarter of the strength of British Royal Navy. By appearing to make all other existing battleships obsolete, the *Dreadnought* nullified Britain's four-to-one superiority over Germany in pre-dreadnought battleships and armoured cruisers. Determined to follow Britain's lead in building large capital ships, Tirpitz obtained amendments in 1906 and 1908 to the basic navy laws that provided increased funding for warship construction. In a single

[15] Jonathan Steinberg, *Yesterday's Deterrent: Tirpitz and the Birth of the German Battle Fleet* (New York, 1965); Ivo Nikolai Lambi, *The Navy and German Power Politics, 1862–1914* (Boston, 1984), 137–54; Volker R. Berghahn, *Der Tirpitz-Plan: Genesis und Verfall einer innenpolitischen Krisenstrategie unter Wilhelm II* (Düsseldorf, 1971), 11–304; and Paul Kennedy, 'Strategic Aspects of the Anglo-German Naval Race', in *Strategy and Diplomacy, 1870–1945* (London, 1983), 127–60.

[16] John Brooks, '*Dreadnought*: Blunder, or Stroke of Genius?' *War in History* 14(2) (April 2007), 157–78.

[17] Holger Herwig, 'The German Reaction to the Dreadnought Revolution', *International History Review* 13(2) (May 1991), 273–83.

legislative stroke, the 1908 amendment ratcheted up the competition by declaring a number of older German battleships obsolete, making them due for immediate replacement by modern dreadnoughts. To carry out this replacement of obsolete vessels, the amended navy law provided for starting the construction of sixteen battleships and battle cruisers over four years.

Germany's rulers were fully conscious that this upswing in battleship construction would provoke Britain. Tirpitz even feared that Britain might respond by launching a preventive war to forestall the German buildup. He warned:

The fact that in the next four years Germany would lay down 16 capital ships of 18,000 tons and in addition the awareness that in the future England would have to reckon with 50 to 60 first-class German capital ships involves such a shift in *real power factors* that even a calm and reasonable English policy *must* come to the decision to crush such an opponent before it reaches a military strength too dangerous for England's position as a world power.[18]

Despite these fears of a British preventive strike, Germany's leaders were not deterred from pressing ahead with their naval buildup.

Of course, the German naval buildup could hardly escape notice in Britain. Quick to respond, Conservative political leaders jumped on the issue of naval defence. Already in March 1908, during debates in the House of Commons about naval policy, the Conservative spokesman on naval matters Arthur Lee spelled out the implications of the newly enacted amendment to the German navy law. In 1918, Lee stated, 'if the present programme is carried out Germany will have twenty-three "Dreadnoughts" and thirteen "Invincibles" – a total of thirty-six'. According to Lee's calculations, to maintain 50 per cent superiority over Germany in battleships and battle cruisers, Britain would need to start at least five large armoured ships each year for the next eight years. Lee castigated the Liberal government for proposing to start only two large armoured ships in the coming year rather than five.[19] In the hurly-burly of Britain's domestic politics, the Conservatives sought to revive their political fortunes by sounding the alarm about the growing German naval menace.

Meanwhile, the Liberal government looked on with dismay at the German naval buildup. Germany's actions endangered the Liberal Party's ambitious political agenda of domestic reform. The Liberals had

---

[18] Quoted in Jonathan Steinberg, 'The German Background to Anglo-German Relations, 1905–1914', in F. H. Hinsley (ed.), *British Foreign Policy Under Sir Edward Grey* (Cambridge, 1977), 199. Emphasis in the original.

[19] *Parl. Debs.* vol. 185, cols. 561–62 (3 March 1908).

come to power determined to tackle the country's most pressing social problems: huge disparities of wealth, growing labour unrest, a militant women's movement, and Irish nationalism. Addressing these problems with a comprehensive reform programme ensnared the Liberals in a partisan political and constitutional fight with the opposition Conservatives, still smarting from their heavy electoral loss in the 1906 general election. A benign international environment would politically benefit the Liberal Party by enabling it to concentrate its efforts on the challenges of reform at home.

The German naval challenge, however, added a serious and distinctly unwelcome complication for the Liberal government's plans. Trying to find the money for both weapons and welfare while maintaining fiscal probity by balancing the budget represented a tall order, which many Liberals feared beyond their means. Additional funding for armaments also threatened to upset the Liberal Party's political unity. Liberals did not want to be known as the party that lavished money on weapons. Nor did Liberals relish taking a confrontational foreign policy stance to contain Germany: the party's dogma instead called for engagement and peaceful resolution of international rivalries. Holding together the party to face the increasing German threat would tax all the political ingenuity of Prime Minister H. H. Asquith.

Not surprisingly, two of the leading advocates of social reform within the government, the Chancellor of the Exchequer, David Lloyd George, and the President of the Board of Trade, Winston Churchill, advocated reaching a settlement with Germany about naval armaments. Both made highly publicized speeches during the summer of 1908 calling for better relations with Germany and slowing down the naval competition. Averting an arms race with Germany appeared essential if Lloyd George and Churchill intended to realize their political ambitions of leading the Liberal reform effort.

In 1908, as a young and rising star on the British political scene, Churchill spoke out for establishing good relations with Germany. He deplored the widely held view that a major war, pitting the European Great Powers against each other, might occur in the near future. Instead of a looming clash of Great Powers, Churchill foresaw 'the peaceful development of European politics in the next twenty years'. Churchill held the conviction 'that the blessed intercourse of trade and commerce is binding the nations together into one solid interdependent mass. During nearly forty years no two great highly-organized commercial powers have drawn the sword upon one another.' In Churchill's opinion, 'the prosaic bonds of commerce, in which all civilized and commercial states are becoming involved ... impose an effective caution and restraint even upon the most reckless and the most intemperate of statesmen'.[20] In particular, Churchill maintained that neither Britain nor Germany would stand to benefit from making the other into an enemy. The two countries, in Churchill's view, were not condemned to become hated rivals, fated inevitably to fight. Churchill told his listeners: 'These two great peoples have nothing to fight about, have no prize to fight for, and have no place to fight in.'[21]

Furthermore, Churchill looked to Germany as providing a model for Britain to emulate in social welfare reform. On a visit to Germany, where he inspected labour exchanges to reduce unemployment and examined the German system of social welfare benefits, he recorded: 'My heart was filled with admiration of the patient genius which had added these social bulwarks to the many glories of the German race, and I was filled with hope that we might soon in our own country, with our much greater national wealth ... establish broadly and forever a system of national insurance which should embody and carry further all the experience which the Germans have slowly acquired and should comprise insurance against unemployment.'[22] In Churchill's view, Britain had much to learn from Germany in ensuring domestic peace and social justice.

Lloyd George, too, admired Germany's achievements in establishing a state-sponsored system for social welfare. He found most unwelcome the prospect of an arms race, whose costs might derange British finances, the Liberal government's reform agenda, the party's election prospects, and his political ambitions. In Lloyd George's opinion, Admiral Fisher's search for competitive advantage by building and trumpeting a new generation of capital ships like the *Dreadnought* spurred an unwanted naval rivalry. He complained: 'Fisher is a great man, but too prone to be always making the pace, so that other nations are urged to do more than they would otherwise.'[23] In a speech to the Universal Peace Congress, delivered amidst disorderly protests by suffragettes who demanded 'votes for women', Lloyd George castigated the Admiralty's policies for provoking a naval arms race. 'We started it', Lloyd George declared. 'We had an overwhelming preponderance at sea which would have secured us against any conceivable enemy, but we were not satisfied. We said, "Let there be Dreadnoughts." What for? We did not require them.' Lloyd George also

---

[20] Speech on Free Trade to the International Free Trade Congress, 4 August 1908, in Robert Rhodes James (ed.), *Winston S. Churchill: His Complete Speeches, 1897–1963* (New York, 1974), 1078–82.

[21] Speech on Government Policy and the Foreign Situation, 14 August 1908, in James (ed.), *Churchill Speeches*, 1082–87.

[22] Randolph S. Churchill, Winston S. Churchill, vol. 2: *Young Statesman, 1901–1914* (London, 1967), 313.

[23] Diary Entry, 25 March 1909, Ad. MSS 62969, Riddell Diaries, British Library.

attacked the Conservative opposition, whose leaders in the House of Lords were standing against the passage of the 'Old-Age Pensions Bill'. He decried the

noblemen who think that we ought to save up a little of the pension money for old people in order to provide more funds for armaments. (Cries of 'Shame.') My principle is, as Chancellor of the Exchequer, less money for the production of suffering and more money for the reduction of suffering (cheers) . . . . It really seems incredible, when you begin to reflect upon it, that it should be necessary in the 20th century of the Christian era to hold a meeting in a civilized country to protest against expenditure by Christian communities of £400,000,000 a year upon preparing one nation to kill another. (Hear, hear.)

There was no cause, Lloyd George claimed, for Britain and Germany to come to blows.[24]

Out of the public eye, Lloyd George also worked for a settlement with Germany. Meeting with the German ambassador Count Paul von Wolff-Metternich, Lloyd George pressed for restraint in warship construction by Germany. Metternich reported that Lloyd George had unfolded his 'pet idea, the slackening down in the speed of naval construction and exhorted me to make use of the time during which the peace-loving Liberal government was at the helm'. Lloyd George warned Metternich of the dire strategic consequences for Germany that would follow if Berlin refused to work toward a settlement. Whatever his personal inclinations and those of the Liberal Party, Lloyd George stated that the government would spend whatever necessary to keep ahead of Germany in the naval competition. Using blunt language, Lloyd George declared his willingness to find £100,000,000 for naval spending. Even worse might be in store for Germany: if Berlin did not work with the current Liberal government in Britain, then the Conservatives might effectively use national security as an electioneering rallying cry and sweep into power in a general election. A Conservative government, Lloyd George warned, would not only keep Britain ahead in the naval race but also might raise a much larger army by introducing conscription, conclude a formal defensive alliance with France, and erect tariff barriers to hurt Germany's trade with the British Empire.[25] Lloyd George could not paint a starker picture of how Germany's strategic position might deteriorate if German leaders did not cooperate with Britain's Liberal government in arms control

[24] 'Mr. Lloyd-George at Queen's Hall', *The Times*, 29 July 1908.
[25] The German ambassador Metternich was already very much concerned about the prospect of the Conservatives coming to power. He singled out the prominent opposition leader Austen Chamberlain in May 1908 for a lengthy discussion about the foreign and economic policies a Conservative government might follow. See Sir Austen Chamberlain, *Down the Years* (London, 1935), 48–58.

negotiations.[26] In this manner, he hoped to convince Germany's rulers that, if they provoked an arms race, Britain was determined to win it.

A scheduled trip to Germany, the ostensible purpose of which was to examine first-hand the administration of its pioneering social welfare programmes, provided Lloyd George with an opportunity to pursue his 'pet idea' of opening discussions about the naval rivalry. Lloyd George broadcast his intentions in an interview, saying he welcomed the prospect of 'an *entente* between England and Germany' that would afford both countries an opportunity to concentrate on 'the tasks of peace, of progress and of social reform'.[27] Clearly, Britain's dynamic chancellor did not consider Germany as an implacable foe with whom conflict was inevitable. Instead, he wanted to engage German leaders in negotiations and forge a closer relationship between the two countries.

Lloyd George's pet project raised the ire of the Foreign Office, which viewed his visit to Germany as amateur diplomacy, trespassing over departmental boundaries into an area where he was not expert and could do harm to Britain's foreign policy. Lloyd George's public statements and attempt to take the lead in bringing about an Anglo-German understanding vexed the Foreign Secretary, Sir Edward Grey. Grey demanded that Asquith rein in Lloyd George's mission to Germany. Given the intransigent attitude of the German government, its refusal to explore arms control that would set limits on Germany's navy, Grey need not have worried. The prime minister assured Grey that reports from Germany 'do not encourage me to be sanguine as to an approaching *détente*'.[28]

Asquith's assessment proved right on the mark. Wilhelm poured nothing but scorn on proposals to curtail the German naval buildup. When the Kaiser read Metternich's dispatch about meeting with Lloyd George, he scolded the ambassador for being too soft in his response. In Wilhelm's indelicate view, the ambassador should have responded to 'that sort of fanatic [that is, Lloyd George] with a kick in the – '.[29] The German government, taking its lead from the Kaiser, refused to discuss

[26] See T. G. Otte, '"What We Desire Is Confidence": The Search for an Anglo-German Naval Agreement, 1909–1912', in Keith Hamilton and Edward Johnson (eds.), *Arms and Disarmament in Diplomacy* (London, 2008), 33–52; John H. Maurer, 'Arms Control and the Anglo-German Naval Race before World War I: Lessons for Today?' *Political Science Quarterly* 112(2) (Summer 1997), 285–306.

[27] John Grigg, *Lloyd George: The People's Champion, 1902–1911* (Berkeley and Los Angeles, 1978), 307.

[28] Asquith to Grey, 28 August 1908, quoted in Matthew S. Seligmann, *Spies in Uniform: British Military and Naval Intelligence on the Eve of the First World War* (Oxford, 2006), 262.

[29] John C. G. Röhl, *Wilhelm II: Into the Abyss of War and Exile 1900–1941* (Cambridge, 2014), 634.

with Lloyd George ways to restrain the naval competition. Germany's Chancellor Bernhard von Bülow turned aside requests to meet with Lloyd George. While Lloyd George did hold talks with Bethmann Hollweg, Germany's secretary of the interior and future chancellor, their discussions went nowhere and even took a bizarre twist. Lloyd George recalled Bethmann Hollweg, after serving 'great tankards of lager beer', grew combative, maintaining that Britain was trying to forge an iron ring of encirclement around the German Empire because 'you hate Germany!'[30] While Lloyd George failed in his mission, he remained committed to preventing an all-out naval rivalry.

The outlook of prominent Liberals, then, hardly showed them as gripped by an inordinate fear of the rising power of Germany. Instead, they wanted to find constructive ways to engage Germany to dampen the naval rivalry. Ideological predisposition and domestic political imperatives drove the Liberal government to avoid spending more than the minimum on naval weaponry and preparations for war. Churchill believed 'that a policy of strong armaments was not popular with the political forces by which we are supported, and that whether as a party or as a Government we had nothing whatever to gain, and much to lose, by creating a sensational [international] atmosphere'.[31] The soul of the Liberal Party was committed to an ambitious agenda of political and social reform, not an expensive naval contest with Germany. A deepening antagonism with Germany would only make their reform agenda at home more difficult to achieve and strengthen the political fortunes of their Conservative opponents. British Liberals soon discovered that, however much they wanted to avoid an arms race, the German naval buildup was not going away and could not be ignored.

## III

Throughout 1908, British naval intelligence began to piece together a disturbing picture that indicated Germany was taking steps to accelerate the timetable for the construction of battleships as laid down in the navy laws. The naval attaché in Berlin warned of a secret acceleration in German warship construction. This acceleration might enable Germany to sprint ahead of Britain in the latest generation of large surface ships. Deeply disturbed by this intelligence, the Admiralty feared a worst-case

---

[30] David Lloyd George, *War Memoirs* (London, 1933), 28–31.
[31] Report by Churchill to Grey of conversation with Metternich, 9 September 1909, CHAR 2/39/86–92, Churchill Archives Centre, Churchill College, University of Cambridge.

scenario was rapidly becoming a threatening reality.[32] Only urgent action in response could avert Britain falling behind Germany in the naval race. The sea lords feared it was a 'practical certainty' that Germany would have seventeen modern battleships and large cruisers by early 1912 and might even have twenty-one. By starting six capital ships in the coming year, Britain would have eighteen on hand to match the anticipated German buildup. They warned: 'we consider the situation is serious, and we wish to emphasise the point that Great Britain's 18 to Germany's 17 DREADNOUGHTS in 1912 is not considered in any way adequate to maintain the command of the sea in a war with Germany without running undue risk'.[33]

Within the government, the First Lord of the Admiralty, Reginald McKenna, sounded the tocsin, writing Asquith:

I am anxious to avoid alarmist language, but I cannot resist the following conclusions which it is my duty to submit to you:

1) Germany is anticipating the shipbuilding program laid down by the law of 1907 [*sic*].
2) She is doing so secretly.
3) She will certainly have 13 big ships in commission in the spring of 1911.
4) She will probably have 21 big ships in commission in the spring of 1912.
5) German capacity to build dreadnoughts is at this moment equal to ours.

The last conclusion is the most alarming, and if justified would give the public a rude awakening should it become known.[34]

That Germany could achieve parity in battle fleet strength with Britain loomed up as a likely outcome to the naval competition. Germany would then have an opportunity to fight Britain on equal terms in the North Sea.

At the end of 1908, to meet the scenario of a German acceleration in battleship building, McKenna advocated that the government authorize the start of six capital ships during the coming year.[35] The navy's leadership considered six ships as the minimum requirement, and given the uncertainty about German intentions, Britain's naval security might require an even greater effort. Additional intelligence at the beginning of the New Year seemed to confirm a secret accelerated German shipbuilding effort. Furthermore, the naval attaché reported that the heavy

---

[32] Matthew Seligmann, 'Intelligence Information and the 1909 Naval Scare: The Secret Foundations of a Public Panic', *War in History* 17(1) (January 2010), 37–59.

[33] Memorandum by the Sea Lords, January 1909, Jellicoe Papers, Ad. Ms. 48990, ff. 16–20, British Library.

[34] Reginald McKenna, First Lord of the Admiralty, to H. H. Asquith, 3 January 1909, Asquith Mss, Box 21, Bodleian Library, Oxford University.

[35] McKenna Memorandum, 8 December 1908, CAB 37/96/164, TNA.

armament of the German battleships would be increased, making them more formidable warships.[36] The Admiralty also received information that the Krupp armaments factory in Essen had undertaken an expansion in their ability to manufacture large guns. The Admiralty's Director of Naval Ordinance, Captain Reginald Bacon, underscored the danger of a surprise acceleration of German battleship construction: 'The secrecy which Krupp is able to maintain is such that, combined with a large plant, it will enable them to spring a new gun or mounting on us in large numbers at very short notice.'[37] The sea lords reported: 'The fact that one hundred 12-inch & 11-inch guns have been counted in Krupp's works, together with the evidence of the immense facilities which exist for manufacture, indicates the ease and rapidity with which their ships can be equipped.'[38] McKenna reported the Admiralty's assessment: 'It is certain also that Krupp's are fully equal to providing armaments for more ships that are included in the Fleet Bill ... could probably achieve the requisite output for eight ships a-year.'[39] With this new intelligence, the Admiralty upped their demands, calling for the immediate start of no fewer than eight capital ships.

The Admiralty's assessment triggered a crisis within the Liberal government. The prospect of an escalating naval arms race with Germany frustrated Lloyd George, who saw his goal of avoiding an expensive naval rivalry with Germany put in jeopardy. He had tried to prevent this competition during his visit to Germany the previous summer. But Germany's leaders had refused to parley with him. Now, the Admiralty was pressing the government for a major increase in warship construction that required the Treasury to find more money for the navy. Lloyd George complained about 'McKenna's fatuous estimates'.[40] He wanted intelligence about Germany shipbuilding from sources other than the Admiralty. He asked: 'Can we not secure reliable information on this through the Foreign Office – or even through the German Embassy as to what the Germans are really doing.' He had reservations about the intelligence estimates that were driving the Admiralty's demands. He contended: 'Frankly I believe the Admirals are procuring false

---

[36] Herbert Heath, reports, 14 January 1909 and 25 January 1909, FO371/671, TNA.
[37] Memorandum by Reginald Bacon, 10 July 1908, ADM 116/3340, TNA.
[38] Handwritten note by the Sea Lords to McKenna, n.d., MCKN 3/19/21–25, The Churchill Archives Centre, Churchill College, University of Cambridge.
[39] McKenna Memorandum, 'Battleship Building Programmes of Great Britain, Germany, France, United States, Italy, and Austria' (June 1909), 14 July 1909, CAB 37/100, TNA.
[40] Lloyd George to Churchill, 21 December 1908, in Randolph S. Churchill (ed.), *Winston S. Churchill*, vol. 2: *Companion Part 2* (London, 1969), 937. Hereafter cited as Churchill (ed.), *Companion*.

information to frighten us.'[41] An exasperated Lloyd George wrote to his political ally Churchill:

The Admiralty mean to get their 6 Dreadnoughts ... [T]he Admiralty have had very serious news from their Naval attaché in Germany *since our last Cabinet Committee* & that McK[enna] is now convinced we may have to lay down *8* Dreadnoughts next year!!!

I feared all along this would happen. Fisher is a very clever person & when he found his program was in danger he wired ... for something more panicky – & of course he got it.[42]

In the government's deliberations, Churchill led the charge in providing a critique of the Admiralty's assessments. He argued that, even under the worst-case scenario, Britain would still remain ahead of Germany in the naval competition. Britain's existing lead in pre-dreadnought battleships would help to compensate for any German acceleration that might be occurring in the construction of dreadnoughts. Even if Britain did temporarily fall behind in dreadnoughts, the Royal Navy would maintain command of the maritime commons. Instead of stampeding into an emergency shipbuilding program for the coming year, Churchill wanted to wait for better intelligence, and then respond to German construction. Churchill's assessment, however, did nothing to allay fears about Germany's actions in upsetting the naval balance of power. While Churchill showed that Britain would retain parity in battle fleet strength if Germany did carry out a crash program of construction, his analysis nonetheless underscored the potential danger posed by accelerated German shipbuilding. If Germany was indeed accelerating its shipbuilding program, then the best Britain could do was to maintain parity, not a pronounced superiority in capital ship strength.[43]

Asquith faced the difficult task of finding a formula to hold together the government and keep the party's loyalty. Lewis Harcourt, the First Commissioner of Works, warned that the public and party 'will be horrified at what every one will realize is a programme of 8'.[44] Lloyd George and Churchill believed that they represented the party's rank and file. Churchill bluntly told Asquith that if he and Lloyd George resigned on the matter of naval spending, '90 per cent of the Liberal party [would be] behind them.'[45] Lloyd George wrote the prime

[41] Lloyd George to Churchill, 3 January 1909, in ibid., 938. Emphasis in the original.
[42] Ibid.
[43] Churchill Memorandum, 2 February 1909, CAB 37/97/19; and, Churchill Memorandum, 8 February 1909, CAB 37/97/27, TNA.
[44] Lewis Harcourt Memorandum, 25 February 1909, CAB 37/98/37, TNA.
[45] George Macaulay Trevelyan, *Grey of Fallodon* (London, 1937), 213.

minister to plead the case for an alternative policy to the Admiralty's proposals. His aim was 'to save Liberalism from the barren mangling up I fear is unavoidable if we indulge in the extravagant and ill-digested policy of the Admiralty. It will disappoint every businessman in the country, it will disgust most Liberals and it will bring disaster to the government.'[46] One prominent Liberal recorded in his diary that Lloyd George and Churchill had formed a 'cabal' with the intention of forcing their colleagues in the government to accept their proposals. If they could not sway their colleagues to agree with them, then Lloyd George and Churchill would 'offer [their] resignation[s] and [wage] a newspaper war on those who remained. McKenna was to be the first victim.'[47] The actions of Lloyd George and Churchill challenged Asquith's leadership. Lord Northcliffe, the influential press magnate, believed that Asquith was 'not nearly strong enough for his job. Hence the continual revolts of Churchill and Lloyd George. I asked Winston the other morning what was wrong with the Cabinet. He was perfectly frank and said they had not got a master.'[48]

The prime minister, too, feared for his leadership and the Liberal Party's unity. The behind-the-scenes moves by Lloyd George to find press support infuriated Asquith, who wrote to his wife: 'The economists are in a state of wild alarm, and Winston and Ll. G. by their combined machinations have got the bulk of the Liberal press into the same camp . . . [They] go about darkly hinting at resignation (which is bluff) . . . but there are moments when I am disposed summarily to cashier them both.'[49] Admiral Fisher also thought that Lloyd George and Churchill would not push their disagreement with the Admiralty to the point of resignation: 'They are not such d—d fools!!!'[50] Nonetheless, the Liberal government and Party appeared on the verge of a breakdown, ushering in a return to power by the Tories.

In keeping together the government and ensuring party loyalty, Asquith received invaluable assistance from Grey. Grey commanded the Party's respect, including even those Liberal leaders – Lloyd George, Churchill, and the elder statesman Lord John Morley – who thought the Admiralty's claims were exaggerated. Grey worked to placate the Admiralty's opponents. To Morley he emphasized: 'If we err at all we

[46] Lloyd George to Asquith, 2 February 1909, Asquith Mss, Box 21, Bodleian Library, Oxford University.
[47] Charles Hobhouse, Diary Entry, 7 March 1909, Edward David (ed.), *Inside Asquith's Cabinet: From the Diaries of Charles Hobhouse* (New York, 1977), 76.
[48] J. Lee Thompson, *Northcliffe: Press Baron in Politics, 1865–1922* (London, 2000), 163.
[49] Asquith to Margot Asquith, 20 February 1909, quoted in Marder, *Dreadnought to Scapa Flow*, 161.
[50] Fisher to Garvin, 11 February 1909, Garvin Papers.

must err on the side of safety: we must be in advance rather than in arrears; for the former error is reparable, the latter is not.' By agreeing to the Admiralty's demands, Grey fully grasped that the government ran the risk of splitting the Liberal Party. Nonetheless, if the Navy's leadership resigned and the Tories made fears of a major German naval buildup into a partisan political battle, the government might lose in the court of public opinion. '[I]f we do *not* promise to lay down 6 [capital ships requested by the Admiralty]', Grey wrote Morley, 'I think with the figures of German building disclosed the feeling of apprehension in the country will be such that the country will become ungovernable. There will not be only scare but *panic*.'[51] In addition, Grey worked to placate Liberal opinion across the country. He met with the newspaper editor C. P. Scott to reassure him that the government wanted nothing more than to find a negotiated settlement to resolve the naval arms race. After their meeting, Scott recorded that Grey 'gave me all possible help & information on the armaments question – he seemed fair & moderate & I was particularly glad to hear his views. His general policy of "Cards on the table" seemed to me admirable & if an understanding could be come to with Germany on that basis it would cut the ground from the feet of the panic-mongers.'[52]

Breaking the deadlock in the Cabinet required that Asquith convince Lloyd George that the danger of German acceleration was a real one and find a formula for new warship construction that would satisfy him. If Asquith could sway Lloyd George, then others opposed to the Admiralty programme would lack a leader and come around. To reach a settlement, Asquith summoned Lloyd George to a small gathering with Grey, McKenna, Admiral Fisher, and Rear Admiral John Jellicoe, the Royal Navy's Third Sea Lord and Controller. In this group, Asquith isolated Lloyd George, subjecting him to a barrage of Admiralty arguments designed to break his resistance. Kept away from the meeting was Churchill, who might have contested the Admiralty's arguments and bolstered Lloyd George's case and resolve.[53] Despite being outnumbered, Lloyd George fought back against the Admiralty's claims, and the meeting grew acrimonious. He complained: 'I think it shows extraordinary neglect on the part of the Admiralty that all this should not have been found out before. I don't think much of any of you Admirals.' McKenna replied: 'You know perfectly well that these facts were

---

[51] Trevelyan, *Grey of Fallodon*, 214.

[52] C. P. Scott to Morley, 25 March 1909, Mss Eur D573/60, ff. 81–82, British Library.

[53] 'Minutes of a Conference Held in the P.M.'s Room, House of Commons on Tuesday February 23, 1909', Asquith Mss, Box 21, Oxford University.

communicated to the Cabinet at the time we knew of them, and your remark was "It's all contractors gossip."'[54]

By the meeting's end, however, Lloyd George conceded that the Admiralty would get what it wanted. Lloyd George would later say that 'Sir John Fisher is a very clever man and very persuasive. When he wants to carry a point he always gives technical details which seem to be overwhelming.'[55] Seizing upon a suggestion made earlier by Lloyd George, Asquith proposed a compromise formula giving the Admiralty permission to proceed immediately with four capital ships and begin preparations for the start of four more if future intelligence showed a need to keep ahead of Germany. This compromise provided cover for Lloyd George to retreat from his opposition to the Admiralty's programme. Churchill made this compromise famous with the clever remark: 'In the end a curious and characteristic solution was reached. The Admiralty had demanded six ships: the economists offered four: and we finally compromised on eight.'[56] By winning over Lloyd George, Asquith ended the struggle within the government, forging a consensus in favour of responding to Germany's naval buildup by constructing eight capital ships. Having achieved a consensus among Liberal leaders, the prime minister could carry the party rank and file. Asquith would later write:

Estimates presented upon the authority of a Cabinet, in which the advocates of peace and economy, and the sworn enemies of militarism, were known to have a powerful if not a predominant voice ... could not ... be opposed by the Liberal Party, to whom they were commended (to cite no other names) by the joint *imprimatur* of Sir Edward Grey and Mr. Lloyd George.[57]

The fight over naval spending nevertheless imparted a legacy of personal bitterness and jealousy, making worse political rivalries that would eventually divide and weaken the Liberal Party. McKenna looked upon Lloyd George and Churchill as political enemies. He confessed to his wife: 'I hate my colleagues.'[58] He told a political ally that he was 'disappointed with Winston in the cabinet – his powers of expression were not associated with constructive ability or helpful criticism. In fact his presence was obviously distasteful to all

---

[54] Handwritten note, entitled across the top: 'Memo from myself to Mr. McKenna 1st Lord after a meeting in Sir E Greys room at Foreign Office' – dated 24 February [?] 1909, Jellicoe Papers, Ad. MSS 48990, f. 21, British Library.

[55] Diary Entry, 25 March 1909, Ad. MSS 62969, Riddell Diaries, British Library.

[56] Winston S. Churchill, *The World Crisis, 1911–1914* (London, 1923), 37.

[57] H. H. Asquith, *The Genesis of the War* (London, 1923), 109.

[58] Reginald McKenna to Pamela McKenna, 1 September 1909, quoted in Martin Farr, *Reginald McKenna: Financier Among Statesmen, 1863–1916* (London, 2008), 165.

his colleagues in the cabinet.'[59] Later, after the war's outbreak, McKenna grumbled that Churchill, who succeeded him as First Lord of the Admiralty, 'is fighting with my ships – the ships he endeavoured to prevent me from building. What a comedy it all is! Where would the nation have been if I had not insisted upon my programme?'[60] The controversy over German shipbuilding, by exacerbating leadership feuds, thus contributed to the 'strange death' of the Liberal Party as a leading force in British political life.

## IV

McKenna's formal presentation of the Royal Navy's budget to Parliament provided a dramatic setting for announcing the government's response to Germany's naval challenge. McKenna's statement and the subsequent debate riveted the country's attention. The newspaper editor J. L. Garvin considered the 'debate last night was the most serious of our time'.[61] McKenna provided a sober assessment about the projected competition with Germany. The government speakers made clear their determination to maintain Britain's superiority in capital ship strength, while decrying the need to increase naval spending.

Despite the government's best efforts to present a reasoned case and measured response, the Conservative press trumpeted the danger posed by Germany's naval buildup. Garvin believed that, despite the government's assurances to keep ahead of Germany, the 'truth is still black'. To Lord Northcliffe, Garvin worried that the construction of eight capital ships might not be enough. He urged: 'The only possible formula is two to one [in capital ships over Germany] – unless we make a somewhat smaller margin possible by adopting universal military training.'[62] Garvin's *Observer* demanded 'the Eight, the whole Eight and nothing but the Eight'.[63] Meanwhile, *The Fortnightly Review* offered its view about the 'naval crisis': 'We were assumed to be decadent. Germany was to succeed us in commercial supremacy, colonial empire, and the mastery of the sea. In a word, "the twentieth century would belong to the Germans." ... Germany had stretched out her hand for the trident which she has now by a sudden attempt tried to wrench from our grasp.'[64]

---

[59] Cameron Hazlehurst and Christine Woodland, *A Liberal Chronicle: Journals and Papers of J.A. Pease, 1st Lord Gainford, 1908–1910* (London, 1994), 111.

[60] Farr, *McKenna*, 260.

[61] Garvin to Northcliffe, 17 March 1909 [incorrectly dated as 28 July 1908], Ad. Ms. 62236, f. 113, Northcliffe Papers, British Library.

[62] Ibid.    [63] Thompson, *Northcliffe*, 163.

[64] 'Imperial and Foreign Affairs: A Review of Events', *Fortnightly Review* 85(508) (1 April 1909), 599.

The opposition Conservatives blasted the government, portraying it as weak in responding to Germany's growing navy. The Tories took the Admiralty worst-case scenario and magnified it. Even level-headed Tories, like the former Prime Minister Arthur Balfour, stoked the public foreboding. As the opposition leader, Balfour pressed the government toward a maximum naval effort. Quoted in the *Daily Mail*, Balfour declared that the country faced a 'Great Naval Crisis', in which 'for the very first time in modern history, we are face to face with a naval situation so new, so dangerous, that it is difficult for us to realise all it imports.' The public debate proved acrimonious. The Tories exploited this issue of national security at a by-election they won in Croydon, where one election poster read: 'Our naval strength has been fooled away by the Radicals and Socialists. What guards your food? Our Navy. Then kick out the Radicals, or when war comes you will starve.'[65]

To support the Conservatives, Admiral Fisher played a devious role in feeding them inside information. He saw outside pressure generated by the Conservatives as strengthening his hand with the government. Fisher supplied questions to Balfour, who was urged to 'press them home' in the coming debate about naval defence. Balfour was told 'that nothing but 8 ordered now can avert catastrophe'.[66] Fisher supplied Garvin with information for his articles attacking the government. 'The beauty of it', Fisher wrote, 'is that though Six are sufficient I am going for EIGHT!!!' Fisher reassured Garvin that Asquith's 'dithering ... was merely to play along the economists'.[67] Metternich reported to Berlin: 'Sir John Fisher has conceded to the German naval attaché in London, it took a little naval scare to carry with him the part of the Liberal Party and those ministers who had inclined against a naval increase.'[68] This brazen intervention in partisan politics would not be the last time that Fisher would work with opposition Tory leaders to intimidate a Liberal government.

In turn, the Conservatives sought to strengthen the Admiralty's bargaining position by promising their support and urging the sea lords not to relent in demanding the immediate construction of eight capital ships. Austen Chamberlain told the Second Sea Lord Admiral Sir William May

---

[65] Frans Coetzee, *For Party or Country: Nationalism and the Dilemmas of Popular Conservatism in Edwardian England* (Oxford, 1990), 133.

[66] Memorandum by Sandars, 15 March 1909, Balfour Papers, Ad. Ms. 49719, ff. 76–77, British Library.

[67] A. J. A. Morris, *The Scaremongers: The Advocacy of War and Rearmament, 1896–1914* (London, 1984), 176.

[68] Metternich to Bülow, 16 July 1909, quoted in Jan Rüger, *The Great Naval Game: Britain and Germany in the Age of Empire* (Cambridge, 2007), 221.

that 'if the Naval Lords stand firm, and are prepared to resign together, they will get their way'.[69] In their partisan attempt to bring down the government, the opposition showed itself willing to abet a revolt by the admirals and breakdown in civil–military relations. This politicization of naval defence added to the pressure bearing down on the Liberal government.

But the government withstood the political pressure. Asquith labelled as ridiculous the opposition's claims that 'this country's superiority over Germany will not be well and adequately maintained'. When the opposition called a vote of censure against the government for failing to make 'immediate provision of battleships of the newest type', the measure was handily defeated by 353 to 135 in the House of Commons.[70] In the aftermath of the debate on naval policy, Lloyd George defended the government's policy in his celebrated speech putting the 'People's Budget' before the Commons. This performance displayed Lloyd George's mastery of political theatre. On the one hand, he demonstrated to the rank and file of the Liberal Party and its supporters throughout the country that the government remained bound to holding down spending on armaments. On the other, he needed to allay fears that the government was weak in providing for the country's security. '[I]t would . . . be an act of criminal insanity to throw away eight millions of money, which is so much needed for other purposes, on building gigantic flotillas merely to encounter mythical Armadas. (Cheers.) . . . We must ensure the complete security of our shores against all real dangers, but we cannot afford to build navies against nightmares. (Loud cheers.)'[71] Although intended to produce funding for an ambitious domestic reform agenda, Lloyd George's budget also paradoxically provided more money for the navy. With the introduction of the government's controversial budget, the naval question moved out of the political limelight for the time being. Consequently, the government proceeded to build without any fanfare the four extra ships because the issue no longer excited as political theatre.

Meanwhile, the panic in Britain reverberated in Berlin. Chancellor Bülow and Metternich could see the damage being done to Anglo-German relations by Berlin's inability to reassure British leaders about Germany's naval ambitions. Bülow recommended to Tirpitz that Germany spread out the construction of capital ships, arguing that it

---

[69] Charles Petrie, *The Life and Letters of Austen Chamberlain* (2 vols., London, 1940), vol. 1, 224.

[70] *House of Commons Debate*, 29 March 1909, vol. 3, cols. 39–149.

[71] David Lloyd George, Budget Speech, 29 April 1909, House of Commons, vol. 4, cols. 478–80.

was their 'duty to take every possible step to reduce British anxiety'.[72] Tirpitz would have none of it. 'I must, as Secretary of the Navy, assert that it is our duty to arm with all our might.'[73] Meanwhile, Metternich sought authority to state accurately German shipbuilding. Wilhelm refused. 'I think it would be better for Metternich to hold his tongue', the Kaiser commented on Metternich's request. 'He is hopeless.'[74]

In the noisy public debate in Britain, Tirpitz saw a conspiracy at work, whereby the British government connived at spreading false information to gain support from the Liberal Party's backbenchers and beat back opposition attacks. Tirpitz asserted to the Kaiser:

The Conservative wire-pullers and navy interests have certainly succeeded in rousing the public with a naval panic, but I think that the government realizes that the idea, secretly and very cleverly spread about by the Admiralty, that we are increasing our speed in construction, is incorrect, but at the same time a very convenient and therefore welcome way for the Liberal Cabinet to shield itself against Conservative attacks by large increases in the navy, and to justify to their own Liberal and Radical followers the expenditure of large sums on armaments.[75]

Reporting about the German navy in the British press also enraged Tirpitz. The British journalist F. W. Wile, working in Berlin for Lord Northcliffe's *Daily Mail*, interviewed Tirpitz, who 'was unmistakably interested' in the newspaper's 'attitude towards German naval development and let me know that he didn't like it'.[76] Tirpitz downplayed British concerns by maintaining that, even if German shipyards had started building capital ships ahead of schedule, the completion dates would not change. In his view, then, no acceleration was taking place, despite the early awarding of contracts to two shipyards and the start of one ship during the winter of 1909.[77]

The Kaiser condemned the views expressed by British political leaders during the debate in Parliament. Fake news, in his view, was driving British actions. On the dispatch from Metternich reporting the debate, the Kaiser derided as 'childish' McKenna's rationale for an increased

---

[72] Bülow to Tirpitz, 25 December 1908, E. T. S. Dugdale (ed), German Diplomatic Documents, 1871–1914, vol. 3: *The Growing Antagonism 1898–1910* (London, 1930), 331–33 (hereafter *German Diplomatic Documents*).

[73] Tirpitz to Bülow, 4 February 1909, ibid., 341–41.

[74] E. L. Woodward, *Great Britain and the German Navy* (Oxford, 1935), 218.

[75] Tirpitz to Kaiser Wilhelm, 8 March 1909, *German Diplomatic Documents*, 345–46.

[76] Thompson, *Northcliffe*, 159.

[77] The Kaiser only learned in August 1909 that one of the capital ships had indeed been started early. He saw 'in this a justification, though only formal one, for the English claim that building is being accelerated ... His Majesty has always emphasized that no acceleration of building has taken place.' Müller to Tirpitz, 4 August 1909, quoted in Marder, *Dreadnought to Scapa Flow*, 178.

British shipbuilding effort. With regard to Balfour's projection that Germany might complete twenty-five dreadnoughts by the end of 1912, the Kaiser wrote: 'The man is a liar – or completely insane.'[78] The Kaiser denied that Britain and Germany were embarked on a naval competition. 'There is no competition', he wrote. 'It exists only in overheated English brains! Who dreams of racing?! Britain is racing against its own self!'[79] But the Kaiser and Tirpitz had themselves contributed to worst-case intelligence projections in Britain. Their truculent attitude played a major part in arousing British suspicions and Britain's response.

The political uproar in Britain led to Germany's rulers falling out with each other over the buildup of the battle fleet. Metternich sounded a consistent note of warning in his messages to Berlin that the German naval programme was antagonizing Britain's Liberal government. Bülow recognized as well that the increase in German shipbuilding was self-defeating strategic behaviour. As Germany's foreign secretary and later as chancellor, Bülow had supported the Kaiser's policy to build up a fleet against Britain. As chancellor, Bülow championed the 1908 amendment to the navy law. But as the evidence mounted that German shipbuilding was damaging relations with Britain, he sought to reverse course. He pushed to settle the naval rivalry. Bülow feared that without a settlement of the naval question the Liberals would lose the next general election. He contended that

the naval scare has reached the point where it hits the money-bags of the English middle classes, otherwise peacefully inclined .... A Conservative government in England would represent a very real war danger for us .... [W]e should do all in our power to keep the Liberal party, to which all peace-loving elements in England adhere, at the helm. Therefore we should meet the aims of this party for a mutual reduction of the armaments burden half way.[80]

Even if a Conservative government did not unleash a preventive war, it might redouble Britain's naval effort, introduce conscription to expand the British army, move toward a closer strategic alignment with France, and adopt tariffs hurting German trade, as Lloyd George had warned Metternich. The panic in Britain broke the consensus within the German government about the strategic wisdom of carrying on with Tirpitz's battleship buildup.

---

[78] Wilhelm's marginal comments on Metternich to Bülow, 17 March 1909, *German Diplomatic Documents*, 347–49.

[79] Kohut, *Wilhelm II and the Germans*, 214.

[80] Report on conversation between Bülow and Kaiser Wilhelm, in Admiral Müller to Tirpitz, 17 April 1909, quoted in Marder, *Dreadnought to Scapa Flow*, 172.

Tirpitz, seeing his life's work threatened, fought back. The loss of Bülow's support marked a turning point where resistance within the German government mounted against naval increases. Tirpitz lamented: 'Bülow has deserted me.'[81] When Bethmann Hollweg succeeded Bülow as chancellor, he also maintained the pressure to limit the navy's buildup. Bethmann Hollweg feared that if Tirpitz refused to reduce battleship construction, Germany could count Britain as a dogged adversary. Wilhelm and Tirpitz, however, rejected significant concessions in the building of a battle fleet that they saw as a precondition to achieving the position of a world power. The Kaiser proved relentless in demanding a powerful navy. If anything, Wilhelm wanted a greater naval effort than Tirpitz. By preventing a genuine accommodation with Britain on naval armaments, by insisting on the construction of a battle fleet that challenged British leadership at sea, the Kaiser and Tirpitz undermined Germany's security before the outbreak of war.

## V

Was this crisis over Germany's naval buildup much ado about nothing, a mock drama fabricated by British leaders to scare one another? After all, the worst-case projections feared by the Admiralty and Conservatives proved mistaken. In the spring of 1912, Germany possessed nine dreadnought capital ships, and not the seventeen or twenty-one projected as probable by the Admiralty or the twenty-five conjured up by the Conservatives. Meanwhile, Britain had ready fifteen capital ships by the spring of 1912. Thus, the 'dreadnought gap' that existed in 1912 favoured Britain and not Germany. In addition, in Fisher's opinion, the battle cruisers included in Britain's building programme represented such a qualitative leap over the ships under construction in German yards that they would guarantee British superiority in a future naval engagement. Admiral Fisher boasted:

*Do you know that the ships that we have just laid down are as far beyond the Dreadnought as the Dreadnought was beyond all before her!* And they will say again, 'D—n that blackguard! Again a new era of Dreadnoughts!' But imagine the German 'wake-up' when these new ships by and by burst on them! *70,000 horsepower!!! And guns that will gut them!!!*[82]

---

[81] Michael Epkenhans, *Tirpitz: Architect of the German High Seas Fleet* (Washington, D.C., 2008), 41.

[82] Fisher to Sir Arnold White, 13 November 1909, in Arthur J. Marder (ed.), *Fear God and Dread Nought: The Correspondence of Admiral of the Fleet Lord Fisher of Kilverstone*, vol. 2: *Years of Power, 1904–1914* (London, 1956), 277. Emphasis in the original.

Jellicoe agreed that Britain should maintain a qualitative edge in the naval competition by building ever more heavily armed capital ships. Jellicoe argued: 'In peace strategy the initiative is probably as important as in war. So long as we retain the initiative we keep our rivals in a chronic state of unreadiness, confuse their building policy, and, by maintaining a perpetual superiority in each individual unit, tend to preserve peace by postponing the moment when they could make war at an advantage.' He warned: 'Had Germany built the first "Dreadnought", and had we followed only when we were assured that she had been a success, we should now be in a lamentable position.'[83] Little danger existed, then, that Germany would acquire parity in battle fleet strength with Britain.

By overreacting to uncertainty about German intentions, Britain gave a clear demonstration of its strength to compete against Great Power challengers, possessing the financial resources, industrial capacity, and cutting-edge technology to build a navy as strong as any in the world. The British sprint to stay ahead of Germany in the race to build battleships underscores Keith Neilson's contention that Britain had the economic resources and political will to defeat naval rivals and remain a world power. In the international contest for naval mastery, Britain had a strong hand to play, and the Liberal government played it to gain strategic advantage over rivals.

This demonstration of British strength has led historians to downplay the German naval threat. For example, Dominik Geppert and Andreas Rose write: 'Among the threats to the British Empire, the German fleet did not occupy a particularly prominent place.'[84] But Germany's growing naval strength loomed up as all too real a menace to British security. British admirals, Foreign Office officials, and right-wing press barons did not invent the German naval threat – Germany's rulers did. While Germans dreamt of world power, they did not sleepwalk into a contest at sea with Britain. In two navy laws and three subsequent amendments, the German government and people deliberated and made conscious decisions to devote considerable resources to the naval challenge. British leaders had good reason to fear that Germany would soon overtake Britain. In 1909, Germany's budget for the construction of warships actually exceeded

---

[83] Memorandum entitled 'A Discussion of the Relative Merits of the 13.5-inch and the 12-inch Gun as the Armament for Battleships', 21 December 1908, Jellicoe papers, Ad. Ms. 48990, ff. 4–9, British Library.

[84] Dominik Geppert and Andreas Rose, 'Machtpolitik und Flottenbau vor 1914. Zur Neuinterpretation britischer Aussenpolitik in Zeitalter des Hochimperialismus', *Historische Zeitschrift* 293(2) (2011), 401–37.

that of Britain.[85] If British leaders had not offset the German navy's buildup, Germany might have before too long overtaken Britain in naval strength. Britain and Germany were contending for command of the maritime commons before the war just as surely as they were to struggle for it in wartime. A generation later, during the perilous 1930s, a less resolute National Government would allow Germany to gain an edge in the arms race between the Royal Air Force and the Luftwaffe, thus contributing to the catastrophic defeats suffered by Britain and France in 1940. Britain's last Liberal government was made of sterner stuff in its determination to prevent Germany from forging ahead in the naval contest.

Even Churchill, a sceptic about the Admiralty's claims, soon began to question his assumptions about Germany's aims and actions. In an interview with Metternich, Churchill stressed 'that the original German Navy Law in itself was [a] formidable fact for British eyes to contemplate, that the revised Navy Law was still more serious, but that the prospects of an acceleration even upon that had been the cause of the deep disquiet which had spread among all parties and all classes in this country'.[86] His department, the Board of Trade, produced a study on how financial constraints might serve as a brake on Germany's ship-building efforts even if German industry could in theory produce a navy to equal the British battle fleet. In a covering memo on this study, Churchill feared that financial problems might confront Germany's rulers with a strategic dilemma: the German government might be forced to choose between curtailing naval construction and seek an accommodation with Britain, or pursuing a more dangerous alternative of 'calculated violence'.[87] Churchill would later write that this memo was 'the first sinister impression that I was ever led to record' about the threat Germany's foreign policy ambitions posed to Britain's security. About Germany's naval building programme, he concluded: 'It was impossible to resist the conclusion, gradually forced on nearly everyone, that if the British Navy lagged behind, the gap [in warship strength] would be very speedily filled.'[88]

Furthermore, the naval contest did not end with the outbreak of war but continued until Imperial Germany's downfall in 1918. Tirpitz's battle

---

[85] David Stevenson, *Armaments and the Coming of War: Europe, 1904–1914* (Oxford, 1996), Table 7, 8.

[86] Report by Churchill to Grey of conversation with Metternich, 9 September 1909, CHAR 2/39/86–92, Churchill Archives Centre, Churchill College, University of Cambridge.

[87] Memorandum by Churchill on Germany, 3 November 1909, in Churchill, ed., *Companion*, 961–62.

[88] Churchill, *World Crisis*, 39–40.

fleet, along with submarines, smaller surface ships, coastal defence artillery batteries, and mines, gave Germany an anti-access area-denial capability which could inflict punishing losses on British capital ships daring to venture into the North Sea. The stealthy undersea weapon of the submarine, in particular, proved at least as revolutionary a platform for waging war at sea as the *Dreadnought*. The submarine limited Britain's strategic options in wartime, making a traditional close-in blockade of German littoral waters a dangerous environment for British battleships to operate. Submarines would also prove an extraordinarily lethal weapon when used in an asymmetric strategy of commerce destruction. During the war, Germany's submarine force came out of the German defensive bastions in home waters, taking the offensive on the high seas to disrupt Britain's command of the maritime commons. German submarines sank almost thirteen million tons of Allied and neutral shipping during the war. By the summer of 1917, the German navy's 'high seas fleet' of submarines proved so lethal that Britain's top naval leaders considered the war as good as lost and urged the British government to negotiate peace rather than continue fighting. Admiral Jellicoe contended that the German submarine offensive was having 'such a serious effect upon the import of food and other necessaries into allied countries as to force us into accepting peace terms'.[89] Jellicoe lamented: 'We cannot go on.'[90] His pessimism was so pronounced that Lloyd George fired him as First Sea Lord.

British Liberals abhorred and wanted to avoid this life-and-death contest for naval mastery. But Germany's rulers gave them little choice, just as German actions at sea would also pull a reluctant America into the war in 1917. What of Lloyd George and Churchill, the two most vigorous opponents of the Admiralty's crash program for a naval buildup in 1909? Both made serious efforts to end the naval arms race and avert conflict with Germany.[91] But their efforts ended in failure. Worse was to follow when, during the July Crisis, Berlin escalated a Balkan conflict into an all-out struggle for mastery in Europe by launching German armies through Belgium on a deep-strike, power drive into the heart of France. The Liberal government, much against its will, then committed the British Empire to waging war against Prussian militarism and Germany's domination of Europe. In their deadly determination to win the war, Lloyd

---

[89] Jellicoe to Balfour, 6 June 1916, Jellicoe Papers, Ad. Ms. 48992, Vol. 4, ff. 61–74, British Library.

[90] Haig Diary, 20 June 1917, in Gary Sheffield and John Bourne (eds.), *Douglas Haig: War Diaries and Letters, 1914–1918* (London, 2005), 301.

[91] John H. Maurer, 'Averting the Great War? Churchill's Naval Holiday', *Naval War College Review* 67(3) (Summer 2014), 25–42.

George and Churchill took up the challenge issued by Germany and, at a time of grave peril, played a leading part in the renewal of British power. As Keith Neilson argued, Britain was no weary titan but a formidable Great Power, fully capable of competing in the international rivalries of that troubled age and beating back challengers, its leaders committed to playing the leading role on the world stage.

# 8    Views of War, 1914 and 1939: Second Thoughts

*Zara Steiner*

Twice within twenty-five years, Britain sent an ultimatum to Germany that resulted in war. A vast literature has illuminated the long-term and short-term causes of Britain's actions, and the number of books and articles continues to increase. In 1972, I gave a seminar paper comparing and contrasting the state of public feeling in July 1914 and in September 1939. In the case of the former, which was my main subject, I looked at the change in British sensibilities since the turn of the century, which I thought pertinent to the public acceptance of war despite the number of those objecting to engagement in a continental conflict. The actual response to the decision for war in July was dealt with in a more cursory fashion. After some summary remarks about the effects of the Great War on public perceptions of war and an examination of the deteriorating international situation in the 1930s, which challenged the movements for disarmament and collective security, I focused on the decision for war in 1939 and the reactions of the political elite and the public to its outbreak. The original paper was critically received; many members of the seminar believed that historians should not deal with the issue of public opinion.[1]

To do so, however, means to ignore the vital nexus of public opinion and political decision making. Indeed, that connection is a vital part of the circuitry that constituted British power in the nineteenth and twentieth centuries. With this in mind, I have revisited this earlier paper in the light of new interpretations and the release of diary material from the Mass Observation and Imperial War Museum files. I have only briefly summarized my earlier account of the changed climate of opinion in the late Victorian and Edwardian periods, which I thought to be substantially correct, and concentrated instead on the examination of 'war enthusiasm' in July 1914 by a new generation of revisionist scholars, which has become the orthodox interpretation of the July crisis. The section on the interwar

---

[1] Zara Steiner, 'Views of War: Britain Before the "Great War" and After', *International Relations* 17(1) (2003), 7–33.

174

period is much expanded. Greater attention is paid to the effects of the Great War in reshaping popular images of future conflicts, and how fear of an air war affected these new perceptions. Comparisons and contrasts between the fictional representations of wars to come in the two periods are highlighted. Qualifications are made to current assumptions about the sea change in public opinion during the last years of peace. Using the new memoir material, it is now possible to provide an introductory analysis of the complex public response to war in September 1939.

## I

A good deal of work, appearing after the writing of my article, had reopened the question of war enthusiasm in 1914.[2] J.-J. Becker and Jeffrey Verhey have written about France and Germany respectively. More recently, British historians, most notably Adrian Gregory and Catriona Pennell, have challenged traditional accounts of the British response to the outbreak of the Great War.[3] Curiously enough, despite the avalanche of studies on the background of the Second World War and the availability of material found in the National Archives, the Imperial War Museum and Mass Observation papers, only a handful of historians have directly addressed the shift in British public opinion during the last year of peace. One notable exception with regard to the longer view has been Daniel Hucker's *Public Opinion and the End of Appeasement in Britain and France,* published in 2011.[4] An article can provide only an introduction to the richness of this material, but I hope to offer possible ways to view the events leading up to September 1939 in the light of these sources.

To understand why the decision for war in 1914 was accepted by the mass of the electorate, one must acknowledge the changes in the British climate of opinion in the late Victorian and Edwardian decades. I argued

---

[2] Jean-Jacques Becker, *1914: comment les Français sont entrés dans la guerre* (Paris, 1977); Jeffery Verhey, *The Spirit of 1914: Militarism, Myth and Mobilization in Germany* (Cambridge, 2000).

[3] Catriona Pennell, *A Kingdom United: Popular Responses to the Outbreak of the First World War in Britain and Ireland* (Oxford, 2012); Adrian Gregory, 'British War Enthusiasm: A Reassessment', in Gail Braybon (ed.), *Evidence, History and the Great War: Historians and the Impact of 1914–18* (Oxford, 2003), 67–85.

[4] Daniel Hucker, *Public Opinion and the End of Appeasement in Britain and France* (Farnham and Burlington, VT, 2011). Terry Charman's *Outbreak – 1939: The World Goes to War* (London, 2009, published in paperback form as *The Day We Went to War* (London, 2010)), offers an excellent selection of Mass Observation diaries. Other countries, as well as Britain, are covered, and there is a connecting commentary. Diarists are identified, but no catalogue numbers are given. See also Stephen Howarth, *August '39: The Last Four Weeks of Peace in Europe* (London, 1989).

in my earlier article that during this period Britain faced a more competitive international environment and a number of imperial conflicts. A new generation of statesmen and officials were more attuned to Britain's seemingly exposed position and the foreign threats to its maintenance. New currents of thought as well as diplomatic and technological changes fanned interest in imperial and military affairs. Darwin's *Origin of Species* created a new vocabulary that coloured the language of politics; its emphasis on change, natural selection, and the survival of the fittest was applied to Britain's imperial role and position in the world's hierarchy of nations. The mass dailies of the period, the *Daily News*, *Daily Express*, and *Daily Mail*, the last 'written by office boys for office boys' according to Lord Salisbury, were primarily profit-making enterprises, in sharp contrast to most of the well-established and more expensive papers read by Establishment figures. 'Our policy', Sir Arthur Pearson wrote in the first issue of the *Daily Express*, 'is patriotism; our party is the British Empire'.[5] The new press was intended to attract a fledgling generation of voters and literate readers hungry for news. Sensational accounts of imperial flashpoints, of arms races and reports of war, sold papers. During the Boer War, the *Daily Mail* sold almost a million copies a day and in 1907 its proprietor, Alfred Harmsworth, commissioned William Le Queux's *Invasion of 1910*, hoping to attract more readers. Exploiting an already popular theme, this serialized version of an invasion of Britain by barbaric Prussians was a huge success. Subsequently published as a book, it was prefaced by Lord Roberts, the Boer War general, who reiterated that a country prepared for war would not be invaded. Le Queux's story opened the floodgates to an outpouring of invasion stories that tapered off only after 1912. It was hardly surprising that P. G. Wodehouse capitalized on the enthusiasm for this new genre in his spoof *The Swoop! or, How Clarence Saved England* (1909). Such publications fed the German spy scare which temporarily swept the nation, including briefly even the king. Some writers, like H. G. Wells, combined images of future sophisticated weapons with stories of invasions from abroad that appealed especially to Edwardian middle-class readers interested in science and technology.

The long life of Queen Victoria, the Jubilee celebrations, naval reviews at Spithead, and the launching of new ships provided a focal point for public gathering and displays of patriotic feeling in a society beginning to feel the alienating effects of industrialisation and urbanisation. At the same time, heightened imperial conflicts in the 1890s created a sense of unease among some politicians, who often publicized their anxieties and

---

[5] Editorial in the first edition of *The Daily Express*, 24 April 1900.

sought to mobilize public support for change. The Boer War, that unusually long and expensive colonial war, brought to the surface many of the often conflicting approaches to the problems it posed. The struggle with the Boers was strongly supported by the Unionists and, within the Liberal party, by the Liberal imperialists who viewed the empire as the bedrock of Britain's strength and supremacy. It also unleashed and revived more traditional anti-imperial sentiments and the association of imperialism with nationalism and militarism. J. A. Hobson and L. T. Hobhouse provided new versions of the economic arguments against imperialism and war which were warmly received by many Liberals and Labour supporters. In general, the war was popular; public demonstrations of loyalty, if less jingoistic than once thought, and the unprecedented outburst of popular emotion at the news of the relief of Mafeking, were noted with some alarm by those concerned with order and control.

The war, too, resulted in a good deal of discussion among politicians, journalists, military commentators and others about the state of the nation. Though the war was won, and no coalition of powers was formed against Britain, many of the political elite shared a sense of providential escape. Critics spoke of the need for 'national efficiency', reform of the military services, strengthened ties of empire, and the improvement of the physical and moral quality of the country's youth. A quarter of those volunteering for military service during the Boer War were rejected on physical grounds; the percentage in such cities as Manchester was considerably higher. It provided a wake-up call for those already fearful that without change Britain would go the way of Rome and lose its empire because it could not defend it.

It was not only that Sir Jacky Fisher, made First Sea Lord in 1904, accelerated the reform of a navy which, after all, had not fired a shot against a Great Power since 1855, but the Liberal secretary of state for war Lord Haldane's more far-ranging reforms from 1906 to 1912 which led to the creation of a professional expeditionary force trained for overseas wars and a volunteer territorial army for home defence. These reforms were accompanied by discussions in technical and service journals, but also in Parliament and Fleet Street about the nature of war, the shape of wars to come, and the kinds of weapons needed to fight them. There was much public interest and pride in the new technology and a far greater awareness of military and naval matters. The naval rivalry with Germany added fuel to this interest; the 1909 'we want eight and will not wait' campaign was a case in point. The Territorial Army attracted 270,000 volunteers, many from working-class backgrounds. Active steps were taken by the campaigners to arouse the public to the new dangers and the need for reform. The Navy League, founded in 1895, actively propagandized for a larger fleet navy that would more than meet any German challenge. The National Service League, created after the Boer War, supported a form of national conscription, which though anathema to many voters, gained adherents in the Lords and Commons and a substantial public following. By 1912, it claimed a membership of 200,000, about half of whom were active. The leagues took their messages of patriotism, duty, and military service to the schools and universities, and, above all, to the public schools, which had already abandoned the Victorian emphasis on 'Godliness and Good Learning' in favour of manliness, athletics, competitive sport, and team spirit. Lord Roberts, spokesman for the National Service League, was a favourite choice for school speech days. Even the Leys school, a Methodist foundation with a strong anti-militarist tradition, joined the vast majority of schools which were expanding or founding cadet and rifle corps, many with direct links to Haldane's Officer Training Corps.

Working-class youths were not forgotten. Many youth groups were founded, some before 1900, but others the result of the Boer War. The Boys Brigades, the Church Lads Brigade, and the British Girls Patriotic League, the Duty and Discipline movement, the Empire Day movement were often initiated or led by ex-officers, clergymen, and school masters, as well as public-spirited individuals, who wanted to improve the health and moral fibre of city-dwelling children. Along with the indoctrination came uniforms, exercises, athletics, singing, parades, and excursions into the countryside. Empire Day was celebrated in state as well as public schools; the half-holidays were naturally highly popular. Its purpose was to create an awareness and sense of pride in the British Empire. Above all, the Boy Scouts, founded in 1905 by Baden-Powell, hero of Mafeking, proved a highly popular and permanent feature of British society. Though with much of the paraphernalia of military life, its emphasis was on scouting, nature, woodcraft, and an appreciation of outdoor life. There were 100,000 scouts in Britain by 1907, and many more read *Scouting for Boys* and the weekly *Scout*, both emphasising physical exercise, good citizenry, and the glory of empire. Baden-Powell intended to attract the thousands of 'pale, narrow chested, hunched up, miserable specimens, smoking endless cigarettes into the countryside' but it was, and remained, mostly a middle-class movement concentrated in the south-east of England. There was high overlap in the leadership of these pre-1914 movements and though their messages differed, for the most part, they shared common aims.

Affiliation to the brigades or scouts, attendance at naval demonstrations or membership of cadets corps does not, as William Mulligan insists, point to a 'bellicose strand in British public opinion which would have supported a war of aggression'.[6] There was a multitude of reasons why these groups flourished and gathered public support. Those clamouring for military preparedness and national service were not, however, successful, and Britain remained committed to a naval strategy which underlined her defensive position. The majority of the working class remained apathetic if not hostile to any concept of military service and pacifist societies, though small in number, were found in both middle-class and working-class circles. It is fair to suggest, nonetheless, that in contrast to the mid-Victorian period, there was a greater emphasis on patriotism and chauvinism, a deeper concern with war, and an often unarticulated belief that 'it was the duty of every Englishman' to render his own country more powerful, richer and larger than any other country.[7]

One other feature of the Edwardian period requires consideration. Changes in the diplomatic scene meant that while there was no wish for war or support for turning Britain into a military state like Germany, there was a sense that Britain and its empire might need to be defended and that the country and its subjects should be prepared to meet that test. There was also an awareness of a new enemy, Germany, though the period of acute Germanophobia was actually short. Both at the ministerial level and in the country at large, after 1912, with the naval race won and the invasion threat dismissed, the German menace seemed to diminish just as concerns about Russia revived. Anglo-German relations improved in the year before the war.

I believe that the general portrait of Edwardian Britain painted in my article stands as an acceptable introduction to the subject. At the time, however, I gave little attention to the public mood in July 1914, and here a great deal of new research requires considerable rethinking. Jean-Jacques Becker's groundbreaking study of France has shattered the conventional view of public enthusiasm for war, while recent studies by Gregory and Pennell suggest that previous accounts of war enthusiasm in Britain have been greatly exaggerated. The mood of the crowds that assembled in London and elsewhere over the bank holiday weekend as the crisis peaked was a mixed one and showed little of the Mafeking spirit that punctuated the latter's relief. It must be remembered that the crisis escalated unexpectedly and war was not on the horizon until late in the day. The public at large had almost no knowledge of the government's deliberations between 24 June, when Sir Edward Grey first brought the subject of the Austrian ultimatum to the attention of the cabinet, and

---

[6] William Mulligan, *The Origins of the First World War* (Cambridge, 2010), 142.
[7] Harold Nicolson, *Lord Carnock: A Study in the Old Diplomacy* (London, 3rd printing 1931), x.

3 August, when he went to the Commons to present the case for intervention. The assassination of the archduke had been widely reported but
few thought it likely to cause war, and certainly not a European one. It was
only with the delivery of the Austrian ultimatum and the Serbian reply
that the press turned its attention away from the Irish question and the
death of Joseph Chamberlain to the new crisis. By 26 July, most of the
London press had come to accept the probability of a European conflict;
a few discussed the possibility and prospect of British involvement. The
main Conservative papers, *The Times, Daily Mail, Pall Mall Gazette*, and
*Daily Express*, urged British engagement. Others were more reluctant to
back involvement; the *Daily Telegraph* and *Evening Standard* remained
ambiguous, the former possibly because of links with the anti-war City of
London, until 3 August. The Liberal newspapers, for the most part,
followed the neutrality line set by the *Manchester Guardian* and *Daily
Chronicle*. The *Westminster Gazette*, regardless of the editor's links with
Grey, changed its position on 3 August. The *Manchester Guardian* and
*Daily Chronicle* reluctantly supported intervention only when the Anglo-
German war began. The Labour papers, the *Daily Herald* and *Daily
Citizen*, began to discuss the crisis on 27 July. Both strongly opposed
intervention, stressing the burden a war would place on the working
classes. The *Daily Herald* backed the Trafalgar Square anti-war demonstration on 2 August and maintained its position into the war. For the
most part, during these days, the provincial newspapers were more anti-
war and anti-interventionist than the London papers. Above all, until
3 August, concrete news was rare and people were anxiously seeking
information. Outside of London, the news of the ultimatum and its
rejection came late, which may partly explain the delayed reaction.

This scarcity of news combined with the decision not to disperse the
fleet anchored at Spithead and Grey's public announcement of his med
iation proposal intensified the sense of unease. On the afternoon of
29 July, even after Austria had declared war on Serbia, Grey told the
Commons that he would continue his efforts for peace. The Liberal
Foreign Affairs Committee, a Radical campaign group in Parliament,
warned the government against going beyond the limited commitments
given to France and Russia. Grey convinced Lord Ponsonby, its chairman, that a declaration of neutrality at this point would be counterproductive, but both he and Prime Minister Asquith knew that the cabinet
was split and that the Radicals and many Liberal backbenchers opposed
intervention. It was not until Sunday 2 August, after Grey had threatened
resignation and a letter had been received from the Unionists pledging
support for a government decision for war, that the Cabinet agreed that
British abstention would depend entirely on the non-violation of Belgian

territory and on Germany refraining from hostile operations in the Channel (i.e. an attack on the French Channel coast). One cabinet minister, John Burns, resigned; three others were about to do so though only John Morley followed Burns. On the same day, a well-attended anti-war rally was held in Trafalgar Square. On 3 August, Grey addressed the Commons stating the moral and strategic reasons for war. Once the ultimatum was sent with an expiry time of midnight on 3 August, most but not all of the opponents of war rallied to the government.

The final days of the crisis have evoked a mass of commentary and debate. We now have a body of evidence, not previously explored, about the mood of the crowds which gathered before Buckingham Palace and along Whitehall and also in provincial cities over the bank holiday weekend. There is some dispute about the actual number who gathered outside Buckingham Palace on the nights of 2, 3, and 4 August. Figures range from 1,000 to 10,000. Much larger crowds turned out on 6 August according to the king, and even more people came out on 9 August. The pro-war hecklers at the Trafalgar Square demonstration appear to have been mainly middle-class youths. Photographic evidence of the crowds assembled on 3 August show far more 'boaters than cloth caps', suggesting that those who gathered were mainly from the middle class. Reports indicate that the younger set did most of the cheering. Just before the ultimatum expired at 11.00 p.m. on 4 August, more people arrived, many spilling out of theatres, perhaps fuelled by drinking. According to H. A. Gwynne of the *Morning Post*, 'you have to bear in mind one thing: this war is not a "Mafficking" war. We all feel it too deeply and too strongly. They do not even cheer the troops as they march through the streets . . . No bells are rung . . .'[8] Revisionist historians suggest that Grey's Commons speech, stressing the importance of the Belgium guarantee, was a catalyst in making interventionists out of many opponents and waverers. Undoubtedly, the expiration of the ultimatum came as a shock and generated outbursts of great emotion. Gregory and Pennell insist that this was, in part, the reaction to pent-up feelings. The general reaction was mixed: shock, anxiety, and fear, as well as excitement and enthusiasm. Many individuals had mixed feelings: worry and foreboding but also anticipation and hope for action.

There is evidence of an upsurge of nationalism and even enthusiasm for war as the crisis reached its climax. The description of the July mood found in Lloyd George's defensive autobiography was not, as Adrian Gregory claims, simply an *ex post facto* recollection. As he and Herbert

---

[8] H. A. Gwynne to Victor Marsden, 1 December 1914, Keith Wilson (ed.), *The Rasp of War: The Letters of H.A. Gwynne to the Countess Bathurst, 1914–1918* (London, 1988), 55.

Samuel made their way along Whitehall, packed with cheering people, he said to Samuel: 'This is not my crowd. I never wanted to be cheered by a war crowd.'[9] Worried officials at the Foreign Office, too, noted with relief the enthusiasm of the crowds following Grey's speech in the Commons. Later commentators may well have exaggerated the unanimity of the public response and the degree to which cheering can be attributed to enthusiasm for war. It is important, however, to acknowledge that being in a crowd, with Germany long identified as an 'enemy' rather than a friend, and with the rising sense of an imminent war, that there would be an upsurge of patriotic feeling and emotive nationalism. There was certainly a mixture of feelings as people waited for news, but an element of war enthusiasm on 3 and 4 August was also present.

A more nuanced view of the public response to war is necessary. The recruitment of volunteers increased after the declaration of war, mainly from the usual recruiting grounds for the Army, the urban unskilled, but as the revisionists point out, the real increase occurred in the four days after publication by *The Times* of the Mons despatch on 25 August. Depicting the battle as a heroic defeat, *The Times* appealed for more volunteers. The response was instantaneous: more than 10,000 men volunteered on each of the next four days. The highest recruitment figure for the whole war was recorded on 3 September when 33,304 men joined the army.[10] This increase cannot be attributed to a new outburst of enthusiasm but resulted from the feeling that the country had to be defended. People went to war in a defensive rather than an aggressive mood. The motivations for those men from all classes and all regions of the country who volunteered for Kitchener's Army were mixed. While there was little talk of a short war among the new recruits, few could have anticipated the war that developed during 1915. The image of war inculcated in the youth of the country, above all, among the public-school boys who officered the New Army, led to expectations that would be tested and exposed only as the war developed into the bloodbath which it became. What remains astonishing, though historians have provided many explanations, is why men continued to enlist and to fight when the true nature of war was revealed.

## II

The interwar scene would be markedly different, in tone and expectation, from that of the pre-1914 decades. Somewhat surprisingly, despite a mass

---

[9] Samuel to Beatrice Samuel, 3 August 1914, quoted in T. G. Otte, *The July Crisis: The World's Descent into War, Summer 1914* (Cambridge, 2014), 499.

[10] Gregory, 'British War Enthusiasm', 80.

of monographic studies of both the domestic and international developments of those years, few historians have attempted the admittedly difficult
task of plotting the changing course of public opinion or the background to
the final decision for war.[11] The most obvious contrast between the two
periods was due to the experience of the 1914–1918 war itself and the long
shadow it cast on the interwar years. Many living in this period actually
fought in that conflict; many more had either lost family or friends. A good
proportion of those who survived were scarred, either physically or men-
tally. The romantic vision of war died at Ypres. The New Army's 'spring
tide of faith and joyous illusion' did not outlast the experiences of 1915.
Few (Winston Churchill was one of the exceptions) thought of war as
a 'picnic' or the 'best fun ever dreamed of'. For many combatants, the
shock of war was disorienting and the 'disenchantment'[12] (the title of
C. E. Montague's memoir) shattering. The lengthy casualty lists of this
four-year conflict brought home the human costs of war to millions of
civilians.

The need to mobilize the nation to fight a war, the political and social
effects of this mobilisation, and an enlarged electorate now including
women meant that British post-war governments were forced to respond
to expressions of public feeling.[13] Apart from some exceptional years,
such as 1931, party politics was less contentious than in the Liberal
decade. The National Governments of Baldwin and Chamberlain
enjoyed considerable majorities and the Conservatives dominated these
coalitions. Nonetheless, post-1918 statesmen were acutely aware of public opinion on foreign policy issues. The previous generation had enjoyed
decades of peace; the interwar generation remembered the Great War.
The main pressure groups before 1914 were those advocating the moral,
physical, and material preparation of the country for the defence of
Britain and its empire. In the interwar decades, it was the anti-war groups
and the supporters of the new collective security system that dominated
the public scene. The largest and most influential was the League of
Nations Union (LNU), founded in 1918 with cross-party support. Its
leader, Lord Robert Cecil, had extensive political connections and
enjoyed a position of considerable influence both as a member of
Cabinet and in the public at large. At its peak in 1931, it had nearly

---

[11] I wish to thank Dr Daniel Hucker of Nottingham University who provided many of the
references for this article and was invaluable as an advisor on this subject. I also want to
thank Paul Horsler of London School of Economics, who is preparing a PhD on these
topics, and who sent me some valuable sources.

[12] C. E. Montague, *Disenchantment* (London, 1922).

[13] See the note by Stephen King Hall explaining why public opinion was considered far
more important in 1938 than in 1919: The National Archives (TNA), Kew: INF 1/712,
Stephen King Hall, 11 July 1938.

407,000 members with 4,400 corporate affiliates including churches, trade unions, universities, schools, and women's groups. The LNU played a central part in marshalling support for the much delayed World Disarmament Conference, which finally met in 1932 only to be adjourned once Hitler left the conference and the League of Nations in November 1934. In 1934–35, the LNU organized a national survey of public opinion, culminating in a huge rally at the Royal Albert Hall in London in June 1935. A total of 11.6 million people (38 per cent of the UK population) responded to the LNU's 'peace ballot'. Women as well as men canvassed, knocking at the doors of households throughout the country. More than 90 per cent of the respondents supported Britain's continued membership in the League of Nations and its commitment to international disarmament. There was also wide acceptance of the need for non-military sanctions; a smaller percentage even backed the use of force against aggressors.[14] The results were read as showing massive public support for 'collective security' and strong doubts about rearmament.

Whatever questions were raised about the phrasing of the ballot and the meaning of its somewhat contradictory results, most politicians assumed that its import was clear. This explains, in part, official reactions to the Ethiopian affair, Hitler's annexation of the Rhineland, and even the Spanish Civil War, which exposed the tensions in the peace movements in Britain and France and split the ranks of the Labour Party which had adopted, in 1933, a 'no-war' resolution. Did support for collective security preclude rearmament and the use of force? To this fundamental question, there was a divided response. LNU membership declined in 1936 and 1937, as the leadership was unable to bridge the gap between the wings in favour of and against sanctions. Other peace groups continued to attract new members. In 1936, Canon Dick Sheppard launched his Peace Pledge Union (PPU), backed by a glittering cast of intellectuals and writers. Bertrand Russell, Aldous Huxley, Storm Jameson, and Rose Macaulay were among its founding members. Because of its broad humanitarian appeal, high profile activists, and brilliant propaganda, it seemed by 1938 that the PPU might become a mass movement. In August 1939, it had a membership of 129,289 men and women. Other pacifist or anti-war societies continued their activities right up to and beyond the outbreak of war.[15] The pre-1914 youth groups, above all the still-popular

---

[14] See Helen McCarthy, *The British People and the League of Nations: Democracy, Citizenship and Internationalism, c.1918–45* (Manchester, 2011), 4 and 30.
[15] R. J. Overy, 'Pacifism and the Blitz, 1940-1941', *Past and Present*, 219 (2013), 206–07.

Boy Scouts, played down any previous association with militarism, the latter stressing its internationalism and world jamborees.

By the late 1920s, a combination of factors including the publication of the volumes of *Die Grosse Politik*,[16] the German documentary collection of pre-war diplomatic correspondence, raised questions about Germany's responsibility for the war. Frequent Franco-British clashes over reparations and responses to German non-compliance convinced some that the Treaty of Versailles was unjust and based on false premises. Revisionism began almost as soon as the Treaty was concluded. John Maynard Keynes's *The Economic Consequences of the Peace*, published in 1919, a highly influential polemic against the Treaty, initiated a considerable and continuing debate about the justice of the peace terms. Between 1928 and 1933 the bulk of what is now seen as 'anti-war' literature was published. The importance and popularity of Erich Remarque's *Im Westen nichts Neues* (1929), translated into English as *All Quiet on the Western Front*, hardly needs mentioning. The works of the 'war poets', Robert Graves, Wilfred Owen, Siegfried Sassoon, Richard Aldington, and others, appeared during these years. The point needs to be made that many of these writers, including Remarque, were far more ambivalent about the war experience than later generations have assumed. Most, like R. C. Sherriff, whose play *Journey's End* ran for 5,593 performances in London and was seen as a protest against war, did not intend to write anti-war tracts, but to provide a realistic picture of what war was like. Writers such as Frederic Manning and Guy Chapman underlined the positive aspects of trench warfare, the comradeship and friendships in an all-male society where class and background lost their meaning. Boys and girls in the interwar period continued to read Henty and Bigglesworth ('Biggles'), the latter updated in the 1930s to depict the air war, and the old messages of patriotism, nationalism, and pride in empire endured. In my previous article, a quotation from John Le Carré's account of his school days, written in 1941, reminds one that these ideas persisted. But they no longer dominated the literary landscape. Anti-war books, though often selling only in small numbers, combined with the highly popular films of the day to give a very different image of war than that found in the works of the Edwardian poets and novelists. The patriotic poetry and prose of Henry Newbolt, Rupert Brooke, and Jessica Pope belonged to a previous age.

A new feature of the interwar period left an indelible mark on official and public attitudes toward war. The air war and the fears it engendered

---

[16] J. Lepsius, A. Mendelssohn Bartholdy, and F. Thimme (eds.), *Die Grosse Politik der europäischen Kabinette, 1871–1914* (40 vols., Berlin, 1922–27).

were markedly different from the fears of a German invasion in the Edwardian period. That possibility had been dismissed by successive government enquiries and faded from public view before 1914. The German air raids of 1917, particularly the two raids on London in June and July 1917, as well as later examples of the power of bombing (China and Spain), came to dominate discussions about future wars. Well before the end of the 1920s, the dangers of an aerial bombardment of Britain became a major preoccupation for the government and the public at large, technology facilitating a 'bolt from the blue' with bombing raids targeting civilian populations. Britain's cities, above all London, were particularly vulnerable to air and gas attacks. The number of anticipated casualties, as accepted in official circles, was considerably exaggerated. In 1932, the Air Staff predicted that a one-week air attack against London would produce 18,750 casualties. The Chiefs of Staff in 1936 argued that there would be 150,000 casualties in London alone in the first week of an aerial bombardment.[17] Fictional accounts of the air war were even more alarmist. There seemed to be no defence against bombing except a counter-bombing campaign. The issue was raised and much discussed in the run-up to the World Disarmament Conference and the National Government was persuaded that the population strongly supported an agreement on air disarmament. Winding up the Commons debate on disarmament in November 1932, Stanley Baldwin provided the disarmers with invaluable ammunition. 'I think it is well also for the man in the street to realise', he warned, 'that there is no power on earth that can protect him from being bombed. Whatever people may tell him, the bomber will always get through.'[18]

During and well after the World Disarmament Conference met and broke up, the National Government tried to secure an air disarmament agreement with Germany. The advent of Hitler to the chancellorship, his open espousal of rearmament, and the creation of an air force with a superior bomber capacity to that of Britain shaped the government's strategic and defence policy until 1939. Once rearmament began in 1934, the fruitless search for an agreement with Germany was paralleled by an augmentation of the Air Force intended to equip it with a sufficient number of bombers to deter Berlin, at the cost of the other two services, above all the Army. This concentration on the Air Force was political as well as diplomatic; the public would accept funding for the Air Force but

---

[17] David Reynolds, *Britannia Overruled: British Policy and World Power in the Twentieth Century* (Harlow, 2000), 23. Professor Reynolds notes that there were fewer than 147,000 casualties from bombing and all sorts of bombardment during the whole Second World War.

[18] *Hansard*, HC Deb 10, vol. 270, col. 632 (10 November 1932).

opposed spending money on the Army. The term 'field force' replaced 'Expeditionary Force', the latter evoking negative memories of the Great War. In 1937, the Army was given the lowest priority of the three services. Its main purpose was to provide anti-aircraft defence at home and secure imperial commitments abroad. Developments in radar technology and the manufacture of modern monoplane fighters like the Hurricane and Spitfire enhanced Britain's defensive capabilities but failed to eradicate fears of aerial bombing. After his second visit to Hitler in September 1938, Chamberlain spoke of his feelings as he flew home up the Thames. According to Cabinet minutes, 'he had imagined a German bomber flying the same course, he had asked himself what degree of protection he could afford to the thousands of homes which he had seen stretched out below him, and he had felt that we were in no position to justify waging a war today in order to prevent a war hereafter'.[19]

A few prescient writers such as H. G. Wells had already turned to the threats from the air before 1914. Wells brought out a new edition of *War in the Air* in 1921, predicting in a new preface that the war would end and reverse the progress of civilisation. His novel of 1933, *The Shape of Things to Come*, written after Hitler had come to power, was far more terrifying. A war arising out of a trivial incident in Danzig between Germany and Poland destroys the existing world order and leaves the world in chaos. Wells, ever optimistic about the power of science, predicted that a new order would emerge, established by technicians who would take over the country's essential services and create a scientific utopia. William Le Queux, whose highly popular *The Invasion of 1910* (1906) had set off the stream of German invasion novels, returned to the theme of a German-led conspiracy in *The Terror of the Air* (1921). The possibilities of a German 'bolt from the blue' wiping out civilian populations was a favourite theme for the multitude of popular, if often unreadable, interwar novels.[20] Not untypical was *The Gas War of 1940*, published in May 1931 (selling 100,000 copies despite negative reviews), in which 'Miles', the pseudonym of the prolific writer Stephen Southwold, responded to and played on public fears of bombing. But as the possibility of war increased, there was a reaction to the

[19] Quoted in David Reynolds, *The Long Shadow: The Great War and the Twentieth Century*, (London, 2013), 238.
[20] Much of this information and the relevant citations for this and other works can be found in Martin Ceadel's important article 'Popular Fiction and the Next War', in Frank Gloversmith (ed.), *Class, Culture and Social Change: A New View of the 1930s* (Brighton, 1980), 180–81.

highly alarmist accounts of its consequences. In 1938, both Eric Linklater's *Impregnable Women* and Nevil Shute's *What Happened to the Corbetts*, while not short of the ghastly details of the air war, pointed to possible chances of survival. Although horrific, the real-life experiences in China and Spain demonstrated that civilian morale was not eroded easily by bombs. German and British wartime expectations that the enemy's morale would be shattered by bombing proved unfounded as did the worst-case scenarios of the fiction writers.

Though these domestic differences between the two pre-war situations had a direct bearing on the decision for war, there were also a variety of external and short-term factors which explain them. The most obvious contrast was the far more dangerous and challenging international environment. The threat to British interests in 1914 was posed mainly by Germany and its possible challenge to the balance of power in Europe, and, because of Britain's global position, the Russian challenge to the empire. The European balance of power and the safety of the empire were intertwined. In 1914, with the German move into Belgium and the existing ententes with France and Russia, national interest as well as morality brought Britain into the war. In the years prior to 1939, Britain was faced with three enemies in different parts of the globe, Germany in Europe, Italy in the Mediterranean, and Japan in East Asia. Germany posed the immediate threat, thought capable of delivering a knockout blow at the very start of the war. The Chiefs of Staff made it abundantly clear that Britain could not fight a three-front war with only France as an ally. The situation was far more immediately alarming and dangerous in September 1939 than in August 1914.

There was also a question of timing. The last year before the Great War, despite the Balkan upheavals and the active diplomacy that ensued, was relatively peaceful and the spring of 1914 unusually calm. In the late 1930s there were crises in Europe, the Mediterranean, and East Asia, where an undeclared war between Japan and China was already underway. After Hitler's march into Austria, the European situation became increasingly fraught. There was a muted reaction to *Anschluss*; it was, after all, Germany's backyard, and the enthusiastic Austrian response to Hitler's arrival quieted many fears. The demands on Czechoslovakia increased tensions through the summer of 1938, though many still hoped that Hitler would be satisfied with redressing the injustices of Versailles by incorporating the lost Germans into the Reich. Britain persuaded Prague to make concessions to the Sudeten Germans and applied pressure on Paris (though little was needed) to prevent the French from taking any precipitant action. The Runciman mission reported favourably on the Sudeten German position. Subsequent German threats to settle the issue by force raised the temperature chart. By late August the situation had reached crisis proportions. Chamberlain's personal diplomacy, his first two dramatic flights to Germany in September, was welcomed by the Cabinet and an overwhelming majority of the country. At the Godesberg meeting on 22–23 September, Hitler demanded an immediate solution to the Czech problem and threatened to invade and occupy the disputed territory. Chamberlain was inclined to accept Hitler's demands but faced considerable Cabinet opposition. The foreign secretary, Lord Halifax, broke ranks and a Cabinet revolt made further concessions impossible. War now seemed imminent. The British fleet was mobilized, people were advised to try on their gas masks, evacuation plans were updated, and trenches were dug in the parks. The majority of the population expected German bombing raids within days or even hours.

The last-minute reprieve, Chamberlain's flight to Munich, and the Anglo-German agreement subsequently signed were greeted with huge relief and enormous enthusiasm by a grateful public. Chamberlain was the man of the hour having secured 'peace with honour'. Nor were the scenes of jubilation restricted to his homecoming. During the next weeks the prime minister received more than 200,000 letters and telegrams as well as gifts 'in embarrassing profusion' from admiring men and women. Only Duff Cooper resigned from the Cabinet after Munich, and though Churchill's Cassandra-like speech in the Commons was widely reported in the press, he had only the most limited parliamentary support. The fear of war had peaked during the Czech crisis. The emotions unleashed acted as a counterweight to the public reaction one year later. Few second crises, coming so swiftly after the first, generate the same level of emotional response. By September 1939 people felt that the country was better prepared to fight than at the time of Munich, although fear of an immediate bombing campaign and concerns about the consequences of war persisted. In the first four days of September 1939, nearly 3 million people were transported from towns and cities in danger from enemy bombers to the relative safety of the countryside. The well-planned evacuation of children began on 1 September, two days before the declaration of war. The evacuation went smoothly; the real problems came in the reception areas where local authorities, left without central guidance, were overwhelmed. Gas masks had been distributed and fitted and a number of Anderson shelters dispatched. In some ways, the Czech crisis in 1938 was a rehearsal for what was to come, and steps were subsequently taken to strengthen the country's defences.

## III

One year earlier, and the post-Munich euphoria proved short-lived. Hitler showed no willingness to fulfil his promises of goodwill and made no secret of his contempt for Chamberlain. Resentment at Hitler's bullying tactics grew stronger. Polls conducted by the British Institute of Public Opinion (BIPO) shortly after Munich revealed growing support for rearmament and an increased scepticism that Hitler's word could be trusted.[21] Despite the prime minister's fears that the burden of armaments 'might break our backs', he had to accept an increased armaments bill, though he was able to resist demands for the establishment of a Ministry of Supply and the return of Eden to the Cabinet. *Kristallnacht* (9–10 November) was strongly condemned throughout the country but no action was taken, not even the recall of the British ambassador in Berlin. Parliamentary by-elections in October, November, and December showed little sign of the strong support that Chamberlain anticipated when considering the date for the next general election, his government losing two seats, one to the journalist and broadcaster Vernon Bartlett, standing as an independent anti-appeasement candidate in a safe Conservative seat. In January, false rumours circulated that Hitler was contemplating an attack on Switzerland, the Low Countries, or even the United Kingdom. Chamberlain was compelled to respond, and in February 1939 he pledged support to France while Cabinet proposals to equip the army for service on the continent, a reversal of earlier 'limited liability' policies, proved acceptable to backbenchers and the public. Yet the prime minister remained hopeful that his policy of appeasement might be furthered through discussions with Mussolini and possible economic concessions to Germany. Indeed, such was Chamberlain's renewed confidence that after some reassuring signs from Berlin, he told the parliamentary lobby on 9 March that the foreign situation 'is less anxious and is giving me less concern for possible unpleasant development than it has for some time'.[22]

Within a week, Hitler's troops marched into Prague. The Cabinet, backbenchers and many members of the public were outraged by Chamberlain's lukewarm Commons response to the Prague 'coup'. Later, at Birmingham, responding to public displeasure, he took a firmer line, though much of his speech was a defence of his earlier policies. The labourite *Daily Herald* and the communist *Daily Worker*, but also papers such as the *Daily Telegraph* and the *News Chronicle*,

---

[21] F. McDonough, *Neville Chamberlain, Appeasement, and the British Road to War* (Manchester, 1998), 128.

[22] Andrew Roberts, *The 'Holy Fox': A Biography of Lord Halifax* (London, 1991), 141.

questioned Chamberlain's commitment to substituting firmness for appeasement. Even the *Daily Express*, one of the Prime Minister's strongest supporters, admitted that 'the policy of appeasement was finished'.[23] There was no question of using force in the face of the German move, but circumstances and political pressure compelled the government to change course by building a dam against further German and Italian aggression. The guarantees to Poland, Romania, and Greece were part of a policy of deterrence intended to warn the dictators from making any further advances in Eastern Europe. It was a political and not a military policy, shifting the trip wire for a British reaction from Western to Eastern Europe. Chamberlain was particularly proud of his guarantee to Poland, which he thought would warn Hitler off without provoking him, facilitating a renewal of negotiations with Berlin. In these hopes, he was out of step with some of his own ministers, backbenchers in all parties, and sections of the public.

'In terms of public opinion', Daniel Hucker writes, 'Prague was not a turning point.'[24] For months, at least since November, opinion had been hardening and the deep hostility to continental engagements had receded. Prague brought a residual opposition to appeasement to the surface, and this stiffer popular mood was shown by public clamour to commence talks with the Soviet Union with a view to inaugurating a 'Triple Alliance'. Contacts had been initiated in January but were pursued with greater urgency after the Poland guarantee. Backing for talks with Moscow was widespread; the hostility of several isolationist newspapers reflected a latent anti-communism that still ran strong in many quarters, but the majority insisted that alliance negotiations should begin. Chamberlain strongly opposed the talks from start to finish but had to yield to Cabinet pressure. The negotiations continued for four months but were hamstrung from the outset on account of mutual suspicion and a fundamental disjunction between what the Soviet Union and the western powers wanted. The talks continued, mainly because Foreign Office officials feared a possible German-Soviet agreement should the negotiations fail, but also because pulling out of the talks would be difficult given the strength of public feeling.

Another indication that Chamberlain and appeasement were losing support was the press campaign in early July for a cabinet reshuffle, bringing in Churchill, a persistent advocate of the Soviet alliance, or Eden (one of the 'glamour boys' as Chamberlain sometimes called them). Chamberlain rode out the storm, which he felt would give the wrong signals to Hitler and Mussolini and might have unwanted political

---

[23] Hucker, *Public Opinion and the End of Appeasement*, 127.    [24] Ibid., 130.

consequences. There were, however, further indications of public opposition at signs of appeasing Germany. When the press leaked details of
talks between Dr Helmuth Wohlthat, a German official linked to
Goering, and Robert Hudson of the Department of Overseas Trade,
contemplating a loan to Germany in order to cultivate good relations,
a public scandal ensued with wide reverberations. Chamberlain was
furious at the leak and Hudson was sacked, but the damage was done.[25]
Awkward questions were asked in Parliament, and Chamberlain's
responses – and those of his close confidant, Sir Horace Wilson, were
found evasive. Despite criticisms of Chamberlain, he kept his hold over
both Parliament and the public at large. Opinion poll data between
October 1938 through July 1939 shows that his approval rating ranged
narrowly between 55 and 59 per cent.[26] Chamberlain's authority was
never really challenged. Summer by-elections, in contrast to some of
those of the previous autumn, were fought on domestic rather than
foreign policy, reflecting a growing consensus that the government was
doing what it could to protect the country. The only time that
Chamberlain was in real danger of losing the House of Commons was
the famous occasion on the night of 2–3 September when he failed to
produce the ultimatum to Germany within the time limit the Commons
was expecting. It was then that Arthur Greenwood made his stirring
intervention and Leo Amery, a former minister from the right wing of
the Conservative party, told the Labour spokesman to 'speak for
England'. Chamberlain was warned that he would lose the House if he
did not proceed to set a deadline. Although this final delay was actually
attributable to the French, the suspicion that Chamberlain was preparing
another Munich was widespread, even in his own party.[27]

The general view of a sea change in popular thinking during the last
months of peace is substantially correct, but a degree of caution is necessary. Most people went about their daily lives concerned with their own
problems. The nearer the danger of war came, the more people retreated
from the realities of the situation into their private worlds. A study by
a Mass Observation team in West Fulham conducted before the by-
election in April 1938 showed a low interest in foreign affairs. Despite
an intensive effort to make foreign policy the central issue in the by-

---

[25] Wohlthat, the deputy head of his own Four Year Plan Organisation, also had talks with
Horace Wilson, one of Chamberlain's closest confidants, see D. C. Watt, *How War
Came: The Immediate Origins of the Second World War, 1938–1939* (London, 1989),
394–403.

[26] G. H. Gallup, *The Gallup International Public Opinion Polls, Great Britain, 1937–1975*
(New York, 1976), 9–21.

[27] See Watt, *How War Came*, 577–82.

election campaign, people failed to take notice, and the victor was the candidate who spoke most about home affairs. A year later, the same full-time interviewers visited the same people in the same houses. About a thousand households were canvassed and observers recorded a rise in the number of those who were vague, doubtful, or bewildered when answering questions about foreign policy. According to the author, bewilderment led to apathy and defeatism. A similar survey in East Lancashire revealed even more striking results, contributing to the following composite conclusion:

The result of the increasingly grave international situation is not to stimulate a wider knowledge of public affairs, though it does stimulate an increased interest of the minority, but rather to make the majority increasingly retreat from the awful reality into the greater occupation of private life with cultivating their garden – unless they happen to be among the millions who have not got gardens in which case cultivating their Littlewoods is the better metaphor.[28]

For many people, the whole world seemed crazy. 'I don't have anything to do with it. I don't study politics. I know it is a blooming worry with my two sons. When I turn the wireless on I don't understand it', a housewife told one observer.[29]

The sea change in the public mood did not amount to a pendulum shift from pacifist-tinged opposition to war to a jingoistic embrace of conflict. Many people were apathetic or sought escapism in domestic mundanity, but a small number were still attracted to the pacifist societies. The PPU's membership continued to grow during the phoney war; the Quakers remained active as did other smaller pacifist groups. Pacifists were treated with respect; there was little of the animosity shown in 1914 and during the Great War. There were relatively few actual Nazis. Oswald Mosley's British Union of Fascists had an estimated 22,500 members in 1939, down from its peak of 50,000 in 1934, though it could still marshal a good crowd at its rallies.[30] The communists, though small in number (18,000

---

[28] Mass Observation Archive, FR A16, *Home or Foreign?*, April 1939, 7. I owe the reference to this report and much of this information to Dr Daniel Hucker, as well as much assistance on other points of reference. A recent book on Mass Observation (James Hinton, *The Mass Observers: A History, 1937–1949* (Oxford, 2013), 104–12) does not refer specifically the *Home or Foreign?* report, but the author suggests that Tom Harrisson compiled the report on the West Fulham by-election in 1938 (94), and Kathleen Box, described as a 26-year-old LSE graduate with communist leanings (102) conducted the surveys on ARP carried out in Fulham in April and June 1939, assisted by Stanley Cramp, who did the statistics (111).

[29] Mass Observation Archive, FR A16, *Home or Foreign?*, April 1939, 9.

[30] G. C. Webber, 'Patterns of Membership and Support for the British Union of Fascists', *Journal of Contemporary History* 19(4) (1984), 577.

in 1939),[31] vigorously supported negotiations between London and Moscow until the signing of the Nazi-Soviet Pact. Even after the pact was signed there was uncertainty and splits over the new Moscow line.

There were also a number of pro-German groups and 'fellow travellers' who sought, until the war actually came, an Anglo-German understanding. The Link, founded in July 1937 on a non-party basis, had at its height some 4,000 members. Its journal, *The Anglo-German Review*, conveyed a more positive cultural image of Germany to a wider group of sympathetic readers. During the summer months its columns included ads from an English girl, aged 20, seeking an au pair position in Germany during October, while a young German student advertised for a similar position in England teaching German in return for hospitality.[32] The Link as well as other organisations continued to sponsor Rhineland holidays, and in the columns of the *Anglo-German Review*, British visitors found much to praise as a result of visits to private German families, complimenting the autobahns and sports facilities offered to Germans and tourists alike. British visitors in the columns of the *Anglo-German Review* reported 'a land of smiles and peacefulness, full of gay music and free from the cares and worries that beset the outside world. Crises may darken other horizons, but not those of Germany, it seems.'[33] Among such organisations, most with small memberships, the most important was the Anglo-German Fellowship, founded in 1935. It had an extremely influential membership of about 500 people which included members of both the Commons and the Lords (Brocket, Lothian, Redesdale, Londonderry, the Earl of Glasgow, and the Duke of Wellington), leading figures in the financial and commercial world (Norman Montagu, the head of the Bank of England), editors and journalists, including Geoffrey Dawson, the editor of *The Times*. Firms such as Unilever, Dunlop Rubber, and Thomas Cook & Sons secured 'corporate membership' to show their support. Many members were not actually Nazi sympathizers, but there were a large number of 'sharks lurking among the shallows'.[34] The 'fellow travellers' varied in the degree to which they would go in order to secure German friendship. Many were known anti-Semites. The activities of the Anglo-German Fellowship were important because members had contact with officials in the German government and either individually or through the Fellowship's sister organisation, the *Deutsch-Englische Gesellschaft*, could influence German opinion. Ribbentrop, the German

---

[31] Andrew Thorpe, 'The Membership of the Communist Party of Great Britain', *The Historical Journal* 43(3) (2000), 781.
[32] *Anglo-German Review* 111(8) 28 July 1939 (marked August on the cover).    [33] Ibid.
[34] Cited with references in Ian Kershaw, *Making Friends with Hitler: Lord Londonderry, the Nazis and the Road to World War II* (London, 2004), 144.

ambassador in London, used some of its members for propaganda purposes.

Among the British visitors to Germany in the summer of 1939 was Lord Kemsley, the proprietor of the *Daily Sketch* and *Sunday Times* and the brother of Lord Camrose, the proprietor of the *Daily Telegraph*, who met Hitler at the end of July. Equally active in trying to reinvigorate appeasement was Lord Rothermere (Harold Harmsworth), owner of the *Daily Mail* and *Daily Mirror*. He sent a message of congratulations to the *Führer* on 29 June hoping that he would use his power to 'inaugurate an era of peace so that the work you have undertaken shall not be undone'.[35] On 2 September he wrote to Chamberlain warning him of the consequences of a war with Germany which would lead only to social revolution in Britain.[36] The Foreign Office deplored Rothermere's continuing interventions but could do little to stop them. These 'amateur diplomatists' encouraged Hitler to think almost to the end of August that the British would accept his advances in Poland without resorting to war.

Rothermere had already voiced concern at the post-Prague shift in British policy, writing to Lord Beaverbrook: 'I don't think there will be war over Danzig. But why British foreign policy should be chained to the chariot wheels of Warsaw baffles my comprehension.'[37] Signs of a possible disinterment of appeasement combined with the protracted nature of the Soviet negotiations raised concerns that Chamberlain was reluctant to abandon his Munich policy. An ill-tempered exchange took place in the Commons on 2 August when Chamberlain moved that the Commons should adjourn until October. Churchill considered it 'pathetic' and 'shameful' that the House might 'write itself off as an effective and potent factor in the situation', and ironically reminded vacationing MPs to take their gas masks with them.[38] Liberal and Labour leaders joined in the demand for an earlier recall date. Chamberlain insisted on a vote of confidence and won the adjournment debate 245 to 129.[39] The fact was that Chamberlain still commanded a majority and was not in danger of a major rejection. People went off on their holidays worried, but not expecting war to break out. Harold Nicolson, a known anti-appeaser, went sailing and did not return until 22 August, his early return due to bad weather rather than the political

---

[35] Telegram from Rothermere to Hitler, 28 June 1939, TNA, FO 1093/87. There are other telegrams sent by Rothermere to Hess, Hitler, and Ribbentrop in June–July 1939. I owe this information to Gill Bennett and to Daniel Hucker.

[36] TNA, FO 1093/87.

[37] Rothermere to Beaverbrook, 22 July 1939, Beaverbrook Papers, Parliamentary Archives, House of Lords, BBK/C/286.

[38] *Hansard*, HC Deb 2, vol. 350, col. 2440 (August 1939).

[39] *Hansard*, HC Deb 2, vol. 350, col. 2523 (August 1939).

situation.[40] Ministers dispersed and left London. August began with a week of humid and thundery weather but was followed by four weeks of sunshine. Temperatures were in the high 70s and those not on holiday made the best of the weather; one school party even left for Germany. Unusually large numbers crossed the Channel to take their holidays abroad. There was nonetheless a continued sense of uneasiness. On 25 July, Halifax wrote to his friend Lord Beaverbrook, 'there is a good deal of nervousness in the county over the international situation, and tension, though it has happily decreased in the previous months, has increased'.[41]

## IV

The final crises that led to war in 1914 and 1939 were relatively short ones. The July crisis in 1914 began with the Austrian ultimatum to Serbia on 23 June and Grey's first approach to the cabinet the next day. The cabinet did not reach a decision until 2 August, and Grey only went to the Commons on the 3rd. The ultimatum expired on 4 August. The Polish crisis had a much longer prologue, although its final phase was also short. The public was more aware of the possibility of war than in 1914, but still little was known about what was actually happening. Although German military preparations were reported, the Poles told the allies little about their dealings with Hitler. German 'tourists' entered Danzig, and Polish reports of German divisions moving towards the German-Polish border kept nerves on edge. The prime minister dismissed these reports as part of the 'war of jitters' rather than serious German preparations. In Britain, signs of war intensified. Work on a National Register began, the calling up of 20-year-old men started, ARP meetings were held, and Territorial Army units marched off for training camps. There was further testing of the barrage balloons. People went on with their normal lives, but the undercurrents of fear were there. Hitler had decreed 'Spannung' to begin on 15 August, 'which means the opening of the "battle of nerves" ... Hope mine will be all right!'[42]

The final crisis began on Saturday 19 August when Lord Halifax, returning from holiday in Yorkshire, alerted Chamberlain, salmon fishing in Scotland, about warnings reaching the Foreign Office via one of Vansittart's informers that Germany would attack Poland between 25

---

[40] Harold Nicolson (Nigel Nicolson, ed.), *Diaries and Letters, 1930–1939* (London, 1967), 410.

[41] Halifax to Beaverbrook, 25 July 1939, Beaverbrook Papers, BBK/C/152.

[42] Cadogan diary entry, 12 August 1939, in David Dilks (ed.), *The Diaries of Sir Alexander Cadogan* (London, 1971), 195.

and 28 August. On Chamberlain's return on the 21st, Parliament was summoned to pass the Emergency Powers Act and the cabinet authorized sending warning letters to Hitler and Mussolini. The Nazi-Soviet pact was signed on 23 August. Contrary to what Hitler expected, the reaction to the news was calm and there was no overthrow of the government. Parliament met the following day; Chamberlain assured Hitler that the pact, whatever its nature, would not affect Britain's obligations to Poland. There followed a period of intense diplomatic activity as well as unofficial and highly secret contacts with intermediaries trying to promote a settlement, which went on almost until 2 September.[43] The diplomatic duel between Hitler and the British reached its height during the last week of August. It was still hoped over the weekend of 25–27 August to salvage something from Hitler's unacceptable bid for an alliance without compromising Polish independence. The exchanges between the Führer and the British went on until 31 August. After the parliamentary and cabinet crises over the sending of an ultimatum on 2 September, the ultimatum was sent and expired at 11.00 a.m. on 3 September. The July 1914 decision had come almost without warning; this was not the case in 1939.

The mood during the first days of September was caught in a contribution in the left-wing British weekly *New Statesman and Nation*: 'I see the nation's keeping cool / the public calm is fine / the crisis can't shake England's nerves / it's playing hell with mine.'[44] 'My nerves have completely gone', wrote Mass Observation's Tom Harrisson, 'we've been waiting a whole year, not knowing if there'll be a war or not. I want a knock at Hitler'.[45] Total calm was the exception but there was no panic. What is interesting is how long people thought that the peace could be preserved. On 28 August, a woman in Worthing recorded in her diary: 'news worse and worse but the people feel everywhere that war will *not* come'.[46] On the 29th, another diarist wrote 'many notes passing between British cabinet and Hitler – we really feel war will be averted'.[47] Joan Strange, a 34-year-old physiotherapist in Worthing, summarising the events of the past week, wrote: 'very few people felt this terrible blow would fall and right up to Sunday morning there was the glimmer of hope ... [On Friday] everyone's spirits sank but rose again when Mr. Chamberlain gave Hitler one more chance in a message sent on

---

[43] A great deal has been written about Birger Dahlerus, a Swedish businessman who was used by Goering to make offers to Britain to keep the peace, having talks with Chamberlain, Halifax, and Cadogan, see, among other references, Watt, *How War Came*, 504–13 and 516–19.

[44] Quoted in Steiner, *Triumph of the Dark*, 1024.    [45] Ibid.    [46] Charman, *Outbreak*, 63.

[47] Ibid., 65.

Saturday.'[48] For some, the invasion of Poland and the bombing of Polish cities ended hopes for peace, but for others the previous year's 'rehearsal' persuaded them that another 'Munich' – another last-ditch reprieve – was imminent.

On the night of 2 September, as the cabinet 'rebels' confronted the prime minister, Moyra Charlton, a novelist living in Takeley, listened to the BBC News on the new Home Service (the two Home Channels had been combined and the number of news bulletins increased). She and her family were not reassured at what they heard: 'From Halifax's and Chamberlain's speeches tonight we gather that England is taking no immediate action against Germany ... We send no ultimatum, in fact we hem and haw and talk of negotiation ... We are mad, mad.'[49] A woman in Bolton told Mass Observation 'no one would stand another Munich'.[50] For some the actual radio announcement by Chamberlain came as a shock, but there was also considerable relief. Guy Chapman MC wrote at the time that 'we had waited in suspense too long. We had been shamed and humiliated, we have regained self-respect.'[51] The fear of bombing and the consequences of war remained. Almost immediately after Chamberlain's speech, the air raid sirens went. A 26-year-old schoolteacher in London on hearing the sirens imagined 'that everything and everybody will have disappeared into bomb-strewn rubble when they finally emerge'.[52] Elsewhere in London a man remembered 'the dire prophecies of scientists, journalists and even politicians of the devastation and disease that would follow the first air raid'.[53] Many were influenced by their reading of Wells's *The Shape of Things to Come*; others had seen the movie and were similarly affected. There was palpable relief when the all-clear sounded some fifteen minutes later. Diarists congratulated themselves on keeping calm or disguising their fears so as not to alarm their families.

The last days of peace were not a crisis in the psychological sense of the previous September. A student in Northern Ireland wrote in his diary: 'Even though war seems pretty close now, I can't get upset about it. I worried a lot last September and find it hard, even foolish to worry twice about the same thing. I suppose most people have the same attitude and this accounts for the "calm of the British people" of which the papers assure us every morning.'[54] There was general optimism about the

---

[48] Ibid., 263. Joan Strange was 'a trained physiotherapist living with her widowed mother, and was a committed Christian who undertook a great deal of voluntary work amongst German and Austrian Jewish refugees' (1).

[49] Ibid., 127–28.    [50] Ibid., 133.    [51] Quoted in Steiner, *Triumph of the Dark*, 1024.

[52] Charman, *Outbreak*, 185.    [53] Ibid., 179.

[54] Mass Observation Archive, Diaries, 1939–1967: Diarist 5102, entry for 31 August 1939.

outcome of the war, which may account for the emphatic vote to continue fighting until the end. Over 84 per cent of those polled thought 'we shall beat the Germans'. Throughout the BIPO survey, replies on the issue of peace and war showed that while 'there is no enthusiasm about the war, the people want to finish the job properly now we have started'.[55] Apart from the purchasing of extra foods and commodities needed for the blackout, there were no great runs on the shops or signs of mass buying. Whereas at the time of Munich people had crowded to church, on 3 September 1939 only the usual congregations assembled. The main sign of war fever was the marked increase in the number of marriages. Most people, however apprehensive, had few doubts that Britain would prevail. A BIPO report in October 1939 (the BIPO was by now working on behalf of the wartime Ministry of Information) reported that men and women of all political shades agreed 'that the war should be pursued'. There was greater divergence with regard to Britain's war aims. Most agreed on the need to 'overthrow Hitlerism but there are several interpretations of what Hitlerism means. The majority do not feel hostile towards the German people but merely towards their government, although a tendency exists to hold the German people responsible for their acquiescence in their rulers.'[56] Differently from the role of the Belgian issue in 1914, few contemporary accounts mention the guarantee or the alliance to Poland. There was unease about the inactivity of the government in the first days of the war, but attention was focused on Hitler and Germany.

The days after the outbreak were ones of calm but also of frustration and irritation, particularly at the behaviour of the BBC. On 5 September, a student wrote, 'Everybody is saying they are sleeping better and eating better; the tension and war of nerves has gone, and mother who had been jittery for a long time has now settled down.' Two days later, he noted that 'the scarcity of news about anything that matters, members of Parliament, like the general public, feel that this unnecessary silence is depressing in two ways, it causes anxiety as to our position and has such a deadening effect that all work is a burden'.[57] A civil servant records on 7 September, 'I find myself impatient at lack of real news in papers and on the wireless. This feeling appears general amongst all I have spoken to.'[58] The BBC was criticized for the lack of news and for its descent into quite

---

[55] BIPO report on public opinion 'War and Peace', surveys from the week ending 30 September 1939.
[56] TNA, INF 1/261: BIPO, 'Public Opinion During the Week Ending 30 September 1939'.
[57] Mass Observation Archive, Diaries, 1939–1967: Diarist 5061, entry for 5 September 1939.
[58] Mass Observation Archive, Diaries, 1939–1967: Diarist 5156, diary for 7 September 1939.

'unnecessary depths of gloom',[59] and 'mournful tones'. There were complaints, too, about the music, 'too little of it, and too much slush'. Some, on the contrary, welcomed this effort to keep people cheerful by light music and popular song. As the days went by without action, there were grumbles about the inconvenience of the blackout, transportation, and other such matters, but always repeated complaints about the paucity of news. Public opinion might have helped push Chamberlain towards war rather than another Munich, but when war came the popular response was characterized by unease and a healthy dose of scepticism with regard to the authorities.

Even allowing for the revised view of the popular reaction to the outbreak of war in 1914, there were in September 1939 very few signs of any enthusiasm for war, but rather an acceptance of what had to be done in the full knowledge that it would be a long and difficult struggle. This time, there was an overwhelming sense of what was to come. The public response was complex – shock, relief, fear, resignation, uncertainty, determination, and greater sympathy towards pacifists and conscientious objectors than practised in 1914. The old messages of patriotism, nationalism, and pride in empire persisted to an extent but they shone far less brightly; as Lord Cecil had written to Halifax in 1936, 'I am quite satisfied that the young generation will not fight on those kind of grounds. When our young friends at Oxford said that they would not fight for King and Country, that is what they meant.'[60] But they would fight if necessary, and as in July 1914, few in September 1939 doubted that Britain would emerge victorious from the coming war. It was assumed both times that Britain was a Great Power with the strength to maintain its moral position as well as to defend its national interest, and to this extent, public opinion was one of the networks that sustained Britain's international position.

---

[59] Mass Observation Archive, Diaries, 1939–1967: Diarist 5182 (25-year-old civil servant), diary for 4 September 1939.
[60] Cecil to Halifax, 20 November 1936, Cecil of Chelwood Papers, British Library, Add. MSS. 51084.

# 9    The Ambassadors, 1919–1939

*Erik Goldstein*

They were the British ambassadors, ambassadors of the largest empire the world had ever seen. In the era stretching from the victorious conclusion of the Great War to the outbreak of the Second World War, there were fifty-one such paladins. Forty-five were career diplomats, five politicians, and one a senior India Office official.[1] The First World War had led to most ambassadors in post being extended, often well beyond normal retirement. Once the war had ended a mass retirement ensued, with a comparative flood of promotions. Only two of the appointments had held such rank previously, Lord Hardinge and Sir George Buchanan. The First World War thus provided a watershed in the rise of a new generation of diplomats to the top posts. The ambassadorial cadre provides a view of the British Diplomatic service during this period, at a time when it was under increasing threat of politicization and patronage appointments. The survival of a professional service and the maintenance of high morale among its most senior officials was an ongoing struggle.

\*\*\*

In family background the career diplomats who served as ambassadors resembled in many ways the previous generation of ambassadors; six of them had fathers who had been diplomats, eighteen had been to Eton (there was an Eton Fives court at the Lisbon embassy),[2] fifteen had attended Oxford, and five Cambridge. Most adhered to the established church, though a few were Roman Catholics. The academic attainments of those who attended the two ancient universities were not necessarily high, many had not bothered to take degrees, and several of those who did

---

[1] The anomaly in this group was Sir Francis Humphrys (1879–1971), who had spent much of his career in the Indian Political Service. He served as the first Minister to Afghanistan (1922–29) and then as High Commissioner of the British Mandate over Iraq (1929–32). When Iraq became independent he remained as ambassador (1932–35). His diplomatic postings are indicative of Britain seeing Afghanistan and Iraq as part of its Indian interests. After Humphrys the Bagdad embassy went to career diplomats, unlike Kabul.

[2] 'Sir Lancelot Carnegie', *The Times*, 19 October 1933, 17.

received third class or pass degrees.[3] The ambassadors, though, saw themselves as the personification of their country. Sir Horace Rumbold was wont to describe himself as an average Englishman. While it might be hard to imagine as an average Englishman an individual who was born in St Petersburg, the son of an ambassador, living most of his life abroad, Eton educated, the ninth baronet, with a tea plantation in Ceylon, the ambassadors nevertheless had a strong sense of themselves as the representatives of Britain, and of British values.

The interwar years saw the transformation and evolution of many diplomatic services into professional occupations, and as part of this process many services underwent various degrees of reform and reorganisation. These developments have attracted a certain amount of scholarly attention. Robert Schulzinger in his book *The Making of the Diplomatic Mind: The Training, Outlook, and Style of United States Foreign Service Officers, 1908–31* describes America's effort to create a career service. For Britain, Zara Steiner has provided an account of the workings of the pre-First World War Foreign Office in *The Foreign Office and Foreign Policy, 1898–1914*, while Roberta Warman has traced the decline of its importance in her article, 'The Erosion of Foreign Office Influence in the Making of Foreign Policy, 1916-18'.[4] The First World War was a watershed for the Foreign Office, seeing it plummet from the apogee to the nadir of its influence.[5] The interwar British Foreign Office's officials found themselves engaged in a struggle to restore the influence of the Office, and to avoid the fate of the nascent American service over politicization of appointments. Through eight governments and ten Foreign Secretaries the Foreign Office fought to retain its place at the centre of foreign policymaking.

The threat of politicization began with the formation of the Lloyd George coalition in late 1916. The perceived failure of diplomacy with the outbreak of the First World War saw not only a diminution of Foreign Office influence but also growing demands for its reform. Lloyd George had a well-known antipathy to the Foreign Office and shared many of the popular preconceptions about it. On assuming office he began a politicization of the ambassadorial corps. He had always had a penchant for using personal representatives to conduct sensitive

---

[3] Notable exceptions were Charles Eliot with a first in *litterae humaniores* at Oxford, and Maurice Peterson (who only became an ambassador on the eve of the Second World War), who took a first in modern history at Oxford.

[4] Zara Steiner, *The Foreign Office and Foreign Policy, 1898–1914* (Cambridge, 1969); Roberta Warman, 'The Erosion of Foreign Office Influence in the Making of Foreign Policy, 1916-18', *Historical Journal* 15(1) (1972), 133–59.

[5] Erik Goldstein, *Winning the Peace: British Diplomatic Strategy, Peace Planning, and the Paris Peace Conference, 1916–1920* (Oxford, 1991).

negotiations. It was only a small leap to move to appointing them to an embassy. He chose as ambassadors to the Great Powers of the time diplomatic laymen such as Lord Derby (France, 1918–20), Lord D'Abernon (Germany, 1920–26), Lord Reading (USA, 1918), Lord Grey (USA, 1919), and Sir Auckland Geddes (USA, 1920–24). This worrying trend was continued by the Conservative government which replaced Lloyd George in 1922. Its first diplomatic appointment was the non-career diplomat Lord Crewe to be ambassador at Paris. The Labour government in 1929 briefly toyed with the idea of sending a non-diplomat to Moscow, but finally decided against the idea.[6] These developments alarmed career diplomatists. Half a year into Lloyd George's government a Foreign Office official wrote to the ambassador at Rome that Lloyd George 'intervenes incessantly in appointments'.[7] In 1920, when the British minister at Warsaw, Sir Horace Rumbold, learnt of D'Abernon's appointment to Berlin, he exclaimed, 'This is one of Lloyd George's vamps ... Lloyd George is taking the heart out of the service and bids fair to destroy it. No diplomat can now hope to get one of the really big Embassies, at least as long as the present regime lasts. The FO struggles in vain.'[8] By now all the big embassies were held by political appointees. The permanent undersecretary at the Foreign Office, Lord Hardinge, who strongly disagreed with Lloyd George's actions, and who left the Office a few months later in frustration, told Rumbold, 'There is nothing to be done as far as I can see, for the prospects of the Service are very poor.'[9] George Buchanan, one of the most experienced ambassadors, then serving at Rome, commented on D'Abernon that while he understood 'the reasons why the Govt. want to have at Berlin an Ambassador who is an expert on financial questions. But why not choose an honest man?'[10]

Hardinge's successor as permanent undersecretary, the redoubtable Sir Eyre Crowe, unsuccessfully fought to keep the Paris embassy in the diplomatic service when it came up in 1922.[11] Hardinge had left the

[6] Dalton Diary, 31 October 1929. Dalton Papers, British Library of Political and Economic Science, London.

[7] Theo Russell (FO) to Sir James Rennell Rodd (Rome). Rennell of Rodd 25, First Lord Rennell of Rodd Papers, Bodleian Library, Oxford.

[8] Rumbold (Warsaw) to stepmother, 27 June 1920. Rumbold 27. Sir Horace Rumbold Papers, Bodleian Library, Oxford.

[9] Hardinge (FO) to Rumbold (Warsaw), 13 July 1920. Rumbold 27; on Hardinge see Brinton Cooper Busch, *Hardinge of Penshurst: A Study in the Old Diplomacy* (New York, 1980).

[10] Buchanan (British Embassy, Posilipo) to Gosse, 16 July 1920, letter 27. Sir George Buchanan Correspondence in Sir Edmund Gosse Papers, Brotherton Library, University of Leeds.

[11] Crowe to N. Bland, 18 September 1922. BLND 9/2, Sir Neville Bland Papers, Churchill College Archives Centre, Cambridge. On the permanent undersecretaries in this period

Office to take the Paris embassy, and when Crowe learnt Hardinge was now retiring from there, he wrote to his old chief, 'I literally shudder at the prospect of seeing the P.M. pushing some "friend" of his onto your embassy.'[12] Despondency as to the future of a career diplomatic service wracked the diplomats. These trends were accidentally halted, however, by the domestic political upheavals of the next few years. The rapid changes of government, from late 1923 to early 1925, allowed the Diplomatic Service to reassert itself, and no further political appointments were made until the eve and early days of the Second World War when Lord Lothian (1939) and then Lord Halifax (1940–46) were sent to Washington, and Sir Stafford Cripps (1940–42) was sent to Moscow.

Ultimately the development of the career service, and the careers of those in it, was dependent on the Foreign Secretary. Relations with the various foreign secretaries of this period were, not surprisingly, varied. Lord Curzon was particularly difficult to deal with. Ronald Lindsay, later to be permanent undersecretary (1928–29) and ambassador at Washington (1930–39), painted a vivid picture of life in Curzon's Foreign Office, which his brother recorded: 'it seems as though all the stories about George's [Curzon's] brutality to his officials are true. Poor Eyre Crowe has to go to the telephone at eleven every morning through which he receives such a series of scoldings that he is exhausted till luncheon time.'[13] Lindsay later observed that 'none but the strongest nerves can stand it'.[14] Sir Horace Rumbold complained that 'Curzon is a man who accepts the cream brought to him by someone and kicks the man who brought it.'[15] After his death, some of his fellow Old Etonians at the Foreign Office and in the Diplomatic Service attempted to raise a subscription for a portrait of the late Foreign Secretary to hang at Eton. A letter was circulated in November 1928, but by the following year, of the necessary £300, only £16 had been subscribed.[16]

---

see Keith Neilson and T. G. Otte, *The Permanent Under-Secretary for Foreign Affairs, 1854–1946* (New York, 2009), 161–257; for Crewe's appointment, John Vincent (ed.), *The Crawford Papers: The Journals of David Lindsay Twenty-Seventh Earl of Crawford and Tenth Earl of Balcarres, 1871–1940 during the Years 1892 to 1940* (Manchester, 1984), 469. On Crowe's career see Sibyl Crowe and Edward Corp, *Our Ablest Public Servant: Sir Eyre Crowe, 1864–1925* (Braunton, 1993).

[12] Crowe to Hardinge, 14 September 1922. U927, file 029, item 10. Hardinge of Penshurst Papers, Cambridge University Library, transferred from the Kent Archives Office. I am grateful to Dr David Kaufman of the University of Edinburgh for this letter.

[13] Diary entry for 30 May 1922 in John Vincent (ed.), *The Crawford Papers*, 422.

[14] Ibid. Diary entry for 8 November 1922.

[15] Rumbold to Nevile Henderson, 29 February 1924. Rumbold 22.

[16] Gaselee (FO) to Rumbold (Madrid), 30 July 1928. Rumbold 35. See also copy of circular letter, 30 June 1929, HDLM Acc 727, file 41. Sir James Headlam-Morley Papers, Churchill Archives Centre, Cambridge.

Life was a little easier under Curzon's successor in the first Labour government, as Ramsay MacDonald decided to also hold the Foreign Office
portfolio. This gave him little time to interfere, and much of the day-to-day
conduct of foreign policy reverted to the Office. MacDonald's hands-off style
caused him to be well regarded. One member of the Office writing to
a colleague posted abroad observed that he found MacDonald ' . . . eminently
reasonable & broad-visioned'.[17]

Foreign Office influence began to reassert itself in late 1924 when Austen
Chamberlain assumed office as Foreign Secretary in the new Conservative
government. He was determined to establish his paramountcy in foreign
policy amongst his Cabinet colleagues. He soon became an admirer of
Crowe, and through him of the professionalism of the Office, which he
used effectively in his battle of wills with the Cabinet. The Chamberlain–
Crowe association lasted only a few months, as Crowe suddenly died just six
months into Chamberlain's tenure.[18] Chamberlain was distressed by
Crowe's death, writing at the time to his sister, 'I did not think I could
have felt so much for a man whom I have only known intimately for a few
months.'[19] This high regard undoubtedly led to Sir William Tyrrell,
Crowe's closest colleague, being appointed to succeed him. This assured
a strong continuity of house style at the Office. Chamberlain's standing with
the professionals was undoubtedly a key ingredient of his success at the
Foreign Office. Tyrrell's successor, Sir Ronald Lindsay, regarded
Chamberlain as 'a great Foreign Secretary' and recalled him, implicitly
comparing him to Curzon, as 'the most companionable chief I ever had.
I never knew a man more interested in those who worked for him.'[20]

The period 1929–31 saw a rapid turnover of foreign secretaries until
Sir John Simon assumed office. He never really settled in at the
Foreign Office, and most of his staff found him profoundly irritating
to work with, as well as ineffective in policy.[21] Lindsay reported that
Simon 'made a practice of asking one ambassador what he thought of
another, and as all of them thought themselves much more important

---

[17] Ingram (FO) to Archibald Clark Kerr (Egypt), 20 February 1924. Lord Inverchapel
Papers, Bodleian Library, Oxford.
[18] Erik Goldstein, 'British Diplomatic Strategy and the Locarno Conference' in M. Dockrill
and B. J. C. McKercher, *Diplomacy and World Power: Studies in British Foreign Policy,
1890–1951* (Cambridge, 1996), 115–35.
[19] Austen Chamberlain to Hilda Chamberlain, 25 April 1924. AC 5/1/351. Sir Austen
Chamberlain Papers, University of Birmingham. Reprinted in Robert C. Self (ed.), *The
Austen Chamberlain Diary Letters*, Camden Fifth Series, vol. V (Cambridge, 1995), 275.
[20] Ronald Lindsay, *Sic Fatuor Nuntius*, 151, unpublished autobiography, Crawford Papers. I
am grateful to the Earl of Crawford and Balcarres for permission to quote from this source.
The sentiments were reciprocated, see Neilson and Otte, *Permanent Under-secretary*, 205.
[21] On Simon see David Dutton, *Simon: A Political Biography of Sir John Simon* (London,
1992).

than a parvenu in foreign affairs like Simon, the Secretary of State was soon stranded and could get nothing out of his chief officials, so suspicious had he made them'.[22] Lindsay recalled that when Simon told him he would like to be called Jack, 'I felt as though I were being subjected to the blandishments of an adder ... All feel the same in the foreign service.'[23] Tyrrell, who was rounding off his career as ambassador at Paris, loathed Simon. Once when Simon was talking at length after dining at the embassy, Tyrrell 'put a hand to his mouth to stifle a great yawn, walked out, and never came back'. He told one of his diplomatic staff the next morning that he 'just couldn't take it any longer'.[24] After Simon's departure in 1935, in the lead-up to the Second World War, there was another rapid turnover of foreign secretaries, and prime ministers, that allowed the career officers to maintain control of appointments. Neville Chamberlain, though, in pursuit of his foreign policy objectives, had begun to take an interest in senior Foreign Office appointments, and had events followed a different course he might well have had a serious impact on the professional ethos of the diplomatic service.

The diplomats did not just have to deal with the Foreign Secretary, but also his political alter ego, the parliamentary undersecretary. Lord Cranborne, on being appointed parliamentary undersecretary in 1900, had written to a member of the diplomatic service:

What a dreadful thing it must be for the members of the diplomatic service when they have to endure the advent of yet another Under-Secretary. What! yet one more ignorant M.P. to educate up to F.O. standard; another clumsy mouthpiece of H.M. Govt. whose utterances will have with infinite trouble to be explained away![25]

Some parliamentary undersecretaries failed to make much impact. Godfrey Locker-Lampson, who served under Austen Chamberlain, was known to officials as 'X the unknown'.[26] In contrast, some parliamentary undersecretaries had definite ideas on the Office. When the first Labour government was formed in 1924, Arthur Ponsonby was assigned to this post. He had formerly served as a career member of the Office in 1894–1903, resigning in a row over lack of reform of the Office and the diplomatic service. Although many of these reforms were subsequently implemented, one member of the Office warned another that Ponsonby

[22] Diary for 10 December 1937, in John Vincent (ed.), *The Crawford Papers*, 585.
[23] Diary for 30 December 1939, ibid.
[24] Interview with Sir Frank Roberts, 27 May 1994, and Frank Roberts, *Dealing with Dictators: The Destruction and Revival of Europe, 1930–70* (London, 1991), 11.
[25] Cranborne to Sir James Rennell Rodd, 25 November 1900. Rodd 30.
[26] Lancelot Oliphant quoted in Dalton Diary 13, 2 December 1930.

'has a swarm of bees in his bonnet'.[27] Hugh Dalton, the parliamentary undersecretary in the second Labour government, exerted a great deal of influence over Office life, and Gladwyn Jebb, his private secretary, told him ' . . . that he had heard it said . . . that I was the first Parl[iamentary] Under-Sec[retary] since Curzon who had shown any capacity to get myself disliked in the Office'.[28]

The official who stood at the interface between the politicians and the career service was the permanent undersecretary of state for foreign affairs. As the senior civil servant the permanent undersecretaries stood at the top of the career pyramid. Until 1919 there had been two distinct services, the Foreign Office staff and the Diplomatic Service. While it was possible to arrange occasional transfers between these two services, it was not very common. As a result, most holders of the permanent under-secretaryship were members of the Foreign Office staff, with no extensive overseas experience, the exceptions being Sir Charles Hardinge and Sir Arthur Nicolson. The amalgamation of services took some time to work through at senior levels. Of the five permanent undersecretaries appointed in the interwar period, three were from the Foreign Office stream, while two had started in the Diplomatic Service. Political preferences of the moment inevitably influenced some of these appointments. Lord Hardinge, the wartime permanent undersecretary, did not get on with Lloyd George, who froze him out of any decision making. Hardinge eventually left the post in frustration. Two of his successors suffered similar political clashes. In 1928, just at the end of the second Baldwin government, Sir Ronald Lindsay was appointed permanent undersecre-tary. A career diplomat, he came from an influential Conservative family, and the arrival of a Labour government in 1929 clearly caused difficulties. The result was the shortest tenure of this post. Lindsay and his new political masters did not get on. Within weeks he was having rows with Dalton, who was hoping to replace him with Sir Eric Drummond, then Secretary-General of the League of Nations.[29] Dalton confided to his diary 'that it will be a good thing when L[indsay] goes'.[30] Eventually Lindsay took the opportunity of going to Washington as ambassador, and Robert Vansittart replaced him. Dalton was happy with this choice, commenting after one difficult round of negotiations that Vansittart had 'displayed wonderful physical endurance, inexhaustible patience and good will and supreme negotiating power'.[31] Vansittart was one of those who warned of the growing German threat, a view which increasingly

---

[27] Ingram (FO) to Archibald Clark Kerr (Egypt), 24 January 1924. Inverchapel Papers.
[28] Dalton diary, 13 December 1929.    [29] Dalton diary, 30 June 1929.
[30] Dalton diary, 10 December 1929.    [31] Dalton diary, 8 May 1930.

brought him into conflict with his superiors in the late 1930s. They wished to move him to a less central post and hoped he would accept an embassy as a prelude to retirement, as Hardinge, Tyrrell, and Lindsay had done. Vansittart, though, refused to accept an embassy. He was eventually moved to the specially created post of chief diplomatic adviser, after which his advice was studiously ignored.

The ambition of most diplomats was to become a head of mission, with the ultimate prize being promotion to ambassador. The aftermath of the First World War had seen an increase in the number of states and the consequent need for more diplomatic representation. The Labour foreign secretary, Arthur Henderson (1929–31), was irritated by this proliferation of states, referring to them as 'All these snuffling little countries', and complaining of having to deal with, 'all these wretched little places. Many of them must only be about half the size of Yorkshire!'[32] Nevertheless, all required some diplomatic presence. Britain maintained a strict classification of states, almost like that applied to fine French wines. Traditionally only a few states were considered of sufficient significance to be graced by a British ambassador, the remainder being dealt with by 'Envoys Extraordinary and Ministers Plenipotentiary' and other grades of diplomatic agents.

The Congress of Vienna (1814) had established the modern nomenclature and hierarchy of diplomatic posts, with ambassadors at the apex. Britain made use of this to indicate the standing of other countries in its diplomatic universe. Rising powers were recognized by the elevation of those missions, with legations being made embassies at Berlin (1862), Rome (1876), Washington (1893), and Tokyo (1905). Diplomatic disapproval could also be indicated by reducing the status of the diplomatic mission. In 1822, Madrid was lowered to a legation, and not restored to ambassadorial rank until 1887, largely due to Britain's strained relations with the tumultuous sequence of regimes in those years. In 1844, in a period of poor Anglo-Russian relations which resulted in the Crimean War, St Petersburg was reduced to a legation and not elevated again until 1860. Austria reduced its representation in 1850, in a diplomatic spat. London again elevated both St Petersburg and Vienna to their old status in the wake of Napoleon III's annexation of Nice and Savoy, and the need for better relations with the continental counterweights. The Netherlands was reduced to a legation in 1836 on the separation of Belgium, in part due to frustration at Dutch intransigence over a final settlement. Subsequent efforts by the Dutch to have

[32] Dalton diary, 27 March 1930 and 17 June 1929.

their status restored were unsuccessful until 1942, when the Dutch government in exile, resident in London, was placed on the ambassadorial level.

When the First World War ended this ambassadorial club was limited to five members, France, Italy, Spain, the United States, and Japan. Subsequently, of the formerly ambassadorial states of the Central Powers, Germany was restored to ambassadorial status on the ratification of the peace treaty, not Austria or Hungary. In 1922 an ambassador received an annual salary of £2,500, while a minister received £2,000.[33] During the interwar years eight further states were elevated to ambassadorial status: Belgium and Brazil (1919), presumably for being loyal allies, followed by Portugal (1924), Argentina (1927), Poland (1929), Chile (1930), Iraq (1932), China (1935), and Egypt (1936). The result was the creation of an informal hierarchy of posts, with the great embassies at the top and the lesser embassies at the bottom. Nobody believed Baghdad was equal in status to Paris. When Sir George Clerk was appointed to Brussels, Rumbold observed that he was 'being fobbed off with what one can only call a courtesy embassy'.[34] The growth of the number of diplomatic posts posed difficulties, and although most ambassadors attempted to maintain the custom of writing privately to the Foreign Secretary, Rumbold noted in 1932 that he had written three times to Simon without any reply. By the Second World War the staffing at embassies had also dramatically increased. Anthony Rumbold, a young diplomat at Washington, informed his now retired diplomat father that 'the Embassy, with its associated agencies, is now such a large enterprise, like a government department, that it's impossible even when one is right in it to grasp everything that goes on'.[35]

Britain was reluctant to increase the number of embassies, both for status and financial reasons, as ambassadors were paid higher salaries and allowances. Austen Chamberlain observed in 1928 in a private letter to the minister to Chile in response to the idea that Santiago might be elevated to an embassy, as Buenos Aires had just been:

I have little doubt in my own mind that sooner or later this change will have to be made, but having regard to the claims of other Powers, to the stringency of the financial situation – which makes the Chancellor of the Exchequer unwilling to part with even a five pound note – and to His Majesty's dislike of the

[33] 'Regulations for His Majesty's Diplomatic Service' 1 April 1922. DHW 9/37.4. Howard of Penrith Papers, Cumbria Record Office, Carlisle.
[34] Rumbold to son, 14 May 1933. Rumbold add V/5.
[35] Anthony Rumbold to Sir Horace Rumbold, 8 December 1940. Rumbold add V/3. Sir Anthony Rumbold Papers, Bodleian Library, Oxford.

multiplication of Ambassadors, it is quite impossible for me to come under any engagement however conditional.[36]

Britain and France maintained an informal understanding not to elevate any more missions to embassies without prior consultation, but this began to break down, particularly in Latin America.[37] Some of Britain's elevation of missions was in response to French actions. Belgium was one such instance, where both France and the United States did so in 1919, with President Wilson making the American announcement in person to the Belgian parliament.[38] A failure to match French actions would otherwise result in assigning the British head of mission to a lesser protocol status. As the pressure to create new embassies continued to escalate, Eyre Crowe wrote:

The creation of fresh embassies everywhere is getting a farce, and it is to be hoped that we will not allow ourselves to be driven to multiplying our British embassies without justification. It is now generally recognised that we made a mistake in allowing embassies to Belgium and Brazil, the latter compelling us to follow the example with Lisbon.[39]

In a minute in June 1924, which was approved by MacDonald, Crowe pointed out that if the current trend continued, which would result in doing away altogether with the differentiation between ambassadors and ministers, the necessity would arise of 'finding some other ground on which our Court could claim to extend rather more favoured treatment to *some* foreign diplomatic representatives than to others. Hitherto there has been the difference between Great Powers and minor powers. But already with Belgium and Brazil and Portugal having ambassadors, this distinction is becoming a patent absurdity.'[40] By 1937, as the trend continued, Vansittart commented 'there will be a revolution in precedence. Is a senior Nicaraguan to rank above a new German representative for example?'[41] Oliver Harvey neatly summarized the sequence of events: 'we raised our Mission to the rank of an Embassy in Belgium, Brazil, and Portugal because they had taken part in the war; on Chile lest the prestige of the latter country should suffer vis-à-vis of Brazil and the Argentine; in

[36] Sir Austen Chamberlain to Clark Kerr, 15 December 1928. Inverchapel Papers.

[37] Phipps correspondence with Sir Malcolm Robertson, 26–28 March 1927. PHPP 3/4. Sir Eric Phipps Papers, Churchill Archives Centre, Cambridge.

[38] 'Brussels to be Embassy', *New York Times*, 24 August 1919, 3.

[39] Quoted in John W. Field, 'Policy of appointing British ambassadors to foreign States', 20 February 1925. FO 370/205/L34/34/405. Foreign Office Papers, The National Archives, London.

[40] Minute by Crowe of June 1924, in John W. Field, 'Policy of appointing British ambassadors to foreign States', 20 February 1925. FO 370/205/L34/34/405.

[41] Minute by Vansittart, 20 February 1937. FO 371/20745/C2189/2189/29.

Iraq and Egypt to suit our own interests; and in China because our hands were partly forced by other countries and partly by our own business men.'[42] In November 1938 the ever thrifty Neville Chamberlain took the decision that no more embassies were to be created.[43]

The Foreign Office, for internal purposes, established a necessary distinction between first-class and second-class embassies.[44] One of the factors in this decision was the Diplomatic Pensions Act of 1929 which decided that all pre-war embassies, plus Cairo, would be first-class missions, with a salary of £2,500 for the head of mission. All post-war missions and any new ones would be treated as second-class missions, with a salary of £2,250. 'The principal object of the change was to ensure that the occupants of the recently created Embassies should not enjoy the same favourable pension rights as those attaching to the older Embassies.'[45] None of this was publicly visible as 'One of the conditions on which these second class Embassies were created was that no notification of this fact was to be made to the public, in order to avoid giving offence to the countries concerned and great care has been taken to conceal the existence of these second class Embassies in any published lists.'[46] As a result, in 1931 Lisbon was demoted to a second-class mission. Sir Francis Lindley was fortunate to have been appointed one month before this change, and so received the higher salary of £2,500. Later, Sir Walford Selby, who was ambassador to Portugal (1935–40), complained of this, as it meant he would not retire on a first-class pension, and the chances of moving to a first-class post were much diminished by the war. Perhaps not surprisingly when he did retire, already embittered by other professional experiences, he emigrated to Southern Rhodesia where he wrote a controversial memoir *Diplomatic Twilight* (1953). During the Second World War ambassadorial representation was extended to ten further states, possibly in response to the need to recognise adequately the various governments in exile and other allies, as well as to find postings for senior diplomats repatriated from enemy and occupied countries.

Within the hierarchy of embassies, Latin America was clearly at the bottom of the list. In 1918 it was decided to elevate Brazil to an embassy. This was a consequence of the 1918 de Bunsen mission to South America,

[42] FO 371/20745/C2189/2189/29.    [43] FO 371/22503/W15852/15852/50.

[44] Minute by Mounsey, 8 February 1937, FO 371/20745/C2189/2189/29. This was in the context of a Dutch desire to have diplomatic relations at the ambassadorial level.

[45] FO 371/24495/C7937/7937/36. One quirk was Brussels, as every ambassador there had been transferred from a first-class post, with the exception of Lancelot Oliphant, who by special Treasury sanction was allowed £2,500.

[46] FO 371/24495/C7937/7937/36.

which was looking at post-war economic opportunities, as well as being a reward for Brazil joining the Allies in the war. The first occupant was Sir Ralph Paget, then Minister at Copenhagen, considered to be one of Britain's best diplomats, from a family with a distinguished diplomatic record and well-connected at court. He had become bored with his work and was desperate to escape the Danish climate, even volunteering for a posting to Mesopotamia or Sudan. He had decided the unless he could get a warmer posting 'I think I had better make up my mind if necessary to sacrifice any further prospects of career (after all having got no further than Minister at the age of 54 I am not likely to do much).'[47] All he longed for was 'an old cotton shirt and old pair of pants, a good horse, the open prairie or desert & rarely if ever to set my foot in a house again'.[48] Instead he was chosen to be Britain's first ambassador to Brazil.[49] As his friend (Odo) Theo Russell, the Diplomatic Secretary to the Foreign Secretary, told him, 'We attach utmost importance to this post and to personality of first British Ambassador at Rio.'[50] Paget accepted with alacrity, writing on the same day he received the offer, and asking how soon he could leave Copenhagen.[51] Paget, however, remained in post at Rio only until 1921, when he opted to retire from the service.[52]

The Latin American embassies were, in many ways, in a category of their own. In 1922 Sir Claude Mallet alerted the Foreign Office to a possible problem with Uruguay. With the inauguration of José Serrato as the new president approaching, Mallet noted:

The former custom of neighbourly South American States being represented on these occasions by Special Ambassadors has become a general practice which, in the cases of Argentina and Brazil, was adopted by all the big European powers. The Uruguayans are very proud of their little Country and extremely sensitive of any act which can be interpreted as a reflection upon their insignificance as a nation.[53]

---

[47] Paget (Copenhagen) to Theo Russell (FO), 23 July 1918. BL Add MS 51256 (Sir Ralph Paget Papers), f.118. British Library.

[48] Paget (Copenhagen) to Theo Russell (FO), 4 September 1918. BL Add MS 51256 (Sir Ralph Paget Papers), f.155.

[49] Balfour to Paget (Copenhagen), 30 August 1918. BL Add MS 51256 (Sir Ralph Paget Papers), f.151. He accepted the offer the same day the telegram was received, 31 August.

[50] Balfour to Paget (Copenhagen), 30 August 1918 (rec'd 31 August). BL Add MS 51256 (Sir Ralph Paget Papers), f.151.

[51] Paget (Copenhagen) to FO, 31 August 1918. BL Add MS 51256 (Sir Ralph Paget Papers), f.152.

[52] Paget had been Minister to Serbia at the outbreak of the First World War, and he and his wife had played a notable role in the events of surrounding the invasion of Serbia. Her heroic nursing efforts are recalled in Belgrade with a street named in her honour. See Čedomir Antić, *Ralph Paget: A Diplomat in Serbia* (Belgrade, 2006).

[53] Mallet (Monte Video) to Agar-Roberts, 29 December 1922. FO 371/8528/A437/400/46.

As Britain had just appointed special ambassadors to Argentina and Brazil, he advised they would never hear the end of it. Mallet was one of Serrato's closest friends and warned that not to be so represented would be viewed as contempt of a small state. He suggested that he be appointed, although this would incur some additional expense as the other special representatives would have to be entertained, and the last time he had done this, in Buenos Aires for the inauguration of President Alvear, he had had to pay out of his own pocket. Mallet was duly provided with the necessary credentials, but with the proviso that they were only to be used if the United States or a European power accredited a special ambassador.[54] There had been an agreement in 1919 between Britain, France, Italy, and Belgium on diplomatic representation in South America, and when France was consulted, Prime Minister Raymond Poincaré objected to granting special ambassadorial credentials to the French minister at Montevideo.[55] It was in fact France that had started the issue when it provided for a special ambassador at the inauguration of the Argentine president.[56] The British ambassador at Paris, Lord Crewe, weighed in by observing that Serrato's brother had been killed during the war fighting in Italy and suggested that an exception should be made.[57] In the end the Allied powers and Spain provided special representatives.[58]

Usually any posting to Latin America was seen virtually as a punishment or a career-crippling event. In 1925, Archibald Clark Kerr, then only forty-three years of age, was offered the post of minister to Guatemala. Walford Selby of the Foreign Office, seeking to convince him to accept, told Clark Kerr that 'I should strongly recommend your taking this very early promotion if it is offered, more especially as the Secretary of State is making a great point about the South and Central American service, which need no longer be regarded as a back-water so far as eventual promotion is concerned.'[59] Given that his predecessor was being sent to be Minister and Consul-General in Albania, this was optimistic advice.[60] Clark Kerr did accept, though as he was informed a few

---

[54] Minute by Sperling, 31 January 1923. FO 371/8528/A437/400/46.
[55] St. Aulaire (French ambassador, London) to Curzon, 6 February 1923. FO 371/8528/A778/400/46.
[56] Minute by Sperling, FO 371/8528/A778/400/46.
[57] Crewe (Paris) to FO # 436, 21 February 1923. FO 371/8528/A1060/400/46.
[58] Special ambassadors were accredited by: Britain, France, Italy, United States, Belgium, Spain, Argentine, Brazil, Chile, Ecuador, Paraguay, and Peru. Envoys Extraordinary and Ministers Plenipotentiary on Special Mission were provided by: Portugal, Sweden, Bolivia, Colombia, and Guatemala. Mallet (Montevideo) to Curzon, 2 March 1923. FO 371/8528/A1817/400/46.
[59] Selby to Clark Kerr, 7 September 1925. Inverchapel Papers.
[60] William O'Reilly served briefly in Albania before being posted as Minister to Venezuela, 1926–32.

days later, 'I am sorry to say that you are, as you feared, accredited also to Nicaragua, Salvador and Honduras and, when you have nothing better to do, you will no doubt visit these interesting localities to present you credentials.'[61] At this time the only means of transport to his new post was via a Fyffes banana boat. The post was not without its compensation, however, as Clark Kerr's predecessor wrote to him offering to sell him quite a lot of champagne which he had bought cheaply from a would-be American bootlegger.[62]

Accepting a post in Latin America, though, never became popular. (Malcolm) Arnold Robertson, when offered the post of minister to Argentina in 1925, noted that he only did so 'after much searching of heart and a long talk with [Tyrrell] of about two hours. Quite frankly, I had fully intended to resign and only changed my mind after seeing Tyrrell.'[63] He was fortunate in that two years later his post was elevated to an embassy, and as he observed, 'Though this place is very far off I am, of course, delighted to be an Ambassador and so to have reached the top of our profession.'[64] Nonetheless, he was hesitant at the idea of staying on, even as an ambassador. His friend and colleague in the service, D'Arcy Osborne, advised him 'to accept & retain liberty to leave when he likes'.[65] Indeed, two years later he resigned at the age of 52 to pursue a career in business and politics.

Given the interlocking nature of appointments, with one transfer or promotion being dependent on another, there emerged a cycle of appointments. As a result, at certain intervals, the chess board of diplomatic appointments would see a great deal of movement. During the First World War it had been felt necessary to retain ambassadors in post, and many were continued beyond the normal tour of duty. With the end of the war Curzon informed the ambassador at Rome that 'now that the war is over we have practically to readjust the whole diplomatic chess board & fix the posts & the men for the next few years'.[66] Curzon, though, had to accept Lloyd George's political interference in the process. While he might not have liked having Lloyd George appointees as ambassadors, Curzon was not averse to the possibilities of having non-career ambassadors. Curzon still aspired to be prime minister, and embassies provided both patronage and a way to remove potential rivals. George Buchanan at

[61] Craigie (FO) to Clark Kerr, 24 September 1925. Inverchapel Papers.
[62] O'Reilly to Clark Kerr, 28 September 1925. Inverchapel Papers; see also Donald Gillies, *Radical Diplomat: The Life of Archibald Clark Kerr, Lord Inverchapel, 1882–1951* (London, 1999).
[63] Malcolm Robertson to Clark Kerr, 10 August 1927. Inverchapel Papers.    [64] Ibid.
[65] Francis D'Arcy Osborne Diary, 24 February 1927. BL Egerton MS 3834A. British Library.
[66] Curzon to Sir James Rennell Rodd, 18 July 1919. Rennell of Rodd 22.

Rome, by now Britain's most experienced ambassador, suspected the reason he was not being extended in post after an unusually short duration of two years was that 'that the post has been promised to an outsider'.[67] Curzon provided public evidence of his thinking when in March 1921, at a farewell event for the American ambassador John Davis, a politician and lawyer, he commented on the American approach to ambassadorial appointments:

They have recourse to bins, the vintages of which are sometimes not sufficiently appreciated in this country. I find, when they want to send us an Ambassador here, they go sometimes to the profession of law, sometimes to literary men and men famous as men of letters, and sometimes to newspaper men and journalists. Is there not something in this that we can imitate?[68]

After Lloyd George's fall, Curzon, having retained the Foreign Office, began to replace the former's appointments.

Curzon first of all planned to replace the Lloyd George-era political appointments. At Washington, he hoped to replace Auckland Geddes with Austen Chamberlain, the former party leader and still a popular figure within it. Curzon succeeded in forcing Geddes to resign, albeit unwillingly, though in the end Chamberlain declined the opportunity. Lord D'Abernon was also high on Curzon's list of political appointees he planned to replace. In October 1923 he informed D'Abernon that he would like to have a new ambassador in place early in the new year, and let the news appear in *The Times*.[69] Political developments in London, though, disrupted Curzon's plans. Much to his dismay the new prime minister, Stanley Baldwin, decided to call a general election. Curzon was opposed: 'But the P.M. having, as I think prematurely started the ball rolling, no one can be very sure where it will stop.'[70] Curzon was indeed prescient, and his plans to clear out the Lloyd George legacies and replace them with his own appointees were frustrated by a Labour victory. As the likelihood of Britain getting its first Labour government loomed, in his last few days in office Curzon hurriedly made efforts to pre-empt a new Foreign Secretary being able to make key diplomatic appointments. After consulting the king, Curzon decided he could make

---

[67] Buchanan (British Embassy, Rome) to Gosse, 21 March 1921. Gosse 47. He suspected Lord Lytton to be the candidate who had been hoping to be Viceroy of India. In the end Lytton was made Governor of Bombay.

[68] 'A True Friend', *The Times*, 1 March 1921, 14.

[69] Curzon (FO) to D'Abernon (Berlin), 31 October 1923. BL Add MS 48925B (D'Abernon Papers). 'Lord D'Abernon' *The Times*, 31 October 1923, 4. The rumoured successor was Rumbold.

[70] Curzon (FO) to D'Abernon (Berlin), 8 November 1923. BL Add MS 48925B (D'Abernon Papers).

these appointments, provided they were from inside the Service, and therefore apolitical. To accomplish his goal, Curzon had only a small window of opportunity.

Ronald Lindsay was told in the last days of December 1923 that he was being sent immediately to Turkey, initially only as Chargé d'Affaires until a peace treaty was ratified, without knowing if afterwards he would be accredited as a minister or an ambassador. Lindsay told his brother, 'Curzon is acting with some precipitation. It seems to me clear that he wants to fill the post up before the Labour party come in fearing that they might appoint some wild man. Personally I doubt if they would in any case do such a thing.'[71] Lindsay remained in post after the peace treaty with the anomalous title of H. M. Representative at Constantinople until March 1925 when, somewhat unwillingly, the post was made an embassy, though this necessitated Britain receiving a Turkish ambassador, which both George V and the Foreign Office 'regarded with great distaste'.[72] Newly married, he was delighted that the promotion brought an extra £300 per year, but also that the Office of Works improved the furniture of the new embassy from his previous bachelor existence.[73]

Curzon planned to remove D'Abernon from Berlin and Geddes from Washington, and of necessity to replace them from within the service. All this would cause a chain reaction throughout the diplomatic service, and Curzon thought 'it was important to do it as soon as possible and to get the new men accepted & if possible installed, if only temporarily, before a Labour Govt. comes in, as it now seems fated to do'.[74] He cabled D'Abernon: 'Change in political situation here renders it important that your successor should be appointed without delay and that he should take over at Berlin before new Government enters office.'[75] Various names were suggested for Berlin. Serious thought of appointing Rumbold encountered opposition from Crowe, who did not hold him in high regard, a view shared by Baldwin. Crowe informed Curzon that 'You may possibly know that Baldwin who was a school fellow of his, has no great opinion of him as regard ability and judgment.' In the end Rumbold

---

[71] Lindsay to Lord Crawford and Balcarres, 1 January 1924. Crawford 97/10. Crawford and Balcarres Papers, National Library of Scotland.

[72] John W. Field, 'Policy of appointing British ambassadors to foreign States', 20 February 1925. FO 370/205/L34/34/405.

[73] Lindsay (Constantinople) to Lord Crawford & Balcarres, 29 October 1929. Crawford 97/10, and Lindsay (C'ple) to Lord Crawford & Balcarres, 31 December 1924. Crawford 97/10. Crawford & Balcarres Papers, National Library of Scotland.

[74] Curzon to D'Abernon (Berlin), 19 December 1923. BL Add MS 48925B (D'Abernon Papers).

[75] Curzon to D'Abernon (Berlin), 14 December 1923. BL Add MS 48925B (D'Abernon Papers).

was sent to Madrid.[76] Crowe attempted to press the case of his close friend Tyrrell, but Curzon instead opted to transfer George Grahame from Brussels to Berlin. However, Curzon's plans ran into an unexpected problem when Grahame unexpectedly declined the move. As Curzon explained to D'Abernon, 'The fact is that I offered the succession to you to George Grahame who declined it on the pusillanimous plea of ill health – the reality being that he thought by accepting he might compromise his chance of getting Paris later on, a chance which I was convinced that by this cowardice he has sacrificed forever.'[77] As a result, Curzon had to leave this matter to the new government. One of the members of the Foreign Office staff noted of the arrival of the first Labour government that Curzon 'had scarcely left the building before there was a complete upheaval of his arrangements'.[78] One of the beneficiaries of this period of political volatility was D'Abernon, whose appointment had caused such anguish amongst the career diplomats. The MacDonald government was too preoccupied with other concerns to deal with filling the Berlin embassy during its brief life, and the Conservative government which came to power in late 1924 embarked on a course of rapprochement with Germany which culminated in the Locarno Pact. As this required stability in the Berlin embassy, D'Abernon survived in post for over six years.[79]

The year 1928 saw another round of ambassadorial appointments. Three major embassies were up for grabs as Horace Rumbold noted at the time: 'Washington, Paris and Berlin are our most important Embassies. We should hate the former.'[80] He also commented that 'I think it is evident that some of the factors which used to enter into appointments to important Embassies such as a presentable wife, private means and a knowledge of how to do things will no longer count for much if at all. Things have changed in our service as elsewhere.'[81] While he possessed all of these advantages, he was also a consummate professional and wanted to see appointments made on merit. In this instance the permanent undersecretary Tyrrell, who was close to both the prime minister, Stanley Baldwin, and the Foreign Secretary, Sir Austen Chamberlain, took the Paris embassy as the capstone of his career, although he had never served in an embassy. Rumbold, who had hoped

[76] Crowe to Curzon (private), 22 December 1923, Curzon MSS, MSS Eur.F112/229. India Office Library.
[77] Curzon to D'Abernon (Berlin), 7 January 1924. BL Add MS 48925B (D'Abernon Papers). Grahame ended his career as ambassador at Madrid, 1928–35.
[78] Selby (FO) to Clark Kerr (Cairo), 18 February 1924. Inverchapel Papers.
[79] On D'Abernon see Gaynor Johnson, *The Berlin Embassy of Lord d'Abernon, 1920–1926* (Basingstoke, 2002).
[80] Rumbold to stepmother, 24 February 1924. Rumbold 35.
[81] Rumbold (Madrid) to stepmother, 24 February 1928. Rumbold 35.

he might get Paris, doubted Tyrrell's suitability, commenting, 'He is very clever – exceptionally so, in fact – but he has no experience of running an Embassy and as for Lady T. Well!'[82] Rumbold was not alone in this view. Sir Ronald Lindsay, then at Berlin and about to become Tyrrell's successor as permanent undersecretary, observed, 'few people would be worse suited as Ambassador than Tyrrell[,] none worse as Ambassadoress than Lady T'.[83] Tyrrell, in fact, left much of the running of the embassy to his deputy Ronald Campbell, but his political network in Paris was extensive and kept him well informed. As Lindsay's older brother, the Earl of Crawford and Balcarres, noted, 'Tyrrell it may be added is extremely fond of Baldwin – Baldwin likes hearing Tyrrell's gazouillements [chirpings], with his quick furtive mouselike movements of mind. Baldwin's stolid temperament is appeased by Tyrrell's picturesque and suggestive chatter.'[84] From Paris Tyrrell was able to stay in close touch with Baldwin.

As for Washington, it was decided to prolong Howard's tenure. As Tyrrell told him, 'You give us a sense of confidence and security which in a post like Washington is vital for the conduct of public business.'[85] Rumbold, who had been cooling his heels in Madrid since 1924, when he had hoped to get Berlin, was now appointed there, replacing Lindsay. Lord Crawford and Balcarres commented on the move, 'I rather like the idea of Rumbold going to Berlin: I am confident that a man who looks so dull and stupid must be a genius.'[86]

Discussion on the next round of changes, planned for 1933, began in 1932. This round would see the loss of Tyrrell at Paris, Rumbold at Berlin, Graham at Rome, and Lindley at Tokyo. Vansittart, now permanent undersecretary, also planned to move Lindsay from Washington to Paris. Vansittart advised Sir John Simon, the Foreign Secretary, that it would be best 'to space the retirements and new appointments a little. If we have too many at the same time, an impression may be given that there is something wrong with the Service. That would be unfair.'[87] Vansittart

---

[82] Rumbold (Madrid) to mother, 24 February 1928. Rumbold 35.

[83] Lindsay (Berlin) to Lord Crawford & Balcarres, 8 February 1928. Crawford 97/10.

[84] Lord Crawford & Balcarres (7, Audley St.) to Lindsay, 25 January 1928. Crawford 97/10. Crawford & Balcarres Papers, National Library of Scotland. The six candidates being considered in London were Howard, Ronald Graham, Ronald Grahame, Lindsay, and Tyrrell, with the possibility that Austen Chamberlain might want Paris for himself. Subsequently George Lloyd's name also was talked about.

[85] Tyrrell (FO) to Howard, 9 January 1928. Howard of Penrith Papers, DHW 9/51. There had been some thought of appointing Sir Eric Drummond. Tyrrell (FO) to Howard, 30 November 1927. Howard of Penrith Papers, DHW 9/51.

[86] Crawford & Balcarres to George (Lord) Lloyd, 29 February 1928. Crawford 97/8.

[87] Vansittart to Sir John Simon, 16 August 1932. Simon 73. First Viscount Simon Papers, Bodleian Library, Oxford.

therefore laid out for Simon a complete set of actions. After Lindsay declined the move to Paris, the post went to George Clerk.[88] As Harold Nicolson observed of Clerk, 'he was impervious to disturbance; he would have mounted the scaffold with the same imperturbability as he mounted the steps of the Turf Club, his spats and monocle shining in the summer air'.[89] Lindsay thought it a bad appointment, but thought Vansittart 'was confronted with the risk of the appointment of an outsider who would also have been of questionable suitability'. Lindsay recognize that Vansittart had 'a passionate desire to keep appointments inside the Service'.[90]

Many ambassadors lived in hope of prolongation or movement to a more important embassy. Sir Francis Lindley at Tokyo, who had had to oversee relations arising from the 1931 Manchurian crisis, made it clear that he would only remain in the service if he could move to Rome, Paris, or Washington.[91] When this was not forthcoming he left for a second career in the City.[92] Many diplomats were puzzled that Rumbold was not prolonged at Berlin in early 1933, given Hitler's recent assumption of office. Even *The Times* commented that his handling of the embassy 'was admittedly beyond all praise'[93] and his reporting of the situation in retrospect can be seen to have been perceptive and accurate, but as he had warned his son, 'Between ourselves I have little confidence in my present masters and shall be surprised if they give me a square deal.'[94] Rumbold's replacement was Vansittart's brother-in-law, Sir Eric Phipps. This round of changes, at a sensitive time in international relations, spurred a negative leader in *The Times*.[95]

The last interwar shuffle of embassies came in 1937. Anthony Eden, who had assumed office as Foreign Secretary at the end of 1935, was concerned about the forthcoming moves.[96] Part of the difficulty was that

---

[88] On Clerk see Gerald Protheroe, *Searching for Security in a New Europe: The Diplomatic Career of Sir George Russell Clerk* (London, 2006).

[89] Harold Nicolson, 'Marginal Comment' *The Spectator* 185, 29 June 1951, 859.

[90] Lindsay (Washington) to Lord Crawford & Balcarres, March 1934. Crawford 97/10.

[91] Vansittart to Sir John Simon, 16 August 1932. Simon 73.

[92] Lindley produced an autobiographical volume at this time focused on his hunting and fishing exploits, *A Diplomat of Duty* (London, 1928), and he would go on to write a biography of his brother in law, *A Life of Lord Lovat* (London, 1935). Besides his numerous business interests, he was involved in politics, served as a Hampshire County Council Alderman, and unsuccessfully contested the Combined Universities parliamentary seat as a Conservative and Constitutional candidate in a 1937 by-election.

[93] 'The Loss of Ambassadors', *The Times*, 26 February 1934, 15.

[94] Rumbold (Berlin) to Anthony Rumbold, 28 May 1933, Rumbold add V/5. On Rumbold's career see M. Gilbert, *Sir Horace Rumbold: Portrait of a Diplomat* (London, 1973).

[95] 'The Loss of Ambassadors', *The Times*, 26 February 1934, 15.

[96] Cadogan Diary, 10 October 1936. ACAD 1/5. Sir Alexander Cadogan Papers, Churchill Archives Centre, Cambridge.

there was a strong desire to move Vansittart, who had been permanent undersecretary for over six years, and the only way to do this was to keep a senior embassy open for him.[97] Vansittart, however, had no desire for an embassy and managed to stay in post for another year. Finally, when it was impossible to wait any longer, Phipps was transferred to Paris from Berlin and replaced by Nevile Henderson at Berlin.[98] Henderson was surprised, and no doubt delighted, to receive such a promotion from the perceived relegation of Latin America, where he was ambassador to Argentina. Cadogan, who would ultimately succeed Vansittart, noted that Eden was 'very jumpy' over the whole business.[99]

The Washington and Moscow embassies presented particular ambassadorial difficulties. Washington had grown greatly in importance with the First World War, and Lloyd George's final appointment to Washington had been Auckland Geddes. Commonly agreed to be an individual of ability, Lindsay, who would later serve in the same post, commented at the time that is was 'not a particularly good appointment. He is a masterful & capable man, but too hairy at the heel for America.'[100] He also proved unpopular with the subsequent Conservative government, which was determined to get rid of him. As there were no grounds for removal, and as the government wished to avoid charges of political interference, Curzon forced him out by severely cutting his expense allowance, knowing that he had no independent means. Geddes sadly noted that 'they were beginning to prize me out. I was always regarded as a Lloyd George man anyway.'[101] When Geddes had been appointed his total emoluments for up to five years had been agreed at £20,000 per year. Curzon, who had himself signed the agreement, now informed Geddes that his *frais* (expense allowance) was being cut by £3,000.[102] When Geddes protested, Curzon, no doubt with some glee, replied, 'you must not forget that there is one item on which you will effect a considerable saving – the wine bill. This is usually a very heavy expense at an Embassy. I do not know that I envy you, but from the point of view of your exchequer there is no doubt that the recent decision of the foreign

---

[97] On Vansittart see Norman Rose, *Vansittart: Study of a Diplomat* (London, 1978).

[98] See Gaynor Johnson (ed.), *Our Man in Berlin: The Diary of Sir Eric Phipps, 1933–1937* (London, 2008) and Peter Neville, *Appeasing Hitler: The Diplomacy of Sir Nevile Henderson, 1937–39* (London, 2000), and also Nevile Henderson, *Failure of a Mission* (New York, 1940).

[99] Cadogan Diary, 10 January 1937, ACAD 1/6. Vansittart had hoped for at least another eighteen months.

[100] Ronald Lindsay, Sic Fator Nuntius, 120.

[101] Geddes to Irwin, 8 December 1922. GEDD 5/1. Sir Auckland Geddes Papers. Churchill Archives Centre, Cambridge.

[102] Ibid.

Embassies in Washington to "go dry" will mean a big gain.'[103] Geddes, a medical doctor, former professor of anatomy, and Cabinet minister, was worried as to his future and asked friends about his suitability for a business career. One of his friends advised him that 'it might be difficult to convince them that Professorial & Ambassadorial arts are not inconsistent with business ability'.[104] Geddes in fact went on to run the Rio Tinto company for twenty-three years and oversaw a dramatic improvement in its fortunes.

Geddes's replacement was already being sought in 1923 when Stanley Baldwin, who had recently become prime minister, offered it to the former Tory leader Austen Chamberlain. Baldwin advised Chamberlain that 'There was no position of greater consequence to the British Empire.'[105] The Conservatives may well have hoped to keep Washington as a political sinecure, but the threat of a Labour victory in 1924 combined with Geddes's imminent resignation forced the hurried appointment of a career diplomat, Sir Esme Howard.[106] Two of his immediate predecessors had been sacked and two had died in post. Nonetheless, his colleague Sir Horace Rumbold congratulated him on having bagged 'the finest post in our service',[107] even if it was a post Rumbold himself would have loathed. Howard went on to serve in Washington for six years, at the end of which he told Rumbold 'Washington did put a severe strain on me & I don't think I could have stood another year of it.'[108] Howard was succeeded by Ronald Lindsay, who was happy to escape from the permanent undersecretaryship, which was made uncongenial by the Labour team of Arthur Henderson and Hugh Dalton that had taken office in 1929.

When Lindsay's name was being mooted for Paris in 1928, he had indicated that the only post he wanted was Washington. At Paris, he felt, 'We should hate being at the beck and call of the F.O. and at the mercy of every second rate Cabinet Minister who paused on his way to Nice or Geneva.'[109] His wife and, as it happened, his late wife were Americans, and he had twice served in the Washington embassy. In the 1933 reshuffle planned by Vansittart, Lindsay was to go to Paris, but he demurred, and

---

[103] Curzon to Geddes, 25 March 1922, replying to Geddes to Curzon, 19 February 1920. GEDD 5/5. Geddes Papers.

[104] Unsigned and undated letter, probably 1922. GEDD 5/1. Geddes Papers.

[105] Memorandum by Chamberlain, 27 May 1923. AC 35/2/116. Sir Austen Chamberlain Papers.

[106] On Howard see both his own memoir, *Theatre of Life* (London, 1935), 2 vols. and B. J. C. McKercher, *Esme Howard: A Diplomatic Biography* (Cambridge, 1989).

[107] Rumbold to Howard, 4 January 1924. DHW/4/personal/19. Howard of Penrith Papers.

[108] Howard to Rumbold (Berlin), 17 July 1930. Rumbold 38.

[109] Lindsay (Washington) to Lord Crawford and Balcarres, 9 June 1933. Crawford 97/10.

in the end Simon acquiesced in his staying on at Washington.[110] It may also have been a consideration that he had known the incoming president, Franklin Roosevelt, since 1919 and had even once played baseball with him. Lindsay understood, 'The early connection was valuable to me through all the last years of my Embassy, and there was always something personal in our relationship with each other. I could always get a personal interview with him whenever I asked.'[111]

Lindsay was due to retire in 1936, but his American-born wife wanted to stay a bit longer, and he asked for an extension, which was granted to 1938. The Foreign Office then asked Lindsay to stay on to see through a trade agreement, and that was followed by the visit of George VI in the spring of 1939, when it was considered important that Lindsay remain in post to oversee the first ever visit to the United States by a British monarch. As a result, he did not retire until August 1939. By 1938, Lindsay, in the wake of Eden's resignation and seeing the likelihood of European war, was ready to retire. He did not see himself as a wartime ambassador, commenting 'I don't think I have the spirit to sit here & fight the Germans with my pen.'[112] But on the eve of his departure he observed of his nine years in post that 'during that time this country has come to a point of friendliness towards us that is beyond anything we could have dreamed of'.[113]

Various names were considered as Lindsay's successor, but in the summer of 1938 Lord Lothian was approached and accepted the post, the first political appointment since Crewe went to Paris 1922. He was related to two previous ambassadors, Lord Lyons and Esme Howard. Both the Prime Minister, Neville Chamberlain, and the Foreign Secretary, Lord Halifax, distrusted much of the career service, many of whom did not share their policy of appeasement. Halifax thought Lothian, a supporter of appeasement, well-suited for the post as he had 'all the requisite qualifications, especially the most important of all, namely antennæ, which the FO conspicuously lacks'.[114] He took up his post on 29 August 1939, four days before Britain's entry into the Second World War.

The Moscow embassy posed very different difficulties. During the interwar years there were three ambassadors at Moscow, and as Keith

---

[110] Lindsay (Washington) to Lord Crawford and Balcarres, 9 June 1933. Crawford 97/10.
[111] Lindsay, *Sic Fator Nuntius*, 160–61.
[112] Lindsay (Washington) to Lord Crawford and Balcarres, 22 February 1938. Crawford 97/10.
[113] Lindsay (Washington) to Lord Crawford and Balcarres, 27 June 1939. Crawford 97/10.
[114] Halifax (FO) to Lothian, 22 November 1938. GD 40/17/369. Lothian Papers, National Records of Scotland. Lothian briefly withdrew his acceptance before finally agreeing, Halifax (FO) to Lothian, 22 November 1938. GD 40/17/369.

Neilson observed, 'None of these men were among the most prominent in the diplomatic service.'[115] The MacDonald government of 1924 had tried to re-establish full diplomatic relations, but this never went beyond chargé d'affaires level, and collapsed with the Zinoviev letter affair, which contributed to the fall of MacDonald's government. MacDonald on forming his next administration in 1929 was determined, if possible, to establish full diplomatic relations with Moscow. Who to send as the first ambassador presented some difficulty. It was hoped that the new ambassador would know Russian and have Russian experience, but after such a lengthy period of no relations the number of senior diplomats with the requisite linguistic skills was extremely small. Among those considered were George Clerk, Eric Phipps, and Esmond Ovey. Clerk's Russian, though, was rusty, Phipps's proved to be nil, while Ovey's was thought excellent. The influential Parliamentary Undersecretary, Hugh Dalton, clearly thought well of Ovey, who, having just been publicly announced as the new ambassador to Brazil, instead got Moscow as his first embassy. He had previously been head of mission when relations were restored with Mexico in 1925, so had that experience of re-establishing a diplomatic mission. It seems to have done his career little good. Although Dalton thought highly of Ovey's work, subsequent National Government ministers clearly thought otherwise. He went on to hold two further embassies, but only the second-class embassies of Brussels and Argentina. His successor in 1933 was the 2nd Viscount Chilston, a perhaps unusual visible presence of the British system in the communist capital. A Roman Catholic, he had a chapel consecrated in the embassy, under the old diplomatic right of embassy. As war loomed, Sir William Seeds was brought out of retirement and took up the post in January 1939.

Few diplomats desired a Moscow posting. One diplomat commented in 1934 about possible new postings, 'Provided they don't incarcerate me in Moscow, I don't much care what they do with my vile body.'[116] The importance of Moscow did grow slowly as a desirable post for those interested in being in the thick of events. Clark Kerr, who was approached about the possibility of going to Moscow in 1937, was enthusiastic, commenting that 'it is one of the few worthwhile posts and ... it will soon be by far the most important embassy in the world'.[117] He was eventually appointed ambassador there in 1942. Life in the new Moscow embassy was difficult, and Dalton recorded in his diary the report that 'The Mission is living under "active service conditions" in

---

[115] Keith Neilson, *Britain, Soviet Russia, and the Collapse of the Versailles Order, 1919–1939* (Cambridge, 2006), 25.
[116] Ingram to Clark Kerr, 24 June 1934. Inverchapel Papers.
[117] Clark Kerr, 9 June 1934. Inverchapel Papers; see also Gillies, *Radical Diplomat*.

a Hotel, largely, I gather, on imports from Fortnum & Mason.'[118] Other embassies also posed a variety of logistical difficulties.

Many of the embassy postings came with special challenges. The embassy buildings in Japan were destroyed by the Great Tokyo earthquake in 1923 and the ambassador was headquartered in a bungalow in the grounds for many months. When Sir Ronald Lindsay encountered the architect of the new embassy building at Washington, Sir Edwin Lutyens, he 'forbore to mention that, because of his use of ceiling heating, ceiling after ceiling at the embassy had collapsed'.[119] It was normal practice to provide ambassadors with a car and driver, but when Archibald Clark Kerr received his first embassy in 1935, to Baghdad, he was informed that given the transport difficulties of the country his new post also came with an aeroplane. The only snag was that he would have to be his own pilot.[120] Embassies were havens of comfort, however, when compared with other diplomatic postings. Esme Howard received the following tempting invitation to stop over at the consulate-general at Lourenço Marques, 'H.M. G. provides us with a dilapidated mansion. The paint peels off the walls, drops of water and flakes of whitewash fall from the ceilings upstairs. Downstairs the white ants are busy, and cockroaches get inside the Government ice-box .... Two rooms are at your disposal if you come this way.'[121] It is perhaps not very surprising that the more inhospitable posts did not attract lay diplomats.

***

As the Great War ended the professionalism of the service was under threat of increased politicization. The war had up-ended many long-standing approaches to government and engendered a period to experimentation and innovation. The 'old diplomacy' was one of the suspects in the quest for culprits in the outbreak of the war, and therefore the practitioners of diplomacy became targets. Major political figures ranging from the Liberal Prime Minister Lloyd George to the Conservative Foreign Secretary Lord Curzon demonstrated a predilection for appointing non-career diplomats as ambassadors. That the practice did not take root, as it had in the United States, the exponent of the 'new diplomacy', was due to a combination of political distractions and upheavals, and at times support for the service by some Foreign Secretaries. As the Second World War approached there were indications that this struggle would continue,

---

[118] Entry for 20 March 1930, Dalton Diary 13.

[119] John Vincent (ed.), *The Crawford Papers*, 609.

[120] Humphreys (Baghdad) to Clark Kerr (Stockholm), 16 November 1934. Inverchapel Papers.

[121] Hall (Lourenço Marques) to Howard. DHW 5/33. Howard of Penrith Papers.

though as one observer of events, the journalist Leo Kennedy, commented in 1936, 'The truth is that I am coming more & more to the conclusion that there was *a great deal to be said* for the methods of the Old Diplomacy.'[122]

After the Second World War, the diplomatic service saw greater challenges with the amalgamation into it of the consular service, and as the empire shrank, of the Indian, Colonial, and Dominions services. The further proliferation of states increased yet again the need for diplomatic representation. Slowly, in line with the general international fashion, most missions were raised to embassy status. The service continued to fight off threats of politicization, though occasionally Paris and Washington received such appointees. This stands in contrast to the United States, which has never developed a fully professional ambassadorial corps. Only one career diplomat has ever been appointed by Washington to the London embassy.

The ambassadors of the interwar years, their high degree of professionalism, and dedication to service were part of the machinery that assisted Britain in maintaining its position as well as it did. They were also part of an empire in transition, as the ambassadorial corps itself began to open its ranks in the interwar years, however modestly. But there was always the tension between the ambassador, as the representative on the spot, and the government in London attempting to maintain a global empire. As Sir Ronald Lindsay noted, 'a diplomat is always carrying on a battle on two fronts – with his own Government, & with the Government he is accredited to'.[123] It also proved at times to be a struggle between professional expertise and the vagaries of political inclination.

---

[122] Leo Kennedy (Geneva) to Howard, 29 June 1936. DHW 5/33. Howard of Penrith Papers (original emphasis).
[123] Lindsay (Washington) to Lord Crawford and Balcarres, 16 December 1932. Crawford 97/10.

# 10 The Tattered Ties that Bind: The Imperial General Staff and the Dominions, 1919–1939

*Douglas E. Delaney*

*It will be wise to take such general measures as will enhance the value of the land forces of the Empire as a whole, without prohibitive expenditure, such as;*

*(a.) The coordination of military thought throughout the Empire, including measures taken to ensure the close co-operation of the Staffs, which was so marked a feature of the recent war.*

*(b.) The standardization of establishments and equipment, so far as this is consistent with local conditions.*

*(c.) The drawing up of schemes in each part of the Empire for the distribution of man-power as between the three services and the industries necessary to maintain armies in the field . . .*

*(d.) The extension in peacetime and the expansion in war of industries intimately connected with the supply of war-like materiel, in order that Indian and Dominion forces may be, so far as possible, self-supporting.*

*(e.) Exchange of information as to the capacity for manufacture in Government factories and by private firms of guns, carriages, trench mortars, rifles, machine guns and ammunition . . .*

*(f.) Examination of the resources of the different parts of the Empire, in order to ascertain the amount of and nature of the raw materials and manufactured articles which each Dominion or Colony could provide.*

*(g.) The distribution of responsibility for the collection of intelligence, and arrangements for coordinating the results.*[1]

Britain's military leadership had every reason to pursue measures to 'enhance the value of the land forces of the Empire, as a whole, without prohibitive expenditure' in 1921. The recent war had shown that pre-1914 actions taken to standardize the armies of the British Empire and make them ready for expansion had paid off handsomely. From the most meagre military establishments, the dominions generated the rough

[1] South African National Defence Force Archive (SANDA), CGS, Gp 1, Box 17, General Staff, 'Suggested Military Subjects for Inclusion in the Agenda for the Imperial Conference', February 1921, 1.

226

equivalent of twelve well-equipped and capable divisions for expeditionary operations, while India assembled thirteen divisions for operations beyond the subcontinent. And Britain might need their help again. Even with the war over and former enemies disarmed or in the process of disarming, the British Army had more commitments and liabilities than had been the case before 1914, any number of which 'may synchronize or spread until a situation develops, straining the resources of this country very greatly'.[2] Senior British soldiers hoped that the burden sharing that had characterized the imperial war effort of 1914–1918 would continue into the post-war period. But, having just emerged from a calamitous war that had cost so much manpower and money, no British, Indian, or dominion statesmen was keen to discuss new military ventures. In fact, the British general staff suggestions for maintaining some semblance of war readiness did not generate much conversation at all during the 1921 imperial conference. Military affairs rated barely three lines in sixty-seven pages of conference proceedings and documents: 'A discussion took place on the Military and Air Defence of the Empire and the views of the General and Air Staffs on the principles which should be adhered to in order to ensure co-operation in these matters were laid before Ministers.'[3] The prime ministers and ministers who gathered in London during the summer of 1921 were far more concerned with matters of foreign policy – how to forge a united understanding and fashion common action in foreign affairs, how to ensure continuous consultation with the dominions and keep them informed, whether or not to renew the Anglo-Japanese Alliance, how to deal with the new League of Nations, and so on.[4] The fullest discussions on imperial defence, in fact, revolved not around army issues but naval ones, and even that devolved into delegates deciding against any immediate action: 'this conference is of the opinion that the method and expense of such [naval] cooperation ... should be deferred until after the coming [Washington] Conference on Disarmament'.[5] No one was keen to discuss military affairs.

---

[2] Ibid.
[3] Conference of Prime Ministers and Representatives of the United Kingdom, the Dominions, and India, held in June, July, and August 1921: Summary of Proceedings and Documents (Proceedings and Documents: Imperial Conference 1921) Cmd 1474 (1921), 6.
[4] On imperial defence and diplomacy in the immediate postwar period, see Philip G. Wigley, *Canada and the Transition to Commonwealth, 1917–1926* (Cambridge, 1977), 96–141.
[5] Proceedings and Documents: Imperial Conference 1921, 6.

Surprisingly though, the War Office got most of what it wanted when it came to measures for maintaining the interoperability of the imperial armies. This was largely because their suggestions did not cost much, financially or politically. Schooling small professional cadres would not break any government treasuries, and agreements to organize and equip military forces to imperial standard did not entail commitments that could cause domestic political problems, especially in dominions with deep cultural divisions, like Canada and South Africa. So, in spite of the near-breakneck demobilization that followed the First World War, widespread war weariness, declining defence budgets, and growing dominion autonomy, the British general staff managed to keep some long-proven strands of military cooperation intact. In particular, the 'close coordination of the Staffs' continued because the Imperial General Staff remained in place and the chief of the imperial general staff (CIGS) kept in close contact with the general staffs of the dominions and India. He passed on British assessments of various 'storm centres' around the globe, updates on the most recent experiments in mechanized warfare, and changes to War Office doctrine and training publications. Indian and dominion military chiefs, in turn, kept the CIGS, and each other, informed about their defence budgets, training regimens, manning levels, equipment development, and defence industries (small as they were). India and the dominions even reaffirmed, at successive imperial conferences, their commitment to the 'standardization of establishments and equipment, so far as this is consistent with local conditions'. The 'co-ordination of military thought' that characterized the First World War and the decade that had preceded it survived even the leanest interwar years, as the dominions still sent their best captains and majors to the staff colleges at Camberley and Quetta; and, from 1927, their top colonels and brigadiers attended the Imperial Defence College (IDC) as well. Interchanges of officers continued, albeit in fewer numbers than had been the case before 1914. And Britain and the dominions even established new legal frameworks for working together, frameworks that were in line with the long-recognized autonomy of the dominions, and which would finally be enshrined in the Statute of Westminster (1931). Together, these measures maintained a foundation for the expansion of all British Commonwealth armies during the Second World War. This chapter explores what those measures were, why they existed, and how they worked.

*** 

Military compatibility was worth keeping, and not just in case the empire should find itself engaged in another great war, although that was always the worst-case possibility. There were more immediate concerns. As the general staff made clear to the Committee of Imperial Defence (CID) in 1920, Britain had more military liabilities than had been the case before the First World War and fewer forces with which to address them. The 3.5 million-man army of 1918 had atrophied precipitously to a paltry 370,000, almost overnight, and it still had to garrison the home islands, bolster the army in India, and be prepared to send expeditionary forces abroad, just as it had done before 1914.[6] But, within eighteen months of the armistice, it was also occupying the Rhineland, guarding the straits between the Black Sea and the Mediterranean, keeping the peace in plebiscite areas, supporting a protectorate in Persia, and administering League of Nations mandates in Palestine and Mesopotamia. Global commitments had increased from ten-plus divisions and two cavalry divisions in 1914 to twenty-plus divisions, four-plus cavalry divisions, and twenty-five Royal Air Force (RAF) squadrons in 1920.[7] What is more, if the military situation in any number of these commitment areas deteriorated, Britain could be on the hook for another nine infantry divisions, four cavalry brigades, and twenty RAF squadrons. It was not as though any of the scenarios that the general staff pondered were long-shot possibilities either. The Iraqis did revolt against British rule in Mesopotamia in May 1920, and Irish nationalists did the same before the end of the year. There was always the potential that nationalist movements in India could lead to a 'second mutiny', just as 'a general rising of the population' in Egypt and the Suez Canal Zone could threaten the link to India and the Far East. And a general strike scare in 1920 reminded War Office planners of internal security threats, as did an actual general strike six years later. These were serious concerns that were beyond the military capabilities of the regular army of the United Kingdom to resolve all at once, as a general staff paper explained: 'Wherever we look we find our garrisons beset by potential dangers which may far exceed their strength.'[8] The CIGS, Field Marshal Sir Henry Wilson, was even more bleak in his 1920 assessment for the secretary of state for war: 'I cannot too strongly press on the Government the danger, the extreme danger, of His Majesty's Army being spread all over the world, strong nowhere, weak everywhere, and with no reserve to save a dangerous situation or to avert coming danger.'[9] To make military ends meet, Wilson recommended temporarily reducing the number of British battalions in India, withdrawing from Persia and the plebiscite areas as soon as possible, shrinking the

---

[6] Brian Bond, *British Military Policy Between the Wars* (Oxford, 1980), 21–22.
[7] The National Archives (Public Records Office) (TNA), Kew, CAB 4/7. General Staff, CID 255-B, Military Liabilities of the Empire, 27 July 1920, Appendix A.
[8] Ibid., 8.      [9] TNA, WO 33/1004. Wilson to Sectary of State, 9 June 1920.

230 Douglas E. Delaney

Army of the Black Sea, and improving railways in Iraq so that the mandated territory could be secured with fewer troops.[10]

And by 1921, the British Army had indeed withdrawn from Persia and the plebiscite areas, but there were no additional resources coming the way of Wilson or the War Office – quite the contrary. The British cabinet was almost singularly focused on economic retrenchment. In August 1921, Prime Minister David Lloyd George established the Committee on National Expenditure for the purpose of reducing government spending and producing surpluses, with which Britain could pay off a mass of wartime debts. To say that the committee, chaired by Sir Eric Geddes, was unsympathetic to Wilson's pleas would be an understatement, as the 1922 committee report made clear: 'During the war, in the case of the Fighting Departments, the Government was obliged to accept the statements of the Naval and Military advisers as to the money required by their Departments. In our opinion, the time has come when the Government must say to these Departments how much money they can have, and look to them to name their proposals accordingly.'[11] Geddes also noted that the estimates for the fighting were actually higher than they had been even before the war. Service estimates had been £80,395,000 in 1914/15, but they were projected to be £175,689,000 in 1922/23, a period during which everyone expected a 'peace dividend'.[12] Manning levels had not dropped either. While there had been a combined total 333,000 for the army and Royal Navy in 1914/15, there were 362,000 soldiers, sailors, and airmen in 1922/23. The 'Geddes Axe', as the committee came quite appropriately to be known, was as indifferent to service arguments as it was savage in its determination to retrench. It dismissed general staff's manpower estimates as 'lavish', and recommended instead a reduction of 50,000 officers and men in the army, which would permit a concomitant reduction in military estimates, from £75,197,800 to £55,000,000 for 1922/23.[13] Bottomed-out budgets forced the War Office to disband twenty-two infantry battalions.[14] The net effect was that, by 1923, the British Army was functioning more or less on the Cardwell system of the previous century – no way of preparing realistically for a continental commitment, just enough men and resources to do some imperial

[10] TNA, WO 33/1004. British Military Liabilities, 30 July 1920. See also the definitive biography of Henry Wilson, Keith Jeffery, *Field Marshal Sir Henry Wilson: A Political Soldier* (Oxford, 2006), especially chapter 12.

[11] First Interim Report of the Committee on National Expenditure, Cmd 1581 (1922), 4.

[12] Ibid., 5.

[13] The Geddes committee also found the Admiralty's manpower estimates to be 'lavish', recommending a reduction in 35,000 personnel and trimming of estimates from £81,000,000 to £60,000,000 for 1922/1923. Ibid., 31–32.

[14] Bond, *British Military Policy*, 27.

policing and provide the overseas units with drafts. The Territorial Army of part-time soldiers was not much help either because its soldiers had no obligation to serve overseas. This manpower-stretched state of affairs persisted throughout the interwar period. Even after the Defence Requirements Subcommittee (DRC) of the CID recommended rearmament and substantial increases to army estimates in 1934, successive Cabinets kept British Army budgets low relative to those of the Royal Air Force (RAF) and the Royal Navy, which in turn meant the British Army remained too small to meet fully all of its obligations and contingencies.[15]

It is not surprising, therefore, that the British general staff wondered 'if the Dominions (and India) were prepared to bear even a small share of the burden'.[16] That hope was badly misplaced, at least in the short term. The dominions had already demurred on a September 1920 request to assist in Mesopotamia and they would do it again two years later during the Chanak Crisis, when they were asked to participate in military operations to enforce the Treaty of Sèvres, a clumsy episode made clumsier by British failure to consult them before making threats of British and dominion action against Turkey. In the dominions, imperial ventures perceived as peripheral to their interests were uphill struggles and in effect precluded by a combination of war weariness and ethnic division in places like South Africa (where an Afrikaner revolt had to be subdued at the start of the Union's involvement in the First World War) and Canada (where a 1917 conscription crisis had left English and French-speaking populations badly divided). The dominions did not have much to offer in any event. Cuts to their military establishments made the 'Geddes Axe' look kind. Canada's 363,000-man wartime expeditionary force dissipated to a peacetime army comprising just 4,125 permanent force professionals and a home-service militia of less than 50,000 by 1921.[17] The Australian Imperial Force of over 300,000 had all but evaporated by 1922, when the military forces of the Commonwealth consisted of just 1,603 members of the permanent force and a maximum of 31,000 Citizen Military Force soldiers for

---

[15] On the DRC, see Keith Neilson, 'The Defence Requirements Sub-Committee, British Strategic Foreign Policy, Neville Chamberlain and the Path to Appeasement', *English Historical Review* 118(477) (2003), 651–84; N. H. Gibbs, Grand Strategy, volume I: *Rearmament Policy* (London, 1976); Brian Bond, *British Military Policy Between the Wars* (Oxford, 1980), 191–213.

[16] SANDA, CGS, Gp 1, Box 17. General Staff, 'Suggested Military Subjects for Inclusion in the Agenda for the Imperial Conference', February 1921, 2.

[17] Colonel G. W. L. Nicholson, *Canadian Expeditionary Force, 1914–1919* (Ottawa, 1962) Appendix D, 547; and J. L. Granatstein, *Canada's Army: Waging War and Keeping the Peace* (Toronto, 2011), 158.

home defence.[18] By 1922, the Dominion of New Zealand, which had fielded a full infantry division during war, had just 474 permanent force soldiers to train three weak territorial brigades that were only allowed to recruit to fifty per cent of war establishment strength.[19] The Union of South Africa had slightly more permanent force troops on strength – 1,372 all ranks in 1920 – but they were largely preoccupied with internal security operations, and the Active Citizen Force militia of approximately 30,000 was almost entirely untrained.[20] In sum, the dominions were in no position to share burdens in the short term.

The Indian Army was also getting harder to use. It did have seven divisions deployed abroad in 1920, but nationalists within the country were increasingly adamant in their conviction that the army was exclusively for the defence of India against external attack and the maintenance of internal security, and the legislative assembly passed several non-binding resolutions to that effect in 1921. The viceroy may have had the final say on the deployment of Indian troops, but popular discontent as expressed by the legislative assembly meant that, in effect, 'the Indian Army, in so far as it is paid out of Indian revenues, is as much the property of India as the armies of Australia and Canada are the properties of those dominions', as the secretary of state for India relayed to the Committee of Imperial Defence.[21] The Indian Army withdrew from its foreign deployments over the course of the 1920s and atrophied, both in terms of quality and quantity. Indeed, the British government had to take on a greater share of the financial burden of keeping it compatible and deployable. By the end of the interwar period, the British Treasury was financing a limited programme for mechanizing the Indian Army's four remaining infantry divisions and three cavalry brigades (at £34,000,000 over five years)[22] and paying an annual subsidy of £2,000,000 in exchange for a commitment of one infantry division for operations outside of India.[23]

Given the shrunken states of military establishments across the empire, retaining and refining the 'machinery' for making and expanding

---

[18] Albert Palazzo, *The Australian Army: A History of Its Organization, 1901–2001* (Melbourne, 2001), 104.

[19] See Peter Cooke and John Crawford, *The Territorials: The History of the Territorial and Volunteer Forces of New Zealand* (Auckland, 2011), 203–17.

[20] SANDA, CGS, GP 1, Box 17. Brink to Chief of the Imperial General Staff, 7 June 1921. By 1928, only 4,000 of approximately 30,000 citizen force soldiers had received training; and Annette Seegers, *The Military in Making of Modern South Africa* (London, 1996), 53.

[21] British Library (BL), India Office Records (IOR), L/MIL/4/5510. Montagu to CID, 23 April 1920.

[22] Seventy-five per cent as a gift and twenty-five per cent as an interest-free loan.

[23] T. A. Heathcote, *The Military in British India: The Development of British Land Forces in South Asia, 1600–1947* (Barnsley, 2013), 197–198.

compatible armies was about all that could be achieved. At home, the British government established a standing interdepartmental subcommittee of the CID in 1920 to consider the issue of manpower mobilization for a national crisis, and this led to the creation of the Standing Interdepartmental Committee on National Service in a Future War, which evolved into the Subcommittee on Manpower in 1924. The manpower subcommittee sketched out principles for mobilizing the human and industrial resources of the United Kingdom in the event of a great war – parameters for national registration and a schedule of industries and occupations of national importance, for example – but another world war would almost certainly require the cooperation of India and the dominions, and nothing that the subcommittee planned would help meet Britain's global commitments in the short term, which is why the War Office remained interested in retaining the ability to integrate and combine Indian, dominion, and British formations.[24] After all, the Indian Army had one cavalry and six infantry divisions deployed abroad in 1920, and the British general staff estimated that, in the event of another great war, the dominions were capable of fielding twelve infantry and four cavalry divisions.[25] It was worth retaining the ability to tap those potential resources in the event of some future crisis, so long as such measures did not cost too much.

One of the cheapest and most effective means of keeping tabs on manpower issues and ensuring military compatibility was the Imperial General Staff. Some historians have dismissed the idea of an imperial general staff. Richard Preston wrote of 'the illusion of an imperial military structure and an imperial army',[26] and Keith Jeffery described the Imperial General Staff as 'more a British aspiration than any effective manifestation of coherent Imperial purpose'.[27] Preston, Jeffery, and other critics of the Imperial General Staff assume that it was supposed to function like the generals staffs of the continent, but it was never intended to work that way. It could never have operated as such. Unlike the unitary nation states of continental Europe, the British Empire comprised many

[24] See, for example, TNA, CAB 4/22. Committee of Imperial Defence, Progress Report of the Sub-Committee on Man-Power, 19 December 1933.

[25] For infantry divisions, the estimate was Canada (six), Australia (four), New Zealand (one), and South Africa (one). For cavalry divisions it was Canada (one), Australia (two), New Zealand (one brigade), and South Africa (two brigades). See Archives New Zealand (ANZ), WA 1/31. Interim Draft of a Memorandum by the General Staff on the Future Organization and Distribution of the Military Forces of the Empire, August 1919, 12.

[26] Richard A. Preston, *Canada and 'Imperial Defence': A Study of the Origins of the British Commonwealth's Defence Organizations, 1867–1919* (Durham, NC, 1967), 467.

[27] Keith Jeffery, 'Kruger's farmers, Strathcona's Horse, Sir George Clarke's camels and the Kaiser's battleships: The Impact of the South African War on Imperial Defence' in Donal Lowry (ed.), *The South African War Reappraised* (Manchester, 2000), 199.

autonomous and self-governing countries. Whitehall could not simply tell Wellington or Ottawa what to do. It could barely tell Simla what to do. The general staff for the British Empire was rather a conduit that functioned largely on consensus and looked after operations, intelligence, training, and administration, and it reflected the constitutional make-up of the British Empire. Local sections answered to local governments, not to London. Membership implied no military obligations and it had only an advisory role when it came to the dominions, as the resolution from the 1907 colonial conference clarified: 'without in the least interfering in questions connected with command and administration [the Imperial General Staff] shall, at the request of the respected Governments, advise as to the training, education, and war organization of the military forces of the Crown in every part of the Empire'.[28] It was established in 1908 as a circuit for the exchange and dissemination of information, ideas, and doctrine, and it remained such throughout the interwar period. The War Office promulgated guidance on how to train for and conduct military operations with publications such as the *Field Service Regulations, Infantry Training,* and *Training and Manoeuvre Regulations,* and the dominions, despite their autonomous positions, generally accepted War Office guidance because they had to organize their military establishments in some way, which might just as well have been the British Army way, especially if it saved them money and entailed no formal commitments.

Few sources give a better indication of how the Imperial General Staff functioned during the interwar years than the periodical letters exchanged between the CIGS, the dominion chiefs, and the chief of the general staff (CGS) India. Initiated by Wilson in late 1919, the quarterly correspondence continued uninterrupted for twenty years. While the correspondents generally avoided discussion of concrete contingency plans or expeditionary forces  anything that might have implied a commitment, in other words – the information exchanged was nonetheless useful for those types of ventures. The subjects discussed were wide-ranging, but, typically, CIGS letters contained lengthy assessments of world trouble spots, updates on the progression of collective and individual training in the British Army, the results of various equipment trials, changes to war establishments for units and formations, observations on experimentation with new organizations and equipment (such as that conducted with the Experimental Mechanized Force, 1927–29), ongoing operations of the British Army, revisions to War Office publications, and the projected

[28] Maurice Ollivier (ed.), *The Colonial and Imperial Conferences from 1887 to 1937: Volume 1, Colonial Conferences* (Ottawa, 1954), 218.

dissemination of new ones. The CIGS often sought input from the heads of the Indian and dominion armies on revisions to War Office publications, and occasionally asked for assistance in particular trials, such as when Sir Archibald Montgomery-Massingberd asked the Canadians about testing service respirators and antifreeze filling for machine gun barrels in cold weather conditions.[29] The Indian and dominion chiefs advised of local defence plans, the conduct of individual and collective training, the results of whatever equipment trials they initiated on their own, defence budgets, and manning levels in their permanent forces and militias.

Sir George Milne's letter of 21 January 1927 serves as a typical example of what was discussed and exchanged.[30] It contained a six-page synopsis on the 'World Situation', which included discussion about the ongoing efforts to verify the disarmament of Germany, Hungary's compliance with a Military Control Commission, Austrian non-compliance with the same commission, the apparent end to a rebellion in Syria, French and Spanish efforts to subdue Morocco, Turkish foreign policy and the advent of 'a better understanding' between Britain and Turkey, Italian support for the Imam in Northern Yemen, the requirement to strengthen the Royal Air Force (RAF) flight in the Aden, and the 'deteriorating' situation in China. There was a section on training manuals that listed thirteen publications that were undergoing revision (*Artillery Training* volumes I and III, Field *Service Regulations* volume I, *Engineering Training* volumes I and II, among them), two revised publications that had recently been issued (*Infantry Training* and *Signal Training*), and two new publications (*Tank and Armoured Car Training* and *Signal Training, volume V)* that were in production. The CIGS also passed on aid-of-the-civil-power lessons learned during the General Strike of May 1926, the results of recent trials with tracked and half-tracked vehicles, efforts to develop a 3-tonne motor transport vehicle, and the decision 'to include Assault Bridge material in the equipment of an Infantry Division'. As enclosures, Milne included his memorandum 'Collective Training of the Army, 1926', a training report by the GOC of Aldershot Command, and a document outlining changes to the syllabi at the Royal Military College, Sandhurst and the Royal Military Academy, Woolwich. He also promised to send the reports of the British committee for Mobilisation Equipment and War Reserves, and he relayed a Dominions Office request that 'Returns of Military and Naval Resources' be submitted by 31 March annually.

---

[29] TNA, WO 32/2399, Montgomery-Massingberd to McNaughton, 26 April 1933.
[30] TNA, WO 32/2374, Periodical Letter No. 1/1927, 21 January 1927.

The Imperial General Staff worked well because the most important posts in Whitehall and the local sections were filled by 'officers trained to *think alike* on all matters of principle', which had been the agreed upon design since 1907.[31] Common staff training was the foundation. Camberley and Quetta graduates populated the Imperial General Staff, produced defence plans, and disseminated what they had learned all across the empire.[32] They had proved their worth during the First World War when a nucleus of 1,433 staff-trained professionals generated a nearly tenfold expansion of staffs and the formations they served, which is a large part of why common staff training endured even during the most austere years of the interwar period.[33] The dominions continued to send their most promising captains and majors to the imperial staff colleges because they needed their own staff-trained professionals, but also because it cost very little to do so. It saved them having to establish and run their own staff colleges for one thing, and the fees were actually quite low for another. In 1922, for example, the annual fee for filling a staff college vacancy at Camberley was just £400, a small sum even in 1922 pounds.[34] The dominions actually tripled their flow of officers through the imperial staff colleges, despite straitened financial circumstances. During the decade leading up to the First World War, only 27 dominion officers completed the two-year programmes at Camberley and Quetta, but during the interwar period some 150 dominion officers earned the designation *psc* (passed staff college), a rate of 75 per decade.[35] It also helped that many dominion staff college graduates forged close working relationships and friendships with their imperial counterparts while attending Camberley or Quetta.[36] The

[31] TNA, WO 106/43. General Staff, Proposals for so Organizing the Military Forces of the Empire as to Ensure Their Effective Co-operation in the Event of War, 17 July 1909, 14. Emphasis in original; see also TNA, CAD 5/2. General Staff, Education of Officers at the Staff Colleges, 23 May 1911.

[32] John A. Macdonald, 'In Search of Veritable: Training the Canadian Army Staff Officer' (Unpublished MA Thesis, Royal Military College of Canada, 1992), 87.

[33] See Douglas E. Delaney, *The Imperial Army Project: Britain and the Land Forces of the Dominions and India, 1902–1945* (Oxford, 2017), 53–54; and Paul Harris, 'The Men who Planned the War: A Study of the Staff of the British Army on the Western Front, 1914-1918' (PhD Thesis, King's College London, 2013).

[34] National Archives of Australia (NAA), A11804/1926/554. War Office Charges for Officers Attending the Camberley Staff College, 30 March 1922. Quetta's rates remained at pre-war level of £300.

[35] Delaney, *The Imperial Army Project*, 165–200.

[36] See for example Mark Frost, 'The British and Indian Army Staff Colleges in the Inter-War Years' in Douglas E. Delaney, Robert Engen, and Meghan Fitzpatrick (eds.), *Military Education and Empire: Professional Education and the Military, Naval, and Air Forces of the British Empire and Commonwealth, 1815–1949* (Toronto and Vancouver, forthcoming).

colleges yielded the bare-minimum cadres that the armies of the empire would need to keep compatibility in peace and expand in war. By 1939, there were 1,419 staff college graduates still serving in the British, Indian, and dominion armies, which is approximately the same-size nucleus that had existed in 1914.[37]

The core of the two-year programs at Camberley and Quetta was staff duties. The curricula kept pace with changes in doctrine, as well as with numerous revisions to the *Field Service Regulations* (FSRs) and the other capstone publications. Tank lectures became a feature of interwar courses, as did instructional modules on signals and the Royal Air Force (RAF), for example. And much of the material was delivered by capable and experienced officers such as J. F.C. Fuller, Philip Neame, Arthur T. Harris, Trafford Leigh-Mallory, and John Slessor.[38] It was all geared to teaching officers how to work in the headquarters of modern brigades, divisions, and corps. Primarily, candidates learned how to function as members of general staffs (operations and intelligence), adjutant-general staffs (personnel), and quartermaster general staffs (or Q-staffs for logistics). The pedagogy included lectures, written assignments, directing staff-led discussions in syndicates, tactical exercises without troops (TEWTs), skeleton exercises, and telephone exercises.[39] Most Camberley and Quetta graduates thought highly of the professional military education they received. Hastings Ismay, who became secretary to the chiefs of staff committee (COS) and principal assistant to Winston Churchill as minister of defence, described his year at Quetta as 'one of the most instructive and rewarding of my life'.[40] The New Zealander W. G. Stevens wrote in 1927 that 'every student on conclusion of his work here [at Camberley] feels that he is right up to date with the latest ideas in the army on such points as Staff Duties, Mechanization, Re-organization, and the employment of the various

[37] Delaney, *Imperial Army Project*, 230–96.

[38] Joint Services Command and Staff College (JSCSC), Staff College: Junior Division (1923); and Lieutenant Colonel F. W. Young, *The Story of the Staff College, 1858–1958* (Surrey, 1958), 27. J. F. C. Fuller (chief instructor Camberley, 1923–27, military assistant to CIGS, 1927–30, armoured warfare theorist), Philip Neame (commandant Woolwich 1937–39 and GOC 4th Indian Division, 1940–41), Arthur Harris (C-in-C Bomber Command, 1942–45), Leigh-Mallory (C-in-C Fighter Command, 1942–43, and C-in-C Allied Expeditionary Air Force, 1943–44), and John Slessor (C-in-C Mediterranean and Middle East, 1944–45 and Chief of the Air Staff, 1950–52).

[39] Tactical exercises without troops (TEWTs) challenged candidates to develop solutions to tactical problems for a particular piece of terrain. Skeleton exercises were field training exercise in which all levels of headquarters went to the field, but only the bare minimum of troops participated. Telephone exercises were headquarters exercises conducted indoors.

[40] General Lord Ismay, quoted in Anonymous, *The First Fifty Years of the Staff College Quetta, 1905–1955* (Quetta, 1955), 54.

arms'.[41] Brian Horrocks, a future corps commander who attended Camberley as a captain in 1931–32, was convinced that Camberley and Quetta graduates were collectively responsible for 'the high standard of staff work in the army during the [Second World W]ar'.[42] Horrocks had a point. They filled the most important command and staff appointments in the armies of the British Commonwealth during the war, and they were essential for teaching staff duties to thousands of other officers during abbreviated wartime staff courses.

The Imperial Defence College (IDC), established in 1927, also helped to foster familiarity and compatibility.[43] Its aim was to produce 'a body of [army, navy, and air force] officers trained to look at the problems of war as a whole, capable of investigating specific defence questions and of forecasting and measuring the dangers to which the Empire may be exposed in the future'.[44] In the twelve years that preceded the Second World War, 291 officers of the three British fighting services, the dominion forces, and the Indian Army completed the one-year program at 9 Buckingham Gate, as did 52 civil servants.[45] The curriculum, designed by Vice Admiral Sir Herbert Richmond, first commandant of the IDC, challenged students to think about 'how the strength of that body of nations we call the Empire could best be developed in its defence, including not only the use of the Fighting Services in co-operation but also all those other elements which constitute the strength of this body of nations – economics, commerce, geography ... command of markets'.[46] Students worked in syndicates to develop solutions to strategic problems set in particular scenarios – war with France in continental Europe or war with Japan in the Far East, for example. Many IDC graduates went on to top-level appointments, where they wielded considerable influence within their military establishments. These included two future CIGS (Alan Brooke and William Slim), a future Commander-in-Chief (C-in-C) India (Claude

[41] ANZ, AD1, 877/39/2/16/1. W. G. Stevens, to General Headquarters New Zealand Military Forces, 31 December 1927. Stevens succeeded Bernard Freyberg as GOC 2 NZEF in November 1945.

[42] Lieutenant-General Sir Brian Horrocks, *A Full Life* (London, 1960), 70.

[43] For this paragraph on the Imperial Defence College, I have relied heavily on Andrew Stewart, '"Necessarily of an Experimental Character": The Inter-War Period and the Imperial Defence College', in *Military Education and Empire* (forthcoming).

[44] TNA, CAB4/9. 'Report of the Sub-Committee on the Institution of a Joint Staff College for Officers in the Three Services', 11 May 1923, 3. See also TNA, CAB4/14. M. P. A. Hankey, 'Institution of a Joint College for Officers of the Three Services', 16 March 1926; and CBA 4/2. Minutes of the 214th Meeting of the Committee of Imperial Defence, 10 June 1926.

[45] Royal College of Defence Studies (RCDS) Register. I am grateful to Dr Andrew Stewart for providing me with this source.

[46] Thomas Chegwidden CB, CVO, 'The Imperial Defence College', *Public Administration* 25(1) (1947), 39.

Auchinleck), and seven future dominion CGSs (A. G. L. McNaughton, H. D. G. Crerar, John Lavarack, John Northcott, Vernon Sturdee, Sydney Rowell, and Edward Puttick). Most army officers who attended IDC were also graduates of Camberley or Quetta, and some imperial and dominion officers, like Brooke and McNaughton, had even worked together during the First World War.

Efforts to impart a common way of doing things did not start with colonels at IDC, or even captains at Camberley Quetta. For professionals, it started at the cadet colleges, which were largely run by staff college graduates, just as they had been in the pre-1914 period.[47] The difference during the interwar period was that the dominions had enough of their own staff college graduates to fill those appointments. From 1923 to 1932, the chief instructor tactics at the South African Military School was Lieutenant-Colonel George Brink, future GOC of 1st South African Division and a Camberley graduate from the class of 1920.[48] The Duntroon commandant in 1924 was Lieutenant Colonel C. G. N. Miles, who had graduated from the first interwar course at Camberley in 1919, while the instructor in tactics was Lieutenant Colonel E. C. P. Plant, a graduate of the 1922 class.[49] At the Royal Military College of Canada (RMC Kingston), the tactics instructors were always staff college graduates and the senior general staff officers were always recent staff college graduates, who also had a hand in delivering the militia staff course, which graduated nearly 400 part-time officers during the interwar period.[50] New Zealand did not establish its own cadet college, but the dominion did send about eight to ten candidates to Duntroon annually. The Indian Military Academy (IMA), which opened at Dehra Dun in October 1932, was also cast in a British mould and driven by staff college graduates. The first commandant, Brigadier L. P. Collins of the Ghurkha Regiment, may not have been a staff college graduate, but his two principal instructors for strategy and tactics (Major R. A. Savory and Captain D. T. Cowan) were both *psc*.[51] The IMA was even divided into a 'Sandhurst' Wing for Indian cadets seeking commissions in the infantry or cavalry, and a more technically oriented 'Woolwich' Wing for cadets

[47] Delaney, *Imperial Army Project*, 44–94.
[48] Carel Birkby, *Uncle George: The Boer Boyhood, Letters and Battles of Lieutenant-General George Edwin Brink* (Johannesburg, 1987), 71.
[49] *The Army List of the Australian Military Forces, part I, Active List, 31st March 1924* (Melbourne, 1924), 13.
[50] Macdonald, 'In Search of Veritable', 83–85; and John A. English, *The Canadian Army and the Normandy Campaign: A Study of Failure in High Command* (New York, 1991), 98.
[51] Brigadier M. P. Singh, *Valour and Wisdom: History of the Indian Military Academy* (Chandigarh, 2007), 21–35, 223; and *Supplement to the Indian Army List January 1939* (1939), 72–74.

destined for the artillery or the engineers. Tactics were a big part of the curriculum at Dehra Dun, as were the usual staples of Sandhurst, Woolwich, Kingston, and Duntroon – drill, physical training, and sports. Indian officer cadets also spent a lot of time learning and perfecting English language skills, as well as academic subjects likes physics and mathematics.

The dominion cadet colleges did not produce vast numbers of graduates during the interwar period – annual rates of production ranged typically between twelve and fifty graduates – but they produced important ones.[52] They generated the officers who trained part-time citizen forces in peacetime and who later took up senior command and staff appointments during the Second World War. A few examples make the point. Canadian Guy Simonds graduated from RMC Kingston in 1925, worked as a subaltern in a permanent force artillery battery, completed the gunnery staff course at Woolwich in 1932, returned to a permanent force battery that was heavily involved with training militia gunners, completed the staff course at Camberley (1936–37), became the instructor of tactics as a major at RMC Kingston in 1938, assumed the appointment of general staff officer, second grade (GSO 2) of 1st Canadian Infantry Division when it deployed overseas in 1939, and eventually rose to the rank of lieutenant general during the war.[53] Simonds was only exceptional as a dominion permanent force officer in that he rose so high during war. Australian Reginald G. Pollard, who graduated from Duntroon in 1924, did not reach the rank of lieutenant-general during the Second World War, but he did become CGS during the Cold War (1960–63), and he fulfilled a number of similarly important staff and training functions during the interwar period. After leaving Duntroon, he served as the adjutant or quartermaster in militia battalions for a combined total of eleven years, trained for a year with British Regiments in Indian during 1927–28, worked in Army Headquarters Melbourne 1936–38, graduated from an abbreviated Camberley course in 1939, and took an appointment as brigade major with the 2nd Australian Imperial Force in June 1940. During the Second World War, Pollard commanded a battalion and

---

[52] The first post-war class of cadets at Roberts Heights was just twelve, the second only eighteen, ten of whom passed. RMC Kingston produced about fifty graduates annually. Ian van der Waag, 'South Africa and the Making of Military Officers, 1902–1948' in *Military Education and Empire* (forthcoming); and Richard Arthur Preston, *Canada's RMC: A History of the Royal Military College* (Toronto, 1969), 250.

[53] Simonds rose through a succession of command and staff appointments to become commander of II Canadian Corps in January 1944 and was acting commander First Canadian Army for a time (October–November 1944). See Douglas E. Delaney, *Corps Commanders: Five British and Canadian Generals at War, 1939–1945* (Toronto and Vancouver, 2011), 189–254.

ascended through a succession of senior staff positions that culminated with his appointment in April 1945 as director of military operations of Allied Land Force Headquarters, South West Pacific Area.[54] South African Evered Poole came through the ranks of the Active Citizen Forces, which he joined as a private in 1920. After transferring to the permanent force in 1922, he took a commission in the South African field artillery in 1923, attended a staff duties course at Roberts Heights in 1927, worked as an instructor for the Transvaal Horse Artillery for two years (1931–32), transferred to the South African Staff Corps, took command of the Special Service Brigade in 1934, went on a six-month attachment to the Brigade of Guards in England during 1935, completed the Senior Officer's Course at Sheerness shortly thereafter, and became commandant at the South African Military College in 1938. During war, his peak appointment was General Officer Commanding (GOC) 6th South African Armoured Division, which he commanded from February 1943 until the end of the war.[55]

`Officer exchanges were another inexpensive means of solidifying compatibility. Loans, interchanges, and attachments had been a feature of imperial military standardization since the Edwardian era. At that time, loans were the primary and most important form of exchange. Under this scheme, the dominions paid for the services of scores of British and Indian Army officers, who filled senior staff and command appointments for which the dominions still had no one qualified. These on-loan officers included the likes of Percy Lake (CGS Canada (1904–08)), Alexander Godley (GOC New Zealand Military Forces (1910–14)), and George Macaulay Kirkpatrick (Inspector General of Australian Military Forces (1910–14)).[56] But, in the post-1918 period, the dominions had plenty of experienced and skilled officers who could fill senior command and staff appointments, so attachments and interchanges were more the norm, and they took place at much lower rank levels, seldom above the rank of major, in fact. There were also fewer of them. Whereas there had been thirty-eight imperial officers serving under some form of exchange in Canada in 1913, there were only six of them in the dominion in 1939, all of them on either attachment or

---

[54] Chris Clarke, 'Pollard, Sir Reginald George (1903–1978)', *Australian Dictionary of Biography*, National Centre of Biography, Australian National University, http://adb.anu.edu.au/biogrpahy/pollard-sir-reginald-george-11442/text20393, published first in hard copy 2002, accessed online, 25 July 2017.

[55] Neville Gomm, 'The South African Military College', *South African Military History Society Journal* 2(3) (1972), accessed online, 27 July 2017.

[56] Douglas E. Delaney, 'Army Apostles: Imperial Officers on Loan and the Standardization of the Canadian, Australian and New Zealand Armies, 1904–1914', *War in History* 23(2) (2016), 169–89.

interchange.[57] The attachment scheme, by which dominions sent officers to British or Indian units, allowed captains and majors, like Pollard and Poole, to gain experience with formed professional units, which their permanent forces did not have.[58] It also allowed dominion officers to gain valuable staff experience. Future First Canadian Army commander Harry Crerar, for example, was attached to the War Office's directorate of military operations and intelligence (DMO & I) in 1925–27, after which time he returned to Canada, where he worked in the Canadian DMO & I in Ottawa.[59] A number of staff exchanges also happened as interchanges, whereby officers were simply swapped in a temporary trade. The British general staff, for example, promoted a program of staff interchanges for second-grade staff appointments (major-level) or lower, to a maximum of two each for Canada and Australia, and one each for South Africa and New Zealand. As part of that interchange, Canadian permanent force officer Maurice Pope was one of several Canadian staff-trained majors who went to work in the War Office's directorate of staff duties (DSD) in exchange for a British army major who served as a general staff officer at RMC Kingston.[60] Pope, like Crerar, took what he learned in Whitehall back to the general staff in Ottawa, where he later worked in the DMO & I, and he no doubt left his War Office and DSD colleagues, two of whom were classmates from Camberley, with a better understanding of Canadian defence issues. 'The mutual benefit derived from these exchanges', wrote Milne in his October 1932 periodical letter, 'is well worth the small extra cost.'[61]

It was well worth it because few soldiers and statesmen in Britain, India, or even the dominions doubted that sometime, somewhere, the imperial armies would be working together. Nothing testified more to this pervasive assumption than the creation of new legal frameworks for multinational operations. At issue was the 'equal status' of the dominions and Britain that was formalized with the passage of the Statute of Westminster in 1931. It established that 'no law hereafter made by the Parliament of the United Kingdom shall extend to any of the said Dominions as part of the law of that Dominion otherwise than at the request and with the

[57] *Canadian Defence Quarterly* 16(2) (1939), Appendix, 238.
[58] Canada's Permanent Active Militia was the only dominion permanent force that had fully formed units.
[59] Dickson, *A Thoroughly Canadian General*, 83–85. Crerar served as a battery commander and instructor at RMC Kingston between his DMO & I appointments in Whitehall and Ottawa.
[60] See Lt Gen Maurice A. Pope, *Soldiers and Politicians* (Toronto, 1962), 74–107.
[61] TNA, WO 32/2397. 091/3034 (M.O.1.), Periodical Letter No. 4/1932, 17 October 1932.

consent of that Dominion'; and, because the British parliament would have to pass legislation to supersede the soon-to-expire Army and Air Force Act, Britain and each dominion had to pass their own acts to lay out the legal terms by which their forces would work with each other. To that end, the Dominions Office took the initiative in 1931 when it circulated a draft 'Dominion Forces Bill', the most important provisions of which defined how the forces of one nation of the British Empire would work with or under those of another. There were two relationships: by which the forces of each nation shared little more than location, and which denoted a relationship in which the forces of one nation had been placed under the control of a commander from another. Canadian troops in the United Kingdom (1939–43), for example, would mostly be in a relationship with British forces in the home islands until the government of Canada assigned them with British forces in one of the active theatres of war, as would be the case when the 1st Canadian Infantry Division and the 1st Canadian Armoured Brigade were placed under the operational command of the British Eighth Army for the invasion of Sicily. Matters of national command, discipline, and senior appointments rested with the parent nation, just as had been the case during the First World War. The bill came to be re-titled the 'Visiting Forces (British Commonwealth) Bill' in response to Canadian objections that the term '"dominion forces" inadvertently suggest[ed] in its wording, a distinction in the relationship between His Majesty and His Forces in the Dominions and in the United Kingdom respectively', something which ran counter to the 'equal status' principle of the Westminster statute.[62] The Dominions Office accepted the suggested revisions and the British bill passed into law in 1933. The Canadian and South African parliaments passed their Visiting Forces Acts in 1932–33, and the statutory framework for working together was finally completed with the passage of the Australian and New Zealand acts in 1939.

***

Still, the situation must have seemed bleak to War Office planners in the autumn of 1939. The British Army was no bigger than it had been in 1914 and it lagged behind its adversaries in terms of modern equipment and organization. The army in India was half the size of its 1914 version and the threat of internal unrest kept most of it in the subcontinent. The

---

[62] TNA, DO 35/94/1. O.D. Skelton (for Secretary of State for External Affairs) to J. H. Thomas, 27 February 1932. See also Douglas E. Delaney, 'Co-operation in the Anglo-Canadian Armies, 1939–1945', in Keith Neilson and Greg Kennedy (eds.), *The British Way in Warfare: Power and the International System, 1856–1956. Essays in Honour of David French* (Farnborough and Burlington, VT, 2010), 200–02.

dominion armies had reverted to their pre-1914 strengths and states of readiness, and there was the very real possibility that at least some of their governments might not be 'all in' for an imperial war effort.[63] And yet the empire put together big armies during the Second World War. Britain was able to mobilize nearly 3.8 million men for the army, and this was on top of another 1.73 million for naval and air services.[64] India assembled eighteen divisions during the six years of war. Canada fielded three infantry divisions, two armoured divisions, and two independent armoured brigades for expeditionary operations, and Australia raised four infantry divisions and one armoured division for the 2nd Australian Imperial Force.[65] The Dominion of New Zealand deployed one complete infantry division to the Mediterranean and a two-brigade division to the Pacific, and the Union of South Africa sent two infantry divisions to the Western Desert, one of which was captured at Tobruk in June 1942, the other of which converted to an armoured division in early 1943. Just as important, the divisions that Britain, India, and the dominions raised during the war were mixed and matched, often and easily, as the military situation demanded and political authorities permitted.[66] None of this would have been possible had there not been an empire-wide commitment during the interwar years to foster military compatibility and maintain the slimmest of foundations on which the armies of the empire could build and expand. The tattered ties that bound the armies of the British Empire and Commonwealth may have been badly frayed during the period between the two world wars, but they never broke.

---

[63] See for example Andrew Stewart, 'The British Government and the South African Neutrality Crisis, 1938-1939', *The English Historical Review* 123(503) (2008), 947–72.

[64] Central Statistical Office, *Statistical Digest of the War* (London, 1951), 1 and 8–9.

[65] Canada also raised another three divisions for home defence, one of which was designated for the invasion of Japan when the war in the Far East ended in August 1945. In addition to the 2nd Australian Imperial Force, the commonwealth raised another two armoured cavalry divisions and eight infantry divisions (not completely manned) for the militia and home defence, two of which fought in the New Guinea campaign.

[66] See Douglas E. Delaney, '"Mixable and Match-able Army Formations": The Roots of Anglo-Canadian Military Interoperability during the Second World War', in Ashley Jackson, Gajendra Singh, and Yasmin Khan (eds.), *An Imperial World at War, 1939–1945* (London, 2016), 118–34.

# 11    Seeking a Family Consensus?
## Anglo-Dominion Relations and the Failed
## Imperial Conference of 1941<sup>*</sup>

*Kent Fedorowich*

In 1941, when the fortunes of the British Empire were at their nadir, pressures were building in London and the dominions for an imperial war conference. The idea was to repeat the apparent successes of the 1917 and 1918 imperial war conferences which helped shape future strategy in the latter stages of the Great War. This little understood episode has been largely overlooked or ignored by diplomatic and imperial historians alike.[1] Yet, the failed imperial war conference of 1941 provides invaluable insight into the inner workings of the Anglo-dominion wartime relationship, and so illuminates a key aspect of British global power. The Australian and New Zealand leadership, led by Prime Ministers R. G. Menzies and Peter Fraser respectively, were especially keen to hold a conference in the aftermath of the failed Greek campaign of April–June 1941. The Canadians, led by the mercurial William Lyon Mackenzie King, and the South Africans, directed by the shrewd Jan Smuts, were not; neither was the doughty British leader, Winston Churchill, who had hesitantly supported the idea of a fuzzily named 'supreme' war council in October 1940. Still, in 1941 three of the dominion prime ministers travelled to England to conduct high-level bilateral talks with their British counterpart.

This essay investigates the governmental pressures behind the demands for a conference and the reasons why it never took place. To fathom the intricacies of this wartime coalition, we must begin in 1939 when the idea of

<sup>*</sup> The author would like to thank the British Academy for a small grant in aid of research in 2010 to conduct the archival work necessary for this essay (SG 090299). He would also like to acknowledge the generosity of the following institutions which provided invaluable support through a series of visiting fellowships to facilitate archival research, especially overseas: Stout Research Centre for New Zealand Studies, Victoria University, Wellington (2011); Churchill College Cambridge (2012); the Australian Prime Ministers Centre, Museum of Australian Democracy, Canberra (2013); and the National Library of Australia, Canberra (2013).
[1] The exception is Andrew Stewart, *Empire Lost. Britain, the Dominions and the Second World War* (London, 2008), 51–62.

an imperial conference was first mooted. When Neville Chamberlain was ousted as prime minister in May 1940 and Great Britain found itself facing invasion, calls from several quarters, at home and abroad, rebounded for an imperial gathering. As we will see, Churchill's initial support for an imperial war council in October 1940, and again in June 1941, was a fleeting gesture motivated in part by domestic political insecurities and internal carping about his own and increasingly dictatorial leadership. Led by Australia, dominion criticism over a lack of consultation was on the rise as well, which, as David Dilks has reminded us, set in train or amplified demands from dominion leaders who were facing their own geostrategic and domestic party-political stresses.[2] However, it was in 1941, when British military failures began to take their toll politically, that serious questions about the direction of the war – which was putting enormous strains on the Commonwealth alliance – once again put the idea of an imperial summit back onto the agenda.

## I

When Churchill returned to office in September 1939 as First Lord of the Admiralty, Euan Wallace, the minister of transport, observed: 'He is in tremendous form in his old office  shirt sleeves, cigar and large whisky and soda.'[3] There was no doubting his euphoria at being back at the centre of events or, indeed, how he savoured the fight that lay ahead. With his typical flamboyance, he summed up the significance of the moment when he told the South African premier, Jan Smuts, who had dramatically brought that riven dominion into the war by the closest of margins: 'I rejoice to feel we are once again on commando together.'[4] From Ottawa, King doubtlessly made the sharpest observation of all about Churchill and the course of his wartime leadership: '[He] sees himself already as War Prime Minister of Great Britain with a name which would probably rival that of his illustrious ancestor Marlborough. It all comes back again to the danger of putting too much power into the hands of any one man.'[5]

As Churchill busied himself with naval matters, demands were raised in the British House of Commons to institute an imperial war council. The South African High Commissioner, Charles Te Water, reported to Pretoria

---

[2] David Dilks, *Churchill and Company: Allies and Rivals in War and Peace* (London, 2012), 85.
[3] Bodleian Library, Oxford, MS Eng hist c. 495, Euan Wallace diary, 7 September 1939.
[4] The National Archives, Kew (TNA), Dominions Office papers (DO), DO 35/587/6, G91/225, Admiralty to British high commission in South Africa, 8 September 1939.
[5] Library and Archives Canada, Ottawa (LAC), MG 26-J13, W. L. Mackenzie King diary, 11 October 1939.

that while Chamberlain was engaged in forming his war cabinet, he was also contemplating a supreme war council in which dominion representation would be determined. The idea received a lukewarm response from the cabinet, who argued that it was not 'immediately practicable'.[6] Noting that there were already close links with the dominion governments, primarily through their high commissions, Chamberlain instead invited each dominion to send a senior minister to London to take part in deliberations about war finance, production and supply, shipping, and the common organisation of their respective war efforts. 'While there is no intention of converting these visits of Dominion Ministers into a formal Conference', reported the dominions secretary, Anthony Eden, 'every advantage' would of course be taken 'to arrange a certain number of joint meetings on matters of common interest'.[7]

Privately, Eden admitted the British government had to 'tread warily', especially with the Canadians. Vincent Massey, Canada's High Commissioner in London, cabled Mackenzie King reassuring him that these multiparty meetings were 'purely informative in character'.[8] T. A. Crerar, minister of mines and natural resources, and the only minister to serve in both of the 'senior' dominion's wartime administrations, led the Canadian delegation.[9] Canberra sent R. G. Casey, minister for supply and development, a portfolio which included specific duties for defence preparations. New Zealand dispatched its soft spoken, Scottish-born deputy prime minister, Peter Fraser, who would quickly establish a convivial but professional wartime relationship with Churchill. South Africa sent the famed author and Boer war leader, Colonel Deneys Reitz, minister of native affairs, who became a popular favourite with Whitehall officials.[10]

---

[6] National Archives of South Africa, Pretoria (NASAP), South African Department of External Affairs, BTS vol. 253, PM 1/54/1A, vol. 1, Te Water to External Affairs, 2 September 1939; TNA, Cabinet Office papers (CAB), CAB 104/247, 'Committee on Dominion Collaboration', minutes of first meeting, 14 September 1939; CAB 67/1/10, WP(G)(39)10, 'Dominions Collaboration: Report by Ministerial Committee', 14 September 1939; *Hansard*, HC, vol. 351, cols. 1061–62, 21 September 1939.

[7] TNA, CAB 67/1/41, WP(G)(39)41, 'Arrangements for the Visit of Dominion Ministers', 18 October 1939; CAB 65/1/54, WM54(39)12, 20 October 1939.

[8] Earl of Avon, *The Eden Memoirs: The Reckoning* (London, 1965), 76; LAC, MG 26-J1, microfilm reel C-3746, vol. 274, Massey to King, 1 November 1939.

[9] J. E. Rea, *T.A. Crerar: A Political Life* (Montreal & Kingston, 1997), 194–97. For the Crerar mission itself see David R. Murray (ed.), *Documents on Canadian External Relations (DCER)*, vol. 7, part 1 *1939–1941* (Ottawa, 1974), 375–408.

[10] W. J. Hudson, *Casey* (Melbourne, 1986), 109–11; Michael Bassett and Michael King, *Tomorrow Comes the Song: A Life of Peter Fraser* (Auckland, 2000), 173–79; TNA, CAB 63/84, Lord Hankey, minister without portfolio, to Colonel E. I. D. Gordon, Cape Province, South Africa, 28 October 1939.

The series of meetings and consultations took place in London from late October to early December 1939. It also included a short trip to France in mid-November to visit the Allies' defensive preparations where it was hoped that the dominion ministers would 'see much of interest'.[11] For the Canadians, the relentless haggling with the United Kingdom about the price for foodstuffs such as wheat, bacon and cheese dominated proceedings.[12] However, there were several instances where discussions that were outside the immediate remit of the conference allowed the dominion delegates to get an invaluable insight into high policy, such as war aims and imperial defence. Crerar noted one such briefing in early November where Churchill explained the convoy system to the dominion ministers, pointing out the location of British naval units and the reason behind their positioning. 'It was a lucid explanation', admitted the Canadian. When Churchill finished, Crerar noted Reitz's witticism: 'I am glad now that we did not shoot you when you were in South Africa.'[13]

## II

Despite the tepid response from British cabinet ministers and many of their dominion counterparts in late 1939, demands for an imperial conference and/or an imperial war cabinet still echoed amongst the lobbies of Westminster throughout 1940. Similar demands were also raised by Lord Lothian, British ambassador to Washington, to Lord Halifax, the British foreign secretary. In late February 1940, Lothian advocated that London push the empire aspect of the war more visibly, demonstrating how critical dominion cooperation as free and equal nations could be more discernibly represented to isolationist America. By resurrecting the imperial war cabinet, it would strengthen the hands of those who advocated that the allies were fighting for the freedom of small nations, the ultimate aim of which was an international system where these small nations, like the dominions, had an equal part to play with their larger counterparts. A reconstituted imperial war cabinet, argued Lothian, would validate dominion equality in formulating

---

[11] Rhodes House Library, Oxford, Sir H.B. Batterbee papers, MSS NZ s13, 6/1, Sir John Stephenson, assistant undersecretary, DO, to Batterbee, UK High Commissioner in New Zealand, 10 November 1939.

[12] For fascinating insights into the complicated and often tetchy negotiations over the price for Canadian primary products see Frederick W. Gibson and Barbara Robertson (eds.), *Ottawa at War: The Grant Dexter Memoranda, 1939–1945* (Winnipeg, 1994), memoranda by Dexter, Ottawa correspondent for the *Manitoba Free Press*, 13–17 and 22–30.

[13] Queen's University Archive, Kingston, Ontario (QUA), T. A. Crerar papers, box 155, series iv, diaries, 6 November 1939.

wartime strategy that would make it more palatable for the Americans to come out of isolation and cooperate with a British Commonwealth of free nations.[14]

The Dominions Office opposed the idea on constitutional grounds, as senior officials firmly believed that the dominions, which had striven for greater autonomy throughout the interwar period, would find the concept of a super-cabinet that took decisions for the United Kingdom and the dominions entirely unacceptable. Even the less ambitious idea of holding a meeting of Dominion leaders was fraught with difficulties. As one insider explained, the Dominion Office's reaction in early 1940 not to support an imperial gathering had to do with genuine pride in the efficacy of existing arrangements that would serve equally well in wartime.[15] And there was the difficulty, observed by Chamberlain, in finding representatives from the dominions who would be a 'valuable addition' to the British cabinet: 'Where is the Smuts?'[16]

Where indeed. South Africa was adamant that such a meeting was both unnecessary and untimely. It stemmed from the fractious and militant nature of the domestic political arena. Unlike its imperial cousins, South Africa was unique in that it not only faced the threat of external aggression; it also had to combat a serious danger to its internal security posed by a number of pro-Nazi, anti-British and predominantly right-wing Afrikaner groups, such as the 300,000-strong *Ossewabrandwag*.[17] Although the South African authorities, including Smuts, continually and persistently played down the scale and risk of the 'cankerous growth' of these fifth columnists,[18] London realized that it could not push Smuts too hard to attend an overseas conference knowing how precarious his position was within the Union.

Always wary of imperial centralization and the subordination of dominion interests to those of the metropole, Mackenzie King, for his part, argued stubbornly right from the beginning of the war that an imperial conference was utterly unnecessary. True, he did not face the

---

[14] TNA, DO 35/998/12, WC 7/1, Lothian to Halifax, 27 February 1940.

[15] Joe Garner, *The Commonwealth Office 1925–1968* (London, 1978), 193.

[16] TNA, DO 35/998/12, WC 7/1, Chamberlain minute, 11 March 1940.

[17] Christoph Marx, *Oxwagon Sentinel: Radical Afrikaner Nationalism and the History of the Ossewabrandwag* (Berlin, 2008); Kent Fedorowich, 'German Espionage and British Counterintelligence in South Africa and Mozambique, 1939-1944', *Historical Journal* 48(1) (2005), 209–30.

[18] Churchill Archive Centre, Cambridge (CAC), L. S. Amery papers, AMEL 2/2/24, Smuts to Amery, secretary of state for India and Burma, 18 February 1941; NASAP, J. C. Smuts papers, A1, vol. 143, interdepartmental committee memo on internal security, c. May 1940; TNA, DO 35/1008/7, WG429/40, E. J. Harding, UK High Commissioner in South Africa (1940–41), to Viscount Caldecote, secretary of state for the dominions, 31 July 1940.

threat of armed insurrection which Smuts confronted in South Africa. The political stakes in Canada were delicately poised nonetheless. At its heart was the preservation of unimpaired national unity. King was also tormented by his own deep-seated insecurities that if he travelled to London for an extended period he would be unhorsed as leader of the Liberal party.[19] He reminded his cabinet colleagues that he had always been opposed to any such conference, 'feeling strongly that a Prime Minister [must] be prepared to deal with the emergent situations as they arose'.[20]

The issue that threatened to divide the country along ethnic lines was conscription, which, in 1917, had almost split the country between the already deeply alienated English and French-speaking communities.[21] However vexing King's isolationism and lack of commitment to British diplomatic efforts had been for Whitehall in the latter half of the 1930s, it was this motivating factor to keep Canada united that drove him to be frustratingly non-committal in the lead up to the Second World War.[22] When Canada did declare war one week after the United Kingdom on 10 September 1939, the Canadian premier, a man 'above all things a lover of peace and conciliation', had succeeded in taking a united but fragile nation into war.[23] His promise not to invoke conscription had staved off (temporarily) a political insurgency from the Quebec wing of the federal Liberal party, aided it as it was by a triumvirate of fiercely loyal and influential Quebec MPs – Ernest Lapointe, minister of justice; Arthur Cardin, minister of public works; and the hard-drinking, chain-smoking but immensely popular C. G. 'Chubby' Power, postmaster general. Parliamentary unity may have been achieved, but Mackenzie King, the shrewdest of political tacticians, knew that national unity was far from secure. As a result, the pledge not to introduce conscription was the keystone in his pursuit of 'limited liability', deliberately calculated to provide a measured

---

[19] QUA, Crerar papers, box 104, J. W. Dafoe, editor, *Winnipeg Free Press*, to Crerar, 5 May 1941.
[20] LAC, reel C-11,789, RG 2, 7C, vol. 2, July–October 1940, minutes and documents of the Canadian Cabinet War Committee, meeting 34, 1 October 1940.
[21] J. L. Granatstein and J. M. Hitsman, *Broken Promises: A History of Conscription in Canada* (Toronto, 1977).
[22] James Eayrs, *In Defence of Canada*, vol. 2, *Appeasement and Rearmament* (Toronto, 1965); Norman Hillmer and Robert Bothwell, '"A Self-Evident National Duty": Canadian Foreign Policy, 1935–1939', *Journal of Imperial and Commonwealth History* 3(2) (1975), 212–33.
[23] TNA, DO 35/586/3, G88/83, Sir Gerald Campbell, UK High Commissioner in Canada, to Eden, 20 September 1939.

commitment to the war by concentrating on hemispheric defence and supplying Britain with the sinews of war.[24]

At the beginning of April 1940, London explored the possibility of another visit by a Canadian minister to London. King, who was also secretary of state for external affairs, warmly welcomed the British initiative as it chimed neatly with a planned trip to London by his minister of national defence, Norman Rogers.[25] Germany's invasion of Denmark and Norway on 9 April intensified demands in some political circles for an imperial conference to discuss the Commonwealth's 'joint war effort in all its aspects'. Chamberlain, in part to fend off growing criticism of the disastrous Norwegian campaign, then proposed a meeting of dominion prime ministers, perhaps in July or early August 1940.[26] Although Eden warned his cabinet colleagues the Canadian leader had showed 'considerable suspicion' about the 1939 autumn meetings, buoyed by his recent landslide at the general election in March 1940, it was hoped King might be in a more positive frame of mind.[27] Lester Pearson, the official secretary at the Canadian high commission, mused whether King would approve: 'It will be a crumb thrown to us for lack of active participation in the week-to-week direction of the war'.[28]

King telegraphed Rogers, who had made it to England for discussions on war finance, that such an arrangement would be 'inadvisable'.[29] His reluctance to leave Canada was outlined to Chamberlain, the gist of which was that Canada's war effort and its 'continued unity' would best be maintained by the prime minister 'being as continuously as possible at the seat of Government in his own country'. The Canadian premier concluded that the existing arrangements for consultation, including the visits of key ministers other than the prime minister to London, would ensure the desired collaboration between the Commonwealth partners. If this was not enough to kill off the idea of a London conference, Mackenzie King added that Chamberlain should not forget the 'peculiar advantages' of Canada's situation vis-à-vis the neutral United States. In other words, the Canadian premier was best suited to continue the vital task of

---

[24] Norman Hillmer, Robert Bothwell, Roger Sarty and Claude Beauregard (eds.), *A Country of Limitations: Canada and the World in 1939* (Ottawa, 1996).

[25] LAC, Records of Department of External Affairs, reel T-2207, RG 25, D1, vol. 825, file 716, Chamberlain to King, 2 April 1940 and King's reply, 3 April 1940.

[26] Ibid., Eden to King, 21 April 1940, and Chamberlain to King, 22 April 1940.

[27] TNA, CAB 65/6/34, WM89(40)12, 12 April 1940; CAB 67/5/45, WP(G)(40)95, 'Consultation with the Dominions', 2 April 1940.

[28] LAC, MG 26-N8, Lester B. Pearson papers, vols. 1–2, diary entry, 24 April 1940.

[29] Ibid., diary entry, 8 May 1940; LAC, reel T-2207, RG 25, D1, vol. 825, file 716, King to Massey for Rogers, 7 May 1940 and Massey's reply forwarding correspondence from Rogers, 8 May 1940.

maintaining good relations with Washington on behalf of the Commonwealth alliance, which his absence from Ottawa could undermine at such a critical juncture of the war.[30]

What of the antipodean dominions? Stanley Bruce, the urbane former prime minister and now Australian High Commissioner in London, thought it imperative that such a gathering take place and was adamant that prime minister R. G. Menzies attend whatever his 'local difficulties' in Australia.[31] Menzies was in two minds. In September 1939 he had broached 'with deliberate casualness' the question of wartime information flows and consultation with Great Britain. Complaints had been made in Australia about the paltry information reaching the dominion about the conduct of the war. Menzies, however, was sympathetic to the practical difficulties involved; what he challenged was the impossibility in the present circumstances for effective consultation on issues of wartime strategy. Dominion representatives in the British war cabinet would improve the consultative process, but there were constitutional and political obstacles preventing his or Bruce's appointment.[32]

The new overtures made by Chamberlain for a gathering of dominion leaders in the summer of 1940 did not, at first, change Canberra's initial thinking. Despite Bruce's enthusiasm for Menzies' presence in London, Canberra responded more cautiously to Whitehall's advances. The timing was problematical because of an impending general election in Australia, which made it difficult for the prime minister to be absent. Menzies, echoing his Canadian counterpart, added that the necessity of 'continual watchfulness' over the Australian war effort was another reason impeding his absence from Australia. Several days later, however, London was informed by its High Commissioner in Australia, Sir Geoffrey Whiskard, that Menzies had a change of heart and intended to accept the invitation to attend a meeting of dominion leaders. Yet, he was still opposed to the idea of dominion representation in an empire war council, arguing that by adding five dominion ministers it would make the new body unmanageable and impractical. Existing air communications now made it feasible to have 'brief conferences in London at comparatively short intervals' at fleeting notice. No reply was received from New

---

[30] TNA, Prime Minister's Office (PREM), PREM 4/43A/11, King to Chamberlain, 10 May 1940, and DO note, 20 May 1940.

[31] H. Kenway, H. J. W. Stokes and P.G. Edwards (eds.), *Documents on Australian Foreign Policy 1937–49*, vol. 3, *January–June 1940* (Canberra, 1979), 218–19.

[32] P. G. Edwards, 'Menzies and the Imperial Connection, 1939–41', in Cameron Hazlehurst (ed.), *Australian Conservatism: Essays in Twentieth Century Political History* (Canberra, 1979), 202–03.

Zealand, which was mourning the loss of its Australian-born bachelor prime minister, Michael Savage, who had died on 27 March 1940.[33]

Events continued to move swiftly. Chamberlain's government was on the verge of collapse, and as such, Pearson correctly surmised that the beleaguered British prime minister did not care much whether the Canadian premier 'came to the July meeting or not'.[34] Chamberlain's tepid offer of an imperial war council was quickly overtaken. The humiliating withdrawal from Norway in late April–early May, compounded by the German invasion of the Low Countries and France on 10 May 1940, put paid to Chamberlain's half-hearted initiative. Forced to resign as British prime minister, the Dominions Office nevertheless left the door ajar if an occasion allowed for the reopening of the question.

## III

Churchill's rise to the premiership marked a seismic shift in Downing Street's attitude towards the dominions. Unlike Chamberlain, who was willing to consult them (even if he had already made up his mind), Churchill wanted supreme control over policymaking. Rightly, he realized that there were far too many committees that tied up too many ministers and did not yield sufficient results. The cabinet secretary, Sir Edward Bridges, was instructed in late May 1940 to reduce these committees by 'suppression or amalgamation'.[35] Churchill was also not prepared to tolerate interference from the dominions' High Commissioners (who collectively did possess an over-exaggerated view of their authority and influence during these early days of the war). The new prime minister was decisive. If he needed to consult the High Commissioners, he would, although his preferred method was to cable their respective prime ministers directly, thus avoiding the Dominions Office, once described rather presumptuously as a sort of foreign office of the empire.[36]

The sway of the High Commissioners was further blunted when Churchill assembled his cabinet. Eden, the popular dominions secretary,

---

[33] TNA, PREM 4/43A/11, Menzies to Chamberlain, 2 May 1940, and DO note, 20 May 1940; *DAFP*, vol. 3, 284; CAB 67/8/77, WP(G)(40)277, 'Imperial War Conference. Proposed Message to Mr Menzies', 29 October 1940.

[34] LAC, MG 26-N8, Pearson papers, vols. 1–2, diary entry, 8 May 1940.

[35] Winston S. Churchill, *The Second World War*, 9th ed., vol. 2 (London, 1971), appendix A, 560.

[36] TNA, DO 35/541/3, C97/42, Stephen Holmes, secretary, UK high commission in Ottawa, to E. J. Harding, permanent undersecretary of state at the Dominions Office, 21 July 1939.

was moved to the war office. His replacement, for a second stint as dominions secretary, was the rotund and unimpressive Lord Caldecote, which several dominion High Commissioners adamantly believed was a second-rate politician who had only been given the post as a sinecure for being a faithful party loyalist. To add insult to injury, Caldecote informed his dominion colleagues in late June 1940 that he would be attending only two cabinet meetings each week, instead of being present at all such gatherings. When the Canadian High Commissioner, Vincent Massey, complained to Churchill about Caldecote's unsuitability, he was ignored.[37] Several small but token concessions were made to the High Commissioners in early July 1940 when they were invited to a briefing in the Cabinet War Room; and then in mid-July they attended a private audience with Churchill and Caldecote to discuss a wide range of issues. 'But this is no substitute for the continuous flow of confidential information', grumbled Massey, 'for which we continued to press and of which we were occasionally deprived.'[38] Bruce agreed. Now that Whitehall was deliberately freezing the dominions out of highly confidential information, they were being denied the opportunity to initiate policy or present their own views with the full knowledge of all the facts or the benefits of continuous consultation regarding the broad conduct of the war.[39]

In October 1940, Churchill was forced to reshuffle his cabinet. That September, a joint British-Free French task force – which, unbeknownst to Menzies, included the heavy cruiser HMAS *Australia* – had botched an attempt to capture the Vichy port of Dakar in French West Africa. Menzies, primed by his High Commissioner, had been deeply critical of the attack and had chastised Churchill for not consulting the dominions (the Commonwealth leaders learned of its failure through the press!). Growing pressure from within Churchill's own cabinet about his autocratic style of government combined with growing public dissatisfaction over recent events forced this change.[40] The idea of reviving the imperial war cabinet now came back into play, in part, as one Australian external affairs officer in London put it, because of the substandard and

---

[37] Kent Fedorowich and Carl Bridge, 'Family Matters? The Dominion High Commissioners at War, 1939–42', *Journal of Imperial and Commonwealth History* 40(1) (2012), especially 7–8.

[38] University of Toronto Archives (UTA), Vincent Massey papers, box 310, vol. 43, diary entry, 17 July 1940.

[39] National Archives of Australia (NAA), S. M. Bruce papers, supplementary war files, M103/1, 1940 JAN–JUN, handwritten note for Menzies, 7 June 1940.

[40] Sheila Lawlor, *Churchill and the Politics of War, 1940–1941* (Cambridge, 1994), 104–11; David Lee, *Stanley Melbourne Bruce: Australian Internationalist* (London, 2010), 145–46.

convoluted methods of (mis)communication between London and Canberra.[41]

Led by Bruce, this gave the dominion High Commissioners (or so they thought) an opportunity to influence Churchill in choosing a replacement for Caldecote, who had been appointed lord chief justice. But Churchill was in a belligerent mood. Menzies' censure was interpreted by Churchill as a personal attack. With his blood up, Churchill asked Bruce whether he was suggesting that the British cabinet 'should never have a private meeting without the Dominions being present'.[42] Bruce emphatically denied that he was trying to dictate policy to the British leader; but as he told Menzies, the real problem in the British war cabinet was that no one stood up to Churchill and 'his judgement is not such as to obviate necessity for some check on his impulses'.[43]

Undaunted, Bruce pushed hard for a meeting of an imperial war cabinet which for him was still the most desirable solution to put the dominion case to the heart of policymaking. Nonetheless, he was realistic in its chances of coming off as 'Smuts could not attend and Mackenzie King would not'. A meeting of ministers other than prime ministers, he argued, 'would be useless and in my view [a] fundamental mistake'.[44] Privately, he now hankered to be Australia's man in the inner councils of London. From Washington, Casey added more grist to Bruce's mill. He told Menzies that he felt 'very strongly' about the advantages which would accrue to Australia if the prime minister insisted that Bruce be made a member of the British war cabinet. 'The simple fact remains that Bruce has [a] sense of reality which is badly needed and will be even more needed before this business is finished.'[45] Churchill, however, continued to resist these Australian entreaties, but did offer an olive branch by suggesting that Menzies visit London.

Churchill also fought off similar pleas from the House of Lords, elements of which led by Lord Davies and Viscount Elibank had been pestering the government since August that vital wartime decisions were not taking the dominions into account, and that the present arrangements for consulting them were not only 'totally inadequate' but were

[41] W. J. Hudson and H. J. W. Stokes (eds.), *DAFP*, vol. 4, *July 1940–June 1941* (Canberra, 1980), 206.

[42] NAA, Bruce papers, M100/1, monthly war files – OCTOBER 1940, Bruce to Menzies, interview with Churchill, 2 October 1940.

[43] *DAFP*, vol. 4, 201.

[44] NAA, CRS A981, item SOU AF 39, Bruce to Menzies, 24 October 1940.

[45] NAA, CRS A3300, item 67, handwritten cipher, personal for prime minister, Casey to Menzies, n.d.

'haphazard and unbusinesslike'.[46] There was also pressure from certain organs of the press.[47]

In November, when it was mooted by the Dominions Office that a sort of 'supreme war council' be convened made up of representatives of those nations who had been recently overrun in Europe and constituent parts of the empire, Churchill rounded on the newly appointed dominions secretary, Lord 'Bobbety' Cranborne. The prime minister argued that such terminology was inappropriate and was contrary to what was discussed at cabinet. Churchill's robustness was in response to a stinging protest from Ottawa, for which he reminded Cranborne that it was quite easy to see how the Canadian premier had been misled: 'With his particular isolation tendencies, this was a puddle at which he would sure to shy.'[48] An apology was immediately forthcoming, but it was clear to King's overweening paranoia this was simply the revival of an imperial war cabinet but on a larger and more dangerous magnitude. The whole scheme, just like Chamberlain's approach in April, was a 'façade and a sham, making the Empire subject to ridicule – a mere show, the absolute hollowness of which would be wholly apparent to the world'.[49]

Menzies and his cabinet colleagues disagreed. Arguing that Canberra was not 'unconscious of the practical difficulties of creating a standing Empire War Cabinet', and that existing methods of communication and consultation were adequate to a point, Menzies nevertheless felt that face-to-face personal contact between Commonwealth leaders was essential if concerted military plans and common strategic ideas were to be updated. Australia already had 'special interests' in the Middle East, but the festering sore which prompted Menzies to accept the British government's invitation to go to London was the defence of Singapore.[50] The Singapore Defence Conference, held in late October 1940 between British, Australian, Dutch and New Zealand military representatives, tabled its report in late November, which revealed ominous concerns in antipodean eyes about the deficiencies of the defence of Malaya, especially Singapore. Both the Australian war cabinet and the advisory war

---

[46] *Hansard*, HL, series 5, vol. 117, cols. 139–40 and col. 161, 6 and 8 August 1940; and series 5, vol. 117, cols. 499–510, 16 October 1940.

[47] LAC, reel T-1807, RG 25, D1, vol. 802, file 557, Pearson to King, 22 October 1940, containing press digest from *Sunday Times*, 20 October 1940 and *Daily Telegraph*, 15 and 16 October 1940.

[48] CAC, CHAR 20/13, prime minister's personal minutes, M 285, November 1940, Churchill to Cranborne, 10 November 1940.

[49] LAC, reel T-1807, RG 25, vol. 802, file 557, King memo to O. D. Skelton, under-secretary of state for external affairs, 3 November 1940; MG 26-J13, King diary, 2–3 November 1940.

[50] *DAFP*, vol. 4, 263.

council unanimously supported Menzies' mission to London to discuss matters of mutual importance. He informed Cranborne: 'I would be willing to go to London or any other nominated place to attend the necessary conference.' Mindful about his perilous position domestically, however, Menzies instructed Bruce to give him a frank report of the value of a visit.[51]

The reaction of Peter Fraser was more measured. Fraser, who had succeeded Savage as prime minister after the latter's death from cancer, was content to leave the initiative for calling a conference with London. If convened, he would do his best to see New Zealand was represented. Then, intriguingly, he confided to Sir Harry Batterbee, the UK High Commissioner in New Zealand, that a meeting *in London* would be an excellent public relations exercise to show the international community 'that London was still functioning as the Imperial capital and that Hitler could not prevent the representatives of the Empire from meeting there'.[52] For Fraser, unlike King, such a gathering demonstrated a unity of purpose particularly to audiences in neutral countries.

In December 1940, Churchill made fresh efforts to restrict the circulation of 'secret matters' within government. Cranborne warned that the antipodean dominions were complaining that they were not being kept as fully informed as they would wish. Sharing important information with the dominions was essential, argued the dominions secretary, as it contributed to dominion confidence in British leadership. It also ensured practical cooperation with London which allowed the dominion governments to frame their own policy and its public presentation.[53] Despite Cranborne's protests Churchill continued his exclusion of the High Commissioners from the inner circle. As a result, Cranborne was becoming progressively annoyed that his duties and responsibilities as dominions secretary were being undermined. As 1941 dawned, the tensions within the Commonwealth alliance began to build.

## IV

The first dominion prime minister to arrive in London during the darkening days of 1941 was Robert Menzies. He had been exercised right from the beginning of the war that the dominions needed an effective voice in

---

[51] Paul Hasluck, *The Government and the People 1939–1941*, reprint (Canberra, 1965), 294–300; A. W. Martin, *Robert Menzies: A Life*, vol. 1, *1894–1943* (Melbourne, 1996), 316; *DAFP*, vol. 4, 263, 320 and 325–26.

[52] RHL, Batterbee papers, MSS NZ s13, 6/1, Batterbee to Sir Eric Machtig, 5 November 1940.

[53] TNA, PREM 4/43B/1, Cranborne to Churchill, 23 December 1940.

London on questions of broad political strategy. In late September 1939 he had broached the idea 'whether those Dominions who were taking or were preparing to take an active part in war ought not to have a seat in [the] United Kingdom War Cabinet'.[54] Although he had prevaricated about the dominions having a permanent place in a reconstructed imperial war cabinet prior to his visit in 1941, it was his experiences while in Great Britain that made him press forcefully for its restoration.

The results of Menzies' four-month trip to the United Kingdom via Singapore and the Middle East (and home via Canada and the United States) were less than satisfactory for Australia. In fact, the strategic blunder of the Greek campaign to which Menzies had committed the 6th Australian Division coupled with his visit to Ireland against Churchill's explicit wish only served to embitter relations between the leaders.[55] Menzies was both dazzled and increasingly frustrated by Churchill as his stay progressed: 'Winston is not a receptive or reasoning animal.'[56] Menzies was also fearful that Churchill's 'real tyrant' was his penchant for the 'glittering phrase – so attractive to his mind that awkward facts may have to give way'. During a war cabinet meeting in early March, Menzies recalled that he had to 'speak plain words about consulting [the] Dominions before grave decisions [were] made affecting them'. Complaining about Churchill's dictatorial style, Menzies unloaded his frustration on the British war cabinet which he called 'deplorable – dumb men most of whom disagree with Winston but none of whom dare to say so'. The chiefs of staff were little better and without exception 'Yes Men'.[57]

Menzies' trip to London between February and May 1941 had convinced him that a return trip to London was necessary. Much has been written about Menzies' motivations. David Day and Andrew Stewart have both argued that Menzies' attempts to return to London were driven by an overweening ambition to challenge Churchill's leadership and replace him as prime minister.[58] Indeed, Menzies had impressed those disgruntled elements within the cabinet, parliament and the chiefs of staff

---

[54] TNA, CAB 21/874, Whiskard to DO, 20 September 1939.

[55] A. W. Martin and Patsy Hardy (eds.), *Dark and Hurrying Days: Menzies' 1941 Diary* (Canberra, 1993), appendix II, 'The Trip to Ireland', 151–58.

[56] Ibid., 110.

[57] Ibid., 71, 112 and 83. There are two excellent analyses of Churchill's style as wartime leader: Alex Danchev, 'Waltzing with Winston: Civil-Military Relations in the Second World War', in Paul Smith (ed.), *Government and the Armed Services 1856–1990* (London, 1996), 191–216; Geoffrey Best, *Churchill and War* (London and New York, 2005), 165–84.

[58] David Day, *Menzies and Churchill at War* (Sydney, 1986), 191–232; Stewart, *Empire Lost*, 60–62.

with his persistence in challenging Churchill's strategic assumptions and doggedly standing up to the prime minister's dictatorial manner. Many, like General Sir John Kennedy, director of military operations (1940–43), were equally captivated by his tenacity to ask uncomfortable questions and not accept being fobbed off by Whitehall mandarins.[59] Undoubtedly, Menzies got caught up in the political intrigue as his opinion of Churchill's leadership became more critical. Equally, he must have been attracted by the opportunity to extricate himself from the fractious and toxic political atmosphere in Australia, elevate himself to a higher political plane and enhance his stature as an imperial statesman. However, as Alan Martin and Peter Edwards have persuasively argued, the desire to return to London was not primarily driven for personal political gain; rather it stemmed from a strong desire to challenge British diplomacy, inject an independent voice into imperial policymaking and broaden the strategic horizons of many British policymakers seemingly transfixed on the European situation.[60]

Menzies was equally critical of his Canadian counterpart. His return home via Ottawa in early May 1941 highlighted the contrasting styles and views of the two Commonwealth leaders, which adds a more nuanced dimension to the conflicting views these two men possessed regarding the need for an imperial conference, and more specifically, dominion membership in an imperial war cabinet. Malcolm MacDonald, the newly appointed UK High Commissioner in Ottawa, told Cranborne that the Australian gave his Canadian audiences 'an impression of vigorous war leadership which they are conscious of missing amongst their own Statesmen'. The result of Menzies' speeches was indeed a personal triumph for him, but what was more remarkable was the demonstration of Canadian enthusiasm for Menzies himself. His oratory, reported MacDonald, had been a 'spur to the Canadian war effort'.[61] King was equally impressed with Menzies, who held a commanding presence, possessed 'great vigour', 'endless confidence' and a 'wonderful gift for speaking'.[62] For the sensitive Canadian leader, Menzies' performance must have been worrying as it re-energized the Conservative opposition and their newspaper allies, such as the *Toronto Telegram* and the *Montreal*

[59] Stephen Roskill, *Hankey: Man of Secrets*, vol. 3 *1931–1963* (Collins, 1974), 499–502; Cameron Hazlehurst, *Menzies Observed* (Sydney, 1979), 209–25; John Kennedy, *The Business of War* (London, 1957), 190.
[60] Martin, *Robert Menzies*, vol. 1, 316–55; Edwards, 'Imperial Connection', 202–04.
[61] TNA, PREM 4/43A/12, MacDonald to Cranborne, 14 May 1941.
[62] LAC, MG 26-J13, King diary, 7 May 1941.

*Gazette,* who had been attacking King since the spring of 1941 for his lacklustre wartime leadership.[63]

Uppermost on Menzies' mind, according to King, was the desire for an imperial conference or cabinet, the idea of which Churchill had evidently asked Menzies to discuss with the Canadian leader. The nub of Menzies argument was that there was no British cabinet; that Churchill ran the 'whole show'. It was Churchill who 'did all the talking and no one dared to say no to anything'. It was vital, argued Menzies, that the dominion point of view be put forward and that there should be someone from the dominions putting their case to the fore. King noted how outspoken Menzies was on this issue: 'I sensed the feeling that he would rather be on the War Cabinet in London than Prime Minister of Australia.'[64] Arguing that the existing channels of communication were sufficient, King told Menzies that there had been 'too much done for the sake of appearance and too little in the way of reality'. Furthermore, what would be the consequences for the dominion prime ministers if they were kept in London for inordinate periods of time? Surely a more effective way was to have individual ministers travel to London and take up matters with their opposite numbers. Then, the Canadian premier rolled out the now familiar trope that his real duty was to ensure that Canada remained united: 'If we failed in that, nothing else would much matter.'[65]

King believed that he had swung Menzies around to his point of view – that a meeting of dominion leaders was only necessary when some 'great decision' was to be made, such as drafting peace terms or post-war reconstruction policies. At the very least, King seemed satisfied that Menzies recognized each dominion had its own special problems. Consultation was critical, but for King that could be accomplished more effectively through the existing machinery.[66] Menzies conceded that his Canadian counterpart had done well in maintaining Canadian unity; and he also admitted that he had kept the United States onside. However, in private, Menzies was forthright about the abilities of his Canadian host: King was not a war leader, and he 'possessed no *burning* zeal for the cause'. Even more damning was that for Menzies, King was a 'politician who possibly prefers to lead from behind'.[67]

---

[63] QUA, Crerar papers, box 104, Crerar to Dafoe, 10 May 1941. For the wartime picture of the Canadian Opposition, see J. L. Granatstein, *The Politics of Survival: The Conservative Party of Canada, 1939–1945* (Toronto, reprint 1970), 58–112.

[64] LAC, MG 26-J13, King diary, 7 May 1941.

[65] Ibid: CAC, CHAR 20/38, prime minister's personal telegrams, T 165, King to Churchill, 10 May 1941 on Menzies' visit to Ottawa.

[66] LAC, MG 26-J13, King diary, 8 May 1941.

[67] Martin and Hardy (eds.), *Dark and Hurrying Days,* 124–25. The emphasis is Menzies.

**V**

Throughout May and June 1941, the Canadian prime minister remained adamant that the unimpaired maintenance of national unity was more essential to Canada's war effort than anything else. Arguing that crucial issues within the domestic political arena such as conscription needed his undivided attention, he refused to see the need for a formal conference. As Cranborne informed Churchill, the Canadian leader was still 'very wobbly' about coming over for an imperial gathering.[68] This did stop the British government from investigating the possibility of a conference to be held that summer. At the end of May, Cranborne told MacDonald that Churchill seemed open to the idea of a meeting of dominion prime ministers to be convened over the summer.[69] In early June, Cranborne, with the assistance of the foreign secretary, Anthony Eden, began formulating the pros and cons of hosting such a get-together. These options were tabled to the war cabinet on 9 June.[70] Cranborne was also cautiously optimistic that Menzies' trip to Ottawa had modified King's views on the need for a meeting. Menzies 'got results' while in Ottawa, reported MacDonald. Although the Canadian premier remained 'resolutely opposed' to anything like an imperial war cabinet sitting continuously in London, he was allegedly impressed by Menzies' arguments for a conference of 'comparatively short duration'. Cranborne revealed if specific, compelling points required collective discussion by the Commonwealth heads, then the Canadian leader would make the trip.[71] Churchill suggested that Smuts and King be sounded out privately about the idea. The timing was opportune for two reasons, argued Churchill. Fraser was about to arrive in the country, and there was talk that Smuts was contemplating a trip to Cairo to visit his troops.[72] Could he be enticed to come to London for a few days?

There were powerful underlying reasons why the British government was once again raising the possibility of an imperial conference. The war was going badly. Censure in parliament was building. The press was

---

[68] TNA, DO 35/999/3, WC8/3, King to Cranborne, 20 May 1941; WC8/2, King to Churchill, 16 June 1941; TNA, Foreign Office papers, FO 371/29119/W 7813, Cranborne to Churchill, 30 May 1941.

[69] Durham University Library, Special Collections and Archives (DUL), Malcolm MacDonald papers, 14/4/13, Cranborne to MacDonald, 31 May 1941.

[70] TNA, PREM 4/43A/12, Cranborne to Churchill, 3 and 6 June 1941; CAB 65/18/37, WM58(41)5, 9 June 1941.

[71] TNA, PREM 4/43A/12, MacDonald to Cranborne, 14 May 1941; CAB 66/16/44, WP (41)121, memo by Cranborne, 4 June 1941.

[72] CAC, CHAR 20/49, prime minister's personal minutes, T 288 and 290, June 1941, Churchill to King, 11 June 1941, and Churchill to Smuts, 13 June 1941; TNA, FO 954/15, Sir Miles Lampson, British ambassador to Egypt, to Eden, 17 June 1941.

growing critical about the direction of the war, especially Churchill's leadership. This had all the hallmarks of Chamberlain's dilemma the year before. The nation needed reassuring and a demonstration of imperial solidarity might soothe these anxieties. It was decided that Churchill address parliament on the war situation. The foreshadowing of an imperial conference would be part of the report. However, the replies from King and Smuts were not favourable. The constraints of domestic politics once again did not allow the two prime ministers to travel.[73] For Churchill, however, this did not stop him from making several personal but unsuccessful appeals to his adored Smuts asking him to trek to London, 'and to give me, at this critical time, the support of your presence and advice'.[74] Smuts appreciated the sentiment, but once again reiterated that the timing was poor, the dangers vast and the decision to concentrate all the dominion premiers in London unwise.[75]

When Churchill rose in the House of Commons on 24 June, he announced that both Smuts and King were unavailable to attend a conference that summer. What seemed an innocuous statement, quickly turned into a highly embarrassing *faux pas* for the British government. Mackenzie King expressed his hurt and annoyance, thinking Churchill was fixing the blame on Smuts and himself for the failure to hold a conference. It also played into the fractious political arena exposing the Canadian leader to attack from his political opponents, who insinuated he was an indifferent and weak wartime leader.[76]

Meanwhile, Menzies again attempted to co-opt the support of the other dominion prime ministers in July 1941, this time suggesting that dominion representation on the British war cabinet should be a permanent feature; especially since the dominions secretary was not a member of the war cabinet and was therefore 'little more than a channel of communication'.[77] With a wary eye on domestic political considerations,[78] Menzies emphasized that there was an inadequate consideration of long-range policy, an insufficiently comprehensive view of how the productive capacity of the empire and the United

[73] TNA, PREM 4/43A/12, Massey to Churchill, 16 June 1941, and King to Churchill, 22 June 1941: CAC, CHAR 20/49, prime minister's personal minutes, T 314 and T 315, June 1941, Churchill to Smuts and King, 20 June 1941.

[74] CAC, CHAR 20/49, prime minister's personal minutes, T 290, June 1941, Churchill to Smuts, 13 June 1941.

[75] NASAP, Smuts papers, A1, vol. 95A, Smuts to Churchill, 16 June and 22 August 1941.

[76] DUL, MacDonald papers, 14/4/27, private and personal, MacDonald to Cranborne, 1 August 1941.

[77] National Library of Australia (NLA), R. G. Menzies papers, MS 4936/581/21, Menzies to Smuts and King, 3 July 1941.

[78] Stuart MacIntrye, *Australia's Boldest Experiment: War and reconstruction in the 1940s* (Sydney, 2015), 47–84.

States could be used and an absence of effective consultation with the dominions over major questions of policy.

Smuts was the first to respond. He agreed that an imperial war conference would be desirable but reiterated domestic considerations compelled him to stay at home. Furthermore, the Allied position in the Mediterranean was far from secure, especially in the western desert where Axis forces had besieged Australian, British and Indian units at Tobruk and were also threatening the Egyptian frontier. He also challenged Menzies' contention that a reconstituted war cabinet involving the attendance of dominion prime ministers in London was the solution. True, the war cabinet in London could be a much stronger body, as it was in the last war. But, were the men available and were drastic changes the right way to set reform? These were questions, he told his High Commissioner in London, Sidney Waterson, that only Churchill and his cabinet colleagues could judge: 'we should concentrate the most loyal support behind him and avoid anything which savours of criticism'. Smuts was also concerned that a dominion prime minister in the war cabinet would not necessarily represent the views of the other dominions. More importantly, dominion prime ministers could best serve the common cause by 'keeping their peoples keyed up to the highest pitch. Occasional visits to London are a different matter', but he found himself agreeing with Mackenzie King, that a 'prolonged absence of Prime Ministers from their countries in our ever-changing world-wide war situation might at any time prove a mistake'.[79]

King took a month to reply and not surprisingly was even less receptive to Menzies' overtures than Smuts. The possibility of war in the Pacific coupled with a worsening situation in the Atlantic made it impossible for him to participate in any protracted conference or take membership in any kind of imperial war cabinet. While he agreed that Churchill's burden was far too great, it was a burden that he carried as prime minister of Great Britain and one that 'can only be relieved or altered by Churchill himself, or by the British Government, Parliament or the people'.[80] Mackenzie King acknowledged that it was imperative that close, constant and continuous consultation was undertaken between the dominion governments to ensure against any conflicts of policy and that the war efforts of the dominions should be as co-operative as possible. Where existing machinery for consultation fell short it should be improved and the manner of this would be something which each dominion government

---

[79] NASAP, Smuts papers, A1, vol. 147, Smuts to Waterson, 16 June 1941; NLA, Menzies papers, MS 4936/581/21, Smuts to Menzies, 11 July 1941.
[80] NLA, Menzies papers, MS 4936/581/21, King to Menzies, 3 August 1941.

could best decide for itself. That said, Mackenzie King believed that it would be difficult, if not impossible, to improve upon the existing machinery for dominion consultation. 'I think it is working more smoothly and swiftly than anyone expected it to work in the middle of a great war.'[81]

What of New Zealand? Like Menzies, throughout the latter part of 1940 Fraser had been worried about the Far Eastern situation and the defence of New Zealand in the event of a Pacific war. New Zealand had also despatched troops to the Middle East to defend imperial communications; and in early 1941 backed initial British assessments about the need to defend Greece as part of a larger strategy to bolster Balkan resistance against the Axis. The 2nd New Zealand division, under the command of Major General Bernard Freyberg, together with the seasoned 6th Australian division was formed into an Anzac Corps under the overall Australian command of Lieutenant General Sir Thomas Blamey. In early April, the Germans came to the aid of their spluttering Italian ally and launched their invasion of Yugoslavia and Greece. By the end of the month Axis forces had reached the southern shores of the Peloponnese, but not before an evacuation of over 50,000 Allied troops to nearby Crete and Egypt had been executed. As Freyberg marshalled his ragtag force to defend Crete, Fraser left Auckland on 3 May 1941 for urgent talks in London.[82]

He arrived in Cairo before the Germans invaded Crete and was in Egypt throughout the island's evacuation, where a personal intervention by the prime minister secured an additional withdrawal of 4,000 more Allied troops, 700 of which were New Zealanders.[83] His presence in Egypt as the disaster on Crete unfolded strengthened his resolve to get to the bottom of the debacle. On 8 June, Fraser resumed his onward journey. Unforeseen delays meant it took twelve days for him to get to England via Khartoum and Lagos. This allowed Fraser and his close advisor, Carl Berendsen, to distil the main features of their exhaustive investigations of how and why the preparation and oversight of the campaigns in Greece and Crete went so badly. Fraser, with the fullest endorsement from his cabinet colleagues in Wellington, had already complained to Churchill about the ill-fated campaigns, and with Berendsen's assistance had prepared a series of pointed questions to be tabled to the British war cabinet and chiefs of staff.[84] As Gerald Hensley

---

[81] LAC, MG 26-J13, King diary, 1 August 1941.

[82] Bassett and King, *Tomorrow Comes the Song*, 213.        [83] Ibid., 215.

[84] Archives New Zealand, Department of External Affairs papers, EA1 264, 87/19/2 part 1, Walter Nash, acting prime minister, to Fraser, 28 May 1941; TNA, CAB 66/16/38, WP (41)115, 26 May 1941; CAB 80/29/5, COS(41)405, 'Notes Raised in Mr Fraser's Questionnaire, 30 June 1941', 1 July 1941.

has noted, the questions were asked not 'in a spirit of recrimination or criticism ... but to get the full facts'.[85]

Fraser arrived in London on 23 June 1941. He stayed in the United Kingdom until 19 August where he attended thirteen meetings of the British war cabinet. He had unfettered access to Churchill, conducted the usual rounds of visiting New Zealand forces wherever they were stationed, however remote (which he relished very much), and gave numerous speeches to a host of audiences to boost morale. Unlike Menzies, Fraser was not a charismatic leader, but this did not make his criticism of British policy any less damning. Some British observers mistook his austere habits, quiet demeanour and teetotalism as signifying an uninviting and 'dull' person.[86] True, he lacked the 'oratorical flair' of Churchill and the 'philosophical basis' of Smuts, but he possessed a critical mind; he was also shrewd, a man of great resolve and acute judgement. As one New Zealand diplomat recalled, 'Fraser was never frightened to oppose Churchill if he thought he should.'[87]

What of the idea of an imperial conference which was re-floated when he was in London? Fraser informed Wellington that he would not leave for home until the question of a meeting of dominion prime ministers had been finalized. This meant he delayed his return home several times over the summer of 1941 as the prolonged but fruitless discussions unfolded.[88] Interestingly, he initially endorsed the suggestion that Menzies might represent the dominions in the war cabinet. This was later retracted.[89] Keeping in mind the political battle for survival Menzies was experiencing in Australia, Walter Nash, the acting prime minister in Wellington, reminded Fraser that 'Visits to London and meetings of the Imperial War Cabinets ought not to be used to solve political problems in any Dominion.'[90] Prescient indeed.

Although disappointed by the response of Smuts and Mackenzie King, Menzies was not prepared to give up just yet. Casey, writing from Washington, supported Menzies' position. British representatives were naturally engrossed with their own problems, which meant dominion

[85] Gerald Hensley, *Beyond the Battlefield: New Zealand and Its Allies 1939–1945* (Auckland, 2009), 133.

[86] David Reynolds, *In Command of History: Churchill Fighting and Writing the Second World War* (London, 2004), 246.

[87] Alexander Turnbull Library, Wellington, Michael King papers, MS-Papers-2096, folder 1, King interview with Alister McIntosh, New Zealand diplomat, 12 August 1978; Alister McIntosh papers, MS-Papers-11090, Professor F. L. Wood and Mary Boyd interview with McIntosh, 1 July 1976.

[88] TNA, DO 121/113, Cranborne to Machtig, 5 July 1941.

[89] TNA, FO 954/4, Dom 41/14, 'Proposal that Mr Menzies should join the War Cabinet', DO minute, August 1941.

[90] ANZ, Walter Nash papers, bundle 2294–0335, Nash to Fraser, 15 August 1941.

issues tended to be overlooked or insufficiently appreciated. This was not motivated by any selfish British point of view, observed Casey, but 'from a lack of understanding on the part of the United Kingdom representatives of Dominion points involved'. Australia needed a strong voice in the British war cabinet, the nucleus of all British war policy. Now that Britain had decided to locate senior cabinet ministers in Cairo and Singapore to facilitate a more efficient coordination of regional views, defence interests and allied responses, why should Australia not have the equivalent in the inner councils in London? The reasons which led to the formation of the imperial war cabinet during the last war, urged Casey, applied even more strongly in the current conflict.[91]

Emboldened by Casey, Menzies complained to Bruce that neither Mackenzie King nor Smuts were interested in his proposals, 'Smuts going so far as to say in substance that we Dominion Prime Ministers should mind our own business and leave Churchill to mind his. This completely overlooks the fact that many matters dealt with by [the] British Cabinet and Foreign Secretary are our business a[s] well as Britain's and that the present Cabinet set-up excludes us from a real voice at the right time.'[92] Menzies announced to Bruce that the Australian cabinet had asked him to return to London due to the deteriorating position in the Far East and thereby ensure that the Australian point of view was constantly pressed upon the British war cabinet.[93] Sensing the precariousness of his own political future, evidenced by a 'disgruntled and personally hostile section of the press' that was calling for his resignation, Menzies turned to Bruce for advice. Bruce remained steadfast that Menzies return to London especially now as Anglo-American discussions focused upon Japan and Allied security in the Pacific. Bruce also hinted that there was a distinct prospect of a meeting of dominion prime ministers in London.[94]

Mackenzie King remained adamant that it was impracticable to hold a formal gathering of dominion leaders in London. Churchill concurred, but he would 'of course defer to Dominion wishes' if, in future, there was a change of heart. This proved to be a clever ploy by Churchill, who then invited the Canadian leader to make a short informal visit to the United Kingdom, something King had been thinking about in the aftermath of Churchill's address to parliament in late June.[95] Was Churchill clearing the ground for the forthcoming meeting with US President

---

[91] NAA, CRS A3300, item 118, Casey to Menzies (and copied to Bruce), 22 July 1941.
[92] NLA, Menzies papers, MS 4936/582/29, Menzies to Bruce, 13 August 1941.
[93] Ibid.    [94] Ibid., Bruce to Menzies, 14 and 18 August 1941.
[95] LAC, MG 26-J13, King diary, 24 June and 14 July 1941; TNA, CAB 120/20, Churchill to King, 26 July 1941.

Franklin Roosevelt to be held at Placentia Bay, Newfoundland, in August 1941? Was Churchill, as David Dilks has suggested, seeking an 'unobstructed opportunity to make acquaintance' with the American leader?[96]

Bridges, the cabinet secretary, had taken soundings whether it was necessary to inform the dominion leaders of the forthcoming summit before it was announced in the press. Would they feel hurt if they were not informed? The complication, as he told Churchill, was that President Roosevelt was planning a trip to Ottawa, but he was unsure if this would occur before or after Churchill met with his American counterpart. In the meantime, if the Canadian leader's 'feelings are not to be seriously ruffled and [possible] political difficulties caused, the least which can be done is to arrange for a message to be sent to him at least 24 hours before the arrival of the party on the other side'.[97] This was rejected by Churchill, who saw no need to inform the Canadian leader in advance, as Roosevelt was not now visiting Ottawa until September. 'It would be a pity if anything happened to lead Mr Mackenzie King to join us in Newfoundland.' He instructed his deputy prime minister Clement Attlee to 'make sure Dominions Office give no encouragement to any such plan'. King, who had accepted Churchill's invitation, now had to be persuaded not to visit Britain until after 20 August.[98]

Malcolm MacDonald was kept abreast of developments, to ensure that nothing should be made public about King's change of departure as this might arouse suspicion about the Argentia meetings scheduled for 8–11 August. In the end, King was not invited let alone informed of this secret offshore meeting which was held on his doorstep.[99] Jack Granatstein argues that Canadian public criticism was generally low key. In fact, MacDonald informed London that the reaction to the joint statement was welcomed and 'warmly approving'; but there was the usual jibe from Mackenzie King that many Canadians would feel that Canada was 'too much left out of these consultations'. MacDonald supported King's desire to visit London. He also told London that at a personal level Mackenzie King might feel disappointed that he had been eased out of the

---

[96] David Dilks, *The Great Dominion: Winston Churchill in Canada, 1900–1954* (Toronto, 2005), 156.

[97] TNA, CAB 120/20, Bridges' memo to Churchill, 31 July 1941.

[98] Ibid., Churchill to Bridges and Cranborne, 3 August 1941; and Churchill to King, personal telegram T 460, 3 August 1941.

[99] TNA, DO to MacDonald, 6 August 1941; J. L. Granatstein, 'The Man Who Wasn't There: Mackenzie King, Canada, and the Atlantic Charter', in Douglas Brinkley and David R. Facey-Crowther (eds.), *The Atlantic Charter* (London, 1994), 115–28.

picture by his two erstwhile allies, 'but I really do not think he is much bothered about that'.[100]

In private, according to the newspaperman and Ottawa insider, Grant Dexter, King's rage was 'unbounded'. Not only had he been 'cold-shouldered', he did not know of the conference until it was in full swing. His position as an alliance lynchpin had not only been compromised, but it also looked as if it had been made redundant. In order to salvage his position and reputation he needed 'with all speed' to travel to Britain.[101] MacDonald remained sceptical about the depth of King's personal disappointment over not being invited to the conference, but he reminded London how 'hurtful to the susceptibilities of the Canadian political public' which King's omission might engender; a public 'who have been taught to take pride in the fact that Canada is a valuable as well as a vitally concerned third party' in the alliance. Compounding the fragile state of Canadian morale, MacDonald outlined the stark fact that their troops had not yet engaged the enemy while their Commonwealth partners had been steadily winning battle honours in East and North Africa and the Mediterranean throughout 1941. MacDonald warned his superiors in Whitehall that so long as they did not offend one of King's many 'sensitivities', he could not only be one of Britain's best, but also one of its 'most reliable and helpful friends'.[102] This snub had deeply wounded King, whatever MacDonald believed. Imagine Whitehall's surprise when Attlee informed Churchill that the idea of an imperial conference was back in play, and that it was being pushed by Mackenzie King himself![103]

Why, then, did the Canadian premier change his mind about going to England? King prided himself on being the great lynchpin between the two larger English-speaking giants of Great Britain and the United States. For him, Canada's role as the conduit between these two great powers enhanced the dominion's (and his) prestige. The Ogdensburg Agreement of August 1940, in which the Americans agreed to safeguard Canadian sovereignty in case of invasion (and which established a Permanent Joint Board on Defence to co-ordinate hemispheric security), and the Hyde Park Declaration of April 1941, which saved Canada from financial ruin by allowing her to participate in Lend-Lease, were proof in King's mind of

[100] TNA, CAB 120/20, MacDonald to DO, 13 August 1941; Granatstein, 'The Man Who Wasn't There', 123.
[101] Gibson and Robertson (eds.), *Grant Dexter Memoranda*, 193–94.
[102] TNA, DO 35/999/3, WC 8/4a, MacDonald to DO, 13 August 1941; PREM 4/44/7, MacDonald to Cranborne, 20 August 1941; DO 121/68, MacDonald to Cranborne, 28 August 1941.
[103] TNA, CAB 120/20, Attlee to Churchill, n.d. probably 14 August 1941; CAB 65/19/18, WM82(41)4, 14 August 1941.

Canada's importance in harmonizing relations within the western alliance.[104] Stern critics in Ottawa and American policymakers in particular may not have attached much importance to King's self-proclaimed role as intercessor. It was, however, an important ingredient in Canada's domestic political arena. In the aftermath of the Argentia conference, a trip to London would salvage his reputation and restore Canada as the conduit between its two larger Atlantic allies.

The political stakes had indeed become self-evident. According to MacDonald, now that American efforts as the arsenal of democracy were receiving immense publicity and seemed to be 'completely eclipsing the valuable efforts of Canada in the sight of the overseas public', this deeply worried the Canadian premier. More alarmingly, this tendency to downplay Canada's contribution so far was, reported the UK High Commissioner, being encouraged from Washington itself. When Canada's war effort was discussed, it was spoken of in very sarcastic terms. 'This sneering is very unjust', reported MacDonald, but it was not helped by King's incessant frowning on anything to do with propaganda. In his view, the 'blame for the world's imperfect knowledge of Canada's war effort' lay primarily with King himself.[105] This, combined with the complaint that exclusive control of the direction of the war by Great Britain and the United States, despite the important contributions made by the smaller participants like Canada, became an increasingly contentious theme with Ottawa as the war progressed. These factors no doubt contributed to the growing frustration felt by many Anglo-Canadian ministers and their electorate that Canada was not doing enough. Pearson, who had just returned to Ottawa from his posting at Canada House, immediately picked up on this growing angst in Canada about its war effort. Ottawa 'is crowded, there seems to be a tremendous amount of activity, and everyone is busy, but I get the feeling that much of the activity doesn't result in anything and a lot of the busyness is fussiness over inconsequential things'.[106]

King's visit to England, which began on 21 August 1941, was engineered to coincide with Churchill's return from Newfoundland. It was a mixed success. Politically, and in terms of alliance politics, several

---

[104] J. L. Granatstein, *The Politics of the Mackenzie King Government, 1939–1945*, 2nd ed. (Toronto, 1990), ch. 4; Galen Roger Perras, *Franklin Roosevelt and the Origins of the Canadian-American Security Alliance, 1933–1945* (Westport, CT, 1998); John Alan English, 'Not an Equilateral Triangle: Canada's Strategic Relationship with the United States and Britain, 1939–1945', in B. J. C. McKercher and Lawrence Aronsen (eds.), *The North Atlantic Triangle in a Changing World: Anglo-American-Canadian Relations, 1902–1956* (Toronto, 1996), 147–83.

[105] TNA, PREM 4/44/10, MacDonald to DO, 24 May 1941.

[106] LAC, MG 26-N1, vol. 10, Pearson to Massey, 27 May 1941.

accomplishments were made, despite the complaint by one close external affairs advisor that the trip was too hurried with too little time spent with British ministers.[107] Canada's High Commissioner was sidelined and took very little part in the proceedings apart from ceremonial duties and public relations exercises. Such petulance was not uncommon for the Canadian leader, but the relationship between Massey and his premier had been strained well before the war, so it was no surprise that Mackenzie King intentionally went out of his way to ignore Massey and Canada House.[108]

But there was one bright moment before his departure home on 6–7 September which pleased King to no end, justifying his self-styled role as interpreter between London and Washington. His Mansion House speech delivered on 4 September 1941 was a triumph. King confided in his diary that J. L. Garvin, editor of *The Observer*, thought the address was the 'best of my life and most important'. Many of the London periodicals were very positive as well; so too were some of their Canadian counterparts, including the *Montreal Gazette*, which hitherto had been an outspoken critic of King's leadership. Perhaps the greatest accolade came from Churchill himself, when, in his reply to the Canadian leader said that Canada, that great dominion, was the 'linchpin of the "English-speaking world" linking the two great branches together by her unswerving loyalty to the British Commonwealth and her friendly, affectionate intimacy with the United States'.[109]

For Massey, the visit had accomplished two things of lasting importance. It had not only put an end to the woolly thinking about a proposed imperial war cabinet (an idea which Massey had never supported); but the Mansion House speech had made a 'profound impression' on the British public, which also embodied a 'perfectly timed' message to the United States about Britain's determination to fight on.[110] This was precisely what Churchill was counting on. His reference to Canada as the lynchpin was just as much about political calculation as it was of King's political intimacy with the American leadership, however genuine Churchill's

---

[107] J. L. Granatstein, *Man of Influence: Norman A. Robertson and Canadian Statecraft 1929–68* (Toronto, 1981), 129.

[108] Kent Fedorowich, 'Directing the War from Trafalgar Square? Vincent Massey and the Canadian High Commission, 1939–42', *Journal of Imperial and Commonwealth History* 40(1) (2012), 87–117.

[109] LAC, MG 26-J13, King diary, 5 and 8 September 1941; MG 26-J1, King papers, C-4866, vol. 312, Massey to King, 9 September 1941; 'Where Canada Stands' and 'Canada "With Us to the End"', *The Times*, 5 September 1941.

[110] LAC, MG 26-N1, Pearson papers, vol. 10, Massey to Pearson, 12 September 1941.

praise of King's speech was.[111] Sir William Glasgow, Australia's High Commissioner in Canada, also noted how the lynchpin analogy was a compliment 'deeply appreciated' by the Canadian public; a public growing weary of the relative inactivity of their troops in comparison to her Commonwealth cousins. King had once again confounded his critics.[112]

Buoyed by his Mansion House success, upon his return to Ottawa, King used the opportunity to rein in his cabinet by limiting the number of ministerial missions conducted to London. King thought it inadvisable to have it appear too much to the Canadian public that all war matters were being settled in London. It was imperative that the Canadian people realized that Ottawa was shaping and managing the national war effort, not merely taking directions from 'mother'. Government ministers should focus on what was being accomplished in Canada and their presence in the dominion was imperative to deal with 'new situations as they arose'.[113] His South African counterpart could not have agreed more with King's sentiment: 'I was glad to see Mackenzie King's outspoken condemnation of the agitation for an Imperial War Cabinet.'[114]

What of Menzies? Although he had procured the assent of his cabinet to proceed to London, he lacked the wholehearted commitment of Labour members within the advisory war council. Menzies, who had a parliamentary majority of one, offered again to form a national government but this was rejected on 26 August. Amidst growing calls for his resignation amongst his own United Australia Party and the Country Party in favour of Arthur Fadden, Menzies resigned, and Fadden was appointed prime minister on 29 August. Prior to his resignation, however, Menzies had announced to the House of Representatives that a minister other than the prime minister would be despatched to London as soon as possible; presumably this could be Menzies once he was relieved of the premiership. Cranborne, who had no sympathy for Menzies or his predicament, concluded that the former prime minister was better out of the way for his 'intriguing was a constant danger'.[115]

---

[111] Bruce Hutchinson, *The Incredible Canadian: A Candid Portrait of Mackenzie King* (Oxford, 2011 [1952]), 294–95.

[112] NAA, CRS A981, item CAN 38, part 2, Glasgow to Sir Frederick Stewart, minister for external affairs, 11 September 1941.

[113] LAC, MG 26-J13, King diary, 10 September 1941; LAC, reel C-4654, RG 2, 7C, vol. 2, meeting 107, 10 September 1941.

[114] NASAP, Smuts papers, A1, vol. 95A, Smuts to Churchill, 22 August 1941.

[115] British Library, Paul Emrys-Evans papers, Add MSS 58240, Cranborne to Emrys-Evans, 31 August 1941.

## VI

It was not until May 1944 that dominion leaders finally met with Churchill at the first ever Commonwealth prime ministers conference in London. This rebranding, so close to the Normandy landings, demonstrated several interrelated issues. In terms of public relations, it validated the importance of the dominions as equals to the imperial war effort and their critical roles in supporting British arms, fuelling its industries and feeding its peoples. Although still insufficiently realized, these vital contributions should not be underestimated.[116]

Clearly, there were key fault lines within the Commonwealth alliance which were initiated during the Second World War or widened because of intense wartime pressures, be they domestic or foreign. One of the most challenging was consultation. As we have seen, with the notable exception of the 'most treasured' Smuts,[117] direct intervention from the dominion leaders on issues of global strategy and military policy was not tolerated by Churchill. His patrician views of empire, based on a Victorian worldview of unswerving colonial fealty, held forth throughout the war.[118] In fact, as David Reynolds has so aptly demonstrated, any mention of the dominions in Churchill's memoirs were perfunctory at best.[119]

What of the idea of an imperial conference? All four dominion premiers agreed that a conference was desirable; the question was the timing and the agenda. Working in tandem, Smuts and King supported the idea provided the issues concentrated specifically on fashioning peace proposals or formulating post-war reconstruction. For them, the war had still to run its course and it was premature to think that a conference was in fact necessary. On the other hand, by 1941, Menzies was convinced that an imperial conference was essential because of the more immediate issues which threatened Australia in the Far East. Fraser was somewhere in between. His concerns about the Far Eastern situation mirrored those of Menzies. But like Smuts and King, he was satisfied with the overall strategic direction of the war provided Wellington was kept abreast of developments. This did not mean, however, that he would not be critical of Churchill or his advisors.

Domestic political pressures also informed the decisions of all four leaders and their differing views on holding an imperial jamboree.

---

[116] See the ground-breaking study by Iain E. Johnstone-White, *The British Commonwealth and Victory in the Second World War* (London, 2017).

[117] John Colville, *Winston Churchill and His Inner Circle* (New York, 1981), 173.

[118] See Cranborne's complaint, Lascelles diary, 6 October 1943, Duff Hart-Davis (ed.), *King's Counsellor: Abdication and War: The Diaries of Sir Alan Lascelles* (London, 2006), 168.

[119] Reynolds, *In Command of History*, 246.

Smuts was far from secure at home. It would not be until the eviction of Axis forces from North Africa and his victory at the general election in 1943 that Smuts felt assured of his position within that unsettled dominion. As for King, he had been consistent in his refusal to leave Canada. His priority, as he saw it, was the maintenance of Canadian unity and that needed his undivided attention. There were times when Whitehall complained that he made too much of his indispensability to remain at home; but as Malcolm MacDonald reiterated in August 1941, whatever King's critics thought of his shortcomings as leader, it was dangerous to underestimate his political dexterity or his commitment to winning the war.[120] Hence, King's visit to London in August 1941 must be seen in this light. Angered at not being consulted about or invited to the Anglo-American talks off the coast of Newfoundland, King's ego had been badly bruised. Ridiculed in the Canadian press for taking such a flaccid role in Anglo-dominion relations, he cleverly used the trip to accomplish three interwoven objectives: regain the initiative in the domestic arena; silence his many critics in parliament and his own party about his leadership; and most importantly, re-establish his cherished role of diplomatic pivot in the North Atlantic alliance.

The Australian desire to have a permanent dominion representative in the British war cabinet was something else entirely. Throughout 1941, the consensus within Canberra was that if Australia was going to directly influence policy it needed someone on the inside. Menzies' desire was to use the proposed 1941 imperial conference as a stalking horse where a resolution would be passed in support of direct dominion representation, the mantle of which would fall on his shoulders.[121] However, the proposal that one of the dominion leaders should act as the representative for all the dominions in the war cabinet was abhorrent to the other three dominion premiers. King was the most vociferous critic arguing that Menzies' reasoning smacked of constitutional impropriety. How could one dominion leader undertake to represent the collective interests of all the dominions in an imperial cabinet? Smuts agreed. The real strength of the Commonwealth system was its decentralisation, which was well situated for waging a world war, where the 'diffused leadership in all [its] parts [was] a blessing rather than a hardship'.[122] Fraser, who had initially warmed to the idea of dominion representation in the war cabinet, drew back while visiting England. It seemed to him that Menzies was using the demand for a permanent dominion presence on the British war cabinet to

---

[120] TNA, DO 121/68, MacDonald to Cranborne, 8 August 1941.
[121] Ibid., Cranborne to MacDonald, 11 August 1941.
[122] NASAP, Smuts papers, A1, vol. 95A, Smuts to Churchill, 22 August 1941.

solve the intractable domestic political problems in Australia which Menzies himself had created. For Churchill, who had always wanted unrestricted freedom of action, he made his true feelings known. In June 1941, his assistant private secretary, John Colville, recalled that while dining at Chequers, the topic of conversation about a proposed imperial war cabinet was raised: "'Well', said the PM, "you can easily turn the War Cabinet into a museum of Imperial celebrities, but then you have to have another body to manage the war.'"[123]

Churchill's droll remark about the administration of the war effort was not far from the political realities he faced daily. Interestingly, the demands made to convene an imperial conference or allow dominion representation in a reconstituted imperial war cabinet were raised at times of acute stress. Compelled by growing criticism of their respective leaderships, Chamberlain in April 1940 and Churchill in October 1940 and May–June 1941 tolerated the idea of summoning the dominions to an empire council to help stave off this pressure. Vincent Massey, who had always believed that the existing channels of communication between London and the dominions were more than adequate, suggested Menzies' advocacy of dominion representation on an imperial war cabinet was not simply about the Australian's overweening ambition and inflated sense of importance; it was just as much about Churchill's enemies using this issue as a '"can opener" to pry the way open for further cabinet changes'.[124]

So what does the failed 1941 imperial conference tell us about Anglo-dominion relations? One consequence of Churchill's rise to power in May 1940 – despite Menzies' Herculean efforts to the contrary – was the dominions' exclusion from the inner circle. Their influence on British foreign policy and imperial strategy was subtle but limited. With America's entry into the war in December 1941, the dominions were firmly placed on the fringes of power; and by the end of 1942, Churchill, Roosevelt and the Soviet premier, Josef Stalin, were fully in charge of Allied strategy. Even Australia's success in being granted a seat in the British war cabinet in September 1941 was a pyrrhic victory. The appointment of Sir Earle Page, a former prime minister and senior figure in the Country Party, proved to be an embarrassing move fraught with all kinds of pitfalls. If anything, the friction between Canberra and London intensified throughout 1942. As the Australians scrambled to defend themselves from the Japanese onslaught, demands continued to be

---

[123] Colville diary, 21 June 1941, John Colville, *The Fringes of Power: Downing Street Diaries 1939–1955* (London, 2004), rev. edn., 350.

[124] LAC, reel C-4866, MG 26-J1 series, King papers, vol. 312, Massey to acting secretary of state for external affairs, 26 August 1941.

made for greater consultation which strained the now brittle relations between the two Commonwealth partners.

Crucially, Smuts was the exception. He was the only dominion leader who had any influence on Churchill; and he was the only dominion premier with whom Churchill could find no fault. Smuts, a stalwart defender of Churchill, did not want to be dragged into the internecine nature of British domestic politics because he had his own pressing problems at home. For him, the decentralized nature of the Commonwealth alliance was its real strength not its weakness. As for Mackenzie King, the fierce guardian of dominion autonomy, he was adamant that any attempts at imperial centralisation had to be avoided at all costs. Like Smuts, as long as dominion consultation was undertaken either through existing conduits such as the high commission in London, or preferably via personal communications with Churchill, there was no need for the concentration of power in an imperial war cabinet. New Zealand was somewhere in the middle – a steadfast but critical friend. The ultimate paradox of the failed 1941 imperial conference was that it demonstrated the individuality of each of the dominions in the conduct of their own foreign policy within an evolving, now multi-centred Commonwealth alliance.

## 12 Imperial Hubs and their Limitations: British Assessments of Imposing Sanctions on Japan, 1937

### G. Bruce Strang

Britain's gunboat diplomacy in the mid-nineteenth century built an important imperial presence in China. The First Opium War and the subsequent
Arrow War opened China to trade, especially to opium imported from
British-controlled India, and compelled the Qing Dynasty to sign the
Treaty of Nanking (1842) and the subsequent Treaty of the Bogue
(1843) – the unequal treaties. The treaties granted Britain extra-territorial
rights, ceded Hong Kong to Britain, required the Qing to pay indemnities,
and ended Qing control over their tariffs on foreign trade. Most importantly,
they ended the Qing Dynasty's Canton trade system that had attempted to
put strict limits on foreign trade. Over the following decades, British investors
built many of the transportation and commercial industries in developing
a Chinese economy more integrated into the world trade system. Major
British companies such as Jardine & Matheson, Hongkong and Shanghai
Bank, Butterfield & Swire, John Swire & Sons, British-American Tobacco,
and the Asiatic Petrol Company played a central role in many of China's most
important industries, from banking, shipping lines on China's navigable
rivers, railroads, chemical industries, soap-making, breweries, mining colli-
eries, lumber, cotton and woolen mills, dockyards, cold storage and ware-
houses, to hotels, while many British subjects owned small property holdings
such as private residences and rooming houses. Investors had placed the
majority of this investment in the vicinity of Shanghai.[1] Although other
nations had joined in imperialist challenges to Qing authority, Britain
remained the nation with the largest investments in China. The China
Association, a network of British businessmen, members of parliament,

[1] I am grateful to the Brandon University Research Committee and to the then Vice-
President, Scott Grills, who helped to fund the research for this chapter. I have compiled
this list from an extensive series of documents in Foreign Office Papers (hereafter FO)
371/21006–21011/F4480/9/10 and ff. For a broader discussion of British interests in
China, see: Bradford A. Lee, *Britain and the Sino-Japanese War, 1937–1939: A Study in
the Dilemmas of British Decline* (Stanford, 1973), 16–18; Wm. Roger Louis, *British Strategy
in the Far East 1919–1939* (Oxford, 1971), 226–31.

and retired civil servants had direct access to lobby leading politicians and Whitehall officials. Although Whitehall officials and, to an even greater degree, British businessmen, hoped to tap the potentially vast Chinese market, British exports to China and Southeast Asia had instead fallen by more than half through the depression years – in part due to an overall decline of world trade, but largely due to increased competition from firms in the United States, Japan, and Germany. Nevertheless, Britain's economic position in China remained an important part of the British Empire, and government ministers and officials were determined to find a way to protect it.[2]

The outbreak of fighting between Japanese and Chinese troops in the Marco Polo Bridge (Lugouqiao) incident in July 1937, therefore, caused consternation in Whitehall. Early reports suggested that local commanders hoped to localize the incident, but both sides rapidly reinforced and the conflict escalated, engulfing much of northeast China.[3] As the fighting spread, both Chinese and Japanese military leaders committed themselves to winning the undeclared war. China extended the fighting by launching an attack on the troops guarding Japanese-controlled areas in the international settlement in Shanghai. The Japanese Diet fully supported the military, and Japan dispatched several divisions to Shanghai initially to defend its position there, and then to take the offensive. Inevitably, the fighting in and around Shanghai and in the Yangtze River basin threatened British commercial interests and took the lives of British subjects caught in bombing attacks gone awry. Japanese aircraft strafed the car carrying the British ambassador to China on his trip from Nanjing to Shanghai, seriously wounding him. The Japanese refusal to apologize for the attack, its dramatic escalation of the war in the northeast and near Shanghai, and its refusal to contemplate peace terms without substantial territorial gains gradually painted Japan as the aggressor in the eyes of most British politicians and Whitehall officials.[4]

---

[2] Treasury Papers (T) 188/162, China Committee, British Policy in the Far East, Frank Ashton-Gwatkin Memorandum, 19 March 1937.

[3] War Office Papers (WO) 106/5309, M.I. 2 (c), intelligence report, 12 July 1937; Air Ministry Papers (AIR) 2/1728, F7855/35/10, Gage to Eden, 8 September 1937. For an account of the incident and the policy considerations that led to the war, see, for example, Rana Mitter, *Forgotten Ally: China's World War II, 1937–1945* (New York, 2013). For a useful general survey of international relations in the Far East, see Akira Iriye, *The Origins of World War II in Asia and the Pacific* (London, 1987), 1–87.

[4] FO 371/20953/F5393/9/10, Ronald Minute, 12 August 1937; FO 371/20956/F7361/9/10, Naval and Military Intelligence Summary no. 28, 18 August 1937; ibid./F7121/9/10, Craigie to Eden, 29 August 1937; Cabinet Papers (CAB) 23/89, 34(37), 8 September 1937. For an initial position that sharply condemned both Chinese and Japanese leaders for their actions in escalating the war, see FO 371/20953/F5164/9/10, Orde to Knatchbull-Hugessen, and Dodds, Vansittart Minute, 14 August 1937. The previous Keelung incident, where Japanese police had beaten three British sailors and insulted a British naval officer, also coloured British perceptions of Japan. It took months of fractious discussion and patient British diplomacy to pry even a minimal statement of

The press and public opinion in Britain shared the view that the Japanese were aggressors who defied international law and 'civilized' standards of behaviour. The government faced pressure from Chiang Kai-Shek, the opposition, and British public opinion to impose sanctions to compel the Japanese to abandon the invasion.[5]

In light of the escalating Japanese aggression and indiscriminate bombing of Chinese cities, Sir Anthony Eden, the British foreign secretary, asked his staff to develop measures that Britain could take to induce Japan to moderate its behaviour. Whitehall officials accordingly turned to the study of the possible effects of economic sanctions against Japan. When President Franklin Delano Roosevelt made his Quarantine Speech on 5 October 1937, the concept of economic sanctions potentially received a powerful supporter. Eden thought that Britain should be prepared to work with the United States to impose sanctions against Japan to force it to abandon its aggression in China should the Roosevelt administration proceed in that direction. Eden pushed for the creation of an inter-departmental committee to try to circumvent lengthy bureaucratic procedures. Strong opposition from the Treasury and the service departments, however, blocked this manoeuvre, and the inter-departmental committee simply referred the question for further study. In the fall of 1937, therefore, Whitehall officials prepared reports and made recommendations, and the Cabinet eventually discussed the issue of imposing sanctions against Japan. After consideration by British officials, the Cabinet decided that it would not impose sanctions, and would instead rely on diplomacy and Japanese goodwill or sufferance to preserve the British imperial presence in China.[6] Although many historians have covered Anglo-Japanese relations and British policy during the

---

regret from the Japanese government. CAB 23/87/5(37), 3 February 1937. CAB 24/267, C.P. 45(37), 1 February 1938; Greg Kennedy, 'The Keelung Incident and Britain's Far Eastern Strategic Foreign Policy 1936–7', in Greg Kennedy and Keith Neilson (eds.), *Incidents and International Relations* (New York, 2002), 135–57. By the end of 1937, Britain's ambassador to Japan, Sir Robert Craigie, and some of his embassy staff were among the few who dissented from the essential conclusion that Japanese policy was fundamentally hostile to British interests in the Far East. FO 371/20958/F8982/9/10, Craigie to Eden, 3 November 1937, Thomas, Orde, and Eden Minutes, 4 November 1937. For an assessment sympathetic to Craigie and often critical of the Foreign Office's views of Japan, see Antony Best, *Britain, Japan, and Pearl Harbour: Avoiding War in East Asia, 1936–1941* (London, 1995), 40–42 and 45.

[5] FO 371/20956/F7343/9/20, Howe (Nanking) to Eden, 1 October 1937; Prime Ministers' Series (PREM) 1/278, Notes on a Meeting of Chamberlain and Cranborne with opposition Members of Parliament, 25 January 1938; CAB 23/89/35(37), 29 September 1937; University of Birmingham, Cadbury Research Library, Neville Chamberlain Papers (NC), NC18/1/1024, Neville Chamberlain to Hilda Chamberlain, 16 October 1937; Tom Buchanan, *East Wind: China and the British Left, 1925–1976* (Oxford, 2012), 61–70.

[6] CAB 23/89/36(37), 6 October 1937, and ibid./37(37), 13 October 1937.

Sino-Japanese war, none have considered the issue of sanctions or the possible escalation to a wider war in explicit detail.[7] In light of the incredible risk inherent in relying on Japanese benevolence, this chapter asks the question of why the Cabinet decided not to impose sanctions against Japan in 1937. The answer lies in the difficulty and inherent risks of imposing sanctions against Japan, Britain's global strategic weakness, and its complex relationship with the other Great Power in the Pacific region, the United States.

\*\*\*

Various British departments contributed to an investigation of the effects of sanctions against Japan, including the Treasury, the Industrial Intelligence Centre, the Board of Trade, the service ministries, and the Foreign Office. A preliminary assessment by the Treasury concluded that the subject merited deeper study, as Japan's reliance on trade with the British Empire and the United States could make it vulnerable to a trade embargo. The report argued that Britain and its empire would be unable on their own to do enough damage to the Japanese economy to compel the Japanese military to abandon aggression against China. An embargo by the British Empire could seriously impede Japanese exports in wool and cotton textiles. Britain could make Japanese imports of war materials such as raw cotton, wool, manganese, rubber, iron ore, and pig iron more difficult. For each of these commodities, however, with the possible exception of nickel, Japan would be able to find alternate sources of supply. The Treasury Department concluded that '*neither the United Kingdom alone nor the United Kingdom and the rest of the Empire could, by themselves, take any action which would effectively stop or shorten hostilities*'.[8] If, however, the United States were to join, sanctions had far more likelihood of being successful. Together, the British Empire and the United States supplied 62.8 per cent and purchased 52.9 per cent of Japanese trade. Japan, therefore, was potentially far more reliant on Britain and the United States than Italy had been prior to the League of Nations' imposition of sanctions in 1935–36.[9]

As the issue of Japanese aggression in China intensified, the Advisory Committee on Trade Questions in Time of War (ATB) assessed the

---

[7] Best, *Britain, Japan and Pearl Harbor*, 42–45; Wm. Roger Louis, British Strategy in the Far East, 242–46; Bradford Lee, Britain and the Sino-Japanese War, 23–78; Aron Shai, *Origins of the War in the East: Britain, China, and Japan 1937–9* (London, 1976), 20–102; Peter Lowe, *Great Britain and the Origins of the Pacific War: A Study of British Policy in East Asia 1937–1941* (Oxford, 1977), 15–32.

[8] Emphasis in the original, T160/1034/F15255/1, Possible Sanctions against Japan, 1937, no date.

[9] T160/1034/F15255/1, Possible Sanctions against Japan, 1937, no date.

efficiency of sanctions against Japan in more detail, but the study suggested that imposing sanctions would be problematic. Potentially, Japan could have been quite vulnerable to Anglo-American economic sanctions. Britain itself exported relatively little to Japan, only 2.9 per cent of Japan's imports, but the British Empire was the largest supplier to Japan, representing 34.9 per cent of its imports. In reality, however, sanctions would take considerable time to be effective. Japan was relatively self-sufficient in food. Large harvests in Japan, Korea, and Formosa meant that Japan would not need to import rice for at least eighteen months. Japan imported all of its raw cotton and most of its wool, with the vast majority of these supplies coming from the British Empire. For these textiles, however, Japan would be able to find alternate suppliers.[10]

In other areas, though, Japan was more vulnerable. It required certain products essential for industrial production, including various kinds of iron. For iron ore, domestic and Japanese colonial production only met 25 per cent of Japan's annual consumption. Britain and America normally supplied 72 per cent of Japanese imports. Japan reclaimed about 45 per cent of its scrap iron, but Britain and the United States provided 92 per cent of its imports. Japan produced relatively few machine tools, and normally purchased most of them from British and American sources. Japan would have a hard time replacing these imports if faced by an Anglo-American embargo, as most countries were consuming their own production or had placed contracts with the major powers that were busily rearming in Europe. Japan needed to import non-ferrous metals: copper, tin, zinc, lead, nickel, aluminium, and brass or bronze. The British Empire and the United States supplied most of these imports for Japan, and British or American companies also controlled most of the alternative sources of supply. Although Japan had been stockpiling non-ferrous metals, British intelligence estimated that these stocks would only sustain normal, peacetime production for two to four months. Accordingly, Japan would have a difficult time importing these strategic raw materials and machine tools if faced with Anglo-American sanctions.[11]

An oil embargo represented perhaps the greatest opportunity to compel Japan to abandon its undeclared war in China. According to British intelligence sources, Japan consumed 5 million tonnes of oil for annual

---

[10] CAB 4/26, Papers of the Committee of Imperial Defence, Miscellaneous B Series, 1365-B (Also A.T.B. 155), Economic Sanctions against Japan, October 1937.

[11] CAB 4/26, Papers of the Committee of Imperial Defence, Miscellaneous B Series, 1365-B (Also A.T.B. 155), Economic Sanctions against Japan, October 1937. T160/1034/F15255/1, Possible Sanctions against Japan, 1937, no date. T160/1034/F15255/2, Ryan (CID) to Waley, 26 October 1937.

peacetime requirements. It produced only 15 per cent of its needs. It therefore imported ¥4,820,000,000 worth of oil annually. Only 5 per cent of its imports came from British sources in Borneo, but Japan derived 65 per cent of imports from sources in the United States. The remainder largely came from the Netherlands East Indies and Venezuela. The Netherlands West Indies refined the vast majority of Venezuelan oil, so the Netherlands either directly or indirectly controlled most of the remainder of Japan's imports. In theory, then, an Anglo-American oil embargo could cripple the Japanese economy. The Netherlands East Indies could theoretically supply Japan with its minimum peacetime requirements, but the Dutch colony would never export all of its oil to Japan unless Japanese forces conquered it. In that case, Britain presumably would have to go to war in any case to protect its vital interests. No other country could supply Japan either through its own production or through entrepôt trade, say, from Italy or Germany, as their needs for oil remained high and the distances were too great.[12]

Two problems weakened the potential effectiveness of an oil embargo. Many American firms conducted large amounts of business outside the United States. It would have been exceptionally difficult to limit that trade, as other non-sanctioning countries would likely be unwilling to impose country of origin rules to support an Anglo-American embargo. The other limit was that Japan had amassed a large stockpile of oil. Intelligence estimates assessed that Japanese commercial firms stored 1,500,000 tonnes of oil, while the Japanese Navy had stockpiled 3,500,000 tonnes. Accordingly, Japan could survive an Anglo-American boycott for a considerable period of time, especially as the war in China did not require a massive expenditure of fuel for naval manoeuvres. Taken in total, estimates suggested that Japan would feel relatively little inconvenience for the first six months of sanctions, and likely would be able to withstand sanctions for at least a year, even if the Netherlands East Indies participated in an embargo, however unlikely it was that that the Dutch colonial masters of the largely defenceless colony would participate in sanctions.[13]

Financial pressure owing to a trade embargo would not appreciably shorten the amount of time that it would take for sanctions to compel

---

[12] CAB 4/26, Papers of the Committee of Imperial Defence, Miscellaneous B Series, 1365-B (Also A.T.B. 155), Economic Sanctions against Japan, October 1937. T160/1034/F15255/1, Possible Sanctions against Japan, 1937, no date. T160/1034/F15255/2, Ryan (CID) to Waley, 26 October 1937.

[13] CAB 4/26, Papers of the Committee of Imperial Defence, Miscellaneous B Series, 1365-B (Also A.T.B. 155), Economic Sanctions against Japan, October 1937. T160/1034/F15255/1, Possible Sanctions against Japan, 1937, no date. T160/1034, F15255/2, Ryan (CID) to Waley, 26 October 1937.

Japan to abandon its aggression. Japan would lose substantial export markets to the British Empire and the United States, and given the intensely competitive nature of world trade during the depression, Japan would be able to find new markets for only a limited amount of its exports. Estimates placed the loss of Japanese trade at approximately ¥1,000,000,000 per year. In addition, loss of the ability to secure loans in Britain or the United States, the world's two greatest financial markets, meant that Japan would lose roughly another ¥250,000,000 from its balance of trade. Counterbalancing these constraints, however, Japan could draw on gold reserves of ¥1,220,000,000, plus another ¥200,000,000 per year in new production of gold. British estimates suggested that Japan would perhaps be able to liquidate some ¥500,000,000 of foreign securities, and it would no doubt default on ¥120,000,000 of loans drawn from Anglo-American banks and commercial firms. The net result would be that Japan would not run out of currency or gold to purchase foreign goods for some two years. These estimates, of course, included certain assumptions: first, that the war in China would not dramatically increase Japanese consumption of required imports; and, second, to counterbalance the loss of trade, the highly centralized Japanese government would not simply resort to driving down wages and increasing the deprivation of its already exceptionally poor farmers. However these factors would play out in the event of sanctions, financial pressure against Japan clearly would not be an immediately decisive weapon of coercion.[14]

Given these various conditions together, the ATB committee concluded that sanctions would likely not be effective in compelling Japan to abandon its aggression for at least a year, and perhaps as long as two years if countries such as Germany and Italy were willing to help Japan evade sanctions and certain other countries were willing to continue to trade with Japan. It was clear throughout the committee's deliberations, however, that certain officials and ministries had developed a strong aversion to imposing sanctions. David Waley of the Treasury Department, for example, deprecated the

---

[14] CAB 4/26, Papers of the Committee of Imperial Defence, Miscellaneous B Series, 1365-B (Also A.T.B. 155), Economic Sanctions against Japan, October 1937. T160/1034/F15255/1, Possible Sanctions against Japan, 1937, no date. T160/1034/F15255/2, Ryan (CID) to Waley, 26 October 1937. The ATB report also considered the possibility that sanctions could limit Japan's ability to supply its troops in China through controlling its automobile and truck production. Japanese firms produced only 9,000 vehicles, of which 6,500 were small cars. General Motors and Ford exported 1,117 whole cars and 1,061 chassis to Japan, but, more importantly, produced 22,000 vehicles in Japan, of which a third were trucks. Even if Japan were to nationalize the American plants it would be unable to use them, as General Motors and Ford exported the vast majority of the components to Japan.

idea of imposing sanctions; in his view, 'an embargo on exports to Japan could to a large extent be evaded by the action of third countries, while an embargo on imports from Japan would not be effective for a long time in view of her own gold production and her considerable gold reserves and reserves of foreign currency'.[15] His greatest objection, however, was that the more effective sanctions were, the greater the possibility that Japan would resort to a wider war to escape them. As he wrote to Sir Frederick Leith-Ross, the British experience in imposing sanctions against Italy showed that it was little use to start 'sanctions unless you are prepared to go to war if necessary'.[16]

This view that sanctions against Japan carried a high risk of leading to war was very common. The service ministries all recoiled from the thought of sanctions. The Lords Commissioners of the Admiralty thought sanctions would be ineffective owing to third-party interference from Italy and Germany; in their view, Japan was a modern state and therefore highly capable of resisting economic sanctions. The Japanese military, supported thoroughly by its government, appeared absolutely determined to follow through on its aggression in China to the end. It would not easily abandon its conquests. Accordingly, the Lord Commissioners feared war against Japan, as Japan could attack Britain and the Netherlands East Indies as a means to try to escape from the effects of sanctions. The United Kingdom alone amongst the League of Nations powers had the naval power to make sanctions work. If Britain sent a substantial part of the fleet to the Far East, then Germany or Italy would be emboldened to seize on Britain's weakness in Europe and the Mediterranean to create some form of further mischief. Planners in the Admiralty dismissed the thought that the United States would come to the aid of Britain in the event that sanctions landed it in a war with Japan, and even less would the Americans help if Britain found itself involved in a European war.[17] Sir Warren Fisher, permanent undersecretary of state at the Treasury, pleaded that 'I earnestly trust that the Admiralty view will be endorsed by the government'.[18]

---

[15] T 160/1034/F15255/1, Minutes of an Interdepartmental Meeting held at the Foreign Office on October 13, 13 October 1937.

[16] T 160/1034/F15255/1, Waley to Leith-Ross, 22 October 1937. For a brief survey of Japanese leaders' understanding of British foreign policy, see Usui Katsumi, 'A Consideration of Anglo-Japanese Relations: Japanese Views of Britain, 1937–41', in Ian Nish (ed.), *Anglo-Japanese Alienation, 1919–1952: Papers of the Anglo-Japanese Conference on the history of the Second World War* (Cambridge, 1982), 57–75.

[17] T160/1034/F15255/1, Captain S. H. Phillips (Admiralty) to E. E. Bridges (Treasury), 4 October 1937, Waley Minute, same date; Captain S. H. Phillips (Admiralty) to the Undersecretary of State at the Foreign Office, 4 October 1937.

[18] T160/1034/F15255/1, Fisher Minute, 5 October 1937.

The Air Ministry was even more abject in its weakness. The Air Council fully endorsed the Admiralty's view. 'Sanctions are unlikely to succeed unless countries concerned are prepared to run the risk of war', the Air Council argued. 'Military sanctions are part of collective security, and in the long run, and perhaps in the short run, cannot be avoided.' Adding an even more defeatist tone, the Air Ministry, in the midst of its own rearmament effort, indicated that the Royal Air Force was in no position to play a significant role in war that sanctions might precipitate.[19] The unified opposition from the Treasury and the service ministries showed a profound aversion to imposing sanctions against Japan. The opposition arose not only from the length of time that sanctions would take to coerce Japan to abandon its aggression in China, but also to the fear that Britain would find itself involved in war in the Far East, and possibly in Europe as well.[20] How well-founded were these fears? What potentially would have happened had Britain found itself involved in a war against Japan?

A military confrontation against Japan did run considerable risks, especially considering that the United Kingdom was in the relatively early stages of its own military build-up. The Cabinet, having approved the Defence Requirements Committee report, was funding rearmament as quickly as it believed it could, given the constraints of economic orthodoxy that governed British thinking of the time. Japan was not even Britain's primary concern. The DRC's central conclusion had been that Germany represented the greatest threat to British security.[21] Accordingly, British planning focused on defence against the German threat. The Air Ministry planned to reach air parity with Germany by the end of March 1939. It first needed to build factory capacity and to train workers, creating an eighteen-month delay in manufacturing new air frames and engines. The development and production of machine tools

[19] T160/1034/F15255/1, J. M. Speight (Air Ministry) to the Undersecretary of State at the Foreign Office, 13 October 1937.

[20] T 160/1034/F15255/1, Minutes of an Interdepartmental Meeting held at the Foreign Office on October 13, 13 October 1937.

[21] For some context on British assessments of Germany and Hitler's intent to dominate southeast Europe, see FO 371/20710/C2857/3/18, Phipps (Berlin) to Eden, 14 April 1937, and Cadogan Minute 21 April 1937; FO 371/20712/C7232/3/18, Ogilvie-Forbes (Berlin) to Eden, 20 October 1937. For Anthony Eden's hopes to buy time by getting on better terms with Hitler, see FO 371/20710/C2947/3/18, Leeper Minute, 14 April 1937, Eden Minute 15 April 1937. For a useful summary of the lengthy attempts to try to use colonial issues to appease Germany, see FO 371/20736/C2618/270/18, CAB Paper F.P. (36) 23, 2 April 1937, and C2619/270/18, CAB F.P. (36), Eighth Meeting, 6 April 1937. For an excellent assessment of the accomplishments and failures of the DRC process, see Keith Neilson, 'The Defence Review Sub-Committee, British Strategic Foreign Policy, Neville Chamberlain and the Path to Appeasement', *English Historical Review* 118(447) (2003), 651–84.

represented the greatest bottleneck.[22] Germany, however, was rearming faster than British officials had projected. For example, forecasts had thought it impossible for Germany to create thirty-six infantry divisions by the end of 1936. Instead, it had not only met that target, but could field three armoured divisions and two additional armoured regiments as well. British estimates suggested that Germany could have 78 infantry divisions and 6 armoured divisions by 1939, with personnel to create an army of more than 150 divisions. Intelligence reports indicated that German war preparations were more serious than those taken before 1914, and Hitler was clearly 'preparing the nation for a totalitarian war'.[23]

In the race to build up the Royal Air Force to match the threat from Germany, Britain seemed to fall ever further behind. By early 1937, the Secretary of State for Air Viscount Swinton had warned that it would be impossible to fulfil the pledge to the House of Commons that the government would establish air parity by 1939. His staff projected that Germany would have 2,500 front line aircraft by April 1939 as opposed to Britain's 1,750. He did not believe that British aircraft would be superior in range, performance, or load compared to German ones, and it was overwhelmingly likely that Britain would be several months late even in reaching its target.[24] By the late fall of 1937, the situation looked even gloomier. Forecasts indicated that by the end of 1939, Germany would have 3,240 front line aircraft to Britain's 1,736. Swinton called for increased spending for an additional thirty squadrons of aircraft and increased recruitment and training for pilots and service personnel in order to try to close the gap by building up British front-line strength to 2,331 aircraft by 1941. In total, this would increase the cost for RAF rearmament for 1938 to 1943 from £540,000,000 to £820,000,000.[25] Even with this

---

[22] T161/836/S40063/2, Inter-Service Committee, Draft minutes of the Second Meeting, 20 March 1936. For discussions on Chamberlain's hopes to limit rearmament within the framework of a liberal, democratic economic system, pressure from the services, the Foreign Office, and government backbench critics, and general naval policy, see: Joseph Maiolo, *Cry Havoc: The Arms Race and the Second World War 1931–41* (London, 2010), 143–47, 158–60, 208–12, and 217–19; Stephen Roskill, *Naval Policy Between the Wars: Volume II, The Period of Reluctant Rearmament 1930–1939* (London, 1976), 164–93 and 322–68; Daniel A. Baugh, 'Confusions and Constraints: The Navy and British Defence Planning, 1919–1939', in N. A. M. Rodger (ed.), *Naval Power in the Twentieth Century* (Basingstoke, 1996), 101–15.

[23] FO 371/20731/C1134/136/18, Committee of Imperial Defence (CID) Paper 1303-B and William Strang Minute, 6 February 1937; C5456/136/18, CID Paper 1345-B, 26 June 1937

[24] FO 371/20733/C676/185/18, C.P. 18 (37), Memorandum by the Secretary of State for Air, 14 January 1937. See also Strang, Sargent, and Vansittart Minutes, 6, 8, and 9 February 1937.

[25] CAB 16/182, CID, Defence Plans (Policy) Subcommittee (D.P.(P)) 12, The Strength of the R.A.F. and Air Defence, 12 October 1937. CAB 24/272, C.P. 256(37), Defence

vastly increased expenditure, however, Britain would still lag rather far behind Germany. In the Foreign Office, William Strang, head of the Central Department, commented that the current RAF was 'little more than a façade'. Britain lagged some two years behind Germany, while the day when Britain would have 'security never comes any nearer, but is successively postponed to a more distant future'. He cited Lord Grey's dictum: 'You must not rely on your foreign policy to protect the United Kingdom'. Strang commented acerbically that 'we've been doing that for years and will have to for years more. We have no alternative, therefore, but to put on as bold a front as we can, and play for time'.[26] Anthony Eden sent the gist of Strang's comments to the Committee of Imperial Defence, citing the importance of accelerating the rebuilding of the RAF. In December, the Cabinet took note of the gloomy international situation and the struggles with British rearmament. In Cabinet, Neville Chamberlain cited a Chiefs of Staff report to highlight Britain's precarious strategic situation:

We cannot foresee the time when our defence forces will be strong enough to safeguard our territory, trade and vital interests against Germany, Italy, and Japan simultaneously. We cannot, therefore, exaggerate the importance, from the point of view of Imperial defence, of any political or international action that can be taken to reduce the numbers of our potential enemies and to gain the support of potential allies.[27]

As events would prove, however, the goal of detaching the potential enemy Japan conflicted directly with the goal of attracting support from the potential ally in the United States.

While Germany remained the primary focus of British rearmament, as Britain needed first to guarantee the survival of the Home Islands, the potential of war against Japan in the Far East represented a desperate scenario for British military planners. During the 1920s, naval staff had based their plans on the understanding that European navies were either dispersed or in decline. With the destruction of the German Fleet and the Versailles Treaty's prohibition of further German construction, combined with the limits placed on naval construction in the 1922

Expenditure in Future Years, October 1937. For the Defence Estimates for 1937, see: T161/754/S15164/37, Army Estimates; S15171/37, Navy Estimates; S15170/37, Air Estimates. Maiolo, *Cry Havoc*, 212–13.

[26] FO 371/21011/C8124/185/18, Strang Minute, 5 November 1937.

[27] CAB 23/89/46(37), 8 December 1937. CAB 24/272, C.P. 256(37), Defence Expenditure in Future Years, October 1937. For an assessment of the comparative strength of Britain's forces and its allies and potential enemies, see CAB 24/273, C.P. 296(37), Comparison of the Strength of Great Britain with that of Certain Other Nations as at January 1938, 3 December 1937. CAB 16/182, CID, D.P.(P) 13, The Strength of the R.A.F. and Air Defence, 25 November 1937.

Washington Treaty, Britain could contemplate sending a fleet to the Far East to deter potential Japanese aggression while remaining certain of having an adequate defence in home waters. Rearmament in Hitler's Germany and the end of the Washington Treaty limits on naval construction on 31 December 1936, however, undermined the basis of these assumptions. With Germany able to build up to 35 per cent of British naval tonnage, the Royal Navy would have to increase its Home Fleet substantially, thus decreasing the number of ships and aircraft that it could dispatch to confront Japan. As a result, the Admiralty had requested the creation of a new standard of naval strength to address its deficiencies. Essentially, it called for a fleet of sufficient size and comprehensiveness that the Royal Navy could defend home waters even if complications in the Far East compelled the maintenance of a main force fleet based in Singapore indefinitely. The Admiralty, recognizing the massive bill of its requirements, scaled back its request, but still wanted a fleet of nineteen battleships, fourteen aircraft carriers, ninety-eight cruisers, twenty-one destroyer flotillas, and seventy-three submarines, plus proportionate increases in support vessels. If one included Italy in the potential list of enemies, then the navy's requirements would increase still further beyond the already sizable list of new construction.[28]

Although the Cabinet had not formally approved the new standard and the entailing new construction programme, the 1936 and 1937 defence estimates had tacitly accepted an increased building programme equivalent to the new naval standard. Without the new construction program, Britain would be placed in a position where it could not react to a Japanese challenge to its imperial interests in the Far East. The problem was that this new construction forecast carried a price tag roughly double previous estimates, averaging £104,000,000 per year, assuming that no cost overruns or inflation occurred. The massive naval expenditure costs would extend for seven years rather than prior estimates of three years of special construction. These requirements would either press the British Exchequer beyond its capacity or would require decreases in spending on the Royal Air Force and the army. Nevertheless, failure to meet naval planners' demands would mean that Britain would be unable to send a fleet to the Far East to defend British interests while facing the threat of German rearmament and the potential of Hitler undertaking a military adventure in Europe. As the Defence Requirements Subcommittee had noted, 'it would be suicidal folly to blind our eyes to the possibility of

---

[28] CAB 16/182, CID, D.P.(P) 3, Memorandum, *A New Standard of Naval Strength*, 29 April 1937. CAB 16/181 CID, D.P.(P) Subcommittee, Minutes of the Second Meeting, 11 May 1937. CAB 24/272, C.P. 256(37), October 1937.

a simultaneous, or practically simultaneous, threat on both fronts'. The leading members of the Cabinet considering the report could only agree that rearmament was stretching British spending to the breaking point, and that British foreign policy would have to work to limit the constellation of forces threatening British interests.[29]

Financing this new standard of naval strength proved enormously difficult. Though all senior Cabinet ministers were committed to facing the challenge of the dictators, the demands of the Navy in particular proved beyond the financial capacity of the country.[30] Naval spending began to crowd out other military requirements. By the fall of 1937, it was clear that the need to speed up aircraft production and to meet a higher naval standard were challenging the government's entire rearmament strategy.[31] Simon complained that the government had determined a budget of £1,650,000,000 for 1937 to 1941. After allotting some money for civil defence, that left £1,570,000,000 for the three services. In Simon's view, this amount already represented an enormous burden for the economy. Nevertheless, the three services had had to accept some level of rationing within this framework. The government could not afford to fund all service requirements given the wide range of the requests. The Admiralty, however, had refused to accept this verdict,

---

[29] CAB 16/182 D.P.(P) 3, CID, D.P. (P) Subcommittee, Memorandum, *A New Standard of Naval Strength*, 29 April 1937. CAB 16/181, CID, D.P.(P) Subcommittee, Minutes of the Second Meeting, 11 May 1937. For a brief discussion of the new standard of naval strength, the complications with Japan, and the exorbitant cost, see Joseph Maiolo, *The Royal Navy and Nazi Germany, 1933–39: A Study in Appeasement and the Origins of the Second World War* (New York, 1998), 133–37. For more on context on the complex series of economic and intellectual constraints on financing British rearmament, see Robert Paul Shay Jr., *British Rearmament in the Thirties: Politics and Profits* (Princeton, 1977); and G. C. Peden, *British Rearmament and the Treasury: 1932–1939* (Edinburgh, 1979). British Foreign Office officials well knew from Government Code & Cypher School decrypted radio intercepts that Galeazzo Ciano, the Italian Foreign Minister, was trying to build a Japanese-German-Italian front directed against Great Britain, designed at a minimum to enable the three powers to extort concessions from the over-stretched British Empire. They also knew that the Japanese government rejected this framework, wanting any tripartite arrangement directed against the Soviet Union. Japan intended that the developing admission of Italy to the Anti-Comintern Pact should only operate against the Soviet Union and against international communism; HW 12/219/ 069143, 3 September 1937 (Hotta (Rome) to Hirota (Tokyo), 27 August 1937); / 069158, 4 September 1937 (Mushakoji (Berlin) to Hirota, 31 August 1937); /069164, 6 September 1937 (Hotta to Hirota, 30 August 1937). HW 12/220/069467, 7 October 1937 (Hirota to Hotta, 30 September 1937). HW/221/069730 (Mushakoji to Hirota, 25 October 1937). For more on Ciano's steps in 1937 to build a triple alliance directed against Britain, see G. Bruce Strang, *On the Fiery March: Mussolini Prepares for War* (Westport, 2003), 92–97, 101–03; Robert Mallett, *Mussolini and the Origins of the Second World War, 1933–1940* (Basingstoke and New York, 2003), 151–54.

[30] For the government's commitment to rearmament, see, for example, PREM 1/210, Eden to Chamberlain, 3 November 1937.

[31] CAB 24/273, C.P. 316(37), Defence Expenditure in Future Years, 15 December 1937.

and instead pushed for the increased naval standard. The new spending would either require the Royal Air Force and the army to cut their spending, or the government would far exceed its current budget. As it was, British manufacturers were finding it difficult to meet the Admiralty's demands for new construction.[32] In light of the time delays inherent in the lengthy process of building capital ships and the tight constraints governing the entire British rearmament effort, and given the ever-present threat of German rearmament in the potential European theatre of war, the Cabinet had to consider very carefully the possibility that, if faced with strong economic sanctions, Japan would resort to war rather than surrender its conquests in China.

The Committee of Imperial Defence, Defence Plans (Policy) Subcommittee was one of the most important committees for determining defence policy. Its membership included the Prime Minister, the Chancellor of the Exchequer, the Secretaries of State for Foreign Affairs and Home Affairs, the First Lord of the Admiralty, the Secretaries of State for War and Air, the Minister for Co-ordination of Defence, and the three Service Chiefs. The Subcommittee had considered the Chiefs of Staff appreciation of the strategic situation in the Far East very shortly after the Marco Polo Bridge incident. The report was not encouraging. The purpose of British planning had always remained to *deter* Japan from war in the Far East and to be able to protect British trade. In the case of war with Japan in 1937, the goal would be to induce Japanese leaders to see reason: to restrain their military and to call off their aggression in China. A central secondary goal, protecting British imperial trade outside of China, would be relatively easy; most of it would be out of range of Japanese aircraft or warships, especially after the arrival of the British main fleet at Singapore. Britain needed rubber and tin from Malaya, but could divert that trade west through the Suez Canal. Trade for Australia and New Zealand would not be problematic. Both countries could adopt alternate shipping routes. For trade with the United States, they could either send shipping on longer voyages or substitute British goods for American ones. India would face significant dislocation of its cotton trade, as Japan bought roughly one-sixth of Indian export goods. British planners were concerned, but thought on balance the effects on British trade as a whole would be minimal, affecting only 2 per cent of British trade.[33]

---

[32] PREM 1/346, Simon to Chamberlain, 24 June 1936, Cooper to Chamberlain, 13 March 1936.

[33] CAB 16/181, CID, D.P.(P), Third Meeting, 13 July 1937. CAB 16/182, D.P.(P) 5 (Chiefs of Staff 596), Strategic Appreciation of the Far East, 14 June 1937.

Britain, on the other hand, could cause serious problems for the Japanese economy. Japan was heavily dependent on imports of a wide range of strategic goods vital for modern warfare, including iron and non-ferrous metals, petroleum, rubber, coking coal, salt, textiles, and timber. Although Japan had a large strategic reserve of naval fuel suitable to fund some eighteen months of wartime operation, it would be vulnerable to economic blockade after that time. Japan imported half of its iron from the British Empire, Europe, or America. It required 500,000 tonnes of salt annually to maintain its chemical industry. It also required some 250,000 tonnes of non-ferrous metals per year. In a war with Britain, Japan would find it problematic to import these materials. Japan also had to export goods to maintain its industrial production, and a British block-ade could significantly interfere with that trade. Although the United States might potentially supplant British trade with Japan, America imported relatively little from Japan, and Japan would find it difficult to acquire enough American dollars to increase its imports substantially. On the other hand, Britain would find it very difficult to interdict Japan's trade with the latter's colony in Korea and with Manchukuo, as the Royal Navy would be unable to project force that far north. British planners concluded that interdiction of Japanese trade would take at least two years to cause sufficient damage to the home economy that it would require Japan to stop its invasion of China.[34]

Obviously, a war of two years' duration, however limited it might prove, while Britain was attempting to rearm to keep pace with frenetic German and Italian military spending was a far from palatable option. The only way to bring the war to a more rapid conclusion would be to defeat the Japanese fleet in battle. The relative sizes of the fleets and their respective resources made that goal difficult. It would take some seventy days from a British decision to commit the fleet to the Far East to ensure adequate fuel supplies, for sailors to work up all the ships, and for the fleet to travel to the Singapore Base. Before its arrival, and depending on the conditions in which an Anglo-Japanese war started, British forces would face massive Japanese supremacy in battleships, nearly two-to-one odds in cruisers, and four-to-one odds in destroyers and lighter ships. Nevertheless, the Chiefs of Staff generally discounted the possibility of a Japanese main force attack on Singapore in the early days of the war. Japan would face potential British submarine and air attack on the fleet, combined with the prospect of a main fleet action as British reinforce-ments arrived. They thought Japan would either attempt to raid British

---

[34] CAB 16/182, D.P.(P) 5 (Chiefs of Staff 596), Strategic Appreciation of the Far East, 14 June 1937.

commercial sea lanes or to try to seize Britain's forward base in Hong Kong.[35]

Even after the arrival of the main fleet, however, Britain would be operating halfway around the world from its home ports. The Singapore base was far from complete, and even when finished would have inadequate docking and repair facilities, limiting the British ability to keep their ships at fighting trim. The Chiefs of Staffs estimated that Britain would have roughly two of its battleships out of commission at any given time. Accordingly, according to the most optimistic set of assumptions, the Royal Navy would be able to count on a narrow superiority of ten battleships to Japan's nine. Britain would also have three battlecruisers, while Japan had none. Both countries would have five aircraft carriers, while Britain would have slight superiority in cruisers and destroyers. As Japan could potentially draw on its entire military strength from its home islands, it would have considerable air superiority in the theatre of operations as a whole. Nevertheless, Japan would find it hard to deploy that air power effectively against Singapore owing to its lack of forward air bases. British planners ruled out the possibility of a Japanese land attack against India, as it would stretch Japanese logistical capabilities and available resources too far. In a purely defensive war, therefore, the Chiefs were optimistic of maintaining Britain's most important imperial holdings and providing an effective shield for Australia and New Zealand.[36]

When it came to defending British interests in China, however, the situation was quite different. Two British battalions, one at Shanghai and one at Tientsin, would be immediately cut off. Unless Britain had plenty of advanced warning, it would have no chance to remove those troops, and they would be surrounded and massively outnumbered. Britain's advance base at Hong Kong was exceptionally vulnerable. Japan would likely be able to use bases on the Chinese mainland for aircraft and naval units to interdict British reinforcements and to attack Hong Kong directly. British forces in Hong Kong had only sixty days' supplies on hand. As the main fleet would take seventy days to reach Singapore, and Hong Kong lay more than 1,400 nautical miles to the north of Singapore, Britain would have no real ability to reinforce Hong Kong for some ninety days after the start of a war. British forces in Hong Kong had little in the way of heavy coastal guns and no aircraft that would threaten a Japanese fleet. The island would be subject to offshore bombardment or sustained air attack from Japanese planes based in China or launched from aircraft

---

[35] CAB 16/182, D.P.(P) 5 (Chiefs of Staff 596), Strategic Appreciation of the Far East, 14 June 1937.

[36] CAB 16/182, D.P.(P) 5 (Chiefs of Staff 596), Strategic Appreciation of the Far East, 14 June 1937.

carriers. The island had plenty of beaches that would enable the Japanese to choose a potential site or multiple sites for landing an invasion. With only four battalions of troops and relatively light artillery immediately on hand, Hong Kong would be unable to resist a Japanese attack prior to the arrival of the main British fleet. If the Japanese succeeded in taking Hong Kong, Britain would have no chance whatsoever to take it back, as Singapore was simply too far away. Britain would lack the air power to cover a fleet action, and it lacked the ground troops to secure forward operating bases.[37]

British prospects would increase substantially if Japan failed to defeat Hong Kong in the first months of the war. With the arrival of the main fleet, the situation would become much more fluid. The main fleet could escort troops and aircraft to Hong Kong to establish it as a serious forward operating base. Even so, Japanese bases in Formosa and the Pescadores provided Japan advanced bases to the northeast of Hong Kong. As the fleet moved north, the Japanese would have excellent reconnaissance, submarine units to attack the fleet, and the fleet air arm would have to engage Japanese aircraft in the region to try to neutralize them. Once in the area of Hong Kong, however, the fleet, operating with air cover, could threaten Japanese sea lines of communications to its troops in China. The goal would be to compel Japan to send its fleet into a main force engagement with the Royal Navy in order to force an immediate end to the war. Even in these relatively optimistic circumstances, however, the Air Staff argued that Japan's ability to concentrate its air force, including large numbers of squadrons from metropolitan Japan, meant that the Hong Kong base and any ships operating in the region would be subjected to sustained air attack. At best, British planners could only speculate whether or not Japan would commit its fleet against the main force of the Royal Navy. Given the inherent difficulties in trying to base forward operations on Hong Kong, therefore, the Service Chiefs concluded that the most promising course of action was simply to use economic pressure to force the Japan government to come to its senses.[38]

As grim as it was, the Service Chiefs' projection was the best-case scenario. In any realistic assessment, Britain could not send its entire fleet to the Far East. In the short run, Germany had little naval strength with which to threaten the British Home Islands, but the Royal Navy would have to thin its margins by maintaining two capital ships, the *Hood*

---

[37] CAB 16/182, D.P.(P) 5 (Chiefs of Staff 596), Strategic Appreciation of the Far East, Annex III, 14 June 1937.
[38] CAB 16/182, D.P.(P) 5 (Chiefs of Staff 596), Strategic Appreciation of the Far East, 14 June 1937, Annex III. CAB 16/181, CID D.P.(P.) Third Subcommittee Meeting, 13 July 1937.

and *Repulse*, in European waters. In those circumstances, the Chiefs argued that it would be unwise to try to defend Hong Kong. If Italy decided to intervene, then the situation was incalculably worse, as sending the main fleet to the Far East meant virtually denuding the entire Mediterranean Sea of British ships. Britain would have to rely on France to contain the *Regia Marina*, which was far from certain.[39] British planners, however, had little choice, as without an adequate defence in the Far East, Japan could potentially capture the Singapore base, opening up threats to India, Australia and New Zealand. The prospect of some two years' blockade against Japan could hardly inspire much confidence given Britain's array of problems in the European and Mediterranean theatres. Even so, the Service Chiefs' appreciation carried a considerable amount of wishful thinking about Hong Kong. Britain could not defend it, but it could not afford to lose it either. Without a shield provided from Hong Kong, the entire coast of China would be vulnerable to Japanese naval gunfire and air attack. With Japanese troops establishing increasing control throughout northeast China and the Shanghai area, Japan could liquidate virtually every aspect of Britain's colonial holdings in China. British businesses would be vulnerable to Japanese harassment or confiscations as the Japanese conquered ever larger areas in China. A war against Japan would see the destruction of Britain's Chinese position – precisely the outcome that Britain would supposedly fight the war to prevent. Even a successful war against Japan, likely lasting around two years, tying up the Royal Navy throughout, was an imposing prospect to contemplate, especially given the increasing challenge of Nazi Germany and fascist Italy in northwest Europe and the Mediterranean Basin. Unsurprisingly, given the grave set of circumstances facing them, the Service Chiefs concluded that the government should do everything possible to maintain friendly relations with Japan and to avoid a war at almost any cost.[40]

The assessment of the risks of an Anglo-Japanese war, however, would have changed entirely if the United States had been willing to make guarantees that it would participate in sanctions *and* would commit to go to war alongside Britain should Japan escalate the war by attacking the Netherlands East Indies or British possessions. In those circumstances, if

[39] FO 371/20960/F10284/9/10, Cadogan Memorandum on conversation with the First Sea Lord, 29 November 1937. For more detailed assessment of British policy in the Mediterranean, see Lawrence Pratt, *East of Malta, West of Suez: Britain's Mediterranean Crisis, 1936–1939* (Cambridge, 1975), 29–58; Strang, *On the Fiery March*, 89–90 and 97–100; Reynolds M. Salerno, *Vital Crossroads: Mediterranean Origins of the Second World War, 1935–1940* (Ithaca, 2002), 23–28, 36–39, and 40–41.

[40] CAB 16/182, D.P.(P) 5 (Chiefs of Staff 596), Strategic Appreciation of the Far East, 14 June 1937. CAB 16/181, CID, D.P.(P), Third Meeting, 13 July 1937.

Japan concentrated its fleet against Britain in the south, then it would leave its home islands or its central Pacific empire vulnerable to an attack by the United States Navy. As a result, the Japanese military would be forced to maintain a substantial part of its fleet and air force to defend against an American attack, and Britain would be able to establish a clear superiority in the theatre of operations off the coast of China. Anglo-American sanctions, backed by close military cooperation and mutual defence guarantees, would almost certainly have led Japan's military leaders to pull back from an open confrontation. American domestic politics and the challenging nature of Anglo-American relations, however, made such a commitment unlikely in the fall of 1937.

In many ways, Britain and the United States represented the two great, world powers devoted to maintaining the status quo in the inter-war years. As American society largely derived from British origins, they shared considerable similarities, but there were also vital differences. Both countries had democratic forms of government. The two had largely solved their naval rivalry, and tension due to the British occupation of Ireland had largely passed into history. Both countries emphasized peaceful trade and sought stability in international relations. They also had their differences. Both resented the other's trade restrictions – British imperial preference on one hand and high American trade tariffs on the other – and trade relations were often highly fractious. Britain's repudiation of its war debt obligations alienated many American citizens and gave proverbial ammunition to isolationists who sought to keep the United States out of any future European conflict, while British officials developed clear contempt for America's political leadership, especially after the Americans torpedoed the World Economic Conference over the issue of war debts. The Simon–Stimson Affair further bedevilled relations. British officials rejected the widely held premise that Sir John Simon, the Secretary of State for Foreign Affairs in 1932, had failed to act under the terms of the Nine-Power Treaty to preserve China's territorial integrity or to support the American doctrine of non-recognition of Japanese gains in Manchuria. In the United States, many influential politicians and journalists (and British opposition politicians and media critics as well) took Stimson's claims as a matter of faith; they argued that Simon's alleged failure showed British perfidy, and the issue furthered support for isolationism. Above all, British security required it to focus its attention on Europe and a resurgent Nazi Germany, while many Americans rejected the idea that the United States should involve itself in the decadent old world of European affairs. British politicians and officials knew that they had the genuine sympathy of President Franklin Delano Roosevelt, but they were much more suspicious of Secretary of State Cordell Hull, whose tendency to lecture the British government about its international duties while failing to provide practical American support annoyed British ministers and officials immensely.[41]

When the Marco Polo Bridge incident sparked the new Sino-Japanese war, Anthony Eden and his Foreign Office officials hoped to work in close cooperation with the United States. The State Department wanted to maintain close contact with the Foreign Office as well, but, as frequently occurred, fears of American isolationist opinion drove Cordell Hull to reject any moves that would look as if Britain and the United States were working together.[42] As a result, the two countries made separate approaches to the Japanese government to urge restraint. Eden affirmed to his diplomats abroad and to his Cabinet colleagues that British policy would support anything that the Americans might wish to do, but that Britain would not proceed on its own initiative. Above all, Eden hoped to tighten Anglo-American ties. In his view, 'We must lose no opportunity of cooperating with [the] U[nited] S[tates] gov[ernmen]t'.[43] In the circumstances, Britain would try to work with the United States while seeking to avoid embarrassing the Roosevelt administration before its isolationist

---

[41] FO 371/20651/A1925/38/45, Eden to Lindsay, 10 March 1937, Lindsay to Eden, 22 March 1937, Troutbeck Minute, 2 April 1937; FO 371/20659/A2992/228/45, Ashton-Gwatkin Minute, 11 March 1937, Eden Minute, 16 April 1937. FO 371/20660/A4165/228/45, Lindsay to Eden, 1 June 1937. On the Stimson–Simon Affair, see Keith Neilson, 'Perception and Posture in Anglo-American Relations: The Legacy of the Stimson–Simon Affair', *International History Review* 29(2) (2007), 313–37; and Harry S. Stimson, *The Far Eastern Crisis* (New York, 1936). On war debts, see Robert Self, 'Perception and Posture in Anglo-American Relations: The War Debt Controversy in the "Official Mind," 1919–1940', *International History Review* 29(2) (2007), 282–312; and Robert Self, *Britain, America, and the War Debt Controversy: The Economic Diplomacy of an Unspecial Relationship, 1917–1941* (London, 2006). For more on British perceptions of Roosevelt's goodwill toward Britain, but also his unwillingness to take action in public, see, for example, the lengthy discussions about Roosevelt's approach to the British government outside of official diplomatic channels in the spring of 1937. FO 371/20710/C2138/3/18, Bewley Memoranda, 23 February 1937 and 17 March 1937, Eden to Chamberlain, 5 March 1937, Chamberlain to Eden, 15 March 1937, Stanley to Lindsay, 16 March 1937; FO 371/20710/C2614/3/18, Lindsay to Stanley, 30 March 1937. For a strong survey of British policy, see Lee, *Britain and the Sino-Japanese War*, 50–78.

[42] Dorothy Borg, *The United States and the Far Eastern Crisis of 1933–1938: From the Manchurian Incident through the Initial Stage of the Undeclared Sino-Japanese War* (Cambridge, 1964), 287–98.

[43] Eden quoted in FO 371/20952/F4890/9/10, Eden Minute 30 July 1937; FO 371/20949/F4087/9/10, /F43012/9/10, and /F4352/9/10, Eden to Lindsay, all 20 July 1937; ibid./F4317/9/10, Lindsay to Eden, 20 July 1937; FO 371/20950/F4160/9/10, Lindsay to Eden, 15 July 1937; ibid./F4203/9/10, Eden Minute, 18 July 1937; ibid./F4301/9/10, Eden Memorandum, 20 July 1937; CAB 23/89/32(37), 28 July 1937; FO 371/20952/F4890/9/10, Vansittart Memorandum, 30 July 1937.

congressional and media critics through any form of public pressure for American cooperation with British policy.[44]

China's appeal to the now-discredited League of Nations was potentially embarrassing for the British government. Chiang Kai-Shek clearly hoped that the League would declare Japan the aggressor and would invoke economic sanctions as a result. British officials well recognized that the Chinese nationalists needed such support, but they thought the appeal to the League ill-advised. The United States would never associate itself with any League action. Furthermore, an appeal to the League might lead Japan to declare war against China, which would require President Roosevelt to invoke neutrality legislation, possibly preventing China from purchasing war material from the United States.[45] British preliminary investigations showed clearly that American support would be vital for the success of any coercive measures aimed against Japan. British diplomats were able to get the League to refer the issue for consideration by the signatories to the 1922 Nine-Power Treaty. At the same time, British officials further studied the possible effectiveness of sanctions, and the British Embassy in Washington sounded out the possibility that the Roosevelt administration would agree to join Britain in taking coercive measures.[46]

Roosevelt's quarantine speech gave greater impetus to the exploration of sanctions, as joint Anglo-American action would be the only way to succeed. Roosevelt's speech, on its surface, seemed to indicate that the administration was open to the idea.[47] Neville Chamberlain, the British

---

[44] FO 371/20955/F6303/9/10, Mallet (Washington) to Orde, 31 August 1937, Cadogan Minute, 13 September 1937; ibid./F6284/9/10, /F6497/9/10, Mallet to Eden, both 7 September 1937; CAB 23/89/35(37), 29 September 1937. To preserve its independence of action and to forestall criticism from isolationists, the Roosevelt administration insisted on making separate representations to the Japanese government, although both the State Department and the Foreign Office had developed similar views of the situation; Greg Kennedy, *Anglo American Strategic Relations and the Far East, 1933–1939* (London, 2002), 211–32; Ritchie Ovendale, *'Appeasement' and the English Speaking World: Britain, the United States, the Dominions, and the Policy of 'Appeasement', 1937–1939* (Cardiff, 1975), 67–69.

[45] FO 371/20954/F5720/9/10, Orde Minute, 22 August 1937; ibid./F5613/9/10, Vansittart Minute, 20 August 1937; ibid./F5717/9/10, Eden to Knatchbull-Hugessen, 25 August 1937.

[46] FO 371/21019/F7240/7240/10, Orde Minute, 30 September 1937, Eden to Mallet, 2 October 1937; ibid./F7310/7240/10, /F7477/7420/10, Mallet to Eden, both 5 October 1937, Jebb Minute, 7 October 1937, Vansittart to Eden, 11 October 1937; *Foreign Relations of the United States, 1937*, vol. 3, The Far East (Washington, DC, 1954) (hereafter *FRUS*); The British Embassy to the Department of State, 1 October 1937, 560; Memorandum by the Adviser on Political Relations (Hornbeck) of Conversation With the British Chargé (Mallet), 2 October 1937, 569.

[47] For the text of the speech, see Donald B. Schewe (ed.), *Franklin D. Roosevelt and Foreign Affairs*, vol. III, August 1937 – November 1937 (New York, 1979), no. 524, Speech of

Prime Minister, however, had his doubts. As he explained to his Cabinet colleagues, 'He could not imagine anything more suicidal than to pick a quarrel with Japan at the present moment the European situation had become so serious'. Chamberlain shared the concerns of the Treasury Department and the Service Chiefs that Germany and Italy would seize on Britain's involvement in the Far East to create further mischief in Europe or the Mediterranean. Chamberlain emphasized the need to consider British commitments throughout the world. Nevertheless, Britain could not afford to give credence to further claims that it had shirked its obligations, thus letting down the United States as had allegedly happened in the Stimson–Simon affair. Accordingly, Chamberlain wanted to broach the subject in its entirety in Washington. Was the Roosevelt administration willing to impose sanctions? Given that economic sanctions could lead to Japanese retaliation and war, was Roosevelt willing to guarantee that the United States would defend British interests if Britain became involved in a war with Japan? If Germany or Italy seized on the opportunity to attack British interests in Europe or the Mediterranean, would the United States still support Britain? While these diplomatic soundings occurred, Chamberlain, Eden, and their Cabinet colleagues agreed that Britain would have to ensure that it publicly kept in line with Roosevelt's declared objectives.[48]

the President, Chicago, Illinois, 5 October 1937 (hereafter *FDR & Foreign Affairs*). For discussions of the speech, see, for example, Robert Dallek, *Franklin D. Roosevelt and American Foreign Policy, 1932–1945* (Oxford, 1979), 148–51; Dorothy Borg, 'Notes on Roosevelt's Quarantine Speech', *Political Science Quarterly* 72(4) (1954), 405–33; and John McVickar Haight, 'Roosevelt and the Aftermath of the Quarantine Speech', *Review of Politics* 24(3) (1962), 233–59. Borg argued that Roosevelt hesitantly aimed to find a means to educate American public opinion in order to allow his administration to take a more active role seeking to secure peace between the democracies and the dictatorships. Haight argued that the President had a far-reaching plan of creating a system of collective neutrality, but that Cordell Hull's innate caution, combined with congressional isolationists' opposition, caused the president to back away from a more forward policy; see also Borg, *United States and the Far Eastern Crisis*, 369–98. In a letter sent the following day, Cardinal Mundelein, Archbishop of Chicago, wrote that Roosevelt had explained to him that the speech referred neither to 'military or naval action' nor to 'sanctions as generally understood', *FDR and Foreign Affairs*, III, no. 526a, Cardinal Mundelein to Archbishop Cicognani, 6 October 1937. In a press conference the next day, the President said that 'sanctions is a terrible word to use. They are out the window.' He indicated that he was seeking a program to ensure peace, *FDR and Foreign Affairs*, III, no. 530, Press Conference, Hyde Park, 6 October 1937.

[48] CAB 23/89/36(37), 6 October 1937. Privately, Chamberlain complained to his sister Hilda that Roosevelt's proposals were vague. He thought Roosevelt was merely sounding out American public opinion. He feared that if Britain took strong action, then the United States would 'somehow fade out & leave us to carry all the blame & the odium', Chamberlain Papers, NC18/1/1023, Neville Chamberlain to Hilda Chamberlain, 9 October 1937; PREM 1/314, Vansittart to Chamberlain, 8 and 11 October 1937.

The following week, Chamberlain and Eden had further clarified their thoughts. Ineffective sanctions would merely serve to annoy Japan to little purpose. As Japan seemed to be rolling up the Chinese nationalist armies, even sanctions designed to be effective might not serve to save China, as Japan might have accomplished its destruction of Chiang Kai-Shek's military and political position by the time economic measures would serve to coerce the Japanese sufficiently. The more effective sanctions proved, the greater the risk that Japan would retaliate by going to war rather than yield its conquests in China. If Britain sent its fleet to the Far East, it could serve to encourage German or Italian aggression in Europe. In these circumstances, Britain would need a clear guarantee that the United States would be willing to defend British interests in the Far East, as well as the interests of the other countries involved in imposing sanctions. Chamberlain and Eden doubted that the Roosevelt administration would make such a commitment and doubted that the American public would have the determination to see any such guarantee through to the end. Accordingly, they hoped that the upcoming Brussels Conference, convened under the terms of the Nine-Power Treaty, would enable Japan and China to come to a peaceful resolution. For his part, Eden emphasized the importance of the United States in recognizing the inherent dangers of sanctions and making ironclad guarantees of military support to ensure that they could enforce any sanctions. Above all, Eden thought it vital to ensure that British policy conform to American policy; the Cabinet had to avoid at all costs placing itself in a position where American critics could blame Britain for the failure of common policy against Japan. The Cabinet agreed that Britain should press for a negotiated settlement at Brussels rather than seeking to secure a consensus on imposing sanctions.[49]

Unfortunately, Roosevelt's quarantine speech promised much more than the Roosevelt administration was prepared to deliver. To British diplomats in Washington, administration officials indicated that the speech merely sought to affirm American principles and educate American public opinion. Roosevelt had wanted to indicate that isolationists could not simply hope for peace – that America would have to be able to use its influence to support democratic principles against the threat to international peace posed by the dictator states. Roosevelt warned,

---

[49] CAB 23/89/C.C. 37(37), 13 October 1937. Chamberlain wrote to his sister Ida that the Roosevelt administration had indicated that Roosevelt's speech merely expressed his ideals and that the Roosevelt administration had no intent whatsoever to impose sanctions, Chamberlain Papers, NC18/1/1024, Neville Chamberlain to Hilda Chamberlain, 16 October 1937.

(1) It [Great Britain] should not speak or think or act as though it were possible for me [Roosevelt] to be in any way an exponent of British Foreign Office policy.

(2) It should never forget that I cannot march ahead of our very difficult and restive American public opinion.

(3) It must not try to push me in any way to the front or to thrust leadership upon me.

Instead of taking decisive measures, the President indicated that he hoped that the forthcoming conference would serve to teach the American public about the dangerous world situation.[50]

Other diplomatic soundings reinforced the sense of deep American caution. Victor Mallet, the Chargé d'Affaires of the British Embassy in Washington, met with Sumner Welles, the Undersecretary of State; Welles said that Roosevelt was merely searching for peace. The President's use of the word 'quarantine' was vague and did not represent an immediate policy. Above all, the United States hoped that the Brussels Conference would lead to a peaceful solution.[51] Eden's conversation with Robert Bingham, the American Ambassador to the Court of St. James's, echoed these sentiments. Bingham reaffirmed that the United States wanted to cooperate fully with Great Britain. At the same time, however, he urged that neither country should take a leading role at the Brussels Conference. He particularly wanted to avoid a situation where the British delegation would rush ahead and seek to drag the United States in its wake. Bingham hoped that the smaller powers would take the lead, and Britain and the United States could then show unity in supporting a broad consensus. Eden could only comment that if neither the United States

---

[50] FO 371/20663/A7441/288/45, Wickham Steed (Washington) to Vansittart, 13 October 1937, Vansittart Minute, 14 October 1937; *FRUS, 1937*, III, Memorandum by the Undersecretary of State (Welles), 12 October 1937, 600–02. Dorothy Borg essentially agrees with this assessment of Roosevelt's intentions, see Borg, 'Notes on Roosevelt's Quarantine Speech', 420–04, and *United States and the Far Eastern Crisis*, 363–98. John McVickar Haight argues that Roosevelt intended to take a much firmer line, but that domestic opposition and Cordell Hull's innate caution caused Roosevelt to draw back from a forward policy part way through the Brussels Conference, Haight, 'Quarantine Speech', 256–59. Ovendale agrees that the harsh response from isolations caused Roosevelt to draw back, Ovendale, *'Appeasement' and the English Speaking World*, 72–73. British and American documents tend to undermine Haight's and Ovendale's views. Maxwell Hamilton, the Chief of the Division of Far Eastern Affairs, drafted a lengthy memorandum that argued against the United States participating in any sanctions scheme, as it would bear a disproportionate cost of loss of trade and American public opinion would not permit the United States to take the lead. *FRUS, 1937*, III, Memorandum by the Chief of the Division of Far Eastern Affairs (Hamilton), 12 October 1937, 596–600.

[51] FO 371/21019/F7732/7240/9/10, Mallet to Eden, 12 October 1937.

nor Britain took the lead, then the smaller powers would be unlikely to do so.[52]

The Brussels Conference met from 3 to 24 November 1937. Hampered from the outset by Japanese and German refusals to attend, by Italian obstructionism, and by the timid Anglo-American approach, the conference ultimately achieved little. In a meeting with Norman Davis, Roosevelt's roving ambassador and the head of the American delegation, Eden emphasized that Britain and the United States needed to avoid any repeat of the disunity that led to the fall out of the Stimson–Simon Affair. Neither party would benefit from a recurrence. Eden argued that sanctions had to be effective. If they were merely a gesture of admonishment, then they would be 'provocative and useless'. If they were effective, they carried the risk of war and it would be foolish to ignore that fact. The British government was willing to consider sanctions along with the United States, but 'with eyes wide open, and with a willingness to share the risks, whatever they might be, right through to the end'.[53] For his part, Norman Davis indicated that neither Britain nor the United States should take the lead role in the conference. American public opinion believed that the United States had much less at stake in China, and it would bridle at any appearance that the Roosevelt administration was being led by Great Britain. Davis thought that the world should first exert moral pressure against Japan and only consider stronger measures if Japan failed to respond.[54]

For a time, Norman Davis did take a more forward role, and he interpreted his instructions so broadly that he indicated at one point that the United States might consider imposing sanctions.[55] As the conference progressed, however, the State Department clipped Davis's wings, criticizing him severely. Cordell Hull flatly rejected the idea that the United States public would consider any association with economic sanctions against Japan. He argued that Davis's manoeuvres during the Brussels Conference contravened the administration's policy. Davis

---

[52] FO 371/20663/A 7748/228/45, Eden Minute, 28 October 1937; see also Kennedy, *Anglo-American Strategic Relations*, 234–35.

[53] FO 371/21019/F9234/7240/10, Eden to Ronald Lindsay (Washington), 6 November 1937.

[54] *FRUS, 1937*, IV, *The Far East* (Washington, DC, 1954), The Chairman of the American delegation (Davis) to the Secretary of State, 2 November 1937, 145–47. Sumner Welles, the Undersecretary of State, warned Sir Ronald Lindsay, the British Ambassador in Washington, that the United States would not participate in economic sanctions, *FRUS, 1937*, IV, Memorandum by the Undersecretary of State (Welles) of a Conversation with the British Ambassador (Lindsay), 152–55.

[55] For Davis's views on possible coercive measures that the conference might take, see *FRUS, 1937*, IV, The Chairman of the American Delegation (Davis) to the Secretary of State, 10 November 1937, 175–77.

objected but had to concede the point.[56] With no natural leadership, the Conference ended in failure to take measures to reach either a negotiated solution or to find ways to cooperate to impede Japan's aggression. The American delegate informed Sir Alexander Cadogan, soon to be Permanent Undersecretary at the Foreign Office, that the United States would not send its fleet west of Pearl Harbor in any circumstances short of a direct Japanese attack.[57]

Without the ability to impose sanctions and given the extraordinary risk of taking unilateral military action against Japan, the British government had little alternative but to accept increasing Japanese encroachment against its interests. Eden tried to console himself that many military observers thought that Japan was far overstretched by its invasion of China. It could prove to be Japan's '1812'. Whether or not that turned out to be the case, Eden thought that Britain should cautiously take such actions as it could to make that result happen.[58] Chamberlain despaired that it was impossible for Britain to put any significant pressure on Japan without the cooperation of the United States.[59] Posing the essential dilemma of British foreign policy, he echoed the Service Chiefs' calls to reach accommodation with potential enemies, though in such a way as to not lose potential allies. Chamberlain commented acerbically that one could not count too much on the United States. It had enormous power, but he could not plan on the Roosevelt administration 'delivering the goods'. Roosevelt eventually would rouse his population to the danger, but it might prove 'too late'.[60] Speaking more directly to the immediate

---

[56] *FRUS, 1937*, IV, The Secretary of State to the Chairman of the American Delegation (Davis), 12 and 15 November 1937, 180–81 and 187–88; *vice versa*, 14 and 17 November 1937, 183 and 200-02. The president's notes of his conversation with Norman Davis to impart instructions before Davis left for the Brussels Conference do not indicate that Roosevelt contemplated sanctions. They emphasized that the British Cabinet needed to be aware of American public opinion, that the United States would not take part in any League action, that the United States would not take the lead in any future action, and that the United States could not appear to be the 'tail to the British kite'. Roosevelt cited the need for common action based on unanimous opinion, with no one nation taking the lead, FDR and Foreign Affairs, III, no. 570, Notes of Conversation with Norman H. Davis, 19 October 1937; Borg, *United States and the Far Eastern Crisis*, 399–441; Kennedy, *Anglo-American Strategic Relations*, 234–38; Ovendale, *'Appeasement' and the English Speaking World*, 79–82.

[57] FO 371/20960/F10024/9/10, Cadogan Minute 26 November 1937.

[58] FO 371/20958/F8982/9/10, Eden Minute, no date (c. mid-November 1937).

[59] CAB 23/90A/43 (37), 24 November 1937.

[60] CAB 2/7, 303rd Meeting of the CID, 2 December 1937; see also CID Papers 1366-B and 1373-B, and also CAB 23/90A/47(37), 15 December 1937. In part, Chamberlain's distrust for the Roosevelt administration derived from American behavior regarding sanctions against Italy during its invasion of Ethiopia. Michael L. Roi, '"A Completely Immoral and Cowardly Attitude": The British Foreign Office, American Neutrality, and the Hoare-Laval Plan', *Canadian Journal of History* 29(2) (1994), 333–52;

Japanese threat to British interests in China, Sir Alexander Cadogan noted that in the absence of an American commitment, Britain lacked any useful power to deploy to protect British interests in China. Even sending the entire fleet to the Far East, save for a small force to defend home waters against Germany, would not provide sufficient force to compel the Japanese to abandon their attack on China, as Britain lacked the ability to damage Japanese trade quickly enough, to force a decisive battle against the Imperial Navy, or even in reality to defend Hong Kong. As a result, Britain would have to risk that the Japanese would encroach on British interests over the following two to three years while Britain tried to catch up to the rearmament efforts of its potential enemies. The only faint hope would be that Chinese resistance eventually exhausted the Japanese. Until that point, Britain's position in China would exist largely at the mercy of the Japanese invaders.[61]

The Japanese invasion of China represented a serious threat to British interests in China, especially after the extension of the war to Shanghai and central China. British politicians and Whitehall officials sought some way to deal with the situation. Some, especially leading officials in the Treasury, sought to protect British interests through an agreement with Japan, but doing so would alienate public opinion at home and abroad, especially in the United States. Officials in the Foreign Office, led by Anthony Eden, hoped to develop some form of resistance to the Japanese threat to Britain's imperial interests. The exploration of the use of economic sanctions, however, showed serious difficulties. The full participation of the United States would be necessary; Britain alone would not have sufficient leverage to damage the Japanese economy and force Japan's leaders to halt their aggression. Even so, estimates showed that sanctions would take a long time to become effective, between one and two years, owing to Japan's stockpiles of important strategic minerals and its ability to marshal its comparatively meagre resources. More seriously, British officials and Cabinet members feared that economic sanctions would compel the Japanese military to resort to war rather than to abandon its conquests in China. Accordingly, they did not want to impose sanctions without the ability to fight and win the resulting war. The slow rate of British rearmament, the dual threat from Nazi Germany and fascist Italy in Europe, and the remoteness of the Singapore naval base meant that Britain would face stagnation or possible defeat in a war against Japan, and it would certainly lose its imperial position in China

---

G. Bruce Strang, '"The Worst of All Worlds": Oil Sanctions and Italy's Invasion of Abyssinia, 1935-1936', *Diplomacy & Statecraft* 19(2) (2008), 210–35.

[61] FO 371/20960/F10284/9/10, Cadogan Memorandum, 29 November 1937; FO 371/20960/F10024/9/10, Cadogan Minutes, 26 and 30 November 1937.

for which it ostensibly would be fighting the war. The direct support of the United States would have changed the situation dramatically. An American fleet able to operate west of Pearl Harbor would have constrained the Japanese Imperial Navy and would have given Britain the potential to establish local superiority off the coast of China. Despite repeated soundings in Washington and the signs of Roosevelt's sympathy for Britain's strategic problems, President Roosevelt and Secretary of State Cordell Hull were still in an agonizingly long process of educating American public opinion to the dangers of the international world. The Roosevelt administration made it absolutely clear that it would not support Britain militarily should it find itself involved in a conflict with Japan. Given the global threats that Britain faced, its government decided in 1937 that it did not have the requisite military or economic power to resist Japan's threat to its position in China.

This debate showed considerable cognitive dissonance among Britain's leaders. Whitehall officials and Cabinet ministers recognized the extent to which British relative decline against Germany, Italy, and Japan and its imperial overreach meant that investment in China was indefensible. At the same time, however, they did not seem to consider the possibility of cutting British losses in the region. They never gave any consideration to cutting loose the businesses in the China Association. Instead, they indulged in wishful thinking and played for time. They hoped that the heroic Chinese resistance would exhaust Japan and the war would then simply go away. This policy did not constitute appeasement, as Britain offered no substantive concessions to Japan, but it certainly did not constitute an effective defence of British interests.

Keith Neilson made close study of British foreign policy and he displayed an encyclopaedic knowledge of British archives. He argued, compellingly, that debates over Britain's relative decline were too heavily based on economic determinism – that although Britain faced tremendous challenges in the interwar world, it remained a Great Power. It had no ability to resort to isolationism, but otherwise had a range of choices to make. At the same time, however, Neilson recognized that Britain's power, whether military, economic, or soft, was insufficient to achieve its aims. In a world of militant Italian, Japanese, and German revisionism, Britain had to choose what and where it could defend, and what it could not. Whitehall officials and the Cabinet had to fight a series of long diplomatic retreats and delaying actions while seeking a broader coalition of powers that could stand against the principal threat – Nazi Germany.[62]

---

[62] See, for example, Keith Neilson, *Britain, Soviet Russia, and the Collapse of the Versailles Order, 1919–1939* (Cambridge, 2006), 6–12, 323, and 332–33.

This study of the potential imposition of sanctions against Japan and the consequent risk of war fits well with Keith Neilson's view of the nature of the international system in the 1930s and the relative decline of British power within that system. Britain lacked the economic and military power to defend its imperial presence in China, so the Cabinet accepted that it would have to bear Japanese encroachment against British interests and, above all, play for time while seeking to convince the United States that its broader interests were at stake as well.

# Index

Aberdeen, George Hamilton-Gordon, 4<sup>th</sup> Earl of, 112
Aborigine Protection Society, 55
Aden, 64, 235
Admiralty, 40, 41, 42, 43, 68, 70, 81, 154, 157, 158, 159, 160, 161, 162, 163, 164, 165, 167, 169, 171, 172, 246, 283, 284, 287, 288, 289
Advisory Committee on Trade Questions in Time of War (ATB), 279, 282
Aehrenthal, Aloys Lexa Freiherr von, 138
Afghanistan, 52, 96
Air Ministry, 284
Alcock, Sir Rutherford, 78
Aldington, Richard (né Edward Godfree Aldington), 185
Alvear, Máximo Marcelo Torcuato de A. Pacheco, 213
Amery, Leopold Charles Maurice Stennett, 192
Amritsar, 16, 57, 61
Ancell, Richard, 94
Angell, Norman, 149
*Anglo-German Review, The*, 194
Argentina, 112, 117, 120, 121, 122, 123, 125, 126, 127, 209, 212, 213, 214, 220, 223
Armstrong-Mitchell shipyards, 83
Army (British) and military power, 11, 24, 44, 48, 50, 51, 53, 55, 59, 63, 79, 84, 85, 87, 146, 155, 168, 177, 182, 187, 190, 196, 227, 229–30, 231, 232, 233, 234, 235, 237, 238, 239, 240, 241, 242, 243, 244, 285, 287, 289
Army Staff College, 20, 236, 237, 239
Arnold-Forster, William, 42
Ashanti kingdom, 16
Asiatic Petrol Company, 276
Asquith, Herbert Henry, 1<sup>st</sup> Earl of A. and Oxford, 30, 153, 156, 158, 160, 161, 162, 163, 166, 180

Athens, 60–61
Attlee, Clement Richard, 1<sup>st</sup> Earl, 267, 268
Auchinleck, Field-Marshal Sir Claude John Eyre, 239
Auckland, 78
Augusta of Saxe-Weimar-Eisenach, Queen of Prussia, German Empress, 138
Austria(-Hungary), 135–38, 139, 180, 188, 208, 209
Australia, 21, 71, 120, 125, 232, 242, 244, 246, 252, 255, 256, 258, 259, 260, 265, 266, 272, 273, 274, 289, 291, 293

Bacon, Admiral Sir Reginald Hugh Spencer, 159
Baden-Powell, Lieutenant-General Robert Stephenson Smyth, 1<sup>st</sup> Baron, 178
Baghdad Railway, 144
Baldwin, Stanley, 1<sup>st</sup> Earl B. of Bewdley, 183, 186, 207, 215, 216, 217, 218, 221
Balfour, Arthur James, 1<sup>st</sup> Earl, 131, 165
Banks
   Bank of England, 122, 125, 126, 194
   Barings Brothers, 31, 117, 118, 119, 125, 126, 127
   City Bank, 122
   Colonial Bank, 121
   Anthony Gibbs & Co., 118
   Hong Kong and Shanghai Banking Corporation, 276
   Frederick Huth & Co., 120
   J.P. Morgan, 119
   J.S. Morgan & Co., 124, 125
   London and River Plate Bank, 121, 123, 124
   National Bank of the Argentine Republic, 118
   Overend Gurney, 124, 125
   N.M. Rothschild, 17, 118, 119, 122
   Zimmerman, Frazier & Co., 118

Baring, Alexander, 1ˢᵗ Baron Ashburton, 116, 117, 118
Barnett, Corelli, 2
Bartlett, (Charles) Vernon (Oldfield), 190
Batterbee, Sir Harry Fagg, 257
Bazarov, Colonel Pavel, 142
Beaumont, Miles Thomas Stapleon, 8ᵗʰ Baron, 112
Beaverbrook, William Maxwell Aitken, 1ˢᵗ Baron, 195, 196
Belgium, 56, 173, 181, 188, 208, 209, 210, 213
Benckendorff, Count Alexander von, 13, 130, 140, 141, 142, 144, 145, 146
Berendsen, Sir Carl August, 264
Bermuda, 78
Bertie, Sir Francis Leveson, 1ˢᵗ Viscount B. of Thame, 1
Bethmann Hollweg, Theobald von, 150, 157, 169
Bigglesworth, James ('Biggles'), 185
Bingham, Robert Worth, 300
Blamey, Field Marshal Sir Thomas Albert, 264
Board of Trade, 34, 39, 105, 154, 171, 278
Bolingbroke, Henry St. John, 1ˢᵗ Viscount, 91
Bombay, 52, 78
Boys Brigade, 178
Boy Scouts, 178, 185
Brazil, 114, 115, 117, 118, 120, 125, 209, 210, 211, 212, 213, 223
Brennwald, Casper, 85
Bridges, Sir Edward Ettingdene, 1ˢᵗ Baron, 253, 267
Brink, Lieutenant General George Edwin, 239
Brinkley, Lieutenant Francis, 83, 85
British-American Tobacco Company, 276
British Broadcasting Corporation (BBC), 198, 199
British Girls Patriotic League, 178
British Guiana, 64
British Institute of Public Opinion (BIPO), 190, 199
British Union of Fascists (BUF), 193
Brocket, Arthur Ronald Nall Nall-Cain, 2ⁿᵈ Baron, 194
Brooke, Field-Marshal Alan Francis, 1ˢᵗ Viscount Alanbrooke, 238, 239
Brooke, Rupert Chawner, 185
Browning, Colonel Frederick, 29, 30
Bruce, Henry, 121, 123, 124

Bruce, Stanley Melbourne, 1ˢᵗ Viscount B. of Melbourne, 252, 254, 255, 257, 266
Brusilov, Captain L.A., 136, 137
Buchanan, Sir George William, 141, 145, 201, 203, 214
Buenos Aires, 112, 113, 117, 118, 119, 121, 122, 123, 209, 213
Bülow, Bernhard Prince von, 157, 166, 168, 169
Butterfield & Swire, 276

Cadogan, Sir Alexander Montagu George, 108, 109, 220
Caldecote, Thomas Walker Hobart Inskip, 1ˢᵗ Viscount, 301, 302
Callwell, Major-General Charles Edward, 50, 54, 55
Cambridge university, 32, 201
Campbell, Sir Ronald Hugh, 218
Campbell-Bannerman, Sir Henry, 55
Canada, xiii, 21, 125, 228, 231, 232, 239, 241, 242, 243, 244, 250, 251, 258, 260, 267, 268, 270, 271, 273
Canadian Pacific Steamship Lines, 69
Canning, Charles John, 1ˢᵗ Earl, 51, 54
Canning, George, 114
Cape of Good Hope, 78
Cape Town, 78
Cardin, (Pierre-Joseph-)Arthur, 250
Casey, Richard Gavin Gardiner, Baron, 247, 255, 265, 266
Cecil, Lord (Edgar Algernon) Robert Gascoyne-, 1ˢᵗ Viscount C. of Chelwood, 35, 37, 41, 44, 105, 184, 200
Ceylon, 59, 202
Chamberlain, Sir (Joseph) Austen, 22, 155 n., 165, 206, 210, 215, 217, 218 n., 221
Chamberlain, Joseph, 180
Chamberlain, (Arthur) Neville, 6, 22, 108, 110, 183, 187, 189, 190, 191, 192, 195, 196, 197, 198, 200, 205, 206, 211, 222, 246, 247, 249, 251, 252, 274, 286, 296, 297, 298, 301
Chapman, Major Guy Patterson, 185, 198
Charlton, Yvonne Moyra Graham, 198
Chelmsford, General Frederick Augustus Thesiger, 2ⁿᵈ Baron, 53
Chiang Kai-shek, 278, 296, 298
Chile, 114, 118, 120, 125, 209, 210
Chilston, Aretas Akers-Douglas, 2ⁿᵈ Viscount, 223

China, 14, 18, 19, 40, 67, 68, 69, 70, 71, 72,
  73, 74, 75, 76, 77, 78, 79, 80, 83, 85,
  87, 113, 186, 188, 209, 211, 235, 276,
  277, 278, 279, 280, 281, 282, 283,
  284, 289, 290, 291, 292, 293, 294,
  296, 298, 300, 301, 302, 303, 304
China Association, 276, 303
Church Lads Brigade, 178
Churchill, Sir Winston Leonard Spencer-,
  21, 28, 110, 153, 154, 157, 160, 161,
  162, 163, 164, 171, 172, 173, 183,
  191, 195, 237, 245, 246, 247, 248,
  253, 254, 255, 256, 257, 258, 260,
  261, 262, 263, 264, 265, 266, 267,
  270, 272, 274, 275
Clapham, Sir John Harold, 3 n., 125
Clark Kerr, Archibald (né Clark), 1st Baron
  Inverchapel, 213, 223, 224
Clerk, Sir George Russell, 209, 219, 223
Cockerill, Brigadier-General George
  Kynaston, 29, 30, 31, 32
Collins, Brigadier Lionel Peter, 239
Colomb, Sir John Charles Ready, 78
Colomb, Vice-admiral Philip Howard, 84
Colombia, 114
Colonia, 112
Colonial Office, 60
Colville, Sir John Rupert, 274
Commercial Intelligence Branch (CIB), 34,
  44, 232
Committee of Imperial Defence (CID), 20,
  229, 231, 233, 286, 289
Commonwealth (British), 20, 21, 57, 228,
  231, 238, 243, 244, 246, 249, 251,
  252, 254, 256, 257, 259, 268, 270,
  271, 272, 273, 275
Communications technology, 8, 15, 24, 25,
  26, 27, 28, 20, 30, 31, 32, 33, 34, 35,
  37, 39, 40, 42, 43, 45, 72, 109,
  147, 264
Conferences and Congresses
  Argentia (1941), 267, 269
  Brussels (1937), 298, 299, 300, 301 n.
  Geneva (World Disarmament, 1932),
    184, 186
  Vienna (1814–15), 208
  Singapore Defence (1940),
    256
  Washington (1922), 227, 287
Consett, Captain Montagu William
  Warcop Peter, 41
Constantinople, 134, 146,
  216
Contraband Department, 27, 34, 35, 36,
  39, 40, 41, 42, 103

Cooper, Alfred Duff, 1st Viscount
  Norwich, 189
Counter-Insurgency, 47, 48, 50, 64, 65
Cowan, Major-General David
  Tennant, 239
Cranborne, James Edward Hubert
  Gascoyne-Cecil, Viscount, 4th
  Marquess of Salisbury, 206
Cranborne, Robert Arthur James
  Gascoyne-Cecil, Viscount, 5th
  Marquess of Salisbury, 256, 257, 259,
  261, 271
Crawford and Balcarres, David Alexander
  Edward Lindsay, 27th Earl of C. and
  10th Earl of B., 218
Crerar, General Henry Duncan Graham,
  239, 242
Crerar, Thomas Alexander, 247, 248
Crewe, Robert Offley Ashburton Crewe-
  Milnes, 1st Marquess of, 203, 213, 222
Cripps, Sir (Richard) Stafford, 204
Croke Park, 16, 57
Cromwell, Oliver, 149
Crowe, Sir Eyre Alexander, 22, 27, 31, 36,
  37, 101, 109, 203, 204, 205, 210,
  216, 217
Curzon, George Nathaniel, 1st Marquess C.
  of Kedleston, 105, 107, 146, 204, 207,
  214, 215, 216, 217, 220, 224
Cyprus, 62, 63, 64, 65
Czechoslovakia, 12, 188

D'Abernon, Edgar Vincent, 1st Viscount,
  203, 215, 216, 217
Daily Citizen, 180
Daily Chronicle, 180
Daily Express, 176, 180, 191
Daily Herald, 180, 190
Daily Mail, 165, 167, 176, 180, 195
Daily Mirror, 195
Daily News, 176
Daily Sketch, 195
Daily Telegraph, 180, 191, 195
Daily Worker, 190
Dalton, Edward Hugh John Neale, Baron,
  207, 221, 223
Darwin, Charles, 138
Davies, David, 1st Baron D. of
  Llandinam, 255
Davis, Henry William Carless, 30, 31, 32,
  34, 41, 42, 43, 44
Davis, John, 215
Davis, Norman Hezekiah, 300–1
De Bunsen, Sir Maurice William Ernest,
  211–12

Declaration of London (1909), 26
Defence Requirements Sub-Committee
     (DRC), 231
Denmark, 251
Department of Information, 95
Department of Overseas Trade (DOT), 44,
     104, 192
Derby, Edward George Villiers Stanley,
     17th Earl, 203
*Deutsch-Englische Gesellschaft*, 194–95
Dexter, Alexander Grant, 268
Diack, John, 86, 87
Diplomatic Service, 201–25
Directorate of Special Intelligence
     (DSI), 35
Disraeli, Benjamin, Earl of Beaconsfield, 70
Dolgoruky, Prince Nicholas
     Serge'evich, 142
Dominions, 147, 226–44, 245, 249, 252,
     254, 255, 256, 257, 258, 259, 260,
     263, 265, 272, 273, 274
Dominions Office (DO), 225, 235, 243,
     249, 253, 256, 267
'Don Pacifico Affair', 95
*Dreadnought*, 15, 151, 154, 169, 170,
     172
Drummond, Sir James Eric, 7th Earl of
     Perth, 207
Dubasov, Admiral Fedor Vassilevich, 134
Durnovo, Petr Nikola'evich, 143
Dyer, Brigadier-General Reginald, 57, 61

Eden, Sir (Robert) Anthony, Viscount
     Avon, 108 and n., 190, 191, 219, 220,
     247, 251, 253, 261, 278, 286, 295,
     297, 298, 299, 300, 301, 302
Edward, Prince of Wales, Edward VIII, 71
Egypt, 56, 57, 58, 209, 211, 229,
     264
Elibank, Gideon Oliphant-Murray, 2nd
     Viscount, 255
Elizabeth I, 90
Emmott, Alfred, 1st Baron, 31, 32, 33, 34
Empire (British), 3, 7, 8, 14, 15, 16, 17, 19,
     20, 21, 23, 25, 27, 46–66, 70, 71, 72,
     89, 93, 111, 116, 145, 147, 148, 150,
     155, 170, 172, 176, 177, 178, 179,
     183, 185, 188, 200, 201, 221, 225,
     226–44, 245–75, 276–304
Empire Day, 178
EOKA, 62, 65
Esquimalt, British Columbia, 78
Eton College, 201, 202,
     204
*Evening Standard*, 180

Extraterritoriality, 73, 87
Eyre, Edward John, 55

Fadden, Sir Arthur William, 271
Fenton, John William, 84
Ferdinand VII of Spain, 114
Fiennes, Gerard, 147
Finance, 4, 5, 6, 15, 70, 111–28, 129, 147,
     247, 251
Fisher, Admiral Sir John, 1st Baron Fisher of
     Kilverstone, 151, 154, 160, 161, 162,
     163, 169, 177
Fisher, Sir Norman Fenwick Warren, 283
Foreign Office, 1, 9, 10, 13, 22, 25, 27, 31,
     32, 37, 41, 68, 70, 80, 81, 90–111, 112,
     113, 114, 132, 156, 159, 170, 182,
     191, 195, 196, 202–25, 278, 286, 295,
     299, 302
Foreign Office (Trade Section), 31–32
Formosa (Taiwan), 80, 81, 280, 292
France, 5, 13, 46, 56, 57, 59, 67, 81, 94,
     112, 114, 115, 126, 127, 129, 131,
     132, 136, 138, 139, 141, 142, 146,
     155, 168, 171, 172, 175, 179, 180,
     184, 188, 190, 203, 209, 210, 213,
     238, 248, 253, 293
Franz Ferdinand of Habsburg-Este,
     Archduke, 145
Fraser, Peter, 245, 247, 257, 261, 264,
     265, 272
Frazer, Nalbro, 118
Fremantle, Admiral Sir Edmund Robert, 75
Freyberg, Lieutenant-General Bernard
     Cyril, 1st Baron, 264
Fuller, Major-General John Frederick
     Charles, 237 and n

Garvin, James Louis, 164, 165, 270
Geddes, Sir Auckland Campbell, 1st Baron,
     203, 215, 216, 220, 221
'Geddes axe', 20, 106, 107 n., 230, 231
Geddes, Sir Eric Campbell, 230 and n
George III, 91
George IV, 94
George V, 144, 216
George VI, 222
George, David Lloyd, 4, 5, 15, 22, 105,
     153, 154, 155, 156, 157, 159, 160,
     161, 162, 163, 166, 168, 172, 202,
     203, 214, 215, 220, 224, 230
Germanophobia, 179
Germany, 12, 13, 15, 26, 27, 28, 40, 41, 43,
     44, 46, 56, 71, 87, 106, 113, 118, 127,
     129, 131, 132, 133, 134, 135, 136,
     137, 138, 139, 141, 142, 143, 144,

145, 146, 147–73, 174, 175, 177, 179, 181, 182, 186, 187, 188, 189, 190, 192, 194, 195, 196, 198, 199, 203, 209, 217, 235, 277, 281, 282, 283, 284, 285, 286, 287, 292, 293, 294, 297, 203, 303
Gibraltar, 59, 78
Gladstone, William Ewart, 70
Glasgow, Patrick James Boyle, 8$^{th}$ Earl of, 194
Glasgow, Sir Major-General Sir (Thomas) William, 271
Godley, General Sir Alexander John, 241
Graham, Sir Ronald William, 218
Grahame, Sir George Dixon, 218 n
Greece, 191, 264
Green, J.H., 122, 123, 124
Grey, Sir Edward, Viscount G. of Fallodon, 113, 146, 149, 156, 161, 162, 163, 179, 180, 181, 196, 203
Gwynne, Howell Arthur Keir, 181

Hakodate, 72 n., 76, 81, 87
Haldane, Richard Burdon, Viscount H. of Cloan, 49
Halifax, Nova Scotia, 78
Halifax, Edward Frederick Lindley Wood, 1$^{st}$ Earl of, 189, 196, 197 n., 200, 204, 222, 248
Hall, Admiral Sir (William) Reginald, 29, 30, 31, 32
Hammond, Edmund, 1$^{st}$ Baron H. of Kirbella, 95
Hankey, Captain Sir Maurice Pascal Alers, 1$^{st}$ Baron, 31
Harcourt, Lewis Vernon, 1$^{st}$ Viscount, 160
Hardinge, Sir Charles, 1$^{st}$ Viscount H. of Penshurst, 102, 104, 105, 145, 201, 203, 204, 207, 208
Harris, Air-Marshal Sir Arthur Travers, 1$^{st}$ Baron, 237 and n
Harris, Commander Frederick Leverton, 28, 34, 42
Harrisson, Major Tom Harnett, 193 n., 197
Harvey, Oliver Charles, 1$^{st}$ Baron H. of Tasburgh, 210
Hawes, Lieutenant Albert G.S., 83 and n
Heigakkô, 68 n., 83
Henderson, Arthur, 208, 221
Henderson, Sir Nevile Meyrick, 220
Henry VIII, 90
Henty, George Alfred, 185
Hiogo (Kobe), 76

Hitler, Adolf, 6, 109, 184, 186, 187, 188, 189, 190, 191, 195, 196, 197, 199, 257, 285, 287
Hobbes, Thomas, 90
Hobhouse, Leonard Trelawney, 177
Hobson, John Atkinson, 177
Hokkaidô, 76
Hong Kong, 14, 59, 68, 69 n., 74, 76, 77, 78, 85, 86, 276, 291, 292, 293, 302
Horrocks, Lieutenant-General Sir Brian Gwynne, 238
House, Colonel Edward Mandell, 150
Howard, Sir Esme William, 1$^{st}$ Baron H. of Penrith, 218 n., 221, 222, 224
Hudson, Robert Spear, 1$^{st}$ Viscount, 192
Hull, Cordell, 295, 300, 303
Hungary, 209
Hurd, Douglas Richard, Baron H. of Westwell, 3
Hurst, Sir Cecil James Barrington, 37
Huxley, Aldous Leonard, 184
Hyde Park Declaration (1941), 268–69

Imperial Defence College (IDC), 20, 228, 238, 239
Imperial General Staff, 19, 20, 226–44
India, 48, 49, 50, 51, 52, 54, 55, 57, 58, 61, 69, 77, 227, 228, 229, 231, 232, 233, 234, 238–39, 242, 243, 244, 276, 289, 291, 293
Indian Military Academy (IMA), 239
Industrial Intelligence Centre (IIC), 44, 279
Information, 8, 9, 10, 25, 26, 27, 29, 30, 31, 33, 34, 35, 37, 38, 39, 40, 41, 43, 45, 90–110, 118, 119, 122, 124, 125, 159, 160, 162, 165, 167, 180, 226, 234, 252, 254, 257
Ingles, Captain John, 83 and n
Insurgencies
  Brunei-Indonesian Confrontation (1962), 64
  Indian Mutiny (1857), 51–52
  Mau Mau (1953), 61
Intelligence, 8–9, 24–45, 80, 99, 100, 104, 109, 148, 157, 158, 159, 160, 163, 168, 188, 226, 234, 237, 278, 280, 281, 285
*Invincible*, 150
Iraq, 201 n., 209, 211, 230
Ireland, 56, 57, 58, 145, 198, 258, 294

Ismay, General Sir Hastings Lionel, 1st Baron, 237
Italy, 43, 106, 188, 209, 213, 279, 281, 282, 283, 286, 287, 288 n., 293, 297, 301 n., 302, 303
Izvolsky, Aleksandr Petrovich, 132, 134, 135, 138, 139, 141, 142

James, Lieutenant John M., 83
Jameson, Storm, 184
Japan, 13, 14, 16, 18, 19, 67–89, 134, 135, 136, 188, 209, 224, 238, 244 n., 266, 276–304
Jardine & Mattheson, 276
Java, 59
Jebb, Hubert Miles Gladwyn, 1st Baron Gladwyn, 207
Jellicoe, Admiral John Rushworth, 1st Earl, 162, 170, 172
Jerusalem, 59
John Swire & Sons, 276

Kagoshima, 72, 74, 79, 88
Kellett, Vice-admiral Sir Henry, 76, 77, 81
Kennedy, Aubrey Leo, 225
Kennedy, General Sir John Noble, 259
Kenya, 61, 63, 64
Keppel, Admiral Sir Henry, 67
Keynes, John Maynard, 1st Baron, 185
King, William Lyon Mackenzie, 245, 247, 249, 250, 251, 255, 262, 263, 264, 265, 266, 267, 268, 270, 275
Kingdon, Nicholas, 79 and n
Kirkpatrick, General Sir George Macaulay, 241
Kitchener, General Sir Herbert Horatio, 1st Earl K. of Khartoum, 53, 54
Kobe, 69, 72 n., 76, 87
Kokovtsov, Vladimir Nikola'evich, 138, 139, 140, 141
Korea, 70, 80, 83, 280, 290
Kuper, Admiral Sir Augustus Leopold, 79

Lake, Lieutenant-General Sir Percy Henry Noel, 241
Lapointe, Ernest, 250
Latin America, 17, 18, 22, 111–28, 210, 211, 213, 214, 220
Lavarack, Lieutenant-General Sir John Dudley, 239
Lawrence, (Alfred) Clive, 42
League of Nations, 184, 207, 227, 229, 279, 283, 296
League of Nations Union (LNU), 183, 184

Le Carré, John (pseud. David John Moore Cornwell), 185
Lee, Arthur Hamilton, 1st Viscount L. of Fareham, 152
Leigh-Mallory, Air Chief-Marshal Sir Trafford, 237 and n
Leith-Ross, Sir Frederick William, 283
Le Queux, William, 11, 187
Leys School, Cambridge, 178
Lidderdale, William, 127
Lieven, Vice-Admiral Alexander, 137
Lindley, Sir Francis Oswald, 211, 218, 219 and n
Lindsay, Sir Ronald Charles, 204, 205, 206, 207, 208, 216, 218, 219, 220, 221, 222, 224, 225
Link, The, 194
Linklater, Eric Robert Russell, 188
Locker-Lampson, Godfrey Lampson Tennyson, 206
Londonderry, Charles Stewart Henry Vane-Tempest-Stewart, 7th Marquess of, 194
Longdon, Commander, 28, 41
Lothian, Philip Henry Kerr, 11th Marquess of, 194, 204, 222, 248
Lowther, Sir Gerard Augustus, 40
Lutyens, Sir Edwin Landseer, 224

Macaulay, Rose, 184
MacDonald, James Ramsay, 205, 210, 217, 223
MacDonald, Malcolm John, 259, 261, 267, 268, 269, 273
Mackinder, Sir Halford John, 147
Mahan, Captain Alfred Thayer, 137, 149
Malaya, 46, 59, 64, 256, 289
Mallet, Sir Claude Coventry, 212, 213
Mallet, Sir Victor Alexander Louis, 299
Malmesbury, James Howard Harris, 3rd Earl of, 112
Malta, 59, 78
Manchester Guardian, 100
Manchukuo, 290
Manchuria, 70, 294
Manning, Frederic, 185
Marco Polo Bridge (Luguoqiao) incident (1937), 277, 289, 295
Masijid i-Sulaiman, 74
Mass Observation, 174, 175, 192, 198
Massey, Charles Vincent, 247, 254, 270, 274
Max-Müller, Sir William Grenfell, 43
May, Sir William, 165–66

McKenna, Reginald, 30, 32, 158, 159, 161, 162, 163, 164
McKenna, Stephen, 30, 32
McNaughton, General Andrew George Latta, 239
Mediterranean, 71, 134, 188, 229, 244, 263, 268, 283, 293, 297
Meinecke, Friedrich, 150
Menzies, Sir Robert Gordon, 245, 252, 254, 255, 256, 257, 258, 259, 260, 261, 263, 264, 265, 266, 271, 272, 273, 274
Mesopotamia, 212, 229, 231
Metternich, Paul Count Wolff-M. zur Gracht, 155 and n., 165, 166, 167, 168, 171
Mexico, 114, 223
Migration, 7
Mikhelson, Colonel Aleksandr, 142
'Miles' (pseud. Stephen Southwold), 187
Miles, Lieutenant General Charles George Norman, 239
Milne, Field-Marshal Sir George Francis, 1st Baron, 235
Ministry of Blockade, 41, 103
Ministry of Economic Warfare (MEW), 44, 45, 109
Ministry of Information (MOI), 199
Ministry of Supply (MoS), 190
Mitre, Bartolomé, 122
Monson, Sir Edmund John, 113
Montagu, Norman Collett, 1st Baron Norman, 194
Montague, Charles Edward, 183
Montgomery-Massingberd, Field-Marshal Sir Archibald Armar, 235
Montreal Gazette, 270
Morier, Sir Robert Burnett David, 161, 162, 181
Morley, John, 1st Viscount M. of Blackburn, 161, 162, 181
Morning Post, 181
Morocco, 235
Mosley, Sir Oswald Ernald, 6th Bart. of Ancoats, 193
Mussolini, Benito, 190, 191, 197

Nagasaki, 69 and n., 72 n., 76
Namamugi Incident (1862), 79
Nanjing, 277
Napoleon I Bonaparte, Emperor of the French, 129, 136
Napoleon III, Emperor of the French, 208

National Service League, 30, 32, 178
Naval Intelligence, Historical Section, 104
Naval Trade Division (NTD), 27, 28, 34, 38
NAVICERT system, 42
Navy (Royal) and naval power, 3, 5, 11, 14, 15, 17, 25, 71, 72, 73, 75, 76, 77, 79, 80, 82, 83, 84, 87, 89, 114, 149–73, 178, 230, 231, 238, 287, 288, 290, 291, 292, 293, 294.
    China Station, 67–89
Navy League, 177–78
Neame, Lieutenant-General Sir Philip, 237 and n
Neilson, Keith Erick, xiii-xiv, 1, 2, 68, 87, 88, 148, 149, 173, 223, 203
Nelson, Vice-Admiral Horatio, 1st Viscount, 11
Neratov, Anatolii Anatoli'evich, 140
Netherlands East Indies, 61, 281, 283, 293
Netherlands West Indies, 281
Newbolt, Sir Henry John, 185
News Chronicle, 190–91
New Statesman and Nation, 197
New Zealand, 232, 239, 241, 242, 243, 244, 245, 247, 256, 257, 264, 265, 275, 289, 291, 293
Nicholas II Romanov, Tsar of All the Russias, 130, 139, 145, 146, 207
Nicolson, Sir Arthur, 1st Baron Carnock, 138, 139, 145, 146, 207
Nicolson, Sir Harold George, 195, 219
North West Frontier, 52, 54, 55, 56, 58
Northcliffe, Alfred Charles William Harmsworth, 1st Viscount, 161, 164
Northcott, Lieutenant-General Sir John, 239
Northern Department, 90
Nyasaland, 64

O'Beirne, Hugh James, 133
Observer, The, 164, 270
Officer Training Corps, 178
Oman, 64
Orange Free State, 53
Orr, Major Sutherland George Gordon, 52
Orwell, George, 11
Osaka, 69, 72 n., 81, 87
Osborne, Sir (Francis) D'Arcy (Godolphin), 12th Duke of Leeds, 214
Osten-Sacken, Count Nicholas Vladimirovich von der, 143
Owen, Wilfred Edward Salter, 185

Ovey, Sir Esmond, 223
Oxford university, 30, 32, 33, 200, 201

Page, Sir Earle Christmas Grafton, 274
Paget, Sir Ralph Spencer, 212 and n
Palestine mandate, 62 n., 64, 65 n., 229
*Pall Mall Gazette*, 180
Palmer, Major-General Henry Spencer,
    86, 87
Palmerston, Henry John Temple, 3rd
    Viscount, 95, 112
Pares, Sir Bernard, 133
Parker, Alwyn, 105
Parkes, Sir Harry, 81, 82
Peace Pledge Union (PPU), 184
Pearl Harbor, 301, 303
Pearson, Sir (Cyril) Arthur, 1st Bart., 176
Pearson, Lester Bowles, 251, 253,
    269
Peel, Sir Robert, 2nd Bart., 112
Penson, Sir (Thomas) Henry, 30, 31, 32,
    34, 35, 41, 44
Persia, 17, 113, 133, 135, 141, 145,
    229, 230
Peru, 114, 115, 117, 118, 120
Pescadores (Penghu) Islands, 292
Phillips, Major, 27, 36, 38, 40
Phipps, Sir Eric Clare Edmund, 219,
    220, 223
Pitt, William the Elder, Earl of Chatham, 91
Plant, Major General Eric Clive Pegus, 239
Plato, 92
Poincaré, Raimond, 213
Poland, 129, 187, 191, 195, 196, 197, 198,
    199, 209
Pollard, Lieutenant General Sir Reginald
    George, 240, 242
Ponsonby, Arthur Augustus William Harry,
    1st Baron P. of Shulbrede, 180, 206
Poole, Major-General William Henry
    Evered, 241, 242
Pope, Jessica, 185
Pope, Brigadier-General Maurice
    Arthur, 242
Portugal, 115, 209, 210, 211, 213 n
Power, Charles Gavan, 250
Procurator General's Department (PGD),
    36, 39, 42, 43, 44
Public opinion, 10, 12, 16, 65, 72, 131, 132,
    133, 134, 138, 139, 141, 145, 162,
    174–200, 278, 297 n., 298,
    299 and n., 300, 301 n., 302,
    303
Puttick, Lieutenant General Sir
    Edward, 239

Rait, Robert Sangster, 33
Reading, Rufus Isaacs, 1st Marquess of, 203
Redesdale, David Bertram Ogilvy Freeman-
    Mitford, 2nd Baron, 194
Reitz, Colonel Deneys, 247
Remarque, Erich Maria, 185
Revelstoke, Edward Charles Baring, 1st
    Lord, 125, 126
Ribbentrop, Joachim von, 194, 195 n
Richards, Lieutenant-Colonel
    Fleetwood, 82
Richardson, Lennox, 79
Richmond, Admiral Sir Herbert
    William, 238
Ricketts, Charles, 115
Rivera, General Fructoso, 112
Roberts, Field Marshal Frederick, 1st Earl
    R. of Kandahar, 53, 176, 178
Robertson, Sir (Malcolm) Arnold, 214
Rodd, Sir James Rennell, Baron Rennell of
    Rodd, 7 and n
Rogers, Norman McLeod, 251
Romania, 142, 146, 191
Roosevelt, Franklin Delano, 222, 267, 274,
    278, 294, 295, 296 and n., 297 and nn.,
    298, 299 and n., 300, 301 n., 303
Rosas, General Juan Manuel, 112
Rosebery, Archibald Philip Primrose, 5th
    Earl of, 55, 70
Rosen, Baron Roman Romanovich, 143
Rothermere, Harold Sidney Harmsworth,
    1st Viscount, 195 and n
Rowell, Lieutenant General Sir Sydney
    Fairbairn, 239
Royal Air Force, 171, 220, 231, 235, 237,
    284, 285, 287, 289
Royal Military Academy, Woolwich,
    235, 240
Royal Military College, Duntroon, 239, 240
Royal Military College, Quetta, 228, 236,
    237, 238, 239
Royal Military College, Sandhurst,
    235, 240
Royal Military College of Canada,
    Kingston, xiii, 239, 240 and n., 242
Rumbold, Sir (Horace) Anthony (Claude),
    10th Bart. of Woodhall, 209
Rumbold, Sir Horace George Montague,
    9th Bart. of Woodhall, 202, 203, 204,
    209, 215 n., 216, 217, 218,
    219, 221
Runciman, Walter, 1st Viscount R. of
    Doxford, 189
Russell, Bertrand Arthur William, 3rd
    Earl, 184

Russell, Sir (Odo William) Theo(philus Villiers), 212
Russia (see also Soviet Union), 1, 4, 5, 12, 46, 67, 87, 98, 126, 129–46, 179, 180, 188

Saga Rebellion, 81
Salisbury, Robert Arthur Talbot Gascoyne-Cecil, 3$^{rd}$ Marquis of, 4, 71, 176
Samuel, Herbert Louis, 1$^{st}$ Viscount, 181–82
Sanderson, Sir Thomas Henry, 1$^{st}$ Baron S. of Armthorpe, 99
Sanford, C.H., 126
Sassoon, Siegfried Loraine, 185
Satow, Sir Ernest Mason, 83
Savage, Michael Joseph, 253, 257
Savory, Lieutenant-General Sir Reginald Arthur, 239
Sazonov, Sergei Dimitrievich, 13, 140, 141, 142, 144, 145, 146
Scott, Charles Prestwich, 162
Scott, George Gilbert, 94
Seeds, Sir William, 223
Seeley, Sir John Robert, 7
Selby, Sir Walford Harmood Montague, 211, 213
Serbia, 139, 146, 180, 196
Serna, José de la S. e Hinojosa, 1$^{st}$ Count of the Andes, 115
Serrato, José, 212
Shadwell, Admiral Sir Charles Frederick Alexander, 76, 82
Shanghai, 14, 68, 69, 74, 77, 79, 86, 276, 277, 291, 293, 302
Sheppard, Canon Hugh Richard Lawrie 'Dick', 184
Shigeki, Tôyama, 69
Shimonoseki, 72, 80, 81, 82
Shute, Neville (né Neville Shute Norway), 188
Simon, Sir John Allsebrook, 1$^{st}$ Viscount, 205, 206, 209, 218, 219, 222, 288, 294, 297, 300
Simonds, Lieutenant-General Guy Granville, 240 and n
Simpkin, O.R.A., 39, 41, 42
Singapore, 14, 68, 69 n., 74, 76, 256, 258, 266, 287, 289, 290, 291, 292, 293, 302
Slessor, Air-Marshal Sir John Cotesworth, 237 and n
Slim, Field Marshal Sir William Joseph, 1$^{st}$ Viscount, 283

Smith, William H., 86 and n., 87
Smuts, Field-Marshal Jan-Christiaan, 245, 246, 249, 250, 261, 262, 263, 265, 266, 272, 273, 275
Soames, (Arthur) Christopher (John), Baron, 62, 64
South Africa, Union of, 228, 231, 232, 242, 244, 247, 249, 250
South African Military School, 239
Southern Department, 90
Soviet Union, 191, 288 n
Spain, 114, 115, 186, 188, 209, 213
Stalin, Yossif Vissarionovich, 274
Stanhope, the Hon. Edward, 48
Stanhope, General James, 1$^{st}$ Earl, 91
State Paper Office, 94
Statute of Westminster (1931), 228, 242
Stevens, Major-General William George, 237, 238 n
Stimson, Henry Lewis, 294, 295 n., 297, 300
Stolypin, Petr Arkad'evich, 135, 140
Strange, Joan Colebrook, 197, 198 n
Sturdee, Lieutenant-General Sir Vernon Ashton Hobart, 239
Sucre, General Antonio, 115
Sudan, 64, 76, 229, 289
Suez Canal, 64, 76, 229, 289
*Sunday Times, The*, 195, 256 n
Surabaya, 60
Sverbeev, Serge Nikola'evich, 144
Sweden, 129, 137, 213 n
Swinton, Philip Cunliffe-Lister (né Lloyd-Greame), 1$^{st}$ Viscount, 285
Switzerland, 40, 190
Sydney, 78
Syria, 235

Taiwan, 80, 81
Teixeira de Mattos, Alexander, 33
Tel Aviv, 59
Tenterden, Charles Stuart Aubrey Abbott, 3$^{rd}$ Baron, 97
Territorial Army, 177, 196, 231
Thompson, Sir Robert, 46
Tientsin (Tianjin), 291
*Times, The*, 52, 55, 85, 180, 182, 194, 215, 219

Tirpitz, Grand Admiral Alfred, 150, 151, 152, 166, 167, 168, 169
Togo, Admiral Heihachirô, 89
*Toronto Telegram*, 259
Townshend, Charles, 2nd Viscount, 91
Toynbee, Arnold Joseph, 2
Tôzenji Incident (1861), 78
Transvaal, 53
Trade, 8, 9, 13, 14, 15, 24–45, 67, 69, 70, 71, 73, 81, 87, 88, 104, 105, 108 n., 111, 114, 115, 118, 127, 137, 141, 142, 145, 147, 153, 155, 168, 184, 222, 276, 277, 279, 281, 282, 286, 289, 290, 294, 302
Trade Clearing House (TCH), 9, 31–37, 38, 40, 41
Treasury, 10, 18, 33, 34, 68, 97, 102, 103 n., 107, 128, 159, 211 n., 232, 278, 282, 283, 284, 297, 302
Treaties
  Anglo-French understanding (*entente*) (1904), 129, 131, 132, 136, 138, 141
  Anglo-Japanese alliance (1902–23), 71, 76, 87, 130, 227
  Anglo-Japanese treaty (1858), 68, 73
  Bogue (1843), 276
  *Dreikaiserbund* (1881–5), 135
  European Convention on Human Rights, 65
  German-Soviet Non-aggression Pact (1939), 194, 197
  Holy Alliance (1815), 115
  Locarno (1925), 217
  Nanking (1842), 276
  Ogdensburg Agreement (1940), 268
  Serbo-Bulgarian Alliance (1912), 140
  Sèvres (1920), 231
  Triple Alliance (1882, 1887, 1892, 1902, 1912), 142
  Versailles (1919), 185, 180, 286
  Washington (Five-Powers) (1922), 287
  Washington (Nine-Powers) (1922), 296
  Webster-Ashburton (1842), 118
Trollope, Anthony, 17
Trubetskoy, Prince Grigorii, 130, 132, 146
Turkey (also Ottoman Empire), 129, 130, 137, 144, 216, 231, 235
Tyrrell, Lady Margaret Ann (née Urquhart), 218
Tyrrell, Sir William George, Baron T. of Avon, 205, 206, 208, 214, 217, 218 and n
Tyrtov, Admiral Pavel Petrovich, 136

Ukraine, 146
United States of America, 6, 17, 18, 21, 22, 28, 37, 42, 118, 125, 127, 128, 131, 142, 209, 210, 213 and n., 222, 224, 225, 251, 258, 260, 268, 269, 270, 278–83, 286, 287, 290, 293–304
Uruguay, 112, 125 n., 212
Uruquiza, General Justo José de, 123

Valetta, 71
Vansittart, Sir Robert, 1st Baron, 22, 31, 32, 108 and n., 109, 207, 208, 210, 218, 219, 220, 221
Venezuela, 213 n., 281
Vickers shipyard, 83, 89
Victoria I, 176
Vladivostok, 76

Waley, Sir (Sigismund) David (né Schloss), 282
Wallace, Captain David Euan, 246
War Office, 43, 228, 229, 230, 233, 234, 235, 243, 254
War Trade Intelligence Department (WTID), 24–45
Warfare, Economic (also blockade), 8–9, 24–45, 103, 104, 109, 112–13, 172, 290
Wars
  Afghan (2nd, 1878–80), 52, 96
  Anglo-Chinese 'Opium' (1839–42, 1856–60), 70, 276
  Balkan (1st) (1912–13), 140
  Boer War (2nd) (1899–1902), 25, 176, 177, 178, 247
  First World War, xiii, 5, 8, 10, 12, 13, 17–18, 21, 22, 24–45, 48, 51, 56, 58, 69, 71, 84, 87, 89, 98, 110, 127, 129, 201, 202, 208, 209, 214, 220, 228, 229, 236, 243
  Napoleonic, 10, 12, 114, 129, 136
  Russo-Japanese (1904–5), 75, 83, 131, 139
  Second World War, 2, 6, 10, 20, 60, 175, 201, 204, 206, 209, 211, 222, 224, 228, 238, 240, 244, 245, 272
  Sino-Japanese (1894–5), 75, 84
  Sino-Japanese (1937–45), 278–79, 295
  Spanish Civil War (1936–9), 184
  Spanish Succession (1701–14), 2
  Zulu (1879), 54–55
Waterson, Sidney Frank, 263
Watson, Captain Hugh, 144
Webster, Daniel, 118
Weihaiwei, 70

Welles, Benjamin Sumner, 299,
    300 n
Wellington, Arthur Wellesley, 1$^{st}$ Duke
    of, 11
Wellington, Arthur Charles Wellesley, 5$^{th}$
    Duke of, 194
Wells, Herbert George, 176,
    187
*Westminster Gazette*, 180
Whiskard, Sir Geoffrey Granville, 252
Whitehead, Trixie Geraldine, 34
Wile, F.W., 167
Wilhelm I of Prussia, German
    Emperor, 138

Wilhelm II of Prussia, German Emperor,
    131, 149
Wilson, Field-Marshal Sir Henry Hughes,
    1$^{st}$ Bart., 229, 230, 234
Wilson, Sir Horace John, 192 and n
Wilson, Thomas Woodrow, 5, 210
Wirgman, Charles, 86 and n
Wodehouse, Pelham Grenville, 176
Wohlthat, Helmuth C.H., 192 and n

Yokohama, 13, 14, 67–89

Zimmerman, Johannes, 18
Zinoviev Letter (1925), 223

For EU product safety concerns, contact us at Calle de José Abascal, 56–1°,
28003 Madrid, Spain or eugpsr@cambridge.org.

www.ingramcontent.com/pod-product-compliance
Ingram Content Group UK Ltd.
Pitfield, Milton Keynes, MK11 3LW, UK
UKHW020431240426
470322UK00017B/465